America 1941

America 1941

A Nation at the Crossroads

Ross Gregory

THE FREE PRESS
A Division of Macmillan, Inc.
NEW YORK

Collier Macmillan Publishers
LONDON

The Free Press
A Division of Macmillan, Inc.
866 Third Avenue, New York, N. Y. 10022

Collier Macmillan Canada, Inc.

Printed in the United States of America

printing number
1 2 3 4 5 6 7 8 9 10

Library of Congress Cataloging-in-Publication Data

Gregory, Ross.
    1941 : America at the crossroads.

    Bibliography: p.
    1. United States—Social life and customs—1918–
1945. 2. World War, 1939–1945—United States.
3. United States—History—1933–1945. I. Title.
E169.G845 1989   973.917   88–16300
ISBN 0-02-912801-3

For
Theresa Marie
Graham Thomas
Darren Matthew

Contents

Preface

This volume carries the story of a year and of an era. It is a story of 1941 and of the late 1930s and early 1940s, the time between the Depression and the war and a time that carried markings of both: America was not exactly in depression, and many Americans still were not out of it; the nation was almost in war and still at peace. It was a time of high drama, of insecurity and indecision, when people had to live their lives as best they could without knowing if their work, their place of residence, or even their family would be the same in September as it had been in January. The prospect of something new was welcome from at least one perspective, for the people had been in a long period of hard times, of worry, suffering, and floundering. Now there was hope it soon would end, perhaps before the year was out. In another sense the new direction caused sadness and apprehension, for Americans lived in a world at war, and each passing month seemed to draw them closer to direct participation in the bloodletting. One citizen, reminiscing about that critical time, described 1941 as "the year we held our breath."

It was a year that offered a view of two Americas: as it existed in the first half of the twentieth century and what it was moving to become in the second half. While parts of the country remained much as they had been for years, the most conspicuous theme of national affairs and personal behavior was change. Americans were moving from rural areas to cities as they had been doing for years, and now the pace was picking up. The people were being carried from an age of pessimism, of national and individual self-doubt, into a time of purposefulness and a confidence that would last for decades. The United States was leaving an era of preoccupation with local and national concerns and heading toward internationalism and an involvement in world affairs on a scale that no one could have begun—or would have dared—to predict. A year marked with quarrels and division would end in unity and full-throated boisterousness.

This volume carries the story of a generation, now rapidly passing from the earth, that had to contend with one of the most troubled and challenging times in the nation's history. Such a study must inevitably deal with major events, political leaders, publishers, opinion-molders, and the spokesmen for interest groups. They received most attention in the press and later were most likely to leave memoirs or to be the subjects of biographies. In large measure, however, this volume is intended as an account of the people, the "ordinary citizen." It is less a diplomatic history than a study of Americans reacting to great events of world politics, less a discussion of religious philosophers than of people practicing their faith, less a story of generals than of privates. It is, in short, a story of how Americans perceived the world of their time, how they lived their lives and tried to solve their problems.

Acknowledgments

I wish to extend thanks to several people who assisted in the preparation of this manuscript. The project was supported by a Fellowship from the Faculty Research and Creative Activities Fund and by the Burnham-Macmillan Fund, both at Western Michigan University. The people in the Interlibrary Loan Office at Western's library obtained many materials needed from other places. Opal Ellis cheerfully worked long hours typing the manuscript several times, and Sylvia Remeta helped in various ways. My editor at the Free Press, Joyce Seltzer, was always encouraging and constructive, and Norman Sloan did a careful job of copyediting. John Houdek added to my understanding of rural life in the United States. Special thanks goes to a colleague, Graham Hawks, who read a substantial portion of the manuscript and whose suggestions were always wise and nearly always usable. My wife, Shirley, read the chapters more than once and criticized them all. Her remarks inspired several changes. Finally, there are the many people with whom I discussed the period before the war, people who either provoked new ideas or confirmed what I thought to be true. Their names do not appear on these pages, but they are there nonetheless.

ROSS GREGORY
Kalamazoo, Michigan

☆
ONE
☆

The Great Dilemma

The tone for the new year was set two days before the old year ended, on December 29, 1940, in a small, hot, oval room in Washington, D.C. A small assemblage of people had gathered there, men in politics mostly, and the experienced observer would be quick to identify Cordell Hull, the aging Secretary of State; Senator Alben Barkley; and other individuals in government. Not far away, however, sat Clark Gable in a chalk-stripe gray suit, and his wife, the actress Carole Lombard, wearing a sombre black dress with black hat and veil. Frequently described as the nation's most glamorous couple, the Gables by their presence were in effect endorsing the occasion, ensuring thereby the attention of people ordinarily indifferent to the doings of politicians.

This evening the movie stars had to take second billing to another skilled performer, President Franklin D. Roosevelt, who now rolled into the room in a wheel chair, placed himself before a row of microphones, and prepared to deliver a national radio address. Roosevelt called his speeches "fireside chats," because he wanted to project warmth, informality, and the trust of a family discussion. Roosevelt's chats were more lecture than exchange of views, for father always did all the talking. The fireside chat of December 29 was to be one of the most important. He did not wish to talk of war, the President said, but in truth he talked of nothing else. He spoke of the danger threatening the United States and the world, of perilous times to come, of the enormous effort to which the people must commit themselves. The message was not as soothing as Roosevelt liked to deliver, but the President saw no soothing way to convey effectively the challenge of the coming year and to call his people to action.[1]

The most momentous fact of life in 1941 was war—two wars, in fact, raging and growing in Europe and Asia. The long struggle between China and Japan—the "China Incident," as the Japanese called

1

it—in progress since 1937, had seemed to drag on endlessly and was spreading to new places, developing from a distant quarrel between Oriental peoples into a war that affected the United States. Most attention remained focused on the closer, more understandable and dangerous conflict in Europe, now in its second year. The armies of Adolf Hitler had swept over most of Western Europe the previous summer, and at the end of 1940 Hitler's *Luftwaffe* had spent several weeks bombing British targets to prepare the island for invasion. If Britain's brilliant defense had delayed the attack, Hitler had given no indication he wished to cancel it. As the new year approached, the most pressing questions remained: When will the Germans strike across the English Channel? When they do, will Britain survive? There remained, moreover, considerable puzzlement about the ultimate goals of Hitler, his appetite for territory and conquest.

Americans had no difficulty keeping up with the war, if they were so inclined; at times it seemed impossible to avoid. They could not in those pre-television days watch battles from the comfort of the living room, but the media then available provided faster, more thorough, and more dramatic information than at any time in the past. Nationwide strikes, disasters, and electoral politics had their brief moments in the journalistic spotlight, but most of the time war news dominated headlines and feature stories. War had become a marketable commodity in the publishing business. *Life* magazine, only five years after rebirth in 1936, became one of the nation's most popular periodicals, its success largely attributable to pictoral coverage of war news. Complaints that journalism had become sensationalist and preoccupied with dismal matters did no good. When a reader asked for more attention to "social gatherings, college life, beautiful women . . . gay things," the editor replied: "This is not the time in world history . . . to present, or for any American to want, only pictures which 'please the eye and soothe the nerves.' *Life* shows the truth . . . the good and bad."[2]

Going to the movies, a popular escapist exercise, offered no certain respite, for the war had entered those halls as well. A growing number of motion pictures had military themes. When they did not, theaters regularly showed action newsreels of battles, air raids, or other war stories. The newsreels stood as forerunner, a sketchy introduction, to the television news coverage that would come a few years later. Even though the films might be days or weeks behind events and gave only hurried glimpses of action, the movies provided visible verification of what journalists were saying in print.

The most exciting new source of war information, of course, was radio. Now more than twenty years old (but too young for the last war), well-established with respect to sponsorship and personnel, with four national networks and hundreds of broadcasting stations, radio by 1941 had surpassed newspapers as the primary supplier of news to the American populace. Networks expanded regular newscasts, interjected special attention to large events, and competed for the most attractive talent. The news analysts, such as H. V. Kaltenborn, Elmer Davis, Lowell Thomas, Boake Carter, Gabriel Heatter, had become some of the newest stars of the airwaves. Radio introduced an extra dimension by sending reporters to the scene of action, where they sought to make listeners a part of events as they happened. The Columbia Broadcasting System led the way. Later to become stalwarts of radio and television, these men of CBS in the 1940s were young, adventurous, dedicated seekers of stories. Larry Lesueur went to the Soviet Union, Howard K. Smith and Charles Collingwood reported from Germany, and Cecil Brown covered the Far East. William L. Shirer had broadcast France's surrender to Germany in June 1940, and at approximately the same time Eric Sevareid first tried his hand at radio, also from France.

The most memorable of all broadcasts had been the reports on CBS by Edward R. Murrow in 1940–41, during the blitz, the continuous German air assault on London. It was a moving spectacle that Americans heard, or tried to hear, described nearly every day on the news broadcasts. A bold, almost reckless pioneer in broadcast journalism, Murrow went to the action, seeking better ways to project events that unfolded before his eyes. He sometimes broadcast air raids from roof tops, with as many as a dozen microphones scattered to pick up the sound. Murrow developed a style that became familiar to all Americans attempting to keep touch with the war: a deep, deathly serious tone, interspersed with live action—sirens, explosions, people shouting—in the background. Tape recording and satellite relay systems remained for the future, so the live broadcasts lost about as much in signal quality as they gained in authenticity. Murrow's normally clear, strong voice often cracked, became scarcely audible, or faded out altogether in the difficulty of long-distance transmission. "This is London," he always began. "This has been what might be called a 'routine night'—air raid at about nine o'clock and intermittent bombing ever since. . . . One becomes accustomed to rattling windows and the distant sound of bombs and then comes a silence that can be felt. You know the sound will return. You wait and then it starts again. That waiting is bad. It gives you a chance to imagine things."[3] Murrow did not set out to sell the British cause to the United States. He wished to tell a story, to report the truth. "He was trying to explain the universal human cause of men who were showing a noble face to the world," a fellow broadcaster explained. "In so doing he made the British and their behavior human and thus compelling to his countrymen at home."[4]

One could hardly feel disinterest in this war, given the daily bombardment by radio and press, the warnings from various quarters that the world indeed was experiencing cataclysm. The most common American reaction surely was relief and gratitude that the war was still more than 3,000 miles away. Americans for the last time could thank heaven for the Atlantic Ocean. There was also a sense of excitement in the tragic drama, a feeling openly conceded by a few and denied by others who did not feel, or refused to admit, a fascination with war.

World War II was a struggle of machines to be sure, but it came at a time when the distance between men and machine was not as great as it later would be. A man still could make a difference, if only through manipulation of a machine. It was perhaps the last romantic war, or at least it had touches of romanticism: heroes and villains, acts of gallantry and cowardice, new weapons and tactics. It gave rise to words that, once one learned how, became almost exciting to pronounce: Stuka, von Runstedt, von Ribbentrop, Blitzkrieg, Mussolini. It produced mystery and suspense, such as the episode in the spring of the *Bismarck*, the mighty German dreadnought that slipped into the Atlantic, overpowered some of the best ships of the Royal Navy, then dropped from sight, heading no one knew where. Some people feared it even might turn up off America's East Coast. One had to feel as much dazzlement with the performance of German forces as sorrow for the people they had overrun. Nearly all people, even the Irish, expressed admiration for Britain's gallant defense against the Germans. More would come in 1941: the continued German advance in the Balkans and, in June, the incomparably massive struggle that began when Germany invaded Russia. Unlike the tedious stalemate of 1914–18, World War II was a war of movement, action, and innovation—the "Big One," as people would call it almost affectionately after it had passed.

All this is not meant to imply that the emotions of Americans rose and fell in step with the latest war news. The United States by that time had been exposed to nearly three years of headlines, 1 inch high or larger, about diplomacy, war, and tragedy. The people had learned to live with stories of bloodshed and devastation, the *Schrechtlichkeit* of war at mid-twentieth century. If slaughtered civilians, bombed-out cities, and conquered nations betokened a dreadful state of the world in 1941, they also served to harden people to the rules—or perhaps the idea that there were no rules—by which nations fought in that day, a sober conditioner for the war Americans soon were to undertake, and for troubles in years to come.

Most people by 1941 had some impression of the belligerents and of what was taking place across the sea. Most unfamiliar, if not necessarily the most complicated, were events in the Far East. In the absence of concrete knowledge and a clear perception of Asians and Asian affairs, Americans acted from impressions hastily conceived and subject to rapid change, formed by comparing glimpses of much different Eastern behavior with their own. Older images of the Chinese as sinister, opium-addicted heathens—projected in films and countless pulp novels—had softened somewhat under the influence of Pearl Buck's classic volume and movie, *The Good Earth*, and a sympathetic press. A powerful spokesman for China for years had been Henry R. Luce, the son of missionary parents and now the owner of a huge publishing empire. His magazines frequently carried pieces on the Chinese, all designed to arouse American respect and admiration. *Life* published in February, for example, a pictorial essay on a college campus at Yenching, showing a placid setting out of the war zone with quiet streams, charming pagodas, and enthusiastic students. "The Chinese people have always had an ancient and rugged feeling for democracy," *Life* explained. "Yenching teaches, above all, self-reliance and self-respect, responsibility and self-expression, the middle class virtues of [the] U.S."[5]

Luce's petitions to the contrary, Americans continued to look upon the Chinese as sheeplike, illiterate, and a good distance from the American concept of a civilized nation. Shanghai was not, as a senator recently had said it could be, "just like Kansas City." But at least the Chinese seemed to be trying; after all, had China's leader Chiang Kai-shek not converted to Christianity, and had his wife, besides being a Methodist, not graduated from Wellesley College in Massachusetts? Because of such purported Americanization of the Chinese and because of the unprovoked punishment they now had to endure, China aroused much pity in the United States. Few Americans had not seen the memorable photograph of a Chinese baby at Shanghai, blackened, frightened and evidently wounded, sitting in the middle of a street and crying as the torture of war continued all around. The government for years had professed sympathy for China's plight, and some Americans, notably religious groups, now thought it should help much more. Volunteers had formed an organization called United China Relief, and in 1941 the film producer Walt Disney agreed to become chairman of a Young China branch of that organization. The "screen juveniles" Mickey Rooney and Judy Garland headed a China Stamp Club of Young China, seeking to raise $5 million.

The more Americans sympathized with the Chinese, the more they experienced puzzlement and disgust with Japan. Acquaintance with that distant island nation came largely from the press and from Japanese products. The toys, trinkets, and cheap manufactured goods exported to the United States seemed almost a characterization of the Japanese nation: small and mobile, hastily assembled, of limited durability. "Made in Japan" had special meaning in the United States. All Japanese apparently had poor eyesight, for cartoons showed nearly all of them wearing eyeglasses, with protruding teeth and a deceitful smile; not very creative themselves, they were said to be adept at copying the West.

They had borrowed Western technology, of course, and for some unexplained reason they had developed a fondness for American baseball. They had copied the game entirely, even down to the team names and English versions of official rulings and exclamations. A pitcher was the "pichah," the catcher was "kyacah," a home run became "homu ran" or "homma." "Battah uppa," the umpire would shout, and then "strik-u" or "brawwr."[6] Baseball fans might have remembered the time seven years earlier when a team of major league all-stars had played in Japan; the Americans had won sixteen straight, and the score of one game had been 23–5. Americans could not decide whether to be flattered or indignant at Japan's taking over "our" game; there probably was some of both feelings. At any rate, both the sparse proficiency of Japanese baseball and their eagerness to adopt it were taken as further evidence of those little people's inferiority.

In military matters as well, Americans refused to take Japan seriously. One story, so persistent that the *Saturday Evening Post* devoted an article to debunking it, asserted that the Japanese could not become good aviators. The practice of carrying babies on the mothers' back reportedly caused the head to wobble so much that by adulthood Japanese men had lost a sense of balance. "Nonsense," the *Post* said, although the article conceded that the Japanese pilot might not have good side vision because of the "way the eye socket is placed in the skull."[7]

The prestigious journal of aeronautics *Aviation* confirmed that Japanese air power produced little reason for worry. Japan was turning out few pilots each year, and the quality of training was reflected in the fact that Japanese fliers had "the highest accident rate in the world." These fliers lacked initiative: "The Japanese are imitators," *Aviation* reported. The planes were "undergunned . . . obsolete or obsolescent," and poor copies of Western models. The quality of Italian aircraft was "strikingly higher." "Japan," the journal continued, "if engaged in a great air war would crumble like a house of cards, dragging after itself the myth of her military prowess and the carefully cultivated daydream of Pacific hegemony and complete world domination."[8]

In other important ways, however, the Japanese insisted upon remaining disgustingly Japanese—secretive and difficult to assess from a Western point of view. They persisted in curious utterings about Japanese destiny, their place in the sun. Reports had it that they worshiped the Emperor: "Hirohito is no longer a man," one author wrote. "All Japanese are expected to treat him as deity."[9] Americans favored China in the Far East, if they took an interest at all. Few people worried that events in Asia threatened danger for the United States, but some observers advised taking Japan seriously, warning that expansion in the Pacific fostered a frightful world movement toward totalitarianism and military rule. One could not ignore the fact that the Japanese had become an ally of Germany by signing the Tripartite Pact in September 1940, a move that many Americans interpreted as placing Japan under the influence, if not the control, of its more able European partner.

Americans had reached more definite conclusions about the war in Europe. Public opinion polls of 1939–41 consistently showed that nearly everyone expressing an opinion favored the Allies, which after June 1940 meant only Britain. Old visions of German militarism, totalitarianism, and brutality—so common during the 1914–18 period—were resurrected and given new sanction by Hitler's racist harangues or pictures of the *Wehrmacht* marching with machinelike precision through some European capital. Germany's government seemed to be a curious lot. *Time* made reference to "beer-bellied, redfaced, medal-chested Hermann Göring," chieftain of the air force and perhaps *die zweiter*, the second in command, this warrior who wore baby-blue uniforms, rouge, and possibly lipstick. Another magazine that compared the "Nazi gang" to a group of racketeers identified the place each official might hold in a criminal organization.[10]

Any discussion of the Third Reich always focused on its omnipresent leader. Hitler had surely the most distinctive face in the world in 1941, at least in the Western world. With the small brush mustache and hair combed across the forehead, he looked like no one Americans had ever seen; yet, with a minimum of improvisation—a comb pressed above the upper lip, swipe of the hair across the brow, and the upraised arm salute—almost anyone could give a recognizable impersonation of *der Führer*. The press had never been flattering in its treatment of Hitler, and in the summer Americans received an authoritative description from William L. Shirer, the familiar radio reporter, with the publication of his *Berlin Diary*. The book, a recollection of several years' residence in the Third Reich, contained the private observations Shirer had never tried to slip past German censors. Shirer reported that Hitler had many peculiar characteristics, such as a "curious walk . . . very ladylike. Dainty little steps . . . every few steps he cocked his shoulder nervously, his left leg snapping up as he did so." He also had a "nervous tic" and "ugly black patches under his eyes."[11]

To most Americans, who could not understand German, Hitler's appearances on radio or in newsreels sounded like bombastic nonsense. He cut such a comical figure that people might have dismissed him as simply a ridiculous little man, had he not become so successful and dangerous. Many Americans saw Hitler as a mixture of genius and madman—genius at military intuition and statecraft, and maniac by virtue of his rumored personal habits and unprincipled thirst for power. "Hitler is no fool," reported a no less competent observer than Walter Lippmann, "he is in fact a man of satanic genius in his understanding of the power of evil in human nature."[12] Already in control of Western Europe, he seemed poised to reach for more. His government's savage treatment of non-German people, particularly Jews, had begun to become public. Hitler's proneness to temper tantrums was evident in his public speeches; in 1941 the press began circulating reports that in fits of rage he threw himself on the floor and began chewing the carpet. Some Germans had taken to calling him *Teppichfresser*, the "Carpet-eater." Surely no sane man could act like that.

Americans had some difficulty deciding what position to take on the German people. As for Nazis and members of the government there could be little doubt: They were maniacs. Shirer described Nazi loyalists during a commotion in the Reichstag at the end of one of Hitler's speeches: "They spring, yelling and crying to their feet. . . . Their hands are raised in slavish salute, their faces now contorted with hysteria, their mouths wide open, shouting, shouting, their eyes, burning with fanaticism glued on the new God, the Messiah."[13] With the ordinary German, however, Americans could reach far less consensus. Some people argued that the Nazi regime was not of the people's doing and even sympathized with them for having to bear a brutal dictatorship. Most individuals of German extraction took this position. Other Americans saw nearly all Germans as potential Nazis, a consequence of militaristic, totalitarian features inherent in the German character. Douglas Miller found the answer in obedience and discipline, the German unwillingness to challenge authority. He related an experience of getting off a train in Berlin to find a large crowd waiting to give up their tickets. The ticket taker was absent, so the people stood there not knowing what to do. Miller threw his ticket on the floor and went on; the Germans timidly did the same. "I expect that if they had not had the example of a foreigner, they might be waiting there yet," he wrote.[14] Americans thus had not decided if Germans admired Hitler or simply endured him. It remained undeniable, however, that they had submitted to his leadership, thereby setting German industriousness, creativity, and discipline on a highly dubious course.

Americans seemed much less worried about the behavior of Italy, if only because the Italians had enjoyed far less success in what they had undertaken. Italy happened to have a powerful partner, but it was stepping out of its class. Benito Mussolini, Italy's bald, blustering *Duce*, looked like a poor imitation of Caesar indeed, a pompous, opportunistic dictator whose foreign conquests came about through his choice of weak countries to attack and through the Germans' willingness to rescue the Italian army from bungled military operations. With his oversized chin and his rooster strut, how could anyone take Mussolini, or his people, seriously? "Poverty-striken, anemic and weak-kneed dagos," ran one uncharitable observation. "Italians since the time of the Romans have never been able to put up a first-class fight anywhere."[15] Detached from Germany, Italy was more worthy of ridicule than fear; associated with Hitler, Mussolini became symbolic of the totalitarian militarism sweeping much of the world.

Such images were of course simplistic and self-serving; they reflected Americans' view of themselves no less than of the world. In their opposition to the totalitarian powers, Americans identified themselves as enemies of oppression and spokesmen for democracy and freedom. The serious economic problems and political divisions of the recent past—by no means now vanished—seemed to leave no unfavorable reflection on basic American institutions, at least not within the context of world politics. Other systems seemed so much worse, and the more the world rushed to tumult, the more Americans stressed their nation's uniqueness as the repository of what was good and sacred in human affairs. America offered the only hope for mankind. That was the message, and it appeared everywhere—in speeches before civic groups, newspaper and magazine pieces, letters to the editor, and such movies as *Mr. Smith Goes to Washington*. A former ambassador wrote: "from what I have seen in Russia and in Europe, I am more than ever grateful for our own form of government. . . . It is the last best hope for liberty and freedom in a threatened world." An editorial put the case as forcefully: "The dirt farmer in the corn belt, the salesgirl behind the counter, the miner at the coal field, the stoker at sea—all believe in our democracy and demand vigorously that it be defended."[16]

How to defend it was the problem, for whatever perception Americans might have had of themselves, there existed other attitudes in that last year of peace which discouraged the logical next step, proceeding toward war with the Axis. German-Americans and people of Italian descent, as fond of the old homeland as they were uncertain about its leadership, found the subject of foreign policy discomforting. They did not want to see the United States go to war against the country of their antecedents. War with the Axis powers would mean alignment with Britain, a prospect displeasing in areas where anti-British sentiment was strong, particularly in Irish settlements and in the Midwest, where Colonel Robert McCormick continued to twist the Lion's tail in his popular newspaper, the Chicago *Tribune*. Angered at the thought of a second war to bail out the British, Anglophobes took delight in assailing His Majesty's empire and misquoting Winston Churchill as pledging "to fight until the last American boy."

But in 1941 the prospect of another "foreign war" repelled most Americans, regardless of national origin. Drawing partly on fear, partly on the notions of American innocence, invulnerability, and uniqueness, partly on recent experience in world affairs, this feeling had dominated opinion polls since the start of war in 1939. At times it seemed to have encompassed nearly the entire population. The horror of war was so obvious, the memory of World War I, now scarcely more than twenty years old, so fresh, as to make the people dubious of all foreign ventures that were not the nation's immediate business. People over forty could think back on their part in the "Great War," perhaps in the mud and trenches of France, perhaps in a shipyard or munitions factory. Experience of the intervening years had left considerable cynicism about the idea of an American world mission, especially for a generation with sons reaching military age.

Who could forget the slogans and high idealism in the crusade of 1917, when another President had sent the boys off to fight for liberty and democracy? With the world in the 1930s and 1940s rushing to totalitarianism, with the United States struggling to survive a long depression, who could claim that anyone had benfited from the experience? Who could deny that that grand effort had been a failure and probably a mistake? "We went over there once and pulled England's chestnuts out of the fire," a lady in Baltimore said. "This time let them stew in their own juices."[17]

At the start, most people had considered this second war a continuation of the first, more of a wearisome European malady, a consequence of too many people living too close together. The message for the United States seemed simple: Do not repeat the error of 1917. Then came the remarkable events of the summer of 1940: the fall of France, the collapse of Europe, the isolation of Britain. Comparison with World War I began to lose meaning. Kaiser Wilhelm appeared almost impotent beside the volatile Hitler, and the Nazi regime unlike anything Americans had encountered. The events were not so simple, and the "lesson of history" notion was at least subject to question.

Feelings thus had changed by 1941 from what they had been two years earlier, but most people had not abandoned skepticism about another bloody war thousands of miles away, a result of forces that seemed to offer at most a theoretical danger. Even though Americans might admit Hitler's greed and brutality, might concede that he threatened American principles, might even question his sanity, they were far from certain about how those conclusions affected the United States or what should be done about them. A British visitor enjoyed hearing American friends express admiration for British courage during the long blitz. They promised friendship, encouragement, and various forms of assistance, until the discussion got around to direct involvement of American forces. Then this Briton encountered "a very definite limitation . . . a fundamental reluctance in the American mind." Later he found the same attitude in "every section of American life, in every state."[18]

If a fateful and costly globalism was to evolve from events beginning to unfold, no such grand design caught the public imagination in 1941. Americans wanted Germany to lose, but they also wanted to remain at peace, and between these lines of thought they found themselves suspended. Any course offered the prospect of great risk, and a satisfactory outcome depended on questions the people were ill-prepared to answer. Assuming that peace was the objective, could the nation best pursue it by detaching itself from Europe or by attempting to influence the war in ways short of intervention? What sort of peace was tolerable—peace at the cost of a German-controlled Europe? Did Germany constitute a threat to the United States now? In the future? Did the United States have a moral responsibility to anyone other than itself? How could the nation best exercise responsibility to itself? On those complicated questions the people could find no consensus. A small minority supported active intervention; a larger minority demanded all steps necessary to keep the United States out of war; the bulk of the population allowed itself to be carried along by events.

In this confused situation the government, particularly President Roosevelt, occupied the decisive position. Roosevelt not only initiated policy; through control of war information and access to almost unlimited press and radio exposure, he possessed an unrivaled opportunity to identify issues and explain the war to the populace. Roosevelt had made the most of it. At no time since the outbreak of the conflict had he made the slightest pretense at impartiality, insisting that Germany constituted a problem of pressing, even desperate concern for the United States. "Never before since Jamestown and Plymouth Rock has our American civilization been in such danger," he had proclaimed. "The Nazi masters of Germany have made it clear that they intended . . . to enslave the whole of Europe, and then to use the resources of Europe to dominate the rest of the world." Roosevelt had moved almost immediately to assist the enemies of Hitler, first by fostering the sale of war material through private American firms, then in September 1940 by sending (officially trading) American warships to Britain. Now early in 1941, he had set the nation astir with the proposal of H.R. 1776, better known as the Lend-Lease Bill, a measure designed to provide almost unlimited arms for the British. "We must be," he said, "the great arsenal of democracy."[19]

But Roosevelt had neither solved the people's problem nor settled the confusion. He had sharpened the issues by insisting that the war affected the United States and arguing forcefully for assistance to one side. But beyond that point his objectives were, if not muddled, at least less convincing. He was unwilling to acknowledge the possible consequences of the action. Roosevelt had set the nation on a course certain to arouse the Germans and possibly leading into hostilities, but one could not grasp this fact from his speeches. Ever the politician, conscious of the polls and fearful of provoking hostile public reaction, he refused to speak of intervention or concede that such action might ultimately be necessary. Only a few months earlier, during the presidential campaign of 1940, Roosevelt had made what sounded like a solid pledge: "I have said this before, but I will say it again and again and again. Your boys are not going to be sent into any foreign wars."[20]

Now, at the start of 1941, Roosevelt held to the same course. The "sole purpose" of national policy was "to keep war away from our people," he promised. "There is far less chance of the United States getting into war, if we do all we can now to support the nations defending themselves against attack by the Axis than if we acquiesce in their defeat . . . and wait our turn to be the object of attack in another war later on."[21] That reasoning made sense—or did it? Who could tell when any course offered such great risk? "The horns of the dilemma are sharp and they may be bloody," one writer warned, and most of the people agreed.[22] Instead of helping the people out of that great dilemma, Roosevelt had chosen to evade the issue, denying that a dilemma existed.

Large decisions nonetheless had to be made, so millions of people had taken sides in a great debate, their positions dependent partly on an understanding of the war in Europe, partly on their willingness to support Roosevelt. Each side contained many shades of opinion, but their clearest division concerned support for or opposition to Roosevelt's aid to Britain.

People wishing to align themselves with an organization found a bewildering assortment from which to choose. One might decide to join, for example, the American Friends of German Freedom, Loyal Americans of German Descent, No Foreign Wars Committee, Student Defenders of Democracy, Mothers of the U.S.A., Paul Revere Sentinels, Women's Neutrality League, Christian Front, Silver Shirts, or another of the hundreds of organizations operating in those confusing days, each seeking to influence the course of national policy. "America today is the scene of a mighty drama," Erskine Caldwell observed. "It is like nothing else that has ever taken place before, because there is no audience to express approval or disapproval. Everyone today is on stage taking part."[23]

Most attention focused on a few well-organized groups with the most influence or the largest following. Among the first organized were those willing to endorse an extreme position: war with Germany. The typical interventionist probably was a person on the non-Communist left, afire with idealism and liberal ideas, who found fascism abhorrent in all respects. The journal *Nation* had proclaimed this conflict "the liberal's war." Even so, several notable businessmen and conservatives joined the crusade in the early stages, and the first effective pro-war organization was a tiny collection of prominent men, some of them wealthy, with mixed political affiliation who formed the Century Group in New York. As it became evident that the organization was too small and elitist to have mass appeal, the Century Group branched out, changed its name to Fight for Freedom, and began furnishing speakers, purchasing ads, and financing such anti-fascist campaigns as "Wanted Dead or Alive" handbills bearing a photograph of Hitler. While all interventionists believed that nothing short of war could crush Hitlerism, they realized that most people in the United States were not prepared to go that far, so they did not hesitate to assist organizations endorsing a less drastic course.

It was far more popular in 1941 to support measures short of war, such as supplying arms and other matériel to nations resisting fascism. That posture could offer potential followers the best of two worlds: protection of the nation and its ideals and exemption of Americans from a direct part in the bloodletting. It also was in tune with American policy, a fact that lent respectability and perhaps a superior claim to patriotism.

Supporters of Roosevelt had moved toward organization during the catastrophic summer of 1940, when all Europe seemed on the verge of becoming Nazi. For leadership they had gone to William Allen White, a respected Republican newspaperman from Emporia, Kansas, and an observer of politics for many years. White brought to the cause seasoned judgment, conservative temperament, at least a hint of bipartisanship, and a homey, colorful style. "The old British lion looks mangy, sore-eyed," he had written. "He needs worming and should have a lot of dental work. He can't even roar."[24] White believed that Britain also needed new leadership, which it acquired in Winston Churchill, and a great deal of help from the United States, and to that end he helped form the organization with a patriotic but cumbersome title "Committee to Defend America by Aiding the Allies" (CDA). The committee believed, as a spokesman put it, that Hitler was a madman, that "America has only one chance to escape total war and that chance is England."[25]

Successful in attracting prominent people in education, business, and entertainment, the "White Committee" soon became the largest and most influential private group concerned with foreign policy. Its members experienced the dilemma in policy most acutely, however, and as each month produced new, more warlike measures, each individual had to determine how long to continue in this position of compromise. Convinced that matters were getting out of hand and that the CDA had become too belligerent, White resigned. Other members gave themselves over to interventionism. Although the Fight for Freedom Committee and the Committee to Defend America remained separate organizations until the end of the year, differences in their programs became increasingly blurred. Even within groups that had taken sides in the great debate, a considerable confusion prevailed.

Many of Roosevelt's supporters had come to view World War II as a struggle of incomparable significance, probably the most important in human history, a conflict that threatened the structure of Western and American civilization. Stephen Vincent Benét argued that the world faced "a new theory of the state of man," of "master and helot, lord and serf."[26] The poet Archibald MacLeish warned of danger "so great, so terrible, so immediate, so close that only the re-creation of the people's will and the people's strength, only the realization of every possibility of the people, will enable the people's government to survive."[27] Rarely in American history had so many people spoken out, and in such intemperate language. Rarely—if ever—had so many individuals active in the arts or prominent for reasons other than politics felt moved to express their views on political issues, seeking, almost straining, to instruct and arouse their fellow citizens.

Opponents of the Administration took the name isolationists, in keeping with their contention that America's stake in the European war was nowhere near as great as Roosevelt had said. They operated under an interpretation of American self-interest and a view of history different from those held by Roosevelt and his followers. The trouble abroad was Europe's problem, a condition that did not endanger the United States, the isolationists said, so the United States should aid no nation, should antagonize no prospective enemy, and should detach itself from foreign problems to concentrate on matters, including the nation's defense, in the United States. A man from Massachusetts put the case bluntly, with no small measure of cynicism: "Let's keep out of this lousy war. It was made by a bunch of crooks on both sides. The poor soldier will be . . . asked to die for slogans as false as hell. . . . We heard it all the last time."[28]

Isolationists objected to the man as much as the policy. From the beginning of his presidency, Roosevelt had provoked strong emotion in the American populace, and while the most common response was favorable, even worshipful, the people who disliked him did so with great intensity. The attitude probably started with a belief that the New Deal had destroyed the American economy, had vastly enlarged government, and had moved the nation toward presidential dictatorship. The President's opponents grew to dislike Roosevelt the man, the tone of his voice, his habits and mannerisms—this cocky, aristocratic Democrat (were aristocrats not supposed to be Republican?) from upstate New York, this clever politician who tried to act like everyone's father. He did not even look like an American. Look at that cigarette holder cocked high in the air, the pince-nez clamped on his nose. Why could he not simply wear glasses, the way real Americans did? And no one used a cigarette holder those days, except possibly a few people in the snootiest Eastern elite circles.

For years rumors had circulated about the secret policies and uncouth personal habits of "that man" in the White House. Russell Baker recalled that his Uncle Harold, who detested the man, claimed to know stories so disgraceful that newspapers were afraid to print them. Harold insisted, for example, that Roosevelt became President only "for the money," that he collected payoffs from everyone who wanted to see him.

"There's a coat rack right outside his door, and he keeps an overcoat hanging on that rack," an astonished young Russell heard his uncle say. "Before anybody can get in to see him, they've got to put money in the overcoat pocket. . . . That's the kind of President we've got."[29]

Uncle Harold might have been notorious among members of the Baker family as a liar, but his story was typical of the vicious personal attacks on the President and his family that circulated among Roosevelt's enemies and often in the general population. *Life* magazine reported in 1941 that "a new disease, sprung up in America during the past eight years is not yet listed in the medical books. But few others have such power to warp and poison a man's mind and soul. The name of the disease is Roosevelt-hatred."[30]

The more the President had to handle large issues of foreign policy, the more distrust spread and intensified. Prevent war by aiding Germany's enemy? It sounded too much like the Roosevelt the critics had known for more than eight years: the soothing simplifier, manipulator of truth, drawer of false analogies (lend-lease, Roosevelt had said, was comparable to loaning a neighbor a hose to extinguish a fire). "What hypocrisy," Senator Burton K. Wheeler, one of the President's most outspoken critics shouted. Wheeler followed a logic different from Roosevelt's: "If it's our war, we ought to have the courage to go over and fight it—but it isn't our war."[31]

Roosevelt's political enemies found an easy explanation for the conflict between the President's words (the promise of peace) and his action (arming Britain): Roosevelt was a liar who would take the nation to war unless they themselves could turn the people against him. Danger came not from Hitler or from world war, they argued, but from a President who used the conflict to pursue secret mischievious objectives, the most reprehensible of which was accumulation of enormous personal power. "Down into the hell of a war—in no sense our war—the President would plunge us," Representative Claire Hoffman of Michigan charged, "to satisfy his ambition to . . . be elected the third time to the Presidency, and in order that he may go down in history as America's first dictator."[32]

Isolationism, no less than war, produced strange ideological bedfellows. In time most isolationists would be conservative Republicans, but the movement always included a small group of Democrats and Midwestern progressive Republicans, such individuals as Wheeler and Senator Gerald Nye of North Dakota. During 1940–41 people had joined from both political fringes. Norman Thomas, leader of the Socialist Party, testified against Lend-Lease, and American Communists, in strict compliance with Soviet policy, maintained a steady attack on interventionism—until June 1941, that is, when Germany attacked the Soviet Union. For several months the extreme American left stood awkwardly in league with the extreme political right: fascists and Nazis, or people impressed with Hitler, Mussolini, and totalitarian systems in general.

Leftist support was at least embarrassing to the Midwestern conservative core of the isolationist movement, but the extreme right proved the most troublesome, for it supported ideas most isolationists considered objectionable, leaving the movement open to the charge that it was fascist itself. Rightists also were the most irresponsible campaigners. One of the most notorious propagandists was Father Charles Coughlin, a renowned "radio priest" from suburban Detroit, who saved his choicest adjectives for the British Empire, Franklin D. Roosevelt, and the President's supporters. Coughlin referred to members of the White Committee as un-American, subversive, "Quislings of America, Judas Iscariots . . . , gold-protected, Government-protected, foreign-protected snakes in the grass who dare not stand upright and speak like a man face to face."[33]

The featured isolationist performer in 1941 was no fascist or radical but Charles A. Lindbergh, "Lucky Lindy," the shy folk hero now moved to lend his considerable prestige to a cause thought more important than a much-publicized penchant for privacy. Though pushing forty, he looked much younger. Tall, trim, with his familiar, boyish face and his ingenuous smile, he spoke with directness and sincerity. Lindbergh was no politician, had no election to win, was driven by no motive beyond love of country. So it appeared to the thousands who gathered to hear his speeches at meetings of the America First Committee. Lindbergh's special contribution, besides his reputation, was an alleged expertise on air power, a development of modern warfare that, in his curious interpretation, guaranteed American security. Otherwise he advanced arguments familiar to most isolationists: The war was not America's business unless America insisted on making it so. Assistance to Britain not only was dangerous but encouraged the British to resist and thus prolonged the struggle. Germany probably could not be defeated, and it was not absolutely essential that the Germans lose. "We are strong enough . . . to maintain our own way of life regardless of . . . the attitude . . . on the other side," he said.[34]

The isolationists proceeded to attack the Administration on every front: fighting measures in Congress, signing petitions, organizing rallies, and using whatever press support was available, notably McCormick's powerful *Tribune*. As the issues became more heated, so did the contestants. Isolationists called opponents war mongers, agents of Britain, and Communists; Roosevelt's supporters associated isolationism with fascism and branded it racist. Rallies attracted counter-demonstrations, creating tense situations and several skirmishes: The leader of one isolationist group, speaking on the radio, challenged his audience to a fight. A rally of the American First Committee in April that drew some 25,000 participants, hecklers, and police to Manhattan Center turned into a minor riot. While the crowds, parades, and scuffles bespoke serious issues facing the nation, they also had started to produce a new mood, a reawakening that came from interest in anything large, an excitement that came from attachment to a cause. The people intimately involved might have found it exhilarating.

The person who seemed to be getting least pleasure from the activity was Lindbergh, and the more he immersed himself in the contest, the more he became the center of controversy and the prime target of the President's backers. Perhaps Americans had expected more idealism from the man who earlier had inspired so many to reach for the stars. Perhaps the opposition feared that the former national idol might be too effective and win the debate for the isolationists. Perhaps Lindbergh was, to some extent, a victim of unsympathetic media. He had quarreled with the press for many years and even had blamed some newsmen for the murder of his kidnapped child in 1932, and he had detested the flagrant badgering that had followed that tragic event. Unfriendly writers now published charges made by interventionist groups and added some of their own, reminding the public of Lindbergh's visits to Germany, his acceptance of a medal from Hermann Göring in 1938, and his admiration for German military efficiency; if they did not say it directly, their implication was that he was probably fascist. One writer called Lindbergh "a leading American Nazi" who deserved "another medal from Hitler for pure devotion and hard work in his cause."[35]

Lindbergh stuck to his guns. He refused to stop or soften his speeches. The most provocative came in September, when he charged that groups responsible for moving the United States toward war were "the British, the Jewish, and the Roosevelt administration."[36] Then came the deluge. Labeled anti-Semitic and perhaps disloyal, he found his credibility in doubt, his effectiveness lessened, and his reputation tarnished beyond recovery. America's love affair with the Lone Eagle had come to an end.

It had been a losing battle anyway, by and large, for Lindbergh and his colleagues. A critical point had come in the struggle over the Lend-Lease proposal that started in January and ran into March. The episode had all the markings of Rooseveltian political maneuver—soothing words, glamorous labels, explanations that muddled the issue without exactly telling a lie. The Administration had started by attaching the title "A Bill Further to Promote the Defense of the

United States and for Other Purposes." Roosevelt had made it appear simple. The United States was going to proceed much as in the past, except with slightly different tactics. "Now what I am trying to do is eliminate the dollar sign . . . the silly foolish old dollar sign," the President had said. He proposed to "loan" supplies to America's friends abroad.

It took little perception to see through the President's jaunty explanation. "The very title of the bill is a fraud," Senator Robert A. Taft of Ohio complained. "Lending war matériel is much like lending chewing gum," he said. "We certainly do not want the same gum back." The President in truth wanted authority to give billions of dollars' worth of military goods to Britain, evidently any kind of matériel, as much as Britain wanted, a remarkable proposal in an age not yet familiar with the concept "foreign aid." The measure also stood to involve the United States in a much larger way in the struggle against Hitler and perhaps foretold of danger to come. "The words of his mouth were smoother than butter," Taft remarked, "but war was in his heart."[37]

The isolationists had used some of their strongest language and had called out their biggest troops in the battle against Lend-Lease. Joseph P. Kennedy, who had been Ambassador to Great Britain, testified against the bill, as did Lindbergh, Norman Thomas, Colonel McCormick, the historian Charles A. Beard, and many others. They gave out familiar warnings about war-mongering, presidential dictatorship, and selling out American interests to the British. Burton Wheeler had been downright nasty: "The lend-lease-give program is the New Deal's Triple-A foreign policy," he said: "it will plow under every fourth American boy."[38]

Giving away war matériel was dangerous enough (and very expensive), but opponents worried as well about what would follow passage of the Lend-Lease measure. What would the government do to see that the goods arrived in Britain: begin using American warships in the Atlantic Ocean, perhaps institute a system of convoys? There were German submarines out there, as everyone knew, slipping through the dark waters, scanning the surface through their periscopes, with no objective other than sinking ships. If the isolationists raised meaningful questions, they were in no position to answer them, and so they could only sound their alarms; offer dozens of amendments, most of which were rejected; and here and there interject a note of sarcasm or cynicism. An Irish Congressman proposed a new battle hymn, to the tune of "God Bless America," which began: "God save America, from British rule." Another legislator recommended that the bill include the following statement: "Nothing in this act shall be construed to authorize or permit the President of the United States to lease, lend, or transfer the original Thirteen Colonies to King George of England."[39]

Even though Roosevelt's critics had enlivened the debate over foreign policy and at times made as much noise as his supporters, they could not control public opinion or muster enough strength to block his policy. When Congress in March passed the Lend-Lease Bill by impressive majorities, Roosevelt seemed to have everything he needed.

The bulk of the people thus continued to follow their President. It had been the American pattern to support the government in foreign relations, of course, but the attitude in 1941 also demonstrated special faith in Roosevelt. In the midst of world war, as during the dreary days of the Depression, they found his presidential messages, the "fireside chats," the only way to make sense out of events nearly impossible to understand. Even if they did not understand all that was happening, or all that the President said, many people trusted Roosevelt to lead them in the right direction. The President helped guide the people to conclusions about the war; he rationalized the nation's perhaps contradictory course of preparing for a war it wished to avoid. A sizable majority continued to support his policies as the year's developments brought the United States ominously closer to full-scale belligerency. Even so, it had been neither an easy nor a comforting decision, and millions doubtless wished they could have chosen between less dismal alternatives.

What Americans were debating, although few people appeared to recognize the fact, was an end of innocence, or the pretense of innocence, in world affairs. The nation had considered the issue a generation earlier, at the end of the other war, and seemed to have decided in favor of remaining apart from the world's problems. They could not guarantee, however, that the world's problems would remain away from the United States. Detachment had not worked well either in making life better for Americans or in solving the world's problems, and so trouble had continued to grow during the beleaguered 1920s and 1930s to this point in 1941, when it seemed ready to turn the world upside down, and the United States was bound to be vastly affected whatever the outcome. "We wasted those twenty years," one observer lamented. "We criticized, preached, exhorted, declaimed, prayed and moaned," and because Americans did no more, "blood is being spilled now."[40]

If innocence was near an end, there appeared little understanding of what its departure would mean, what place the United States would have in the world of the future. In that respect the isolationists did better than their critics, for now and then spokesmen warned that once intervention had started it never would end, that the United States thereafter would seek to police the entire globe. "We have thrown ourselves squarely into the power politics and the power wars of Europe, Asia and Africa," Senator Arthur Vandenberg, an isolationist, said on passage of the Lend-Lease Bill. "We have taken the first step upon a course from which we can never hereafter retreat."[41] The isolationists seemed mostly interested in attacking the deviousness of Roosevelt and offering an unconvincing promise that life in a world that included Hitler's Europe would be tolerable. The only alternative they suggested was to avoid all involvement, a proposal that ignored the nation's far-flung interests and concerns, not to mention its principles, and the impact of world events upon the United States.

Now and then a columnist, an academician, or an observer of world affairs sought to forecast the future in terms of American ascendancy. The most ambitious scheme came from Henry Luce, powerful owner of the publishing empire of *Time*, *Life*, and *Fortune* magazines, and an interventionist. Luce decided that the American people needed to face the hard but potentially glorious facts of world affairs. He had easy access to a public forum, three of them in fact, and so he chose a February edition of *Life* for a forceful essay entitled "The American Century." Luce's thesis, simply stated, was that the United States could dominate the earth if the people would recognize the opportunity and move to exploit it. The foundation of Luce's new world was American capitalism: "It is for America and America alone to determine whether a system of free economic enterprise— an economic order compatible with freedom and progress—shall or shall not prevail in this century. . . . There is not the slightest chance of a free economic system prevailing in this country if it prevails nowhere else."

Luce contended that in some measure the world already had begun to revolve about the United States. American jazz, slang, Hollywood movies, American machines and goods of many kinds were familiar to all areas of the world, from "Zanzibar to Hamburg." "Blindly, unintentionally, accidentally and really in spite of ourselves," the United States already had become the artistic, intellectual, and scientific capital of the world. Why not extend this domination to politics and economics, he asked, and put it forcefully into effect?

With the benefits of world domination, of course, came some hefty responsibilities. Luce did not flinch from those. "We must undertake now to be the good Samaritan of the entire world . . . to feed all the people of the world. For every dollar we spend on armaments, we should spend at least a dime on a gigantic effort to feed the world." "We are the inheritors of all the great principles of Western Civilization—above all Justice, the love of Truth, the ideal of Charity," Luce concluded. It had now become time for the Americans to lift "mankind from the level of beasts to what the Psalmist called a little lower than Angels."[42]

There was more truth and prophecy in "The American Century" than most people knew or cared to admit. The United States had begun a movement toward something resembling the dominance of which Luce had written, and yet the nation was so clouded with uncertainty, so devoid of clear-cut objectives that few people—perhaps not even Luce—could detect what was happening. The nation moved not by deliberate design toward an identifiable goal, but by default, to prevent certain events from taking place. "The American Century" thus encountered at best a mixed reception. Many conservatives who might have enjoyed the ideal of an American capitalist order objected to Luce's proposal to begin his century with war against Germany. One critic could not repress a note of cynicism: "We shall raise our boys not only to be soldiers and sailors, but as great transoceanic bearers of our culture and religion to the outermost places of the world. . . . If that doesn't produce the millennium, why—but of course if will. God's chosen people . . . will produce a world that will make heaven seem shoddy indeed."[43]

Such liberal journals as *Nation* and *New Republic* attacked the article as chauvinistic and pure imperialism. If most internationalists assumed that some form of American century was at hand and that involvement in world politics would continue after 1941 and after the war, virtually none were prepared to endorse the blatant *Pax Americana* projected in Luce's article. They generally were pressed to explain where intervention, if it should come, would lead, and so they rarely tried. It was safer and more inspiring in those perilous times to concentrate on issues at hand. Roosevelt helped not at all. Trying to look like the respondent, not the maker of events, he carefully avoided indications of planning or even thought about the future. "I have not the slightest objection toward your trying your hand at an outline of the post war picture," he told an aide, "but for

Heaven's sake don't ever let the columnists hear of it."[44] Cautious and insecure with public opinion, he seemed content to muddle through, doing only what was necessary to prevent the situation from getting out of hand. The future, apparently, would have to take care of itself.

How could one worry about tomorrow, about the future of the United States in world affairs, when problems of today were so large? How could one know what the problems of the future would be? "If Hitler should win decisively, we shall be in a world for which we need not plan," *New Republic* said; "that will be done in Berlin for us, and we won't like it."[45] Of course, Roosevelt and his followers were pledged to prevent that catastrophe. Defeat of Germany and Japan, on the other hand, also would cause enormous, if undetermined, readjustment. Some isolationists forecast a resurgent Russia and a rampaging Communist movement, but after Germany attacked in June many people came to doubt there would be a Russia, at least a Communist Russia, at the end of 1941. American military leaders gave the Soviet Union two months.

And what did the American people think about their future in the world? No more than necessary. They had not sought to dominate world politics, and if considerable influence was being thrust upon them, they did not take it as an altogether pleasant experience. They continued to struggle with personal problems and with that huge dilemma in foreign policy. William Allen White put it directly: "I am one of those . . . 75 percent of Americans who, for a year, have been . . . favoring the President's foreign policy. I am also of the 95 percent who have been . . . for the same period wishing to avoid war."[46] It was indeed a perplexing set of circumstances, a damnable dilemma. "I wish I knew more than I know . . . where the national ship of state is going, what will happen to it in the end," Carl Sandburg wrote in April. "I agree with anyone who has a headache."[47]

☆
T W O
☆

Building the New American Army

The train had pulled in during late afternoon in January 1941, and the engineer had left the passenger cars at a prescribed place on the siding. Inside the coaches, the passengers started to stir without hurrying. They seemed uncertain whether to remain seated or to get up, and, if they were supposed to get off, in what direction they should go. Someone told them to move, so, wrinkled and sluggish from the trip, they walked through the coach, down the steps to the ground, where they mingled uncomfortably, looking out of place.

The destination they had reached could have been any of a number of spots around the country, all of them barren, without color, cheerless, almost hostile, particularly during the gray days of winter. The older establishments at least had paved streets, an occasional tree, and buildings—albeit drab and cold looking—which appeared to have been standing for some time. The newer ones presented all the disarray and ugliness of a construction site. The ground was bare, and when it rained it was muddy. Off to one side, long rows of tents popped and snapped in the wind. Another section had rows of drab, recently built identical buildings. Nearby one could see the same type of building still being constructed, and the air smelled of the fresh pine and tar paper used in their construction. Whether in Georgia, Missouri, or Florida, the places showed an unwelcoming aspect to the recent arrivals, and their dismay underscored the knowledge that this was to be their home for at least the next several weeks.

The travelers from the train represented the most profound evidence of the ways the world war had begun to affect the nation and people's lives. They were inductees, some of the first people called to be a part of America's new Army of 1940–41. Arrival at this destination was the second step of their journey: They had come from an induction center to their basic training post. Most had come at the government's command, yet the Army did not appear happy to have them. The people who met the train were less than gracious hosts. "Get in line, you stupid bastard!" and similarly uncivil orders were routinely shouted in unnecessarily harsh tones. It seemed unwise to challenge these loud and overbearing people with the stripes on their sleeves, so the young men did as told. With belongings cradled in their arms or slung over their backs, they formed themselves into ragged lines and followed the soldier down the muddy strip he called a company street. He insisted on shouting cadence—"hup, tup, thrip, fo"—but the men, in the Army only a few hours, moved each to his own rhythm. If they resembled soldiers at all, it was stragglers from a lost battle.

Involuntary military service had come to the American people in 1940–41, a change in national policy destined to cause disruption in hundreds of thousands, eventually millions, of families. The decision to resurrect the draft had been neither easy nor painless, for conscription was no more a part of the American tradition than a large standing army. Never had the government drafted men in time of peace, and some people persisted in the belief that it must never do so. The tumultuous events of the summer of 1940, however, had signaled extraordinary times. Whether the nation expected to go to war or not, its deplorable state of military preparedness had to be remedied.

While the Navy was not exactly ship-shape, it at least seemed respectable. If published statistics were to be believed, the United States had one of the largest fleets in the world, and Roosevelt had asked for enough new ship construction to provide a "two-ocean Navy." Three new battleships, the *North Carolina*, the *Washington*, and the *South Dakota*, prepared to join the fleet in the spring, and keels were being laid for more than a hundred other vessels. The Administration had shifted a large part of the fleet to Pacific waters, first for maneuvers and then to remain on station at the base at Pearl Harbor, to let the Japanese know it was there. A pictorial essay in *Life* featured operations of the aircraft carrier *Enterprise*, a "brand-new battle device," launched three years earlier. Planes from the *Enterprise* were pictured flying toward Hawaii. "This is just a mock attack," the essay noted with remarkable prescience, "but if the facts were turned about, they might be enemy bombers from an alien aircraft carrier coming in to attack the great Pearl Harbor base."[1] Because the Navy operated mostly with machines, it did not require massive manpower, perhaps 300,000 or so, and through 1941 it managed to keep its ranks filled through enlistment.

The ground forces faced an entirely different situation. In the summer of 1940 the regular Army ranked eighteenth in the world, with barely 250,000 men, a far cry from Germany's 6 million to 8 million. Poorly equipped, with officers who ranged from excellent to aged, Army units were scattered through outposts abroad and camps in the United States, many of them a legacy of the Indian Wars. The National Guard claimed to have nearly as many soldiers as the Army, but to the seasoned military man, and to many civilians, the guard hardly represented a trained and effective force. Roosevelt in June 1940 had authorized increasing the Army to 375,000, but, inasmuch as few young men offered themselves for service, it was an empty gesture. The solution for one of the problems of defense seemed painfully clear: conscription.

The President had considered selective service politically explosive in that election year, so neither he nor members of his Administration had taken the lead in establishing it. The movement for a draft had started with former military officers and private citizens, notably Grenville Clark, a devoted advocate of military training. The measure had come to Congress in June under the sponsorship of James W. Wadsworth and Senator Edward R. Burke, neither of them a member of the Administration's congressional team. Fearing that the draft "may very easily defeat the Democratic National ticket," as he told a friend, Roosevelt did not support the bill openly until August.[2]

The Burke–Wadsworth Bill had aroused a storm of protest from isolationists, and Roosevelt's belated endorsement made the cries all the more intense. Critics found the measure undemocratic and unnecessary; a larger army if needed could be raised through voluntarism, by offering inducements. Isolationists saw conscription as an extension of the President's foreign policy. To Senator Burton K. Wheeler of Montana, it represented totalitarianism come to the United States: "Hushed whispers will replace free speech," he warned. "Secret meetings in dark places will supplant free assemblage. . . . If this bill passes, it will slit the throat of the last great democracy still living—it will accord to Hitler his greatest and cheapest victory."[3]

However impressive those arguments might have seemed, however regrettable the idea of compulsory service, most people could find no acceptable alternative. The Burke–Wadsworth Bill attracted much bipartisan support, including the Republican presidential candidate,

Wendell Willkie; by August public opinion polls showed 86 percent in favor. The measure had moved through Congress in the heat of Washington in late summer, less than two months before the election. Only a few days earlier Roosevelt had announced a destroyer deal with Churchill. France had fallen in June, and the Battle of Britain now raged at full intensity in the skies over London; Hitler had begun to move landing barges to the northern coast of France. In those circumstances the terms of the law were remarkably optimistic. Although all men of ages 21–36 had to register for a lottery, the government contemplated calling to service less than a million in the first year. The unfortunate young men with the highest numbers picked out of a bowl could expect to serve "twelve consecutive months."

Thus, by the start of 1941 conscription was a fact of American life, and the wheels of selective service had started to turn. On October 16, 1940, more than 16 million men offered themselves for registration. Several thousand failed to appear, but the government eventually would prosecute only 627 for violation of the law, a remarkable display of patriotism and obedience. It soon became apparent, however, that while most men were willing to do their duty as defined by law, many did not object to using the law to stay out of the Army.

One method of avoiding the draft was classification as conscientious objector, which required the petitioner to convince authorities that he was "by reasons of religious training and belief . . . conscientiously opposed to participation in war in any form." Some individuals obtained c.o. status by simply proving adherence to a certain religious faith, such as the Quakers or the Mennonites, and accepting assignment to nonmilitary alternate service. Others underwent the harrowing experience of filling out numerous forms, appearing before a local board and later an appeal board, and having their petition rejected by examiners. A few individuals, citing religious objection, refused to register or accept alternate service, for which they earned a prison sentence. In the first thirteen months of conscription, some 5,700 would receive exemption on grounds of conscientious objection; 109 would be convicted of violation of the law, most of whom would serve sentences ranging from six months to five years.[4]

A more common escape route was through deferment. Local draft boards as a rule based deferment on occupation and family status, granting exemption for critical work or to men whose departure would cause hardship to the family. The need to define essential occupations inevitably led to arbitrary decisions and charges of favoritism; draft boards could recite stories of men claiming exemption as the sole support of a lover, a cat, or, in one case, an old truck. When it became apparent that local boards preferred not to take married men, marriage license bureaus reported a surge in business in late 1940 and during 1941, perhaps as many as half a million more marriages than usual. Although the government threatened to require couples to show they married "in the ordinary course of events," nearly every married man could expect deferment.[5] Still not feeling secure, apparently, many newlyweds got busy creating a child, as attested by an increased birthrate in 1941, the sharpest surge coming in July, some nine to ten months after passage of the conscription act. Evidence that draft avoidance activity continued through 1941 could be seen in a much larger increase in the birthrate the following year.

If a quick marriage was either impossible to arrange or more objectionable than entering the Army, the possibility of physical disability remained. Not many men deliberately maimed themselves, feigned homosexuality or lunacy, or drugged themselves to foul up the Army's tests—the young men of that day were neither as determined nor as ingenious as their counterparts thirty years later. But they did not mind putting their worst foot forward, drawing attention to some ailment that would make them unfit for service. The quest for physical disqualification led to strange goings-on at examination stations, such as acquisition of a mysterious limp or difficulty reading the eye charts. Bed-wetting was a favorite tactic. Some tried having all their teeth pulled, until the government announced that toothless candidates, if otherwise fit, would be inducted anyway.

Such antics were not unique in American military history. One observer, reminded of similar activity during the Civil War, resurrected a piece by David Ross Locke, who wrote under the pen name Petroleum V. Nasby, a fictitious illiterate Kentuckian. Nasby, who wished to stay out of Mr. Lincoln's army, presented his case as follows:

I'm bald-headed, and hev bin obliged to wear a wig these 22 years. . . . I hev lost, sence Stanton's order to draft, the use of wun eye entirely, and hev kronic inflammashen in the other. My teeth is all unsound, my palit ain't eggsactly rite, and I hev bronkeetis 31 yeres last Joon. . . .

I'm holler-chested, an short-winded, an hev alluz hed pains in my back and side. I am afflicted with kronic diarrear . . . am rupchered in nine places, and entirely enveloped with trusses.

I hev verrykose vanes, hev a white swelling on wun leg and a fever sore on the other; also wun leg is shorter than tother, though I handle it so expert that nobody ever noticed it. I hev korns and bunyons on both feet, which wood prevent me from marchin.

The above reasons why I can't go, will, I make no doubt, be suffishent.[6]

Avoiding the draft proved not a difficult task after all, for of the 17 million involved in the first two registrations, more than 12 million received deferment, mostly because of dependency. Of the first million called for induction, more than 40 percent failed to pass the physical examination.

Having failed to qualify for exemption on any ground, most men accepted their fate, albeit with little enthusiasm. A few even volunteered, either to broaden choice of duty through enlistment or to "get their year over with" by volunteering to be drafted. Most men, however, preferred not to go. They found no satisfaction in the thought of leaving home, being subjected to military regimentation, and, if war should come, the prospect of being injured or killed. Virtually all objections could be set aside in the face of a threat from an identifiable enemy. Americans could understand the threat Hitler posed to Europe and his theoretical challenge to the principles of American civilization; philosophically they could appreciate the need for a much larger army. But they could not grasp the idea that the nation faced direct danger, no matter what Roosevelt had said, and until such danger became undeniably clear, they experienced no pangs of conscience at leaving the soldiering to others.

The obligation of registration had affected almost half the nation's families, and while only a small portion of those registered faced early induction—the Army would call 921,722 in the first thirteen months—the draft seemed to touch almost everyone in some way. If a member of the family was not preparing to go, perhaps it was a distant relative, a friend, or a friend of a friend. Those unfortunate souls found no shortage of advice. A mother, troubled that her boy never would be the same again, offered tearful urging to be careful and good and perhaps an insistence that the young man take along a Bible or Testament or Missal. He probably took the little book to please Mom, whether he intended to read it or not. From fathers, an uncle, or father's friends, almost 5 million of whom had seen service in the last war, came words of wisdom about how to make it in the Army and, recalling a much different time of their life, added confidential, albeit embellished, stories of their military experience, ranging from the rigor of the trenches in France to off-duty devilry with girls from Georgia or Paris.

If American youth appeared less than thrilled at the prospect of military service, the nation as a whole had responded with enthusiasm, almost as to a new fad. Patriotic symbols had become the order of the day in the fall of 1940, and the mood continued into the following year. The flag popped out in front of businesses and houses; public gatherings featured either the National Anthem or Kate Smith's resounding "new" rendition of "God Bless America." Songwriters rushed to produce music appropriate to the public mood. Perhaps most to the point was a "hillbilly" tune written for draftees and their girl friends, a mixture of patriotism, sadness, and optimism entitled "I'll Be Back in a Year Little Darling." The publication media had swung into action on all fronts. Newspapers introduced a regular column devoted to "our men in uniform," "Southland Soldiers," or some such rubric. The cover of *The Saturday Evening Post* carried for the first time in 1941 Norman Rockwell's representative of the Army: an innocent-looking, rosy-cheeked youngster named Private Willie Gillis, Jr. Rockwell's productions were always full of optimism and good cheer, and his characterization of Private Gillis, to be used many times in the future, was no exception. Each edition of the *Post* also now carried a cartoon, "Private Breger," featuring lighthearted tribulations of a recent inductee. Ham Fisher had his cartoon hero, Joe Palooka, join the Army (a gesture that earned Fisher personal thanks from Roosevelt), and other cartoonists contemplated sending their characters to join the colors, allowing artists to claim their share of patriotic honors, not to mention opening up countless new avenues for their heroes' adventures.

Hundreds of newspapers and magazine articles heralded the "new" American Army, many of them optimistic—if not trivial—pieces purporting to describe transition from civilian to military life. The American lad might resent such inconvenience as tedious drills, rising early, submitting to orders from an inconsiderate sergeant, so the stories often ran, but he would find the venture into military life a rewarding, character-building experience. "He will eat simple foods at regular hours . . . ,tumble into bed . . . each night at exactly the same time," one account said. "He will straighten his posture. . . . He will trudge a post at night and find new wonder in the heavens. He will, whether he likes it or not, communicate with nature in all her moods."[7]

Amid the enthusiasm, however, appeared expressions of concern and skepticism. Not that many writers challenged the need for an army or even a draft, but some were troubled with the possible consequences of the new surge to militarism. "The buck privates will know their places," one author warned. "The officers will strut about in polished leather puttees, hoping that promotions continue and the emergency never ends." Will recruits be subjected to a rigid caste system, even brutality, all under the guise of discipline? And what will become of the men after military service? "Will they come out as robots trained only in the use of force, jobless, an easy prey to some home-grown Fuhrer?"[8]

Perhaps the most interesting remarks came from a professor of sociology, a dyed-in-the-wool Darwinian, who suggested some social and genetic effects of America's military development. He explained that the draft and especially war, if it should come, would delay or prevent marriage, reduce the birthrate, and create a surplus of women without mates. One recourse, though he did not openly endorse it, was polygamy. While the draft drained away, and war killed off, the fittest young men, "the near-sighted, the hard of hearing, those with weak hearts, are turned down . . . left free to marry and have children and perpetuate hereditary weakness." The logical conclusion, and Herbert Spencer could not have put it better: a civilization of weaklings. This scholar hastened to add, however, that modern warfare might level off these evolutionary consequences, because "the aerial bomb" brings death "also to those rejected." The bombing of cities, from this standpoint, was good for the human race. The writer concluded that the positive effects of military service—exercise, fresh air, and good food—would be likely to offset genetic consequences, and the "net effect" would be "greatly to improve the quality of the people."[9]

There was no need to be uncertain about what the young soldier would face, given the rash of handbooks that appeared in libraries and stores during the first year of the draft. It was almost as if the nation never had had an army. Bearing such titles as *What the Citizen Should Know About the Army*, those little volumes undertook to describe rules, organization, and nearly all aspects of military life. Like the Army itself, they took nothing for granted. Witness, for example, advice appearing in *The Soldier's Handbook*:

Do not drink liquor. If you do take a drink sometimes anyway . . . don't guzzle, or you are liable to come to in the guardhouse or some place worse.

Avoid venereal disease. . . . Nearly all regular whores are infected with one or another of diseases and other women who permit sexual liberties from men are very liable to be. . . . Select for your female companions decent girls or women and keep away from whore houses and "jook joints."[10]

In *Your Year In The Army*, Major John D. Kenderdine offered the inductee two gems of wisdom: "Stand close to the urinal," he recommended, and "after breakfast and before drill period, try to move your bowels."[11]

The act of getting into uniform became for some men a trying experience. If the decision to expand the Army enormously in little more than a year delighted military chieftains, it also sent procurement and planning agents scurrying in search of places to put all those men and equipment for their training. The order in September 1940 to induct the National Guard, more than a quarter of a million troops, quickly absorbed the available space and threw the conscription service into confusion. The process of induction involved a complicated routine of review and examination at local drafting stations, staffed by civilian volunteers, and a second examination at the induction center. Having passed the first test, some men quit their jobs and gave up their residences, only to be either rejected in the second phase or sent home to wait until the Army had room. The Army frequently complained that local draft boards sent men too old or physically unqualified.

Pronounced fit for military service and having taken that step forward at the induction center and repeated the oath, the recruit discovered a new set of problems. If permanent barracks were not yet finished, he had to accept impromptu lodging, most often a five-man squad tent heated by a squat, hissing Sibley stove—miserable quarters at any time, but especially in winter in the North or rainy spring in the Southern states. Factories were turning out more military items each month, but the United States in 1941 was far from mobilized for war; much of the new material went to Britain, and the American Army had to live with shortages of most items, including clothing. Private Thomas Strickland of Atlanta reported that he wore his only shirt and trousers—one can assume, in those days before automatic dryers, without laundering—thirty-two consecutive days. He did not smell too bad, he said, because he had entered the Army in winter, and his unsanitary appearance had the advantage of keeping him off KP duty.[12]

Shortages of equipment led the soldier off into a world of make-believe. "Simulate" was the Army's word for it: The soldier who did not have a rifle must simulate a rifle by aiming a mop, broom, or other long object. Wooden poles became artillery pieces; trucks or other vehicles—if any were available—passed for tanks. Such pretense reached its height during the aptly titled "war games," when it became necessary to devise, and apply, rules for all phases of simulated warfare, from destroying tanks to imitating the sound of a machine gun.

The Army of 1941 was in a state of transition in equipment and tactics as well as in size. Uniforms had changed since the last war, but they still included cumbersome laced leggings and steel helmets exactly the same as "doughboys" had worn to France in 1918. The air force was a part of the Army; the Army manual listed a coast artillery and a field artillery, and the standard field piece still was the 75 mm cannon. Traditionally the term cavalry referred to mounted soldiers, but World War I and the intervening years had elevated the importance of armored vehicles to the point of making mounted warfare obsolete. Old horse soldiers would not concede defeat, however, so the Army contained both "mechanized cavalry" and "horse cavalry." In 1940 it created a special "armored force." The horse soldiers seemed alive and well in 1941, for the Army had one mounted division, purchased 20,000 horses, and began organization of a second division. Horsemen still had their place in the military scheme, so the thinking went. They could be used for reconnaissance and even in combat under certain circumstances. No officer proposed sending horsemen armed with lances to charge the enemy, as Poland had done with Germany in 1939, but one article insisted that on rough terrain the cavalry "could lick its weight in enemy tanks" (which incidentally would not be very many), as long as it had proper support from artillery, armored units, and airplanes.[13]

Perhaps a better explanation is that tradition died hard in the military, that Army men felt comfortable doing things as they had been done. Officers who still savored the romance of George Custer and J.E.B. Stuart could not bear to see the horse soldier die. Even people in the new cavalry, the tankers, still wore the boots and breeches suited to horse operations, and some people liked to quip that the generals would have put saddles on the tanks if they could have gotten away with it.

Despite lessons of the war in Europe, the smashing success of Hitler's *blitzkrieg*, the Army moved slowly toward mechanization. Virtually all American tanks were light machines; one version—the Stuart—weighed in the neighborhood of 12 tons and was armed with a 37 mm cannon. The standard M1 tank, a converted combat car of 9.7 tons, carried only machine guns and no periscope so the machine maneuvered toward a target with the commander's head sticking out of the turret. He directed the driver with kicks; one on the right shoulder meant turn right, for example, and a kick in the back meant forward. Such a vehicle could not last long in the battle conditions of 1941; it was small, light armored, and potentially deadly for the commander, who was face to face with the people trying to shoot him.[14]

Mechanized weapons nonetheless became the most glamorous and significant instruments of modern warfare, and some of the most publicized members of the Army were men who knew their way around armor. George S. Patton moved from horse cavalry to tanks in July 1940 and within seven months jumped in rank from colonel to major general. Well on the way to becoming one of America's most colorful military leaders, Patton scowled from the cover of *Life*'s "Defense" edition of July 7, 1941. Stories already circulated about his dynamism and his uncivil tongue. One of the cleaner versions had Patton's men in the 2d Armored Division compare their commander to God, which Patton apparently did not discourage: "Like God he had the damnedest way of showing up when things went wrong. Unlike God, he had been known to dash headlong into a creek, get a stalled tank and its wretched crew out of the water and back into the line of march practically by the power of his curses." Delighted with the recent course of events, Patton wrote a friend that "all that is now needed is a nice juicy war."[15]

Through it all the new soldier had to adjust to doing things the Army's way, which meant rising early, marching and drilling, endless inspections, and listening to pompous officers and noncoms whose vocabulary, some men would swear, amounted to no more than fifty words. As with soldiers before and after him, the recruit of 1941 learned that the Army had a special jargon, some of it not suitable for use in front of ladies. Food was chow, of course, and, curiously, a dining room was a mess hall. The word fatigue did not mean being tired, but various exercises in cleaning. There were "details" of all kinds. Men who smoked—and the Army behaved as if nearly everyone would—acquired the practice of "field-stripping" finished cigarettes, a simple exercise in that day before most cigarettes had filters. Family publications reported that payday in the military was called the day "the eagle flies," a version that every soldier knew was correct in all but the last word.[16]

The soldier learned in his first week that kitchen police had no authority whatsoever, that KP carried the sorriest reputation in the military lexicon, and was probably the occasion of the soldier's hardest work. While that duty could be dealt out as punishment, everyone had to take a turn. On the assigned day, the man who reported first to the kitchen—at some remarkable hour, such as 4:00 A.M.—had a choice of jobs and probably selected the cleanest duty, DRO: dining room orderly. The man who arrived last would probably be stuck with the hardest job, that of the "pots and pans man." Most soldiers never understood the connection between kitchen police and learning to be a warrior.

One word the men heard a great deal was discipline. It seemed to be the Army's favorite word. The Army needed more discipline, all the officers and some of the noncoms said. They never defined the word, but it seemed to have to do with accepting one's lowly position. The recruit soon learned that the disciplined soldier would follow orders, say "sir" to the right people, march in step during close-order drill, do a snappy manual of arms, scrub floors until they looked bleached, and shine shoes until they looked like glass. Anything that might seem purposeless and boring fell into the category of discipline. Even KP was for discipline. The Army needed more of it.

The Army of 1941 was still a bugler's army. The bugler remained one of the beloved symbols of tradition in the military, almost as if this were the army of Custer and "Useless" Grant. To have an army, you had to have a bugler, and the feeling extended beyond the men in service. A song about a "boogie woogie" bugle boy had become a successful record. The frantic "reveille" was the worst, if only because it came so early in the morning; thank heaven the men did not always hear it but were awakened by the CQ, the man in charge of quarters. Other calls were recall at 11:30 for the noon meal and retreat about 5:10 P.M. Taps was the best—or was it the worst? It was slow, soothing, and restful and usually came at 11:00 in the night, the time for rest; it also was melancholy and sad and could mark the end of the day or of life. Taps was funeral music for the military, a standing reminder that this business after all was serious. It was difficult to be jovial during taps. One hardly ever heard the words but, the few people who had learned them knew they were as touching as the music:

> *Day is done*
> *Gone the sun*
> *From the lake*
> *From the hill*
> *From the sky.*
> *Rest in peace*
> *Soldier brave.*
> *God is nigh.*

It was not all drudgery. There were satisfying times in the barracks and tents. The men witnessed hoary practical jokes and stood ready to play them on comrades or the next group of inductees: the trick of "short-sheeting," for example, or ordering a greenhorn to stand guard at the latrine, allowing no one to pass. Their letters home contained stories—the cleaner ones—that probably had been a part of the Army for decades.

Much comfort came from knowing that all the men shared similar circumstances, and the most popular pastime was the "bull session," the long conversation about girls, home, and what each man wanted to do when he "got out." Young men who had never been outside the home state came to know people from many places. It was enriching to meet a boy who boasted of being from the "Maine" part of the U.S. of A. or from West "By Gawd" Virginia, to learn that Georgia boys still were sensitive about the Civil War and about William Tecumseh Sherman—a sensitivity resharpened with continuing success of the film *Gone With the Wind*. These provincial young men might have marveled at how much they had learned without even trying—about the United States, for example, or Catholics and Jews, city people and country people (but not, because of segregation in the Army, much about black people and whites). They learned about themselves as well. Eager as they were to see them, the old house and the people back home would never look the same.

The Army's food was at least tolerable; if the recruit had happened to enter the service from unemployment or a low-income family, it was probably a vast improvement over his diet in civilian life. In 1941 the Army shifted to a program of master menus, a system designed to offer each soldier 5,000 calories a day. Most men found that they ate more in the Army; exercise sharpened appetites, of course, and mealtime was one of the few parts of the day free of harassment, a time eagerly awaited. Men in the 127th Infantry at Camp Livingston showed an average gain of 12 pounds in the first five months.[17]

It was not fashionable to praise the Army's food, however. The most a recruit could say was that it was not bad; he was more likely to complain, or "bitch," as they liked to put it. He might have passed on the rumor that in combat the Army's cooks were shot at from both sides. One soldier went so far as to send an unappetizing steak—it was too tough—to General George C. Marshall, Army Chief of Staff. Marshall considered the matter serious enough to write the soldier's commanding officer, explaining that he could not produce the evidence because the steak had reached the stage "where it had to be disposed of." "Do not kill him until you have looked into it," Marshall ordered.[18]

Although the Army had to struggle with shortages, mistakes, and lack of preparation throughout the year, some problems gradually eased. Each month led to more completed barracks, more paved streets. In spring the Selective Service System acquired a competent new director, General Lewis B. Hershey; local draft boards resigned themselves to drafting men no older than twenty-five years; and the recruits had taken on a somewhat better appearance. Accustomed to the shock of rising at 5:45, they had learned how and whom to salute, how to march in step, how to make a cot so tight that a quarter would bounce on its taut surface. With few exceptions, the men appeared more healthy, knowledgeable, and confident, though not necessarily happier. If the passing of fright from the first few months developed experience and confidence, it also left the soldiers more acutely aware of shortcomings in their new life.

By late summer, with Army personnel now well past 1 million, a disturbing attitude began to emerge. Virtually every reporter who had been on the scene found intense dissatisfaction and rebelliousness spreading among the troops. An observer from the *Post* reported that, while they were "potentially the finest soldiers on earth . . . most of them want to fold up their uniforms and go home." Another reporter claimed that 50 percent of the men he interviewed had threatened to desert if not released at the end of their year's obligation.[19] Some of the complaints had to do with the haphazard circumstances in which the new Army came to life, others with character of the military itself. The Army had an absolute fetish for cleanliness that seemed to serve no purpose other than harassment. The soldiers were angered with so much waste of time—"hurry up and wait" was the standard cliché—with poorly planned exercises and meaningless hours spent on close-order drill. "You don't stop a tank by doing present arms in front of it," one recruit said. "We have been told, 'stick a crowbar in the treads or throw a Molotov cocktail,'" said another. "Who carries a crowbar . . .? What does a Molotov cocktail look like?"[20]

Most draftees found it difficult to comprehend or tolerate the rigid military code of conduct. The authoritarian organization and stratified social system were unlike anything the men had encountered in civilian life and totally un-American, it seemed. An officer was by definition superior, deserving of strict obedience and a great deal of childish pampering—to be saluted and addressed as "sir," regardless of age or competence. They lived and ate segregated from enlisted men, seemed incapable of driving cars or opening doors. Officers of high rank used enlisted men as butlers, maids, and baby-sitters, all masked behind the title of military aide. Officers who considered such behavior infantile and refused to conform to it were likely to receive a reprimand and a lecture on the dangers of fraternization. Triviality usually crumbled in face of combat, but after more than twenty years of peace, hard-pressed to establish an identity, the Army had become status- and tradition-ridden. It was all, the men were told, for morale and discipline.

The situation was worsened by the haste with which the Army had been put together. Many officers from the National Guard and the Reserve Officers Corps had scarcely any more training than the troops they were supposed to command. Few seemed deserving of the respect the Army demanded for them. "You want to know what's wrong with army morale?" a draftee in Virginia remarked. "They hike us fifteen miles on the hottest day with a full pack over sandy roads. . . . Then this colonel comes up in his staff car, see—with his two dogs! He hikes our legs off, and he rides with his poodles with him in a staff car."[21]

Noncommissioned officers, the sergeants and corporals, fared little better with the draftees, though for somewhat different reasons. Virtually all NCOs were volunteers, Regular Army men. The Army of 1941 remained home for Private Prewitt, Sergeant Warden, and other hard-drinking, whoring career men later portrayed in James

Jones's novel *From Here to Eternity*. The stereotype of the professional soldier was a man of limited ambition and initiative, often a drunk who probably could not make a living "on the outside." Scarcely 25 percent had finished high school. The long, listless interwar years that had hardened professionals in a routine of life and thought now had been interrupted by the draft, which brought in huge numbers of "citizen soldiers," many of them different from the volunteer: 40 percent had high school diplomas, and several had gone to college. Tension between old-timers and amateurs—expected at almost any time—had become more pronounced. The sergeants considered their charges undisciplined, disrespectful, and lazy; the draftees looked at NCOs as illiterate, stupid, and mostly incompetent.[22]

Boredom was another plague of the Army of 1941. Not only did the soldier face the tedium of training camp routine, he also had a shortage of off-duty time and satisfying activity when he was free. The government's efforts to provide on-post recreation—books, movies, pool tables—came late in the reconstruction process, and when available they offered little genuine relief for the high-spirited draftee in his early twenties. Professional entertainers who had started to tour the camps seemed remarkably inept at knowing what the boys wanted. At Fort Belvoir, Virginia, the comedian Ed Wynn tried to inspire the men with a quarter-hour "introductory address." Another entertainer started to lead group singing until unruliness in the ranks, the "Bronxian treatment," caused him to stop. Irritated, he challenged hecklers to do better. The soldiers then pushed a protesting recruit, a Private Louis Salmon of New York, on stage. Salmon proceeded to display "excellent voice" leading the troops singing the "Beer Barrel Polka." Spirits rose considerably with the appearance of the singer Jane Froman and the dancer Betty Bruce.[23] Could it be that here was the answer?

Of course it was. What the soldier wanted most was, in vernacular of the day, booze and broads. Booze was usually available, often too easily so, albeit in unattractive places. One could obtain inexpensive beer at the local Post Exchange (the PX), assuming one had been built, but in that noisy, smelly, crudely furnished place, surrounded by uniforms and all those males, one hardly felt free. Drinking in the PX only made one want to drink. The towns closest to camp seemed to have the most dilapidated stores and taverns on earth, and proprietors often treated military customers as anything but citizens of the first order, granting service with a wary glance for more than the customary price. "There are two things the boys miss, girls, and beer," a reporter wrote from Camp Bowie, Texas. Although nearby Brownswood was dry, one could purchase whisky as "medication" at the drugstore. A doctor was always available to write a prescription for 25 cents.[24] The price of hard liquor soon drained a draftee's salary, however, and alcohol could introduce problems of a different sort. "If we don't do something about it," another observer wrote, "the servicemen will work out their own amusement—like the three I found on King Street in Norfolk, who were so highly spifficated they had invented a new game. The idea was, one of 'em would go out of the room, and the other two would guess which one had left."[25]

An even more difficult proposition was the matter of girls. However well the public understood the need for having men in uniform, in involuntary servitude of sorts, public sympathies did not extend to offering daughters as recreation. Girls from respectable homes were instructed to avoid the soldier like the plague. Putting on a uniform did something to a young man, so went the popular conception. Removed from the restraints of parents, peers, and community, seeking quick release from tension pent up during weeks in fields and barracks, he now was totally irresponsible if not indecent. Above all he wanted sexual satisfaction and would to go considerable effort to obtain it. As for the poor girl who succumbed to the adventure of it all, what could she expect for her efforts? A shattered reputation, a broken heart, perhaps even disease or pregnancy. Not all nice girls obeyed their parents' admonitions; the uniform had taken on a certain glamour, and girls from a state like Georgia might find excitement in meeting a man from New York or Massachusetts, but liaisons of this sort remained the exception. "We didn't expect to be treated like heroes," a soldier at Fort Bragg complained, "but, hell, you'd think we had the smallpox."[26]

That left prostitutes or bar girls (who often doubled as prostitutes) as the most reliable companions for servicemen on a weekend pass. Even prostitutes had become risky business. While the going rate was not out of reach—two or three dollars in some places—the enterprising professional found ways to finagle more than the standard fee. The recruit by the summer was earning $30 a month, a raise from $21 after four months, and even that increased salary would not go far in buying a month's entertainment. If the soldier dared indulge in poker, craps, or some other on-base gambling activity, the money might last scarcely a day.

The soldier might encounter other obstacles. Nice girls were expected to avoid the troops, and the local citizenry often tried to keep away girls of the "other type" as well. The Chief of Police of Battle Creek, Michigan, reported a continuing struggle against forces seeking to corrupt his town and the 15,000 men camped nearby at Fort Custer. Conditions were worse than the last war, he reported, "by 40 percent," and all because of outsiders: "One bunch from Chicago started a house here and we raided them and the girls were fined. But they went back in business again." While he had shut down another outfit from Detroit "right in the heart of town," he had heard reports of other girls coming from Chicago, Detroit, Jackson, Indianapolis and Fort Wayne. "I look for it to get a lot tougher when the warm weather comes," the chief said.[27]

The government was not doing much to make the troops' sex life easier. Military officials could not forget the distressing experience of the previous war, when venereal disease had been a more dangerous enemy than the Germans. Some 400,000 men had been affected. Venereal disease literally could lay an army low. In truth the military tried to be understanding. The Army wanted its men to be men, and that attitude implied certain social behavior, all of it heterosexual. "The army estimates that 15 percent of its men are incorrigible, another 15 percent are total abstainers, either being married, engaged, fearful or disinterested. The remaining 70 percent are subject to occasional lapses of virtue, and this group the army is particularly interested in protecting," ran one account.[28] To protect its people the Army offered instruction, urging physical examination, treatment, and proper prophylaxis.

What else to do remained an issue of some controversy. One view had it that prostitution remained reliable and uncomplicated, perhaps the safest method of meeting a natural, probably irrepressible function. The United States Health Service reported in November that only 6 percent of soldiers with venereal disease had received infection from professionals. The Chief of Police of Honolulu reported that with 40,000 military people in the area, prostitution was absolutely necessary. Sixteen houses operated cleanly and efficiently. For that reason, the chief concluded, Honolulu had virtually no rape, and women could travel safely in any part of the city at any time.[29]

Such logic carried little weight in an issue with the moral impact of prostitution. The boys must be protected from weak moments and scavengers who sought to prey upon them. Congress in the spring had prohibited houses of prostitution near military bases. That action had slowed the traffic and made it more inconvenient, but by no means had it brought the practice to a halt. The girls now had taken to operating out of automobiles, trailer homes, and other movable locations. The connection between moral laxity and troop concentrations remained strong in the public perception, and many people accepted one journal's warning that every new camp in the United States had attracted a "veritable carnival of vice."[30]

Not the least of the soldier's problems was the prospect that his obligation might extend beyond the twelve months specified at time of induction. With the year's service rapidly approaching an end, the reasons for having the men in service had become all the more compelling. International tension had increased markedly, and just as the United States seemed on verge of war with Germany on the Atlantic Ocean, the nation was about to lose the bulk of its Army. The solution seemed simple enough, however regrettable and unpopular the action might be: extend the time of service for men already in uniform. With great reluctance Roosevelt had the Department of War prepare a bill, and the President added a vigorous personal endorsement. The measure aroused an expected outcry, with isolationists accusing the Administration of war-mongering, dishonesty, and breaking a promise to the draftees. Few, however, expected the vote would be as close as it was: The bill passed the House in August 1941 by a vote of 203–202. With a stroke of the President's pen, the obligation of twelve months grew to thirty, bitter news for hundreds of thousands of men and millions more in their families who had accepted a distasteful experience largely on the assumption that it would be short.

The vexation of military obligation, and even the extension of service, would have been more tolerable if the soldiers had had a clear indication of purpose. "The trouble has come from the fact that we have [been] trying to train an army for war without any declaration of war by Congress and with the country not facing the danger before it," Secretary of War Henry L. Stimson noted.[31] Interviews with the troops confirmed his conclusion. One reporter who spent ten days on Times Square talking with more than three hundred soldiers discovered an alarming amount of hatred. They hated Roosevelt, officers, Congress (the extension bill had recently passed), and most of all, Negroes. "They weren't unpatriotic," the reporter explained, "and their confidence in themselves was truly amazing." "The Germans ain't so tough," the soldiers assured him. "We can lick them." The fundamental reason for anger was that few recruits understood the reason for being in the Army: "They were simply confused." As one soldier put it: "the Nazis haven't crossed the channel, have they? How are they going to cross the ocean?"[32]

As summer turned into fall, and relations with Germany and Japan as well continued on a worsening course, the nation seemed to have an unhappy army on its hands. For men pressed into service the supreme expression of dissatisfaction had become the scrawled appearance in conspicuous places of the acronym OHIO: "over the hill [that is, desertion] in October."

By October, as it turned out, many of the soldiers were recovering from an exercise that, while neither easy nor pleasant, offered a change from routine in the cantonments. Although much larger than at the start of the year, the Army remained inexperienced and only partly trained. A standard training device had been simulated conflict or, in military terminology, maneuvers or "war games." Some units had engaged in small operations during previous months, and authorities decided to try the same idea on a massive scale, involving nearly 500,000 troops, approximately one-third of the men then under arms. The idea was to give the soldiers practice, to detect problems, to discover competent officers, to reinstitute pride in the new Army, and to attract the attention of Congress.

The Army attempted to make the maneuvers meaningful. It set aside more than 13 million acres, mostly in Louisiana, created the fictitious nations of Kotmk and Almat, and put them at war with each other; it was the Reds against the Blues, or more specific the Second Army of General Ben Lear and the Third Army commanded by General Walter Krueger. The Third Army had more men in the first phase of the two-part operation, but the Second was much better equipped with armor and thus, according to military odds-makers, favored to win. The Army drew up a set of rules and assigned umpires to determine when a soldier was dead, a bridge destroyed, or any other outcome of the simulated hostilities.

Playing war had never been a precise undertaking, either for neighborhood youngsters or for grown-up generals and colonels. Was it possible to make rules realistic? Was it fair, for example, for the opposition to attack a tank while a crewman dismounted to open the gate to a cow pasture? If not, how long must the enemy wait to open fire? Being "killed" or "captured" in war games was not the same as in real life, and some men took pleasure in being labeled "prisoner" or "casualty." They could lounge about the enemy camp, perhaps for duration of the maneuver; a man killed in action received the same food as a soldier on the firing line. Umpires reported being offered as much as ten dollars for a casualty or prisoner tag.[33]

The terrain in the deep South proved extraordinarily inhospitable. Besides having to do battle with the enemy, soldiers also had to contend with cyprus swamps, pine thickets, chiggers, mosquitoes, cottonmouth snakes, and torrential rain from the fringe of a hurricane that happened to sweep by the area. Shortages continued to plague the new Army, so wooden poles stood for anti-aircraft guns and aircraft used bags of flour on bombing runs. Most soldiers were able to fire weapons with blank ammunition, but some had to utter an agreed-upon sound, such as "bang," and wait for an umpire to deliver a decision.

Local citizens acquired at least a hint of the novelty of living in a battle zone. Airborne troops descending with blue, green, and yellow chutes frightened unprepared residents, some of whom had never heard of such creatures as paratroops. The first assault created a "mild panic" with cotton workers, who dashed to find a place to hide. In time people adjusted to troops scrambling across the pasture or tanks rumbling down the back road. It even became exciting. Through its efforts to give the operation broad publicity, the Army invited new problems, for spectators and people from the news media were all over the place, frequently disrupting operations. It was difficult to launch a surprise attack, for example, if advancing troops were followed by a string of press cars, newsreel cameras, and townspeople out to watch the spectacle.

Invariably there were arguments over close calls by umpires, and of course one always could find participants who would not play fair. The Lousiana State Police had to be called in to separate patrols from the competing armies, particularly aggressive warriors who took their assignments seriously indeed. They were ready to fight. Each claimed to have captured the other. Paratroops of the Second Army refused to stay captured. Generals tried to pull rank on beleaguered umpires who ruled against their side.

George Patton, flamboyant commander of the 2d Armored Division, distinguished himself, as many people suspected he might. A general in the opposition army offered fifty dollars to the man that would bring in Patton "dead or alive." A strict disciplinarian with his men, he did not mind stretching the rules himself. Patton, who liked the light tank, believed that armor should operate in much the same way as horse cavalry: hit and run, "avoid a fight and put their energy into disrupting the rear areas of the opposition."[34] Late in the second phase of the games his tanks suddenly appeared in a position to threaten Shreveport, the defensive assignment of the Second Army. An investigation exposed some startling facts. Patton had sent his vehicles nearly 400 miles dashing along darkened backroads, causing numerous accidents and, incidentally, several civilian deaths. He had refueled along the way, paying for the gasoline out of his own pocket, scarcely the sort of activity one could expect in battlefield conditions.

Just as Patton's forces and other units of the Third Army seemed prepared to assault Shreveport, the director of the operation, General Lesley J. McNair, declared the maneuver over. Observers agreed that Krueger's forces had won the first phase and that his Third Army seemed to have the best of it in the second part. Even so, the Second Army claimed victory at the end, and citizens of Shreveport cheered General Lear for saving their city. Officially the issue stood unresolved. Lear did concede some shortcomings: His army lacked "snap, dash, spit and polish." What the troops needed, he said, was "more equipment . . . harder work and initiative," and of course, "stronger discipline."[35]

Despite obvious problems, the Army was not disappointed with the war games of 1941. While officials had expected 136 deaths from the operation in Louisiana and perhaps 40,000 cases that would require hospitalization, only thirty-four had died, mostly from accidents; one man had committed suicide. The Army gained experience in battlefield conditions, particularly in the relationship between armor and other ground forces. McNair seemed determined to prove tanks not invincible, and he allowed the rules of combat to reflect his bias. The *Umpire Manual* gave a tank little chance when faced with conventional antitank guns; even a 50-caliber machine gun could stop armor at 1,000 yards. Later, in maneuvers in the Carolinas, McNair would rule that an infantryman could destroy a tank with a hand grenade, represented by a small bag of flour. Protests from the tankers found little support at General Headquarters.[36]

The operations demonstrated a need for better leadership. In what some called the "October Purge," several officers, mostly older men in National Guard units, had to accept retirement. Other officers found the situation a godsend for their military careers. Dwight Eisenhower in 1940 had expected to be lieutenant colonel another three years; serving as Krueger's chief of staff, he would receive his first star before the end of 1941.[37] Eisenhower's path to military success, and to the presidency, started in the swamps of Louisiana.

Reports varied about morale, but most observers agreed that the Army's largest problem was not attitude of the troops. Eric Sevareid, recently returned from observing the armies of European nations, observed one setting where paratroopers argued with an umpire.

They behaved as in a baseball game, challenging a disputed call. The men pleaded, cursed, and threw their caps on the ground; one young sergeant broke into angry tears. "Some reporters decried it as a 'mess,'" Sevareid reported. "I was elated and astonished. What gave them this drive and spirit?" "What the new soldier lacks is not morale but incentive," another reporter added. "He is not war-minded as the soldier of 1917 was. . . . Windy lads who had threatened to 'go over the hill in October'—desert, that is," he wrote, "crawled on their bellies in . . . mud night and day, and came up grinning." Threats to desert largely had been bombast, if only because the young men understood and respected the compulsive powers of government. After all, as one soldier pointed out, OHIO invariably led to GIN—guardhouse in November.[38]

The great dilemma of 1941 manifested itself no less in the attitude toward military issues than in approaches to foreign policy. Most people regretted the thought of a large military machine. They wept when bidding farewell to sons who boarded that early morning bus or train on the way to induction. The young men entered service only because they had to. Americans nonetheless acknowledged the need for military rebuilding and looked upon the armed forces as a symbol of strength and of the nation's enduring qualities. If the Army's broad-brimmed hats and 9-ton or 12-ton tanks seemed old-fashioned next to the equipment of modern warfare, few Americans doubted that their army, fully trained and equipped, would be a match for any, even, if it came to that, Hitler's mighty legions.

Better equipment already was on the way. In April the Army rolled out a pilot model of its new 28-ton tank, a clumsy-looking beast with guns protruding all around. The M3—the Grant or Lee—had a 75 mm cannon sticking out the right side (it would not turn all the way around), a 37 mm gun, four machine guns, and holes through which the crew could point pistols. The M3 had problems almost from the time of its introduction. The machine had too high a silhouette and showed a vexing tendency to turn over on a hillside. The big gun had to be mounted in a turret. Nonetheless it was a far cry from the obsolete little Stuarts and combat cars and looked impressive to the people gathered to watch a demonstration. The first production model M3 appeared in July; by December the Chrysler Corporation would turn out five hundred, although most went to British forces in North Africa. Production had started on a new helmet, modeled somewhat after German headgear; the air wing continued to receive B-17s, probably the world's best long-range bomber. Development continued on the P-47, the P-38, and other sturdy pursuit planes that would fight World War II. The Army intended to equip troops with Garand rifles, new semi-automatic weapons to replace the bolt-action Springfields and Enfields used during World War I and still the infantryman's standard equipment. For more than a year ground forces had experimented with a different sort of machine, "a stubby, bouncy 2,200-lb. crossbreed between the half-ton command car and the motor-tricycle . . . ugly as a bullpup," called a bantam scout car, midget truck, blitz buggy, iron pony. The name that stuck was "jeep."[39]

The people did not know it at the time, but the United States was embarking on a course from which it would not soon, or perhaps ever, depart. The tradition of a small standing army was being stripped away. Security demands had begun to shape the nation, determining what goods were to be produced, and how and where people would live. Some thoughtful people viewed the changes with misgiving, realizing that once the country had taken up arms it would be difficult, this time, to lay them down. Yet such reservations seemed almost irrelevant amid the continuing international crisis. "There is no need here to berate the evils of militarism and war," one author wrote. The perception of the military had changed and would continue to change. No longer was the Army looked upon as a group of mindless drunks, people trying to avoid getting a "real" job. Now it included a neighbor's son or someone even closer. No longer could the Army be treated as a necessary evil, barely visible, starved for funds, short of manpower, and held up to derision. Democracies had to have armies if totalitarian states had them. In fact, the military establishment might be "the means for the continuance of our culture and the way through which we may ultimately maintain . . . the values of Western civilization."[40] Was American militarism the only way to resist the surge toward a world militarism? It was an idea so obvious as to be simple, and yet so novel in the American experience as to be revolutionary.

Uncertainty continued to mark the national attitude toward military affairs for the rest of 1941. The novelty of the new Army had worn off; the press, having exhausted angles from which to view the Army had lost some of its exuberance. Public opinion continued to be of two minds about rearmament. Among the most significant facts for many families was where draftable sons stood in the lottery. The nation seemed to be marking time. As it developed, events within a few weeks would make previous decisions on military matters seem unsound only in their conservatism, make objection to military service irrelevant if not unpatriotic, and establish a military course for many years to come. The coming of war would bring political obligation that would translate quickly into military need. The coming of the American Century—or at least a few decades of preponderance—would mean that America's sons would wear uniforms long after the war with Hitler had ended. The manner in which war came would provide advocates of large standing military forces with a virtually unchallengeable example of the danger of weakness. Long after it ceased to be a rallying cry, "Remember Pearl Harbor" was a lesson to be applied to military matters, perhaps for the life of the Republic.

The people most directly involved, the nation's draftable youth, in 1941 had become part of an endless cycle, a repetition of the ordeal the first inductees had confronted a year earlier. Following the maneuvers in Louisiana and North Carolina, the Army returned to the routine of drafting men, starting them on basic training, building more camps, and pleading with the government to let it have more of the weapons coming out of the factories. A reporter for the New York *Times* described in November what had become a familiar scene:

> Tomorrow night in training centers throughout the country, more troop trains will pull into sidings at dusk. Tall, short, slim and fat, the new men will jostle one another like tired cattle. They will be bowed under the weight of new barracks bags and their uniforms will bag at the knees. Non-coms will bark at them and eventually get them into some form of formation. The new men will try to size up the camp in the dark.[41]

Homesick and confused, perhaps hundreds of miles from home, a ragged line of young men would begin to march on this gray November evening down the company street, heading into a vastly different (for some it would be the last) phase of their lives.

THREE

Spurts and Sputters in the Economy

Americans lived in two worlds in 1941, the world at war and the world of their individual environment and experience. While they hoped to keep them separate, the world of war persisted in intruding on the other, closing in, affecting how the people thought, where they lived, and what they did. Was the war a blessing or a curse? Americans, of course, preferred to label it a curse and habitually remarked about the terrible events across the sea; but the war added other, not altogether objectionable, dimensions to their lives. It gave them something fascinating to talk and think about. Even though they hated to see him go, parents did not hesitate to show the latest pictures from the boy at Camp Chaffee or Breckinridge; and the young man, when he came home on leave, wore the uniform with pride remarkable for one said to hate the new experience. Americans also had to admit that the country seemed to be coming alive, that more people now were working and making more money.

Millions would have to agree that because of the war their lives were changing. People who had jobs might find themselves asked to work more hours; with more hours came more money and a need to decide how much to spend, how much to save. People without work might contemplate how and where to get it. At least there was hope. If they lived in the country or a small town, it might be necessary to go to the city or any place that offered the prospect of a job. The people involved faced a new kind of work, the need to relocate to a new social environment. For many people the move did not come too soon; for millions of others the change did come soon enough, for in 1941 their Depression had not yet come to an end.

Americans might have noticed that they were hearing more and more about Roosevelt, Congress, and what was going on in Washington; perhaps to their surprise, what they were hearing was not all bad. The government might already have taken away a son; from people at work it was taking a piece, or a larger piece, of their pay. Although widely unpopular, such actions were accepted as logical and necessary in the extraordinary circumstances of the day. No one could doubt that prospects for work depended much on decisions coming out of the capital. It followed that the government should handle problems arising from the new circumstances. Change in the people's relationship with their leaders, especially in the national government, was one of the most momentous developments of the year and of the era.

It all happened in the natural order of events of the time. The business of military production had started to increase in 1939, when, to assist enemies of Germany, the government had authorized sale of war matériel abroad. The pace had quickened during Hitler's easy conquest of Western Europe in 1940, when Congress had appropriated more than $4 billion dollars for defense, with more soon to come. The impact extended beyond companies engaged in production of military goods. Factories needed material to feed their machines, thus stimulating steel, coal, and other related industries. Businessmen felt greater inspiration to invest, consumers a greater willingness, and ability, to spend, reversing the spiral of a few years earlier, when Depression had overtaken the United States.

Gross National Product nudged upward each month; by year's end it would exceed $125 billion, an increase of $25 billion from the previous year and more than double the lowest point of the Depression in 1933. Factory workers who a few months earlier might have been unemployed now could count on $30 a week, and in some industries more. Wheat reached almost a dollar a bushel wholesale, and the nation wanted more of it; in 1940 the price had been eighty-seven cents.[1]

While those statistics suggest a general economic recovery, some places revived more quickly than others. The people most affected by the changes of 1941 included the more efficient mechanized— usually larger—farmers, who benefited from rising prices, and people who lived where military goods were produced. Most large cities had factories already engaged in producing war matériel, and even more were undergoing conversion. Here and there one found a small town that for reasons often difficult to discover became the site of a military-related project. At tiny Charlestown, Indiana, for example, the government and the DuPont Corporation decided to build a mammoth powder plant. Seattle came under the influence of a bustling Boeing bomber factory, and several cities on or near the Pacific Coast in California were well on the way to becoming aircraft or shipbuilding centers.

The city that came to symbolize the transition, already claiming the title "arsenal of democracy," was Detroit. By May 1941 Michigan showed a 14 percent increase in employment over the previous year, much of the change traceable to an industrial boom striking metropolitan Detroit. January was the best month in the history of automobile production, and forecasters anticipated that the trend would continue through the year. The accuracy of that prediction depended less on consumer demand than on shifting national priorities, for factories ordinarily busy producing Chevrolets, Plymouths, or Hudsons were logical sites for making war machines.

With automobiles selling well, manufacturers were hesitant to change over to military production. But government pressure and appeals to patriotism, not to mention the lure of lucrative contracts, were causing them to reconsider. Almost weekly, it appeared, came news that one company after another had agreed to build some military item: Buick accepted a contract for Pratt & Whitney aircraft engines, and Packard agreed to build power plants for Rolls-Royce. Hudson started making guns and torpedoes for the Navy, and Willys-Overland produced the new Jeep. The huge Chrysler tank arsenal would begin to turn out "land battleships" in the summer, and at Willow Run, some 30 miles west, construction proceeded on schedule on a massive structure where Henry Ford would build long-range B-24 bombers. For a time, Detroit had both guns and butter, but with the demand for military goods steadily growing and a labor shortage of 10,000 expected in a few months, it was clear that a choice would have to be made between the two.

Other cities would have accepted the problems of a semi-wartime economy if they could have had the benefits. A few people complained that the expansion was going too fast, but more said it was too slow and was neither well-planned nor fairly distributed. There were charges that officials were ignoring the unsolved social and economic problems or complications growing out of it. Just as the economic program of the 1930s had been a maze of improvisation, so the economy of 1941 emerged without long-range plan, other than eventually to build a large number of military items. The government provided the boost and much of the money. Private industry was to undertake production, and labor did the work, with conditions to be set, in no identifiable proportion, partly by government, partly by the businesses, and to a lesser extent by labor unions, all without application of a concrete philosophy; the economy was what it became, however one chose to define the product.

The result, not unexpectedly, was a flurry of activity, interspersed with confusion, mismanagement, and delay. Factories might spring up in places unable to handle the growth in population, while larger urban areas continued to languish, waiting for their turn. As Charlestown, Indiana, with pre-boom population of 936 was bursting at the seams, several miles down the Ohio River the much larger community of Evansville reported unemployment of 2,500 industrial workers, and few people active in defense industry.

New problems emerged as the defense industry siphoned away material needed in consumer goods, creating not only unemployment but also scarcity of certain commodities. Shortages and rumors of shortage had become a sign of the times, and while genuine hardship developed from want of key material, the press enjoyed giving attention to frivolous items. "Chicago women stormed several Loop stores," a local newspaper reported. "By noon the customers were standing seven or eight deep . . . shouting and demanding." The cause of the calamity had been a shortage of silk, a standard component of stockings, apparently a more urgent matter than the trouble with Japan that had cut off the supply and caused the government to freeze remaining stocks. Once supplies had vanished, women would have to make do with rayon, the "despised cotton," or an unperfected synthetic fabric called nylon, not yet produced in large quantities. Meanwhile the country would expect "the longest stocking run in history."[2]

Other difficulty developed in areas anything but frivolous. A short supply of steel threatened production of thousands of items. Secretary of the Interior Harold Ickes provoked a furor in July by ordering filling stations closed at night on the East Coast. The problem was a shortage not of fuel but of tankers to carry gasoline to market. Ickes had to rescind the order. A government agency estimated that without drastic changes, absence of key materials would increase unemployment by 2 million people, and by the end of summer perhaps one-third of American industry would have to shut down or change over. "Doesn't this mean," the Chicago *Tribune* asked, "that amidst the greatest industrial boom the country has ever seen the worst depression will be visited upon whole communities in which non-defense industries are located?"[3]

Not unexpectedly, much of the responsibility for the confusion was laid at the President's door. The criticism seemed valid. For all his grand pronouncements about the threat of Hitler, the responsibilities of the United States, and national production goals, Roosevelt was taking a meandering path toward his objectives. He seemed anxious to please all factions and was impossible to pin down. Donald Nelson, a member of the administration's production team, explained his experience dealing with such a man. Nelson had taken a two-month leave from Sears, Roebuck in 1940 to help organize the defense program. After six months he went to tell Roosevelt that the time had come for him to return to Sears. Entering the President's office prepared for "sentimental farewells," Nelson encountered the "Roosevelt charm" working at "high voltage." Each time he started to speak, Roosevelt broke in with discourses about the war, yachting, the Russians, and anything else that came to mind. The meeting lasted an hour, and Nelson had spoken scarcely a sentence when Pa Watson, guardian of the outer office, announced that Cordell Hull was waiting to see the President. "Don, I really didn't get a chance to hear what you had to say, but I have decided that I very much want you to stay," Roosevelt said, holding out his hand. "I'll be seeing you."[4]

Reporters put the problems of production to Roosevelt in the press conferences the President seemed to enjoy so much. In customary manner he joked about trivial matters, evaded questions, twisted others until indistinguishable, and claimed that some problems were being solved. He resisted pressure to place the mobilization program under the command of one man, as he put it, a "Czar" or "Poohbah," or "Ahkoond of Swat." Now and then he created a new agency. Early in 1941 came the Office of Production Management, presumably to streamline and centralize the defense effort. At its head Roosevelt had placed not one man but two: Sidney Hillman, a labor leader, and William B. Knudsen, former president of General Motors. Why not appoint a "single, responsible head"? a reporter asked. "I have a single, responsible head; his name is Knudsen and Hillman," said the President, and the reporter could get no better answer.[5] The nation continued to face critical shortages of steel, copper, rubber, and other materials, and virtually all aluminum available was in the hands of a single firm, Alcoa. The American people, Walter Lippmann complained, "are not being dealt with seriously, truthfully, responsibly and nobly." And in the judgment of Senator Tom Connally: "we are in a mess."[6]

By no means the least important reason for the erratic performance of the American economy was continuing conflict between labor and management. While the military war continued in Europe and Asia, an industrial war raged in the United States, a struggle also marked with theaters of operation, an armed soldiery, pitched battles, and even lists of casualties. If the war in Europe produced the lead stories for radio and the press, the industrial war easily ranked second, in some cases crowding the battle against Hitler off the headlines. In 1941, 4,288 work stoppages plagued the United States, nearly double the previous year's total. The strikes affected more than 2.25 million workers, a fourfold increase, and caused almost four times the man-hours lost in 1940.[7]

The economic reawakening of 1941 coincided with a transition within the labor movement. The change had started in the early 1930s, at the depth of Depression and economic distress; armed with what appeared to be government support, many of the nation's workers began to organize unions and prepared to do battle with employers. The passage in 1935 of the National Labor Relations Act—the Wagner Act—and Supreme Court decisions upholding the law came as a blow to leaders of industry, for they now faced a mandate to bargain with unions properly organized under supervision of a National Labor Relations Board. For the first time in American history, the national government had placed its weight behind the principle of unionism.

It took some time to determine how and by whom this huge new power should be wielded. Encouraged by remarkable victories in the automobile and steel industries in 1937, John L. Lewis and a group of aggressive upstarts had gone on to break completely with the American Federation of Labor and form a rival organization, the Congress of Industrial Organizations, or CIO. At the start of the 1940s, the House of Labor not only continued its conflict with management but also battled itself, as the two organizations maneuvered, grappled, and waged virtual outright warfare in a great struggle for the allegiance of various groups of workers and dominance of the union movement.

While labor by 1941 could look back on the most productive decade in American history—a threefold increase in membership in less than ten years—many problems remained and new questions emerged from the circumstances of that critical year. Millions of workers remained unorganized, with the so-called Little Steel companies (Youngstown, Republic, National, Bethlehem) and the Ford Motor Company receiving special attention. Labor faced a bitter battle with those determined companies and probably a struggle between the rival organizations. An expanding economy broadened and intensified all issues of labor–management relations.

Many issues remained unresolved with firms that had accepted at least minimal unionization. While the law demanded that management under certain circumstances recognize representatives of labor, it did not specify the extent of union power or numerous other items, including, of course, wages, that went into a contract. The most recurrent issue of collective bargaining was "maintenance of membership," which usually involved the demand for a union shop or closed shop—some form of compulsory membership.

Labor troubles revealed that sharp divisions continued to plague prewar America, that in this time of crisis powerful groups did not hesitate to put self-interest first. Patriotism did not exactly stop at the factory gate or the mine portal, but the issue seemed too important for either side to sit aside, and the uncertain posture of the United States in world affairs left room for differing views of loyal behavior. The international crisis magnified all labor disputes and at the same time frequently made contestants recalcitrant, each side seemingly convinced that the government would act on its behalf rather than allow a critical industry to shut down.

Among the most dramatic and significant disputes were struggles that developed at Ford and in the coal mining industry. In both cases dominating personalities set much of the tone of conflict; both were reflective of changing tides of labor relations in the United States. The case of Ford was an expression of times past, a personalized corporation, still headed by a founder determined that truth and justice in American capitalism remain what he long ago had conceived them to be. John L. Lewis, President of the United Mine Workers, came to represent unionism gone rampant, an irresponsible tyrant obsessed with the exercise of power recently gathered into his hands. Ford and Lewis, two giants on the landscape of industrial America, showed similarities as remarkable as their differences. Both were isolationists, both apparently Republican and believers in capitalism, both as headstrong as an angered bull and prepared to press their case to hell and gone. Ford appeared to have the admiration of nearly everyone except the people who worked for him; Lewis drew the condemnation of almost everyone but the people he represented.

Henry Ford in 1941 was a far cry from the man who had established a worldwide reputation as a dynamic, creative, caring captain of American industry. He turned seventy-eight that year, was in failing health, mood-ridden, paranoid, and probably senile. He trusted almost no one, the principal exceptions being his wife and Harry Bennett, his chief lieutenant and enforcer. He nonetheless insisted on running his company and the men who worked it his way. Ford's pride and joy was the mammoth industrial complex at River Rouge in Dearborn, which at peak capacity would employ more than 90,000 people.

The Ford Motor Company for years had struggled under such anachronistic leadership. Slow or unwilling to adapt new management techniques or such vehicular changes as coil springing, Ford ran far behind Chevrolet in annual competition and did close battle with Plymouth for second place in individual automobile sales. The company as a whole ranked no better than third, behind General Motors and Chrysler. Ford Motors probably would have weakened even more but for buyer loyalty, the reputation of the founder, acquired long ago, and Henry's last great innovation, the V8 engine.[8] Fords were rattletraps, many people believed, rode like a bucking steer and started burning oil before they should. Those V8s at least were fast and "peppy."[9]

For years working conditions in Ford plants had been the worst in the industry. The company hired and fired whom it wanted. There were no rest periods; the pace often was frantic, especially during the hated periods of "speed-up" to hasten production. The most notorious branch of management was the Ford Service Department, headed by Bennett. Officially charged with plant protection and personnel supervision, in the factory Bennett's men were brutal and omnipotent, "mercenaries," as a scholar of the labor movement put it, who "mastered every tactic from the swagger of the Prussian drill sergeant to outright sadism and physical assaults." Off company property, Ford Service acted as antagonists and spies, and a worker who drove off in a Chevrolet or Plymouth was deemed traitor and candidate for dismissal.[9]

Organization of the workers, needless to say, had no place in Ford's scheme of things. Henry had said that labor unions were "the worst things that ever struck this earth," and Bennett had labeled the new union of automobile workers "irresponsible, un-American, and no God-dam good."[10] It was Ford's company, and he would take care of the men, as he earlier had done by instituting the five-dollar day. The old man probably believed his argument, given his narrow vision, but it was equally true that he did not want to surrender power. He had come to hate such labor leaders as John L. Lewis and Walter Reuther as much as he hated Franklin Roosevelt. Whereas Chrysler and General Motors had buckled in 1937 and agreed to bargain with the United Auto Workers, Bennett's army of thugs had left such organizers as Walter Reuther and Bruce Frankensteen battered and bloodied near the Rouge plant. Ford's attitude in 1941 remained as it had been during the "Battle of the Overpass." There were not going to be any unions around his place.

The Service Department continued its pattern of activity, patrolling the plants on the lookout for "loafing," "singing," even "smiling" on the job, which would warrant dismissal. If Servicemen could not find offensive behavior, they sometimes provoked it by starting a fight with a man they wanted out. By 1941 more than 4,000 had been fired on suspicion of union activity. Henry seemed to grow more paranoid with advancing age (he had had a stroke in 1938); the growing international crisis served to feed his anti-Semitic and anti-British attitudes. He had refused an offer to build Rolls-Royce aircraft engines; he would produce war matériel for the American Army, he said, not for the British. The order went to Packard.

The UAW continued its struggle mostly in the courts and before the National Labor Relations Board. Virtually every ruling found the company guilty of some illegal practice or sustained the union's right to forge ahead. In February the board ordered Ford to stop "threatening, assaulting, beating," or in any way interfering with workers' organizational rights.[11]

Ford again geared for battle, determined no less than in 1937 to keep the union out. First, the company launched a campaign designed to win over public opinion. "There is no labor trouble within the Ford organization," a full-page statement in the Detroit press announced. "The false propaganda and agitation comes from a few outsiders . . . who live off the workers by collecting millions of dollars in dues from the men and women who ring factory time clocks." Bennett blamed the situation on "communist-led and influenced labor agitators." In a rare public statement the old man himself reiterated that "a union is like a big spider's web. . . . American industry should be free to function; American workmen must remain free to do as they will. . . . We do not intend to submit to any union."[12]

Bennett increased the ranks of Ford Service, preparing if need be to do battle again at the barricades. Bennett's army this time consisted largely of black men recruited in Paradise Valley and other ghettos of Detroit. Ford had become probably the most popular American capitalist among black people of the urban North, a man said to have generous heart and sympathetic mind—a paradoxical reputation in view of Ford's strong ethnic and racial prejudices. Critics said Ford was being opportunistic, recognizing that black people's hunger and desperation for work made them a convenient tool against union organizers. Whatever the reason, black people had been allowed into Ford in large numbers, and many demonstrated their gratitude. "When it comes to Mr. Ford this writer is a 100 percenter," a columnist in a black newspaper asserted. "If the unions take over Ford's, goodbye, goodbye to bright cheerful things of the past."[13]

The Rouge plant became the center of controversy near the end of March. As workers enlisted in the UAW by the thousands, Ford Service continued to operate, ferreting out organizers and here and there firing a man—a union man—for "loafing," "fighting," or some such charge. The lid blew off the night of April 1, when Ford Service refired eight men recently ordered reinstated by the Labor Relations Board. According to Bennett, the men had run "rampant in the plant, cursing people who didn't feel of the same mind as they did about the union. . . . So we fired them again."[14] Workers then streamed from the factory, began setting up picket lines outside entrances, and called for reinforcements from men on other shifts. It soon developed that there were two groups of Ford workers: the strikers in the streets, nearly all white, their numbers growing each hour, and hundreds of other people inside, mostly black, sporting buttons that proclaimed them to be "100 percent for Ford." The striking workers, recalling the disaster of 1937, were ready this time. With weapons comparable to those of their assailants, they repelled two attacks by the loyalists and proceeded to surround the factory and block all access to the inside. The huge plant at the Rouge was shut down.

There followed several days of stalemate, maneuver, and name-calling. Bennett blamed the strike on "a gigantic Communistic conspiracy to paralyze the industrial life of our nation." "Cheap buffoonery," a spokesman for the CIO retorted, "the UAW is dealing with Hitler's Henry—the dictator of Dearborn. . . . What the Ford

Motor Company fears is . . . the abolition of its infamous spy system and its storm troopers. It fears the destruction of its industrial dictatorship."[15] Calmer heads, notably the Governor of Michigan, in time helped produce a compromise. The workers agreed to return to the factory while preparation continued for a referendum supervised by the NLRB to determine which union, if any, the Ford people wanted.

On May 21, after some five weeks of campaigning and bickering between the rival unions, the workers voted. Some 70 percent endorsed the CIO, with 28 percent supporting the AFL. Less than 2 percent voted to have no union. It was a great victory, a chagrined Harry Bennett said, "for the Communist Party, Governor Murray Van Wagoner and the National Labor Relations Board."[16]

Exactly one month later—one day before Hitler attacked Russia and two days after Joe Louis, a local hero, had fought Billy Conn—the press announced that Ford had agreed to a contract with the United Auto Workers. One piece of news was almost as remarkable as the next. The saddened old man had instructed his negotiators "give 'em everything—it won't work." After negotiations lasting only twelve days, Ford's workers received easily the best contract in the auto industry, more than they had expected. Not only did the contract guarantee higher wages and the union shop, but the new union also acquired the controversial "checkoff" clause whereby the company agreed to deduct union dues from workers' wages. The contract with Chrysler and General Motors had no such provision. Most astonishing of all, the notorious Ford Service Department—the "Goon Squad"—was to be disbanded.[17]

Unknown to the public at the time, the matter almost did not stop at that point. The beleaguered patriarch, fearing that his empire would be pulled down around him, considered rejecting the agreement his agents had signed and closing all thirty-four Ford plants, putting some 120,000 people out of work. The decision to follow a different course, to keep operating and deal with the union, was attributable partly to wise counsel from Ford's son, Edsel, and above all to Henry's wife, who threatened to leave if Henry insisted on wreaking havoc on Detroit and other communities.[18]

The settlement of labor problems at Ford would be more important for the future war effort than for military production in the summer of 1941. Ford's heavy participation in military contracting was fast approaching, however, particularly with construction of the bomber plant at Willow Run continuing at steady pace. The settlement was of great significance to longer-term relations between labor and management and for continued progress of the union movement. If Ford, with all its power, resources, and determination, with the founder's status as a folk hero and still large public support, could not hold out against worker organization, could any corporation hope to withstand the tide of unionism?

While the Ford Motor Company stood on the periphery of military production in 1941, the coal industry occupied the center. Coal in fact represented the heart of national economic activity, an indispensable source of energy for heating more than half the nation's homes, supplying most of its electricity, driving all but a few locomotives, forging steel, and fueling almost everything associated with heavy industry. And yet the more critical coal became to an awakening economy and to national defense, the more quarrelsome the men who went into the pits became. If they dug coal at all, they seemed determined to work on their terms, only at the behest of their leaders. To most Americans, the coal miners and their leadership came to represent the epitome of greed, irresponsibility, and a blind quest for power. The miners viewed their behavior differently. They saw themselves as participants in a drama, or a tragedy, with many previous acts, and now it had become their time, their duty, to carry the performance forward.

The miners were reacting to the history of coal-mining in the United States as well as to issues encountered in 1941. Mining had had its ups and downs, its good times and bad, but for the workers it had been a mostly unpleasant story, a century of long hours, low wages, cave-ins, explosions, and autocratic, ungenerous management. If the miner had managed to escape being killed or maimed in an accident, he faced the prospect of life shortened by black lung or some other respiratory disease. The wages he received, frequently paid in special company money called scrip, soon returned to the source, for the company owned the building where he lived, the store where he traded, and just about any other place where the worker might spend his money. "Not all operators force their employees to buy their food at company stores," one student wrote in 1941, "but . . . a great many of them do. Uncounted miners have lost their jobs because they traded at the A. & P., and few and far between are the company stores that sell at A. & P. prices. . . . A miner . . . is lucky to have enough left for a bag of Bull Durham when the commissaries and that fiend 'deduction' gets through with him."[19] Merle Travis' catchy tune, "Sixteen Tons," popular a few years later, recounted the role of the company store in the miner's financial plight.[20]

Not surprisingly, the coal fields had given life to the Molly Maguires and other radical organizations, and to some of the bloodiest industrial conflict in American history. When the miners rose up, operators used virtually any device to retain control of their domain. They recruited private armies of Pinkerton and Baldwin-Felts detectives and supplied them with armored cars, rifles, and machine guns; they sought court injunctions and on a few occasions managed to enlist the state militia in their bloody cause. The "Ludlow Massacre" and "Bloody Williamson County" were but two legendary episodes in the miners' long struggle for respect and a tolerable standard of living.

Coal mining had changed in several ways by 1941. For the most ominous development one could go to southern Illinois, to an area called "Little Egypt," so named because the principal town was Cairo. The visitor would have no problem knowing he had arrived, for the signs were everywhere: huge mounds of yellow clay, destroyed vegetation, and ugly scars left in the earth by the open-pit diggers. The activity here was not mining as the traditionalist understood it to be, and the people who operated those huge machines were not truly coal miners. Strip-mining produced less than 10 percent of the nation's coal in 1941, but the amount was growing each year, and each year those earth-eating monsters with 30-cubic-yard diggers crawled over new fields and started tearing the ground apart.

To find more familiar mining, the method used most frequently on the eve of the world war, one would go to the Appalachian Mountains, to such states as Ohio, Pennsylvania, West Virginia, and Kentucky. Here one would find helmeted men who each day were swallowed by the earth, in mines that followed the veins horizontally through the mountain. The men might travel 5 miles or more to the place of work, the coal face, on what they called the "man trip." "If it is a large mine," one reporter explained, "they ride a coal train, banging, grinding, bumping, constantly careening around curves, and lurching up and down through long, seemingly never level, endlessly dark subterranean passageways." At their appointed spot they climbed out and watched the train roll off leaving a trail of flashes from the electrical connection. "For a moment they stand there, ankle deep in water, surrounded by a darkness so black they can feel it," the reporter continued. "It is a darkness dripping with the oily black slime of the guts of the earth."[21]

Mechanization had found its way into the underground mines also. While the union contract of 1941 still contained references to the use of mules, most mines had small electric railways that carried men back and forth between the portal and the coal face. For many years most coal had been loosened from the vein partly by dynamite (a process called "shooting") and by cutting machines. Such expedients were a mixed blessing: Although they reduced the tedious "picking" of coal from the wall, they also curtailed the number of jobs and presented hazards of injury from working close to machinery, increased coal dust, and sparks that could ignite explosive methane gas. Mechanical loaders now moved approximately 40 percent of the coal; a smaller proportion of miners worked with pick and shovel, but much work remained for those elementary tools and many tasks in the mine required strong arms and backs.[22]

Coal mining remained difficult, dirty, and dangerous. A miner who started at eighteen and kept a job faced chances of one in three that he would be killed by age fifty. Chances of losing an eye, both eyes, an arm, or a leg were much larger. "Do you see that fellow sitting over there in that dilapidated rocker on the porch?" a student of the business observed. "His back was broken in a slate fall. He's just thirty-seven, but he'll never enter a mine again. For $200 he signed away all claims against the company." Nearly 1,300 would die in mine accidents in 1941, and more than 61,000—approximately one man out of eight—would suffer some sort of injury.[23] Clearly the miners' struggle had not ended.

Visitors to a mining area might wonder why the men did it. A mining camp in an Appalachian "holler" seemed the drabbest and dirtiest place on earth, with clotheslines and outhouses, with kids, dogs, and other animals running about at will. The unpainted three-room houses, probably owned by the company, all had warped roofs, sagging steps, and walls with no covering other than newspapers. "Many . . . are almost past description," an observer confirmed. "One can't put smell on paper."[24] Arriving at a mine portal, one encountered men emerging at the end of a shift, blinking as they walked into the bright light of day, a huge aluminum dinner bucket swinging from the arm, filthy from black dust on face and clothes. A visitor bold enough to venture into the miner's world experienced the eerie sensation of entering sudden darkness and going deep into the ground, perhaps the terrifying thought of a ceiling collapsing, a gas explosion, or something that would prevent going back.

Why did they do it? They probably would answer that it was what they did, what they knew. Going into the mines was what people did in the hills, almost all there was. A few young people were leaving those days, going to Pittsburgh, to Portsmouth, Ohio, across the mountains to Washington, or even up to Detroit or Chicago. The older fellows, with little education and no desire to leave friends, relatives, and the familiar culture of the mountain country, stayed in the pits. Why, after all, should they leave? They liked mining coal. The hottest summer, the coldest winter, the deepest snows made not the slightest difference underground, where the temperature was always pleasant, in the 60s. One found in the mines a camaraderie more intense than existed in the factories—partly a consequence of shared danger, one must suspect, and partly a tradition formed in the long struggle against near-serfdom.

Conditions, after all, were better than they used to be. Largely because of the war, a mine almost never stopped operation these days unless the vein gave out altogether or the men shut the place down themselves. Approximately 18,000 more men went into the pits in 1941 than in the previous year, reversing, if only temporarily, the trend toward the use of ever fewer miners. The standard wage reached almost $1.00 per hour, more than one could earn in many places up north; the standard work day in a union mine was seven hours, although because of twice traveling the "man trip" a worker might have to spend up to two unpaid extra hours in the mine. Safety standards still had a good distance to go, but at least many mines had better lighting. The perilous, hissing open-flame carbide lights probably were anachronistic in this age; a few men still used them, although most miners wore safer electric cap lamps. For the first time this year, government inspectors obtained authority to go into the pits.[25] If miners no longer thought of themselves as indentured servants, they knew it was because they had kept the faith, supported the union, and followed the orders of John Llewellyn Lewis.

Lewis was not an easy person to defy. The son of a blacklisted Welsh miner, having spent time in the pits himself, he seemed made for the job, a tough man in a tough business. With barrel chest, a massive head adorned with large piles of unruly dark hair and eyebrows to match, and an expression almost frozen in a frown, he cut a figure one could not forget. If Lewis could not overpower an adversary by force of personality, he did so with rhetoric. Who could have guessed that he had not finished the eighth grade? Listeners might swear he had had instruction in the Bible, Shakespeare, all the classics, public speaking, debate, and acting. Lewis's appearance on stage, addressing an important issue, was a sight to behold:

Expressions chased themselves across his face like clouds across a storm sky—it was now beaming and radiant as if at dawn; now somber and tinged with melancholy as if at sunset; now black and threatening, like thunder. His eyes burned with fire and contempt, and his great voice . . . declaimed, bewailed, taunted, condemned in a series of stately and pounding periods.[26]

Seizing an opportunity created by the Depression, a receptive public opinion, and government patronage, Lewis had moved to make the United Mine Workers the dominant force among the nation's miners, recruiting members and eliminating competing unions. He then led the break with the AFL, and as president of the CIO he earned credit for humbling two giants of American industry, General Motors and United States Steel. By 1937 he had become the hero of the labor movement and one of the best-known—albeit most controversial—individuals in the United States.

Lewis unfortunately was no less adept at provoking enemies than in inspiring supporters. Leaders of the AFL hated and feared him, and he proceeded to antagonize lieutenants in the CIO and the President as well. A much-publicized split with Roosevelt was said to stem from a number of origins. Lewis thought Roosevelt had not supported labor enough during the strike-plagued 1930s. Many people suspected that Lewis felt betrayed for not being offered the vice presidential nomination in 1940. Lewis would proclaim his opposition to virtually all aspects of Roosevelt's foreign policy, a position that leaders of many CIO unions found embarrassing and impossible to follow. In a radio broadcast near the end of the 1940 presidential campaign—heard, it was estimated, by 30 million people—Lewis reiterated his support of Willkie and announced somewhat foolishly that he would take Roosevelt's reelection as repudiation of his leadership and would resign as head of the CIO. Three weeks later he held true to his promise.

While at the start of 1941 Lewis continued to inspire awe, hatred, and fear, his power had dwindled to leadership of fewer than 500,000 people in the United Mine Workers. Many people came to believe in the following months that his actions stemmed from a desire not so much to win benefits for the miners as to wield what power he had left, to humble big men in industry, and to taunt and defy his enemy in Washington. To the great issues of the day—the war against Hitler, the defense effort, emergence from the Depression—he seemed oblivious.

Moving first against what became known as the "wage differen-

tial"—40 cents less per day for miners south of the Ohio River—
Lewis called his men from the pits in April, setting the stage for the
next act in a long drama.

It was a good bet that the trouble would start in Harlan County,
Kentucky. Crunched down in the far southeastern part of the state,
almost in Virginia and almost in Tennessee, Harlan was, as people
in those parts liked to say, the damnedest county in one of the
damnedest parts of the United States. The land was hilly, barren,
and not worth much except for the veins of coal. The people were
lean, wary, and combative. The workers harbored suspicion and hatred for mine operators which often erupted in open warfare. The
company men were an even nastier lot. Nowhere else could one find
employers, as one observer put it, "with the damnable perversity that
nature crammed into the carcasses of the leaders of Harlan's operators."[27] In the hills around the area people still knew the little song
that grew out of the pitched battles of the 1930s:

> They say in Harlan County
> There are no neutrals there.
> You either be a Union man
> Or a thug for J. H. Blair.
> Which side are you on?
> Which side are you on?[28]

Some conditions had changed since the time that song had been
written. The union had made considerable gains. J. H. Blair, the
man who had virtually declared war on "these Communists" in the
union, no longer was Sheriff of Harlan County. What had not
changed was that management of the mines still was in hands of
"men born to hate the very sound of the word union."[29] Sure enough,
Harlan's owners led the way in opposing wage increases, particularly
an end to the differential, and when the old contract expired the
Harlan Coal Operators Association announced plans to keep its
mines open, using nonstriking workers. It was their coal, by God,
and one way or another they were going to get it dug.

Trouble began almost immediately. On April 1, Earl Jones, a
guard at the Mary Helen Coal Company in Harlan County, was
killed, and a union picket was shot in the leg. Later that afternoon
some 250 union men exchanged gunfire with guards at the R. C.
Tway Coal Company, and the next day four men were killed and
five wounded in a shootout at Crummies Creek. The Governor of
Kentucky demanded that the "disgrace must stop," but he seemed
powerless. He could not have sent the state militia—as governors

had done in the past—even had he wanted to, for at that time Kentucky had no state militia. The National Guard was in the Army, and its commander was Roosevelt. Two weeks later, at Fork Ridge, just across the border of Tennessee, the mine fields broke into a pitched battle fought with shotguns, rifles, and submachine guns. It was a familiar story: The mine had kept operating, and approximately one hundred cars and trucks full of union men had come to demand that it stop. A survey of license plates suggested that most of the vehicles came from Harlan County, Kentucky. When the shooting stopped it was possible to count at least twenty-five wounded men. Among the dead were a miner, a deputy sheriff, and President C. W. Rhodes and Vice President E. W. Silvers of the Fork Ridge Coal Company of Clairborne County, Tennessee.[30]

Southern operators sought to convince the public that the controversy involved much more than 40 cents a day. A full-page ad in selected newspapers warned of a threat to deprive the nation of most of its heat and light, and nearly all its railroads, subways, and streetcars, as well as a threat to the defense program and all industry. Who was responsible for the danger? "One man, John L. Lewis. . . . While America slept, he has craftily gained a death-grip on the one industry which affects the destinies of all others. Now he apparently is using that death-grip for the dictator's crown."[31]

For all their expostulation and warning of impending danger, the operators could see that a threat from John L. Lewis and the UMW was not idle chatter. They signed the agreement in July and, by their admission, granted virtually everything Lewis had demanded. While Southern operators stressed that they had acted as "patriotic citizens" seeking to do "everything in our power . . . to further our . . . defense program," they surely were influenced by warfare in the coalfields.[32]

For the rest of the summer, Lewis remained a man of mystery. He said little and seemed to enjoy the attention he attracted riding in his Cadillac from home to office in Washington or walking the city's streets. Now past sixty, the added years and pounds made him appear larger, and the hair, while generously splashed with gray, still was wild and bountiful; the eyebrows had become bushier, the jowls heavier, the frown meaner. After the German invasion of Russia on June 22, Communists in the American labor movement began to level their guns at Lewis the isolationist. Leaders of industry and government surely cast more than an occasional glance toward the building of the miners' union, wondering what the bulky patriarch would do next.

Lewis decided in the fall that the time had come to take up the old issue of the "captive mines" owned by seven large steel companies. While those companies recognized the UMW, and while at least 95 percent of the workers had become members, the contract did not specify a union shop, the requirement that all workers join the union. Troubled about the prospect of losing another battle to this powerful adversary and provoking a similar demand from the much larger steel workers' union, the steel firms held out against the union shop.

Lewis called 53,000 workers out of the pits in September, shutting down the captive mines and touching off a dispute that would last almost to the end of the year. The miners returned after one week, then quit working again (for three days) in October. On November 17, after the National Mediation Board refused to sanction a union shop, not only did captive miners strike a third time, but they began to be joined in sympathy by workers in the commercial mines. Soon 200,000 had stopped work, and more seemed likely to follow. At a time when the United States was virtually at war with Germany and relations with Japan were growing steadily worse, it appeared that nearly all coal production—fuel for the entire economy—would come to a halt, and all over an issue so picayune as union membership for 5 percent of the captive miners, perhaps 2,500 people.[33]

As most people saw it, the person responsible for this calamity was the arrogant and irresponsible director of the UMW. Denunciation of Lewis came from almost all quarters. "Dastardly . . . a betrayal of America," an official of the AFL said. "It is intolerable and America will not stand much more of it," Walter Lippmann wrote. "Congress should legislate and when it does Lewis will be dealing . . . with the government of the United States."[34]

Almost alone in dissent from the national uproar were the miners themselves. Virtually to a man they walked when Lewis ordered, returned when Lewis sent them back, and demonstrated loyalty to the UMW. As they saw it, their action constituted not merely a drive for an immediate goal but payment of a debt to martyrs from a bloody past and to brothers who would follow them into the pits. Amid the many expressions of outrage, a defense of the miners' case appeared here and there. One "letter to the editor" of a Southern newspaper reminded readers of how it used to be: how miners had been under company control from cradle to grave—from delivery as a baby by a company doctor to being put to rest with prayer from a company preacher. During the time in between a miner was "once a man and twice a breaker boy," entering the mines at eight or nine as a coal breaker or doorkeeper; taking a man's job at fifteen or so; and by the time he was fifty or sixty being fit only to join the breaker boys again. What changed those conditions, the writer explained, what broke the miner's chains, was the mine workers' union.[35]

When someone asked Ludie Barnes, a miner in western Kentucky, what he thought of the situation, he replied: "I got four young'uns an' an old lady at home with Christmas coming on but I was gonna stick by the union because they already gimme what I got."[36]

Such loyalty and determination doubtless had an impact on Roosevelt. Frustrated and angered with this man he could not manipulate or threaten into doing his bidding, Roosevelt refrained from ordering the Army into the pits. He knew that only the miners could dig coal, and they would not work until Lewis ordered them to. He issued veiled threats through the press, wrote to Lewis and officials of the steel companies, met with them personally, and offered to write each nonunion worker, urging him to join. In the end he solved the problem by yielding to the labor chieftain.

The President was no slouch at maneuver himself. If he could not win, he at least could manage his surrender to avoid the appearance of defeat. He appointed an "arbitration" tribunal to consist of Lewis, Benjamin Fairless of United States Steel, and John Steelman of the United States Conciliation Service, a supposedly impartial participant. Lewis accepted the proposition, knowing full well, as did Roosevelt, that Steelman was a strong supporter of labor. The board voted 2–1 to award the union shop to workers in the captive mines. Lewis had won again, although events prevented him from fully enjoying the glory of victory. The board reached its decision on December 7; the press published the news the next day, when Americans were preoccupied with a different news story.

En route to that historic event, however, the nation had to endure a year of economic spurts and sputters, many of them traceable to discord between labor and management. Major strikes occurred in Allis Chalmers in Milwaukee; International Harvester at Richmond, Indiana; Bethlehem Steel in Bethlehem, Pennsylvania, and Lackawana, New York; Midlands Steel Products; Federal Motor Truck; and many other places involved in production of military goods. Efforts by management to keep operating, encouraging workers not to strike or seeking replacements for those who did, often led to conflict between strikers and nonstrikers or between pickets and police.

Overturned and burning vehicles were a common sight outside factories and in the coalfields.

With factories reopening and more people working, union leadership moved to ensure that wages at least kept pace with economic change and that as many workers as possible were lodged under the union tent. There seemed to be little danger in those exceptional circumstances that management would revive an old threat of moving to another state or that government would allow a strike to last indefinitely. Some of the same reasoning caused industry to resist union demands. If many large firms had conceded more than Henry Ford had at the start of 1941, few were willing to go as far as he grudgingly did in the contract signed with the UAW in June. Both labor and management understood that while special conditions helped cause the current controversy, the effect of a settlement would last long after circumstances had changed.

In the course of this long struggle, labor scored important gains. The victories at Ford and in the coal industry were complete and clear-cut; membership rolls grew by almost a million in 1941. The victories did not come without considerable loss of support in public opinion. Polls showed that a substantial majority considered labor leaders irresponsible, too powerful, and probably Communists and/or racketeers.[37] The people demanded action, and when on rare occasion the government used force to break a strike, the public seemed to approve. Such a case emerged at North American Aviation in Inglewood, California, a producer of medium-range B-25 bombers. The trouble grew out of a complex situation involving rivalry between the AFL and the CIO, as well as conflict within the union and with the company. The upshot was that rebellious workers, some of them reputedly Communists, struck on June 5 in defiance of the government and the national leadership of the CIO, putting the plant out of operation, according to one account, "as effectively as if it had been bombed."[38]

Not for long. Local draft officials began proceedings to revoke deferment for striking workers, and in a short time Roosevelt dispatched more than 2,500 soldiers to occupy the premises. Many townspeople turned out to watch, perhaps in support of a policy thought long overdue, perhaps to take this first opportunity to observe America's new Army in action. The press could not conceal satisfaction in describing the spectacle: "Down the highway the soldiers came in a menacing silence. . . . The front line of unsmiling soldiers held guns with bayonets. Behind them were stern-faced sergeants and officers. Then soldiers with riot guns and automatic rifles. Then another wave of bayonets. Then tanned men with machine guns." When one angry picket swung at a stocky trooper, the butt of the soldier's rifle landed squarely on his chin, and the man went down "like a log."[39]

By year's end John L. Lewis had become the most hated man in America. It seemed inconceivable that he could defy the government, disrupt military production, ensnarl the economy, and experience nothing worse than public disapproval. One could not even be certain that popular hostility represented punishment to Lewis, for it constituted a recognition of power that the labor chieftain seemed to relish. Demands for stringent action had become commonplace. "Outlaw the closed shop and defense strikes," was a typical proposal. "Send to the penitentiary union leaders fomenting strikes and induct strikers into the defense forces."[40] Representative Hatton W. Summers of the House Judiciary Committee insisted that in dealing with "enemies of the nation in the factory" his committee "would not hesitate one split second to enact legislation to send them to the electric chair."[41] The United States, of course, did not execute striking workers in 1941, but events of that year nourished an antiunion sentiment that would last many years.

Industrial strife was in some measure a reflection of foreign affairs, an indecision that left officials unprepared to demand a course of action and private citizens doubtful that they had to do what the government wanted. While the Administration had established a Defense Mediation Board to deal with labor disputes, it never became clear whether the board's proposals would be binding. Lewis showed no inclination to accept any ruling with which he happened to disagree. Roosevelt much preferred persuasion and pressure to compulsion, and while that attitude might have been admirable from an ideological perspective, it did not always produce the results the economy needed and the public seemed to want. There were no guidelines to specify when the government could or should use force. Occasionally Roosevelt did act: In June he had moved in at North American, and in August the government seized Federal Shipbuilding and Drydock after the company rejected a proposal for a union shop. But such action was rare. Other leaders of labor and industry did much as they wished, and it was not clear what the government could do to stop them. Labor troubles cost valuable time in the rearmament program, although the remark of Donald Nelson probably was an exaggeration. "Nineteen and forty-one will go down in history," he recalled, "as the year we almost lost the war before we ever got into it."[42]

☆

Military and diplomatic considerations aside, Americans had other reasons for wanting a vigorous economy. Many people needed help. Economic indicators appeared most impressive in comparison with the dismal years of the Depression and in several ways gave a misleading picture of national economic health. Unemployment might have showed an impressive decline from the past year and amounted to nearly 10 million less than ten years earlier, but at mid-year it still stood at more than 5.5 million, a disturbing 10 percent of the work force. For millions of people the Depression remained almost as intense as it had been in the mid-1930s.

The standard economic yardsticks—unemployment, gross national product, per capita income—told nothing about differences in income or the millions of people nominally employed but earning scarcely enough to get by. The sharecropper in Alabama, the shoeshine "boy" in Harlem, and the worker in one of Georgia's turpentine plants had no place in the statistics of people without work. Such people were "employed," no matter how little they made. Some individuals, notably people in business and entertainment, did very well indeed. Louis B. Mayer of the Loews theater conglomerate, who had a foot in both areas, had topped the list with an income of $678,048. The best-paid film performer, Gary Cooper, earned approximately $500,000; before going to work for the government, William B. Knudsen had made $350,000 as president of General Motors. The highest paid baseball player, Hank Greenberg of the Detroit Tigers, earned at a rate of $55,000 before being drafted in 1941. The one-fifth of the population with the highest earnings received almost half the nation's family personal income.

In the upper middle class, unsalaried lawyers and doctors averaged appoximately $5,000 (lawyers slightly less), although a few people in each profession earned a great deal more. Public school teachers could expect a salary of $1,500–1,600 a year, and miners and workers in manufacturing earned approximately the same amount, about $30 a week—enough for them to live no better than "frugally." A laborer with the Tennessee Valley Authority received fifty cents an hour, or $20 a week, and while his family struggled to survive on that wage, he probably felt fortunate to have it. Many people he knew made much less.[43]

It is impossible to determine how many people deserved to be classified as living in poverty, or even what it meant to be "poor" in prewar America. Millions of people had been simply "getting by" for so many years that they did not bother to consider whether they were poor or not. Many places were comparable to parts of rural Texas where, as Lyndon Johnson later would put it, poverty was so ordinary that folks did not know it had a name. While earnings provided the first clue to standard of living, individual status also had to do with such factors as location, availability of food from farm or game, medical care, and size of family. Each case of deprivation did not stand as a measure of national economic conditions. By failing to obtain education or skills and refusing to abandon old habits or move to a new area, people locked themselves into a social and economic box. Families often had more children than they wanted or could support, and yet the kids kept coming. In many cases, the largest families had the smallest earnings.

The highest proportion of poverty-stricken people lived in rural areas, notably in the Southern states or the region of the Appalachian or Ozark mountains. Here people who were not coal miners sought to survive any way they could, by hunting, trapping fur, or making moonshine liquor; most of them tried to scratch out a living farming their little plots of land, or land owned by someone else, long since overcropped and worn out. There could be no doubt that those people were poor: The average cash income from farms in Knott County, Kentucky, for example, was $56 a year, and many black and white farmers in such states as Alabama, Arkansas, and Mississippi earned less.

Neither the government nor private institutions gave much help in defining poverty or measuring its scope. The Works Progress Administration (WPA) had determined in June 1940 that "maintenance" income for an urban family of four, which would permit "simple" food, "rather meager" clothing, and no car or telephone, was approximately $1,350, or $1,500 in New York City.[44] One author observed that $1,500 a year would pay for no better than substandard housing in most cities, "minimum diet," and no telephone or automobile. "It can hardly be maintained," the author concluded, "that existing on $1,500 is living on the 'American standard.'"[45] These calculations did not speak well for the American standard of living, no matter what statistics one used to measure income. Nearly 50 percent of all "consumer units" (a family was a consumer unit) earned less than $1,500 "cash" income in 1941. To use another statistic, nearly 25 percent had "consumer family income"—which takes into account earnings and income of all kinds, including goods consumed on the farm—of less than $1,000. The *Tribune* remarked that in Chicago an income of $3,000–4,000 a year "is regarded as not wholly unsatisfactory."[46] Surely not, but less than 25 percent of the nation's families could claim earnings that large.

Roosevelt had proclaimed four years earlier that one-third of the American people were "ill-nourished, ill-clad, ill-housed." He had proceeded to patch up the old economic mechanism, replacing a part here and there and applying occasional lubrication. The operation had not worked very well. The machine had chugged and sputtered in the 1930s. If in 1941, under stimulus of war, it ran at a higher speed, the performance still was not acceptable. The people suffered from many years of malfunction. Of the first million men called for the draft in 1940–41 approximately 40 percent failed the physical examination. In Tennessee the rejection rate was more than 47 percent, and in some counties well over half. The most common cause for rejection nationwide was bad teeth, despite regulations that called for only "6 serviceable opposing posterior teeth" and "6 opposing anterior teeth." Other deficiencies dominated different localities and different groups. More than one-fourth of the blacks summoned in Tennessee had syphilis.[47]

A national nutrition conference reported in the spring that only 25 percent of the people had "excellent" diets and that 45 million were at least "mildly malnourished." The problem arose less from simple starvation than from failure to obtain, or inability to afford, good nutritional balance. *Fortune* magazine advised readers to plan diets carefully, calculating that a family of five could obtain proper nutrition for thirteen dollars a week, if wisely spent.[48] That estimate seemed reasonable, given food prices of the day, and readers of *Fortune* probably could follow that guide. But the laborer on TVA could not spend that much on food, and neither could millions of other families.

Improper diet fostered medical problems that often remained uncounted, and sometimes undetected, unless by chance the carrier came in contact with a government program, such as the draft. Medical and dental care, particularly preventive treatment, was delayed as long as possible, laying foundation for serious trouble later. Toothache, a common malady at that time, usually resulted from failure to have a cavity filled. Most families knew of such home remedies as hot cloths and placing cloves or aspirin in the affected area, all designed to help the seige to pass. The condition might be painful but was not usually critical, and professional treatment could be put off for years. The consequence of such neglect might be, besides intermittent pain, early dentures or costly bridgework. Otherwise the stricken individual might go through life with an unsightly mouth or pretending to chew while in fact only rolling food around the back gums. For many men the catalyst from traditional habits to better nutrition and medical care would be the Army. Even with substantial improvement in earning during the previous year or two, it seemed a reasonable estimate that on the eve of war at least one-third of the people still lived in a state of poverty or very close to it.

As the year progressed, however, the nation and government seemed to worry less and less about people in need. Economic statistics and the preparedness campaign were driving concerns about human welfare into the background. America appeared to be moving toward a genuine economic boom. By the end of year retail sales had reached $54 billion, a remarkable $10 billion more than 1940. Sears, Roebuck & Company, the retail giant, reported for the first seven months a sales increase of 33 percent over the same period the previous year. The largest gains came in consumer and durable goods—automobiles, washing machines, refrigerators—which might be in short supply if war should come to the United States.

As sales increased, so did the volume and variety of advertising, as businessmen moved to promote their products in an enlarging market place. Advertising always had been an inherent part of American capitalism, of course, as a means of selling goods and as the primary supplier of revenue to radio, newspapers, and magazines. A visitor from Britain explained that he came to learn the "daily setup of American life" in the hour before breakfast, when radio heralded the new day with "blasts of music . . . laughter . . . short spasms of news about the European War" and dramatized plugging of Old Gold cigarettes, Bosco, Postum, White Owl cigars, and many other products.[49]

Scanning newspapers and magazines of that day, the reader would be struck by the number of products endorsed by screen performers and professional athletes, a practice that indicated the esteem in which such people were held and the alliance conveniently formed between entertainment and business. "I have been eating Wheaties since 1936 when I first joined the Yankees," said Joe DiMaggio, leaving the reader to find a connection between the cereal and DiMaggio's talents in baseball. Somewhat more dubious, because of a possible impact on youngsters, were testimonial advertisements of cigarettes. "When you're in there throwing everything you've got,"

Kirby Higbe of the Brooklyn Dodgers reported, "there's nothing that hits the spot like a Camel." DiMaggio, who apparently had a wide range of tastes, also liked Camels, because "in his own words, 'they're milder.'"[50]

An intriguing form of testimonial was the use of upper-crust people whose class marked them as sophisticated, refined, discriminating, and cosmopolitan. Whatever prejudice existed against the snobbery and pretension of the social elite, ordinary people still wished to be like them. And what were their identifying characteristics? Rich-sounding names, for one thing, the longer the better, each preferably with more than one syllable, and participation in activities only the leisure class could afford. "Blood lines count . . . in cars as well as horses," said "Mrs. Priscilla St. George Duke, of New York and Tuxedo Park, formerly Mrs. Priscilla St. George, famed as one of America's youngest dog show-judges." Mrs. Duke was fond of her Studebaker automobile, and so was "socially prominent" Mrs. Pierpont Morgan Hamilton. Mrs. Algernon Sidney Buford III, a Southern lady expert in horsemanship, cast a vote for Maxwell House Coffee.[51]

Businessmen had long ago discovered the power of sex as a tool of salesmanship. Both men and women appeared in sexually inspired advertisements, although women were far more common. A scantly clad female was a logical way to dramatize stockings, corsets, and other undergarments; to show the garment it was necessary to show the body. Women also appeared in shorts, bathing suits, and various states of dress or undress to adorn ads for cigarettes, vitamins, yeast (to be taken independently, as a type of vitamin), toothpaste, soap, and automobiles. Through conspicuous placement of the ads and coverage of pretty girls as news items, sex also was used to sell the newspapers and magazines in which the advertisements appeared.

What advertisers hoped to accomplish, of course, was the transfer of a subject's glamour to the product, creating demand for something customers otherwise might not want. It worked best with nonessential items, such as cosmetics and perhaps cigarettes. The practice also fostered sameness and standardization of culture, an ironic development in a society that ascribed much of its attractiveness to pluralism and individualism. The fashionable woman in 1941 should use Lux soap, like "nine out of ten movie stars." Max Factor would color her lips, preferably bright red. Spencer corsets were guaranteed to hide "all those ugly bulges." There was even hope for that sorrowful beauty in the Listerine ad who asked, "Why have I never married?"

It probably was inevitable that as the year went on more and more commercial messages would draw a connection to world affairs. War had become an instrument of merchandising. Testimonial ads showed engineers, workers in defense plants, and anonymous people in military uniform praising the merits of such items as cigarettes or razor blades. Automobile companies regularly reminded the public of their contribution to national defense, and a huge ad appearing near the end of the year almost suggested that buying from Chrysler constituted an act of patriotism. The construction of automobiles mobilized engineers and technicians, the sort of specialists needed to produce military goods. "Anyone buying a new Plymouth today," the ad maintained, "has the satisfaction of not only obtaining the finest car in Plymouth history, but of knowing he has also given support to the defense production structure."[52] Many businessmen saw nothing objectionable in putting the war to good use with a little profit-taking along the way.

Most conspicuous in the developing consumer culture, as in years before and times to come, was the automobile. Americans had been in love with cars for years, and now an upswing in the economy permitted many people to pursue the romance with full vigor. By end of the first quarter, new car sales had increased almost 128 percent over the previous year. Besides the "Big Three," which produced twelve makes of automobiles, one also could select from eight independent models, ranging from the classy Packard to a tiny Crosley, scarcely larger than the driver it had to carry. Counting the English Bantam and the Hupmobile (which soon would cease production), the market offered twenty-one kinds of cars and twenty makes of truck. Competing with the automobile giants had been an almost impossible undertaking, as dozens of bankrupt producers previously had discovered. In 1941 General Motors, Chrysler, and Ford would take approximately 90 percent of the market. The companies that had survived now encountered a stroke of good fortune. Extraordinary prewar conditions had induced an unprecedented demand for new machines and had created additional business in military goods, which made it possible for such firms as Hudson, Studebaker, Nash, and Willys-Overland to show a profit and last a few more years of life in the glamorous automobile industry.[53]

One could not tell from looking at the cars that such problems as scarcity or priority existed: They were large, heavy, and shiny. Producers had rounded and smoothed out body styles and lowered the center of gravity, continuing a movement away from the boxlike appearance of earlier years. For the 1941 models, as in every year, there had been new features. General Motors introduced "concealed running boards"; Studebaker in 1941 pioneered a "concave" windshield; Chrysler's cars featured a safety rim. Nash claimed that its cars could obtain 30 miles per gallon of gasoline, although a more typical performance for the bulky machines of that day was somewhere in the teens. With fuel costing eighteen to twenty cents a gallon and an apparently inexhaustable supply, few people worried about mileage. The standard engine had six cylinders, although several large cars were powered by "straight-eights." Most of Ford's machines—the Ford, Mercury, and Lincoln—and some Cadillacs had V8 engines.

The most exciting new device was a mechanism that allowed one to drive without shifting gears. General Motors had experimented with such a gadget since 1937, but not until 1941 did it become a standard feature of competition. No producer wished to call it simply automatic transmission; a device this novel had to have an exotic title. DeSoto offered Fluid Drive with Simplimatic Transmission; in Chrysler it was Vacamatic (for $38 extra), in Hudson Vacumotive; Packard had Electromatic ("no jerk, no slip, no creep"); in Lincolns and Mercurys it was Liquamatic. The most successful was General Motors' Hydramatic Drive, which Oldsmobile claimed as the "greatest safety development since 4-wheel brakes." Drivers did not easily give up the familiar method of changing gears, however, and so most vehicles offered the option of manual transmission, with the shift lever mounted on the steering column.

In relation to prices and wages of that day, the new cars were not inexpensive. A 1941 Plymouth with no extra equipment (such as radio or heater) went for approximately $750. A new Packard cost anywhere from $907 to $5,500, and Cadillac advertised its lowest-priced model, a five-passenger coupe, for $1,345—not a bad price for a Cadillac, but to millions of families a sum larger than their income for the year. Most buyers had to settle for a used car, with cost ranging from nearly the price of a new car to almost nothing. Perhaps the most practical investment would be a Model A Ford, available in most areas for $50–$75. "She ain't much to look at," a sheriff in Kentucky remarked about his 1929 Model A, "but . . . she's got a good bit o' go in her yet. They can all but climb trees."[54] It was a sturdy little vehicle, even though more than ten years old; if the engine ran well it would hold together a long time. One had to be on the lookout, however, for a "pretty iron," a defective machine doctored by an unscrupulous dealer—by putting sawdust in the crankcase, for example, or by mixing ether with gasoline—to make it seem in good repair.[55]

Americans registered nearly 34 million vehicles in 1941, approximately three-fourths of all cars in the world and an average of nearly one per family. While not every family owned a car, most did—especially outside large cities—and foreigners continued to express amazement at the number of Americans with neither house nor job who remained committed to supporting a four-wheel machine. A sociologist in Illinois observed that when a boy graduated or quit school he first looked for a job and then "he begins to figure out ways and means to buy an automobile. . . . To have a car is the all-important thing." If the young man could not afford a down payment, he might buy a junked car for $10 and set to putting it in running order with parts from other disabled machines.[56] Abandoned vehicles, or pieces of vehicles, had become a blot on the landscape of rural and small-town America. Perhaps nothing better reflected the nation, the economy, or the individual American than the attitude toward cars. In addition to being utilitarian, the automobile enhanced mobility, individualism, and freedom. It stood as a symbol of prestige and personality owners could take wherever they went.

Inevitably the demand for cars and the desire to produce them began to conflict with needs emerging from the international crisis. The manufacturers held their ground as long as possible. Oldsmobile announced an intention to combine an "extensive defense program" with continuance of regular production so that "jobs, the security and well-being of everybody everywhere may be maintained and strengthened, and the American way of life preserved."[57]

The models of 1942 appeared on schedule, as if nothing had changed, late in 1941. With few exceptions they resembled the previous edition. Running boards now had vanished from sight on nearly all makes. They were still down there, covered over by a slight protrusion at the bottom of the door. Grillwork on the new Chrysler stretched all across the front end, almost resembling a huge smile. The headlights of the DeSoto had disappeared altogether, hidden behind two nearly undetectable flaps, which gave the machine an appearance of going around blind. The 1942 Buick was so streamlined that the front fender reached along the side until it bumped into the rear fender, and the large vertical bars of the grill might have reminded oncoming motorists of a shark's teeth.

How many 1942s would be available for sale? That was a problem. The first hint of trouble had come in April, when Knudsen had ordered a 20 percent cutback in production, to begin August 1. It was a conservative step, not as harsh as producers had feared it might be or many observers thought it should have been. The action nonetheless foretold more stringent measures ahead, when the international crisis partly responsible for the boom in the automobile industry would make it impossible to produce any new cars.

The curtailment of automobile production, of course, would be temporary, an expression of wartime expediency, but other changes in the economic system were destined to continue long after the war had ended. However reluctantly some firms converted to the manufacture of war-related materials—and some companies showed not the slightest reluctance—virtually all were to become accustomed to the practice and to understand the relationship between government contracts and economic health. Seeds of a military–industrial complex had started to sprout. The most enduring legacy of the last year before the war was growing participation of the national government in all aspects of economic life. "We are passing in swift steps farther and . . . deeper into a system of government planning," one writer warned near the end of the year. "Next to the outcome of the war itself the dominant question . . . is how far this movement is going and what the final results will be."[58]

The movement had not started in 1941 or with the outbreak of war in Europe. For nearly half a century government had been expanding its activity in economic matters. During the 1930s the government had lurched into many new areas and had apparently assumed a vague, largely unfulfilled responsibility for the public welfare. The international crisis now had established a virtually unchallengeable rationale for more activity, the limits of which no one could define. One might raise philosophical objections about the government's responsibility in pursuit of social and economic justice but there could be no doubt about its obligation for national security. It had become no less clear that defense and economics were inseparable; in raising an army and procuring weapons, the government also was creating jobs, helping establish conditions of employment, and moving the nation toward a period of widespread prosperity. It would be impossible to forget the connection.

Critics' charges to the contrary notwithstanding, the condition did not grow out of greed or lust for power within the Roosevelt Administration. Isolationists, most of whom were economic conservatives, found the President guilty of grievous sins, including being power-hungry, although they could not deny that the rearmament program had to continue. Individuals who found their interests threatened might challenge the legitimacy of the power they had come to encounter. Faced with government pressure for the union shop or some other concession, they probably raised the banner of private enterprise. Far more common than charges of coercion, however, were complaints about government slowness in controlling scarce and essential material, and failure to command production of needed items or to force recalcitrant workers into line. Critics might differ in the ways they found the government negligent; but in economic organization most agreed that timidity was the most persistent shortcoming of the Roosevelt Administration.

Not everyone objected to the government's undertaking new duties. Many liberals continued to cheer expansion of national authority, finding in such activity the only avenue to something resembling social and economic justice. The alternative—which in this time of crisis was not realistic after all—seemed reversion to leadership by the same private individuals who had been so conspicuous in the recent economic collapse. Curiously, big businessmen again were assuming positions of authority, although they now acted as agents, or servants, of government.

Some liberals found a special social message in the political chaos of the age. The antidote for oppressive government—Hitlerist totalitarianism that seemed to threaten the world—was not small government, but large government that functioned for benevolent purposes. One official put the case as follows: The success of dictatorship in Europe created social as well as military challenges for the few democracies that had managed to survive. If the American political system could not care for the people, it would probably collapse from the pressure (and promises) of the new totalitarianism. "To be worth dying for, a political system must make possible a society that is worth living in," the report continued, and that demand might include "provisions for the millions of people . . . dependent . . . upon socially provided income." In other words, democracy has to do some of the things totalitarian systems promised (and do them better), or it would be supplanted by its devious challenger. Thus, in the highly charged political environment of 1941 government leadership, even social welfare programs, went beyond "mere . . . sentimental humanitarianism." They made hard practical sense and constituted "the first line of national defense."[59]

Other observers found a different message, and much reason for concern, in the trend of the times. "Can we go on step by step, adopting the techniques of totalitarianism and still retain the essential freedoms of democracy?" asked a writer in the *New York Times Maga-*

zine. "What is to be the final outcome and will it be good or bad?" The author presented no answers—only his resignation to the fact that the trend would continue. A different course would lead to even more unacceptable consequences. "If we do not enter the war and the Nazis win," the United States would need "indefinitely a tremendous military establishment costing $30–50 billion a year" and "a drastic system of . . . totalitarian controls."[60]

The more the government became entangled in economics, the more responsibility the government—and the politicians who ran it—had to accept for the outcome. If the government could claim partial credit for improving economic conditions in 1941, it would also have to accept blame in the future when the economy might undergo a downturn, and that would establish the rationale for even more government activity. The path to the government's becoming the central force in economic life ran directly through the special circumstances of 1941, and those who governed in Washington could move through that year of crises knowing that as they accumulated power and responsibility they faced the blessing, or at least passive acceptance, of the people they served.

FOUR

☆

On the Road and Into Town

Even with pains of economic rebirth, the embarrassing pockets of poverty and of listless citizenry, the United States remained the world's richest and (next to Germany, perhaps) most energetic nation, a focal point of world affairs, and the nonbelligerent in which all states involved in the world war were most keenly interested. Besides possessing seemingly boundless resources and an industrial machine of unimaginable potential, the United States was one of the earth's largest and most populous nations. Estimates set the population in 1941 at 133,402,000. The most recent census, in 1940, offered detailed information about the people. Americans were predominately white—nearly 90 percent. The largest minority group, black Americans, made up less than 10 percent of the population. What the Census Bureau referred to as "all other," largely American Indian, Japanese, and Chinese, comprised less than 0.5 percent of the people. Officials classified people of Mexican extraction as white Americans. Nearly 9 percent were foreign-born, and total "foreign white stock," which added persons of mixed or foreign parentage to the foreign-born, made up nearly 30 percent of the population.[1]

The nation's centers of economic activity and political and cultural power were the Northeastern region and the area then referred to as the Midwest. Nearly 60 percent of the people lived in fourteen states east of the Mississippi River, north of the Ohio and the Mason-Dixon Line, and in Texas and California—two states that were beginning to emerge as challengers to Northern and Eastern domination of the country. New York State had by far the largest population; California ranked fourth, only 225 behind Ohio in the census of 1940, but barely half the population of New York.[2]

Many people were not satisfied with where they lived or, probably more important, with how much they earned, and so were on the move. Americans had been traveling about for some time, particularly during the previous ten years, and now in the 1940s they had started an internal migration that would be greater than in any previous decade in American history. Unlike later years, when Florida and states of the Southwest would attract retirees and people seeking a warm climate, migration at the start of the 1940s was largely economic, driven by the search for better work or simply for a job.

A few trends already had become noticeable. People continued to move from countryside to town. The farms were to lose more than 600,000 through migration during the year ending in April 1941, and in the following year nearly 1,500,000 more would leave. Black and white people from the economically sluggish—if not still Depression-ridden—farms and small towns of the South and border states left for the industrial North and the far West. The states growing most rapidly included California, Michigan, Washington, and Ohio. The city that gained the most people in 1941 was Washington, D.C. By 1943 the nation's capital would have more new residents than all but five of the states. The places losing the most population were the border states, the region of the Great Plains and Rocky Mountains, and, curiously, New York. The traffic from the South, the Southwest, and, to lesser extent, everywhere else in the nation to the West soon would grow to almost a torrent, largely attracted by aircraft factories and shipyards growing up on the Pacific Coast. California would move into third place among the states in 1941 and soon would be in a position to challenge Illinois for the second spot.[3]

The newcomers, wherever they arrived in substantial numbers, did not always encounter a warm welcome from natives and other longtime residents. The locals had names for the migrants, roughly associated with place of origin. To be known as an "Arkie" or a Tennessean carried a stigma in Chicago or Detroit; the people of Evansville, Indiana, had no use for Kentuckians, even though they came from only a few miles away, across the Ohio River. They all were "hillbillies." Intruders in California still were "Okies," whether they came from Oklahoma or not, and Californians had known about them for years. "These Okies who came out here, who weren't anything before they left, don't amount to anything," a resident of the Golden State remarked. "They're filthy dirty—you give them a decent house and in a couple of weeks they are spitting through the cracks."[4] While for many such people the move would be permanent, the lure of the old home remained strong. If it was close enough, they would go back on weekends to visit relatives, to show how they were making it in the big city, or simply to relax in a familiar environment. It remained for the second generation, the children, to feel fully a part of the place their parents had adopted.

The method chosen for traveling the country varied, of course, with distance, purpose, individual circumstances, and other factors. The motor bus (as it was called) remained a common form of commercial transport, if only because it was inexpensive and flexible. The bus could go anywhere the highway led; it was best for short distances. The age of air travel had not arrived for the United States. Airplanes carried approximately 4 million passengers during 1941, a modest increase over the previous year but only a tiny proportion of all commercial transportation. Buses, for example, carried 435 million in intercity traffic. Air travel simply was too new, too expensive, and too frightening. Despite the recent success of the DC-3, the airlines did not offer a fleet of aircraft that inspired public confidence. Many people continued to look upon pilots as "daredevils"; airplane accidents were national front-page news and were regarded as what one could expect in the vulnerable environment of thin air. The war had caused an increase of air traffic, as many more military craft went up on training missions. More planes meant more crashes, an average of more than three a month, counting accidents of military planes that caused multiple deaths. The climax came October 30 when separate crashes of two civilian aircraft killed thirty-four people.[5] It surely seemed safer to travel on the ground.

Even so, travel by air was enticing for some. Even skeptics would have to admit that airplanes were remarkably fast—the trip to Europe took less than thirty hours—and if one could surmount the original fear, flight was a great adventure. It was exciting to drive out to the airports, to LaGuardia in New York, Midway at Chicago, or other big-city terminals, to watch the big birds come and go. Lucky watchers might get a glimpse of Pan American's massive Boeing clipper, which had beds and a dining room and could land in the water. The war would affect the airline industry, as it would change so many other aspects of American society, by inspiring the development of better aircraft and increasing confidence in the safety of flight. The revolution in civilian air travel was not far away.

For people planning a permanent change of residence, the logical transport and the cheapest was by automobile, assuming the family car could make the journey. Travelers often encountered jalopies stalled on the shoulder of the road, the passengers stretching and peering at a flat tire or under the hood. Steam billowing from the engine probably indicated a blown water hose or stopped-up radiator, common problems in that day. Sometimes the old machine simply would not work, and the driver, even though he might be an amateur mechanic, could not fix it on the spot. Vehicle trouble could be almost catastrophic to people involved in the "great defense migration," for it could wipe out whatever funds had been scraped together for resettlement.

Motorists in 1941 faced other conditions that people of a later generation would have found perplexing. Virtually all concrete or asphalt roads, including the principal highways, had two lanes (one going each way), no more than 18 to 20 feet wide altogether, which often meant long traffic backups, impatient passers, and the deadliest plague of driving, the head-on collision. Most states had speed limits ranging from 45-60 miles per hour; in Massachusetts it was 30. Three states—Louisiana, South Dakota and Wyoming—did not require a driver's license.[6] Highways led travelers winding through (not around) county seats and major cities, making them subject to— and a part of—inner-city congestion.

Wider, divided highways had barely begun to appear. A breakthrough had come in 1940 with the opening of a section of the Pennsylvania Turnpike, the first modern thoroughfare, without intersections or traffic lights, featuring curves designed for speeds up to 90 miles per hour. By 1941 Connecticut had opened the Merritt and Wilbur Cross Parkways and California the Pasadena Freeway. Officials in several states were contemplating similar projects. For the most part, however, expressways and urban bypass systems remained for the future.

Sensing that they were living in a momentous time, reporters and advertisers had begun to travel the land in quest of the "pulse of the people." Erskine Caldwell undertook such a venture to gather material for a new book. When he pulled into a gasoline station in Missouri, the popular novelist found he was digging in overworked soil. The attendant, with a bored expression, handed him a neatly printed card that answered anticipated questions:

> I am 36 years old. I smoke about a pack of cigarettes a day . . . take an occasional drink of beer. . . . I shoot a 12-gauge shotgun and have a 27-inch crotch. I vote for F.D.R., pull for Joe Louis, and boo Diz Dean. I wouldn't have anything against Hitler if he stayed in his own backyard. I don't know any Japs, but I've made up my

mind to argue with the next one I see about leaving the Chinese alone. I'm in favor of the A.A.A., the C.C.C., the I.O.U., and the U.S.A. . . . I thank you. Hurry back.[7]

People who did not travel by car probably took a train. Although the railroad industry continued to struggle with high costs, mismanagement, and dwindling passenger patronage, it remained an indispensable part of the national transportation system. Railroads easily dominated the movement of freight and in 1941 carried nearly a half-billion passengers. Travelers could find much to recommend going by rail, especially over long distances. The passenger was not confined to a seat, as in an automobile or a bus. Like ships at sea, the train traveled through day and night and did not lose time on a long trip. One could ride the Santa Fe's majestic "El Capitan" from Chicago to Los Angeles in less than forty hours for $65 round trip. Passengers who could afford the cost also could enjoy food, drink, and a pullman berth.

Railroads had been a part of American culture for so long that it would have been impossible to imagine the nation without them. A familiar part of the landscape in all parts of the country was the steam locomotive, with its shrill whistle, its plume of smoke when moving, and the hisses and puffs of steam when stopped. Tracks often paralleled the highways in open country, and drivers liked to race with, or at least clock the speed of, a fast-moving passenger liner. If the engineer was a good sport, he too enjoyed the chase. He could not truly race the automobile, but he might respond with a cheerful wave and a toot of the whistle.

The railroad stations were as distinctive as the trains. Nearly every town with a few thousand people had one, probably built during an earlier era, when a town was no place at all unless the railroad came through. Small stations offered little more than a ticket booth, a waiting room, perhaps out-of-date magazines, and a set of scales along the wall that for a penny would give one's weight within 20 pounds or so. The wooden floors creaked, and the sturdy, high-backed wooden benches shined with the latest coat of varnish. Nothing could feel as hard as a bench in a railway station. Several large cities could boast of railway palaces with arched girders and ceilings that seemed to ascend to the sky. Pennsylvania Station in New York, which covered two city blocks, had marble columns four and a half feet in diameter and a vaulted ceiling fifteen stories high at the top. In busy times the metropolitan stations emitted a cheerful buzz. When there was little traffic, perhaps late at night, each step on the stone floor created an echo that carried through the building, and the immensity of the indoor space could be fully appreciated. The city terminals were monuments to the age of rail.

To meet competition from cars and stay in the business of passenger service, railroad managers had introduced recent changes. They first had dressed up the steam engines with cowlings over the cumbersome-looking machinery to give them a streamlined appearance. Travelers between New York and Chicago who could afford the last word in speed and comfort climbed aboard New York Central's prestigious Twentieth Century Limited, the most famous of all trains, pulled by a massive, hooded Hudson steam locomotive. A more radical innovation had come in 1934, when the Burlington introduced a train called the Zephyr with a sleek diesel-powered engine. Other streamlined trains followed, all bearing exotic names: Meteor, Super Chief, Dixie Flyer. While the steam engine remained the backbone of rail transport, the lines were adding streamliners with diesel traction as rapidly as they could.

The passing of a diesel locomotive through town was still novel enough to cause people to stop and watch. The diesel announced its arrival far down the track with a blast of its mellow-toned horn, easily distinguishable from the shriek of the steam whistle. The engine hummed rather than chugged and hissed steam, and the streamlined body had the look of modernity then being pursued in automobile design. By the summer of 1941 more than a hundred trains were diesel-powered; approximately one-fifth of the coaches and most pullman cars had air-conditioning.[8] Lighter than a steam engine, thus easier on the tracks, much quieter, cleaner and smoother-starting, the diesel locomotive was visible evidence of progress and changing times.

Unfortunately for railroaders and for romantics of the age of rail, the changes in cars and engines would not be enough. Although rail passenger traffic would show a slight increase in 1941, it was still less than 40 percent of the business in 1920.[9] The war years would bring a brief remission in the decline, as the nation overloaded all available means of transport. The extraordinary circumstances of wartime would delay the time, not far in the future, when hissing steam engines and most of the diesel streamliners, even the legendary Twentieth Century Limited, would pass from the stage and remain no more than fond, nostalgic memories. The places where they stopped, from quaint little structures to gargantuan metropolitan terminals, would turn into objects of curiosity or anachronistic ghosts destined for new functions at best or, at worst, demolition.

But that remained for the future. In 1941 terminals all over the country bustled, as people moved about and urban areas came alive. The cities differed in several ways from what they would become a few years later. The people who lived there were overwhelmingly white. Of the great metropolitan centers of the East and Midwest, only Philadelphia and Washington had black populations of more than 10 percent. Of almost 7.5 million residents of New York, less than 500,000 were black; Detroit, with a population of more than 1.6 million, had 150,000 blacks. The farther west one moved, the lower the percentage became. Some 64,000 black people lived in Los Angeles, less than 5 percent of the total number. The highest proportion of black population could be found in the South, in such cities as Atlanta, 34 percent black, or Birmingham, more than 40 percent.

The largest cities also were homes for the foreign-born. In all large cities outside the South (excluding Washington, D.C.) foreign-born residents outnumbered the black population, often by massive proportions. More than 2 million New Yorkers were from other countries, and three-fourths of the city's population comprised first- or second-generation immigrants. Ethnic composition differed from city to city: In Chicago the largest number came from Poland, and in Boston the Irish predominated. New York's largest national component came from Italy. (There were more Jews than Italians in New York, but the census counted only country of origin, so Jews, who came from several countries, mostly Germany and Russia, did not appear in published statistics as a nationality.)[10]

Most immigrants lived in large cities, and here their influence was most profound. They added, on one hand, richness and variety in culture, and, on the other, the potential for suspicion and divisiveness. The people who landed at Ellis Island wanted to be Americans but did not intend to stop being Italian, Irish, or whatever else they had been, and rarely did they do so, at least not in a single generation. The character of the cities—or sections of them—thus depended upon what immigrant groups had collected where. They adopted residential districts and over the years came to occupy almost all the houses and tenements there. In New York, the South Bronx belonged to the Italians, Brownsville and much of the rest of Brooklyn to the Jews. Hamtramck was Detroit's Polish settlement, and in the Boston area some 65 percent of the residents of Charlestown were Irish Catholic.

Ethnic groups set the tone for neighborhoods; they established clubs, foreign-language newspapers, periodicals, and radio programs; in time they produced politicians expected to represent their people in city government and in Washington. The ethnic pattern of a city told the visitor where to go for Sicilian spaghetti or authentic wiener schnitzel and bratwurst, where to hear a lively Polka played on the accordian (although all groups seemed to like the Polka), a Jewish folk song, or a melancholy Italian tune. In the neighborhood the people felt secure, protected from that huge, mysterious world beyond. They could live much as they had lived in the old country. It was a good idea to learn English, but one did not have to. Many foreign-born people passed from life knowing only the few English words their children or neighbors had taught them.

It would not be accurate to say that urban America consisted wholly of first- or second-generation immigrants. The large cities had sizable populations of "native" Anglo-Saxon stock and descendants of much older immigrant families who had long ago abandoned the language and many of the ways of the old country. Other Americans living outside the city came in during the day to work or to shop; some of them were owners of the city's commercial and residential property. The farther one moved from New England, the Middle Atlantic states, and the population centers of the Midwest, the farther immigrants declined as a force in the life of the cities. In towns of the Midwest, in the South, and beyond the Mississippi River, one was likely to find a backbone of Anglo-Saxon or older Germanic people; in the South they would be intermingled—except in certain places—with many blacks. Atlanta, with a black population in 1940 of 104,533, had only 4,293 foreign-born. Many small and middle-size cities had been filled by immigration not from abroad, but out of rural areas within the state or region. Cities of the West had few foreign-born residents, yet almost everyone seemed to be from somewhere else. New people were coming into the cities every day with the war boom taking place.

Cities of the South were smaller than those in the North—the largest, Atlanta, had 300,000—and slower-moving. Visitors from the North could not help but notice the large number of black people in Southern towns and the sharp status boundary between the races, which, on the surface at least, blacks and whites fully accepted. The power structure was entirely white, of course, and most of the manual labor, the servant jobs, and lifting and clean-up work fell to the black people. Little black boys with shoeshine kits seemed to be everywhere: "Shaaane, Mistuh?" they would ask, hoping to earn a penny or two.

While small towns of the interior might contain an industry or two, most relied, in part if not fully, on the surrounding agricultural community. Somehow the farm-based economy put a stamp of sameness on thousands of towns and small cities around the country. The smaller the town, the fewer the amenities, of course, and the smallest places, which in truth were extensions of the countryside, offered almost none at all. If they provided little else, at least they could offer hospitality. Small-town America, except possibly in New England, took pride in being "friendly." "I guess we're all just ignorant hillbillies," a resident of a town in Missouri said, "but I bet you never found friendlier people anywhere."[11] To the less charitable observer it meant only that everyone knew "everyone else's business."

In places large enough to support several levels of enterprise—ranging in population from several hundred to a few thousand—one could find some of the sharpest social stratification in the land. Everyone knew there was an upper crust made up of the most prosperous merchants and property owners, the higher managers if a factory happened to be close by, bankers, doctors, and some lawyers. Everyone else was beneath those people, although by no means all at the same level. While differences might have something to do with religion and ethnic background (and certainly race), economics remained at the heart of the system, from which emerged the accepted distinctions in education, attitude, and status.

The upper echelons were much more likely to send their children to college, expected them to marry in their circles if they stayed in town, and chastised those who did not. Members of the elite were assumed to have influence with people in power, including judges and police, giving them superiority before the law. Somehow cases of favored treatment never reached the newspapers. A scholar of "Elmtown," a small town in Illinois, discovered a notorious class structure that extended to giving higher grades, less discipline, and other favoritism to children of elite families. Joe Brummit, the son of a carpenter, had been the brightest student in his class and should have received the "Special College" scholarship. It had gone instead to Willa Cross—"her dad's in the inner circle." "I used to be a reformer and stood for high ideals," the Superintendent of Schools confessed, "but you have to work with people, and so at times you just have to wink at things." Joe Brummit was now working down at the mill.[12]

Local residents found it nearly impossible to break into higher social circles, if they were so inclined; many, indeed, were not. They simply wanted better jobs. They could improve their chances by leaving for a larger city. "Get out of town; you can't cross the railroad tracks here," a man remembered his father saying.[13] Another possibility for change might come from trying to work one's way through college, which again was probably a decision to leave town. Such an undertaking was difficult for a young man in those days and nearly impossible for a girl. The coming war and military service would be a welcome catalyst for many young men from small-town America. It opened the door to higher education and broke down reluctance to try something new.

Change came slowly to the villages and small towns, but it did come. By the start of the 1940s a grocery store might have taken on new refrigeration equipment: a shiny red Coca-Cola box and a white meat counter with a glass window. The most modern even boasted of "self-serve" facilities, with carts for customers to push around. If a factory opened nearby, people went over to look for a job; if one opened right in town, newcomers arrived like an invading army.

Urban life in the United States was becoming both better and worse at the same time. As one moved out from the center of the city, the housing by turns began to look acceptable, good, and finally fashionable and expensive. The flight to the suburbs was well under way, and the traveler through such places as Park Ridge and Oak Park, outside Chicago, Shaker Heights near Cleveland, or Grosse Pointe Park, Michigan, could tell that he was no longer in the city proper. Even during the Depression years of the 1930s the population of suburban Washington, D.C., grew twice as fast as the center of town. The edges of Seattle expanded by 53 percent during the decade ending in 1940, and Houston's suburbs experienced a growth of 137 percent.[14]

As the upper middle class took its money and its notions about property out of the inner city, the area it left behind deteriorated. Urban decay, the growth of slums and the semi-slums then called "blighted areas" (the label "ghetto" had not yet caught on) remained the foremost problem of urban America on the eve of World War II.

The slum was a consequence of urban evolution fostered by a seemingly inexhaustable supply of land in the United States. Instead of restoring worn-out parts of cities, the people who could afford to do so simply stretched the city farther out, perhaps retaining title to the older property, leaving dilapidated sections of the inner city to people who could afford no better residence. For many years immigrants had occupied most of the slums, and some still did. In the meantime, another impoverished group, the black people, had begun to move in beneath the immigrants or the children of immigrants now edging up the economic ladder. Not all the decayed areas of Northern or Southern cities were residences of black people, but the urban residences of most black people were slums.

Whatever their origin, whoever the residents, the slums were eyesores and a breeding ground for poverty and most social vices. Whether called The Bowery, Skid Row, or some other name, in New York, Los Angeles, or Birmingham they had many common characteristics. "We think of the slum," one study reported, as "a place of poverty, wretchedness, ignorance and vice . . . where the conditions of life are . . . squalid . . . and a liability to the community."[15]

A popular magazine series, "How America Lives," described the plight of a family of eight living in Harrisburg, Pennsylvania, in what probably could be described as "blighted" conditions. The husband worked for the WPA, the wife did housework and babysitting, and neither brought in much money. Their house had a furnace, but the family could buy only enough coal to keep the pipes from freezing. They could afford $40 a month for food, although the children in school did get one free meal and dental care because their father was on WPA; they had no money for medicine. The husband and wife had rotting teeth; he suffered from vertigo, fatigue, and discouragement at being sixty and only nominally employed. She had anemia, low blood pressure, and congested lungs. A sixteen-year-old daughter had infected tonsils, a twelve-year-old son defective feet—"I'm a cripple," he explained. There were "at least" two illegitimate children. "You just gotta use your head to get along in our fix," the man of the house remarked.[16]

Prompted by Senator Robert Wagner of New York and other advocates of urban renewal, the Administration of Franklin Roosevelt had begun to look into distress in the cities. Agencies of the New Deal had provided funds and supplies, and others took elementary steps toward improving places of residence. By 1941 the government had contracted for more than 160,000 low-rent housing units and had even built three new towns from scratch, the controversial "greenbelt" communities outside Washington, D.C., Cincinnati, and Milwaukee.

Even so, the New Dealers had identified the problem much better than they had solved it. They eliminated no slums, and it is not certain that the rate of deterioration had slowed much, if at all. The census of 1940, which came at the end of the New Deal, classified nearly 30 percent of urban dwellings as in slum or blighted areas. In some places, such as Mobile, Alabama, the estimate was as high as 50 percent. The same report showed that 12 percent of urban residences had no refrigeration, 23 percent lacked a private bath, and 42 percent were without central heating.[17] All indications suggested that the problem could only worsen in months to come. At a time of world war, neither the government nor private industry intended to place much emphasis on slum clearance. The people now spilling into the cities were not the kind to buy a house in the suburbs or anywhere else.

Even in better parts of town, people had to do without facilities they later would consider commonplace. Dean Acheson recalled that when he returned to government service in 1941 in the old State Department building, he "stifled under the full blast of the summer sun . . . unabated by any such newfangled contrivance as air conditioning." Roosevelt did have an "apparatus" in his study and bedroom, but according to an aide "he hated it and never to my knowledge, turned it on."[18] The President sweltered along with the rest of the people of Washington in August, when the heat was so intense that it melted tar on Massachusetts Avenue. It was much the same in other parts of the country during the summer, for while a few modern businesses had cooling systems, air-conditioning was virtually nonexistent in private residences. The idea was so novel that theaters advertised being "20 percent cooler inside."

The absence of air-conditioning considerably affected the way people lived. Fans of all sizes and shapes helped somewhat, although on the worst days they managed only to move hot air from place to place. Urban residents had much less inclination to shut out the world, as they would do in the air-conditioned homes of years to come. They were forced to join it, to get out of the house for a walk to the nearest park, waterfront, or other place that might be cool. On summer evenings people could be found walking the streets, riding the porch swing of a private residence, or perched on the front steps of teeming tenement buildings.

Even when people had to go in for the evening, they kept their windows open, allowing the noise of engines, neighborhood radios, and voices and the smell of exhaust fumes, industrial smoke, or the cooking next door to drift in. They had to be able to sleep through, or contend with, such noises as cats quarreling and police sirens. Near a busy intersection people might awaken to a newsman shouting the morning headlines. Elsewhere the paperboy "whopping" the paper against the door or the tingle of quart glass bottles from a milkman making his rounds might disturb their sleep. Residents of prewar urban America had to be a part of their world, whether they wanted to or not.

While most urban areas provided public transportation, systems varied. In the towns and the small and middle-size cities, the old staple of public transport, the electric streetcar or trolley, had vanished or was being phased out. In Chattanooga only four lines remained at the end of the year. The largest city to end trolley service altogether was Seattle, with a population of 368,000, although Los Angeles seemed to be moving in that direction. The Pacific Electric Company announced a plan to eliminate streetcar lines to Santa Monica, Venice, and Hollywood.[19]

The automobile doubtless was one reason for the change. As the number of autos in town increased, so did their drivers' resentment toward the trolley. The streets were crowded enough without those red, green, or yellow coaches clanging down the middle, going where the tracks took them, arrogantly oblivious to the impatient motorists who milled about them on all sides. The tracks created a bumpy surface, of course, and sometimes automobile wheels would follow along the steel rail in defiance of the steering wheel. The costs of maintaining cars, track, and live overhead lines—the source of power for the electric railway—made streetcars an expensive operation. Cities that abandoned the trolley turned mostly to the bus, although a new device called the trolleybus—an electric bus powered by a hot line—had attracted much attention. Without tracks, the lines could now be more flexible, passengers could board at the curb, and, by no means least important, the streets were smoother. More than two-thirds of cities with at least 10,000 people used only buses.

In large cities electric-powered systems continued to dominate public transportation. Wide streets made the streetcar a less obtrusive part of traffic. A scarcity of parking downtown made the individual car more often a burden than a convenience. Heavier passenger loads made it easier to turn a profit. In Chicago, for example, the streetcar carried nearly 58 million passengers in June (at seven cents each); another electric system, the elevated railway (the "L" or El) carried 12 million. New York had been using underground public transportation for a long time. Boston and Philadelphia also had subways, and Chicago was building one. In the largest urban areas, such as St. Louis, Baltimore, Philadelphia, Pittsburgh, and Washington, the trolley was alive and well.[20]

Even in the largest cities, however, buses had begun to carry increasing numbers of passengers. Motor transport seemed to be the wave of the future. Given the noise and the foul-smelling exhaust issuing from diesel engines, along with a breed of bus drivers no less overbearing than the streetcar drivers and far less predictable, it was not absolutely certain that the passing of the trolley represented progress for urban America.

The places experiencing the most profound change in 1941 were the boom towns, cities and villages that woke up one morning to find a facility related to rearmament—probably a factory or a new Army camp—on their doorstep. If the locality happened to be a small town, the effect was near devastation, a social and economic convulsion that caused villages to buckle and bulge, and permanent residents to look on in confusion, not knowing whether to praise the boom or damn it.

Falmouth, Massachusetts, a town of 15,000 on Cape Cod, had withstood the summer tourist rush of 1940 and was preparing for a long winter's lull when the Army decided that the area nearby would be suitable for a training camp. The Walsh Construction Company came to town, put out word of its intention to hire carpenters at $1.17 ½ per hour, and hinted that it would not inquire deeply into an applicant's qualifications. "Never in the history of the ancient and honorable profession of carpentry," one observer remarked, "have so many sins of omission and commission been done in its name." Among people passing themselves off as carpenters were clergymen, a lawyer, cooks, an undertaker's assistant, and a reporter who had come to write the story of the boom. Tool boxes could be anything from egg crates to gunny sacks. Stories of shoddy workmanship and waste circulated freely (the only way to distinguish between trucks carrying material to the site and those carrying away scrap, went one standard joke, was to note the direction they headed). Walsh Construction did not seem to mind. After all, the government was paying for it.[21]

Business in Falmouth experienced such an extraordinary surge that restaurants had to extend hours to accommodate new customers. Living conditions became intolerably crowded. The local citizenry found it almost impossible to have a light switch or leaky faucet repaired, for most tradesmen had taken jobs at the camp. Many policemen agreed to work a second daily shift at Walsh Construction and "of 86 call firemen hardly enough could be found for a game of checkers."[22]

Much the same story occurred in dozen of cities and communities: in East Hartford and Bridgeport, Connecticut, for example, and Newport News, Virginia, or York, Pennsylvania. San Diego's population increased by 50,000 in a year, and Waynesville, Missouri, near Camp Leonard Wood, grew from 17,000 to 40,000. "Money is being made hand over fist," came a report from Jacksonville, Florida, "but when you ask a local citizen how the boom has affected the lives of the residents, he answers, 'lives? We don't have lives any more.'" "It's insane," a man in Bridgeport said. "But what is sane about war?"[23]

No city felt the effect of the defense movement more than the nation's capital. By the summer of 1941 people were entering Washington at the rate of almost 50,000 a day to do business, 3,000 a week to stay. One Washingtonian said, "anyone who has been here 28 days is a veteran."[24] The city grew by nearly 100,000 in a year to more than 750,000, and by end of 1941 had become the nation's tenth largest city. Servicemen from nearby encampments roamed the streets looking for amusement of any sort, preferably girls, and they often found it in bars, with secretaries who worked in government agencies or the ever present prostitutes. "The town is full of gimmick guys, promoters, gals and the like who follow the easy money," one visitor remarked. "One cannot walk down 14th street without being grabbed by a sidewalk siren and the hotel lobbies are full of them."[25]

Blacks from the South mingled uncomfortably with poor whites who had crossed the Appalachians or had moved in from neighboring states, all hoping to find jobs with the government. Washington had the highest ratio of black population—at least 25 percent—of all cities outside the deep South, and many probably wished they had not come. Black people had little chance in the scramble for employment. Whites were taking even many of such traditional services jobs as waiters, servants, and "Red Caps," the porters who served the trains.

Perhaps the most curious mixture took place in Washington's higher echelons, where managers of the New Deal, now almost permanent fixtures in the city, came in close contact with new men from private corporations. There were contracts to be had and money to be made, and these businessmen were anxious not to be left out. Some men had come because Roosevelt had asked them to help manage new agencies growing out of the defense effort. To show their patriotism—and also to let everyone know they were better than well-heeled—several had insisted on being paid a mere trifle, a nominal stipend. Thus the dollar-a-year man was born, and his presence often obscured the fact that many government-employed businessmen continued to draw good salaries from the government, from their old businesses, or from both. The new tycoons in government could take satisfaction in the honors accorded them by Roosevelt and his New Dealers, who a few years earlier had delighted in denouncing them as "economic royalists."

As in other cities, growth in Washington had taken place with haste and little attention to social consequences. Public transportation sagged and creaked under the weight of so many fares. Some people drove to work at 6:00 A.M. to find a parking place, then waited two hours for the office to open. Landlords jumped the price of rental property, and in many cases divided houses to rent as separate rooms, often crowding families into an area meant for a single person. This city of grand boulevards and ambassadorial palaces still contained the infamous alley dwellings, 1,700 buildings that needed razing, now more crowded than ever. At least 15,000 homes had no inside toilets, and black people at Marshall Heights lived in shanties pieced together from beaverboard and castoff strips of lumber and tin. Sleezy entertainment districts hinted at the dark realities of the inner city: pool rooms, dance halls, fried-fish joints, racket barons, and numbers runners. Cluttered alleys attracted noisy crap games and men reeking of whisky, with switchblades and revolvers barely out of sight. Some alleys carried the label "no man's land," unsafe for black or white, and "John Law" would enter them only in force.[26]

And still the migrants continued to come, wandering with wide eyes through the spacious caverns of Union Station, crowding the bus terminals, sprinkling the roads into town with overloaded jalopies, feeling that whatever the problems in Washington, they could be no worse than conditions recently left behind.

☆

The United States was a land of open spaces, towns, small cities, and great metropolitan centers, each projecting a mood and an image, carrying the signs of what America was and would become. When one thought of a Western city, it was likely to be Los Angeles. The largest municipality on the Pacific coast, Los Angeles was a parvenu among American cities, a place of motion and change that lacked the history and tradition of a city like Philadelphia. The city could not shake its reputation (if, indeed, it even tried) as a gathering place for bizarre people, for cranks and eccentrics. Was it not in Los Angeles, less than twenty years before that Aimée Semple McPherson chased the devil around with a pitchfork? Sightseers could still visit Angelus Temple, her "Church of the Four-square Gospel" at 1100 Glendale Boulevard, with seats for 5,300 and a tower where prayer had gone on continuously since 1923.

Much of Los Angeles's image emanated from nearby Hollywood, seat of the glamorous movie industry, the workplace of famous people with no small flair for outlandish living and a town of "big breaks" and instant fortunes. Americans could follow the "Hollywood scene" in the newspapers and fan magazines: the marriage of Brenda Marshall and William Holden or Judy Garland and David Rose. Leading contenders for the title of "happiest young marrieds" were Ronald Reagan and Jane Wyman. Divorce made even better news, especially the case in 1941 of Marion Talley, "the farm girl who became an opera singer," and Adolph Eckstrom, her former teacher, which received front-page coverage for more than six weeks.

The press lost no opportunity to draw attention to peculiar activity in Southern California. One Samuel Brummel, for example, charged that his wife had rented him to another woman for $10,000 a year.

"She told you that?" asked his attorney.

"She told me that," Brummel answered.

"And what did you say?"

"I said all right." Now Samuel wanted a divorce and half of the $10,000.[27]

Do not be misled by lurid stories, cautioned the Reverend Norman Vincent Peale of New York, who had come to town for a lecture. Hollywood was "just a nice, hard-working little city. . . . The people there are . . . just wholesome, friendly, home-loving folks."[28]

Angelenos, at any rate, had to make a living, and while unorthodox behavior continued to be a trademark carefully nurtured by local publicists, most residents had no time for such antics. Los Angeles County remained one of the nation's most important agricultural areas. The city was a seaport, an oil-refinery, and an industrial center. As the city nudged outward, more and more orange groves, lemon orchards, and cabbage patches fell to the bulldozer's blade to make way for new housing or manufacturing sites prompted by the boom striking much of the Pacific Coast. No less than five aircraft firms—North American, Northrup, Douglas, Vultee, and Lockheed-Vega—had plants in the area, and the city had surpassed even Detroit in acquisition of defense contracts.

Los Angeles was a symbol of the exploding West, of the fact that America was moving west. The city had jumped from twentieth largest in 1920 to fourth in 1941, behind only New York, Chicago, and Philadelphia, with a population well past 1.5 million and still growing like an amoeba around its suburbs. One could discern from the City of Angels that America changed as it moved west. The houses were of different design, showed more colors, and were farther apart than in Philadelphia. The cars moved faster and confronted fewer traffic signals than in New York. Except in the dead center of town, it was fairly easy to find a parking place. To serve a mobile clientele, "drive-in" restaurants had sprung up almost everywhere.[29]

The racial mix differed from cities of the East. Most Angelenos were American-born whites, of course, and only about 60,000 were black, although the number was rising. The position occupied by blacks in other areas belonged mostly to Mexicans in the West. There might have been 250,000 in the area, living in seedy neighborhoods like Mexican Town or slums with unpaved streets farther out in the country. Local whites considered them lazy, degenerate, and dirty. Mexicans and blacks could swim in city pools only on Wednesday, and on Thursdays the water was changed. The Los Angeles area also contained approximately 25,000 Japanese and 5,000 of Chinese extraction and the same number of Filipinos, nearly all men.

Raw, lusty, and still being built, Los Angeles could revive a vision—perhaps now stifled in cities of the East—of America as a land of endless space, where freedom truly prevailed and one might still strike it rich.

Chicago was capital of the Midwest, and loyalists probably would argue that it deserved a loftier title. Chicago was big, or so everyone seemed to say. Some years back, Carl Sandburg had called it "City of the Big Shoulders." A foreign visitor in the fall of 1941 readily concurred: "Mightily prosperous, bursting with confidence . . . progressive, dynamic . . . big."[30] Chicagoans liked to think of their home not as the "second city" but as a leader in many respects. It was the nation's foremost rail and air terminal and the center of meatpacking. If the tag "stockyard city" or "cattle-town" was a little short on grandeur, well, anything to be first. Publicists still called Chicago the City of Skyscrapers after the Tribune Tower and Wrigley Building, but for ten years now these landmarks had been overshadowed by the Empire State Building in New York, the nation's tallest. Only a few steps from the lake began the bustling Loop with converging "El" tracks, fashionable stores, and the intersection of State and Madison Streets, which Chicagoans claimed was the busiest crossing in the world. The downtown area had to contend throughout the year with construction of the subway; approximately 7.5 miles would be finished by the end of 1941, mostly in the area of State and Dearborn, but the international crisis left the opening of that grand project in question.

Stretching north of the Loop and for many miles to the south and west (directly east was Lake Michigan) were dozens of sprawling residential districts and shopping areas built to serve nearly 3.5 million residents. In many places the city limits marked the inner edge of a suburban town, and so Chicago truly comprised of dozens of communities, a metropolitan area much larger than the census of the city suggested. Along Halstead Street lived numerous ethnic groups, the Poles, Irish, and Czechs among them, and in recent times Chicago had received increasing numbers of Hoosiers, Tennesseans, and Kentuckians—not as many immigrants as New York, but enough to provide a labor force, diversify culture, and enliven politics. The days of Hinky Dink Kenna, Bathhouse John Coughlin, and other colorful politicians had passed, but the machine still functioned, and the Irish still mostly ran the city. The Mayor's name, appropriately, was Kelly.

Chicago had struggled for years with a reputation as the nation's capital of crime, home of Al Capone, site of the St. Valentine's Day Massacre and the gangland wars of the 1920s and 1930s. While many Chicagoans hated that image (a few, who relished distinction of any kind, found it exciting), and city fathers denied its validity, the reputation persisted. The press seemed determined to promote the perception by giving conspicuous, detailed coverage to acts of crime and violence.

Chicago's most famous newspaper was the *Tribune*. As the international crisis grew, so did the *Tribune*'s renown, and Americans more and more identified the city with its newspaper. Did the *Tribune* truly speak for Chicago, even the entire Midwest? Not likely, but one person who thought so was the newspaper's publisher, Colonel Robert McCormick. To his critics, "Bertie" McCormick appeared hopelessly behind the times, "one of the foremost minds of the fourteenth century." Now sixty-one years old, "six feet four, muscular and mustached," McCormick esteemed himself a supreme patriot and spokesman for "genuine" American ideals, which usually appeared in form of Republican politics and conservative economic principles. People still chuckled about the day in January 1935 when McCormick had ordered the flag pulled down from the Tribune Tower. When it went back up, it had only forty-seven stars. The star taken out designated Rhode Island, where a recent Democratic victory had led to total overhaul of state government. Advised that mutilation of the flag was a crime (and certainly un-American) McCormick grudgingly restored Rhode Island to the Union.[31]

McCormick had many reasons for opposing the government of Franklin Roosevelt. He considered the New Deal no less than a betrayal of America and Roosevelt a seeker of dictatorial authority. His suspicion that the President had given favors to a competitor, Frank Knox of the *Daily News*, seemed to be confirmed in 1940 when Roosevelt took Knox, even though a Republican, into the Administration as Secretary of the Navy. The *Tribune*, it was often said, had its own foreign policy; McCormick believed it his duty to lead the people away from Roosevelt's disastrous policy of intervention in the European war. "I'm willing to let Britain have whatever she needs," he liked to say, "and I think she doesn't need anything."[32]

McCormick's newspaper did not always measure up to professional standards of good journalism. The *Tribune* covered most news impartially, but in politics, as one observer remarked, "its reports often have the brash partisan tone of frontier journalism."[33] He gave the news the way he saw it, or wanted it to be. The most grievous betrayal of professionalism involved the practice of intermingling analysis and reporting, the splattering of editorial comment throughout a news story until the reader could not distinguish news from opinion. The *Tribune* was given to casual labeling such as "Dictator [Harold] Ickes," "War Monger [Henry L.] Stimson," and the latest "war-measures" of the Administration, often on the front page.

McCormick understandably attracted the attention of groups supporting the President's foreign policy. "Hitler likes him," propagandists of the Fight for Freedom organization said. Critics had begun organizing a boycott and circulating a sticker that bore a red-circled Swastika superimposed on a drawing of the Tribune Tower and the slogan: "Billions for defense, not 2 cents for the *Tribune*." McCormick replied in kind. The *Tribune* will not be intimidated, he retorted, especially not by "communists . . . cookie-pushers and fighters of the marshmallow set who bay for American participation in the European war."[34]

The *Tribune* was not—as it claimed—"the world's greatest newspaper," but it outsold anything in the Chicago area, and with weekday circulation of more than 1 million it ranked second only to the New York *Daily News* as the nation's most-read daily. Its success might be attributed to a good sports section or woman's page, its generous pages of comics, or Colonel McCormick's views on national and international affairs, but no one could be sure. Attacks on the *Tribune* suggest concern over its influence. Several of the opposition forces joined together at the end of the year to assist the millionaire Marshall Field in starting a new liberal, internationalist paper, the *Sun*, to compete for the morning market.

Dirty from industrial smoke and winter's grime, Chicago showed signs of age and wear. In this era before toll roads sent travelers dashing around the city and expressways named after presidents headed them downtown, the city streets bore all means of public transport. Traffic jams remained legendary, and policemen abusive. No one contended, however, that the best times belonged to the past. Still the nation's hub, magnet of the great interior, Chicago continued to give off signals of an almost brutal vitality, offering rewards for those strong enough to endure the struggle.

For all Chicago's bustle and boisterous self-confidence, it remained only the second city, and nothing Colonel McCormick or anyone else could do would change that fact. And it was a distant second. New York City, with 7.5 million in its five boroughs, had more people than any state but its own, the true national capital in all ways except official. A seaport and an industrial center, the headquarters of international finance, it set the tone for much of the nation's culture and intellectual life, its fashion and some of the entertainment. New York's many distinctions fostered an understandable arrogance in some of the native citizenry. "You could drop all of Hollywood's people, parties, and night clubs into New York," one observer said, "and no one would ever notice them."[35]

A virtual land unto itself, New York at the start of the 1940s towered far above its American sisters. One sensed the power in the Empire State Building and structures uptown. Grace came from the Brooklyn Bridge, now past fifty years old, its sides lined with huge fishnet walls of stretching steel cables. The bridge had been built mostly for pedestrians, but now, as seemed to be happening in so many places, the automobile had taken over. Walkers still could stroll along the wooden promenade that ran snugly between two rows of cables and safely above and between the traffic lanes. Even the much newer and larger George Washington Bridge, built specifically for vehicles and an attraction in its own right, could not diminish the charm of the old structure stretching across the East River.

Some of the most fascinating sights in town were in the haunts of New York's "ordinary" people: Ebbetts Field, where the Dodgers played on summer afternoons, or the slums of Harlem and other parts of town. On the Bowery one could find cheap liquor, beds for twenty cents a night, tattoo shops, and almost any service imaginable. Missionaries stood ready to persuade passers-by to give their souls to God. The streets were cobbled, and the El still operated. The noise from cars, trains, and trolleys might be intolerable to the outsiders but was hardly noticed by the native citizen. The Bowery was "a place where bums get a sour laugh out of the fact that the flophouses where they sleep in have de luxe hotel names—like Belmont . . . or Plaza at No. 25 or Gotham at No. 356."[36]

New York abounded with impressive reminders of its seafaring heritage. Salt water seemed always to be close by; it came right up to the city's front porch. The seven bays gave off all the signals of a bustling seaport, with the smells of coffee beans or other cargo, fish, and rotting timbers. Exhaust fumes rose from the vessels that churned the water, trying to point themselves in the right direction. The way to get to (or arrive from) Europe for almost any reason still was by ship, and most of the ships came to New York. The city took approximately half the nation's trade and most of the passenger traffic. Every day nearly two hundred vessels would tie up for some reason. One could go down to the French Line pier at any time and find the liner *Normandie*—next to the "Queens" of the Cunard Company, the largest ship built for the Atlantic passenger service—in silent majesty at her berth, interned since the start of the war.

The business district of New York and the famous places represented only one part of the city. Downtown New York did not truly belong to the New Yorkers; they simply helped service it for the rest of the nation and, to a lesser extent, the world. The other parts of the city were home for more than 7 million people. Residential New York was largely immigrant. To an even greater extent than Los Angeles reflected what America would become, New York suggested that America had been a land of transplanted Europeans—Italians, Irish, Jews, Germans, and a generous sprinkling from many other countries. Social and cultural life in dozens of communities drew its character directly from the nations from which the people or their parents came to the United States. On the Lower East Side, for example, Jewish neighborhoods proclaimed themselves in the rows of small shops with signs in Yiddish and English advertising dry goods or meat (mostly chicken) or religious books and such articles as *tallesim*, yarmulkes, and mezuzahs.

New York's approximately 1 million Italians congregated in a dozen communities, of which Mulberry Street was probably the best known. Social life consisted almost entirely of association with other Italians. The women usually stayed home to gossip. The men occupied themselves in dozens of small clubs playing poker, their cigar smoke billowing under a red 300-watt bulb, and drinking mellowing red wine. "The mystifying drawn blinds or half-painted windows one sees on so many store-fronts," a former resident explained, "conceal nothing more sinister than tired men seeking to escape the female chitchat at home, enjoying their oaths without censorship, and arguing about whether Il Duce was or was not a socialist before he took a size 48 in a duce's uniform."[37]

The times of grandest celebration came on religious feast days, when communities gathered ostensibly to honor a patron saint— each group of paesani had its own—but in fact to have a good time and seek to outdo a neighboring community: "The Madonna Immaculata is exhorted to perform miracles superior to those of the Madonna del Lauro." The principal street was decorated with colored lights and other ornaments to prepare for the parade, featuring an effigy of the saint carried on a large board. Down the street they would go, the saint leading the way, followed by an army clothed in dazzling attire. Former Sicilian peasants, now urban laborers, became colonels or generals for a day, donning uniforms bedecked with red ribbons, clanking medals, and Napoleonic hats with plumes of two colors. A long sword dangling from the side became more hazard than decoration; the general had to take care not to trip. Spectators tossed coins as the saint's stretcher passed by; others dashed up to pin currency on the plaster effigy. The parade continued to the church steps, where the procession turned saint and contributions over to the priest. At night the street would be roped off for dancing and merrymaking. The saint's day came to a glorious end in a blaze of rockets and fireworks.[38]

Ethnic background had provided the original basis for New York's cultural diversity. Over the years a connection had developed between ethnicity and occupation and economic status. Although not all Jews belonged to the professional classes, a good many doctors, lawyers, managers, and factory- and restaurant-owners were Jewish. Germans frequently became white-collar professionals or entered the ranks of skilled and semi-skilled workers. A step down in status were the Irish, and at the bottom, except for black people, stood the Italians. Italians did practice such special trades as barber and shoemaker, but the bulk of immigrants who came from southern Italy with few skills and little money or education had no choice but to enter the labor force at the bottom. If the entrepreneur was likely to be Jewish or Anglo-Saxon, the people who worked for him came from other ethnic groups.[39]

International politics inevitably would leave a mark on a city with such diversity. The Irish, Germans, and Italians inclined toward isolationism, while Jewish Americans, the largest ethnic group, were for obvious reasons internationalist.

The contest for mayor in the fall of 1941 was partly a classic confrontation of ethnic groups, partly a struggle between isolationists and supporters of the Roosevelt government, and partly a test in popularity of a lively, nationally known politician, the incumbent, Fiorello H. LaGuardia. The Irish-dominated Democratic Party, chafing from being out of power eight years, nominated still another Irishman, William O'Dwyer. LaGuardia had touched nearly all ethnic and political bases. Born half-Jewish and half-Italian, he had become an Episcopalian. Running as the candidate of the American Labor Party, he had the endorsement of the Republicans and the Fusion and United City parties. President Roosevelt, although a Democrat, had urged LaGuardia's reelection. One of the most outspoken advocates of resistance to Hitler, the Mayor also served as the national Director of Civil Defense and wanted to do more, preferably as an appointed general.

LaGuardia was a man of boundless energy, given now and then to colorful behavior—he enjoyed riding fire engines—and remarks bordering on overstatement: "We had a dream to make New York the greatest city in the world—yes we had a dream," he said during

the campaign, "and now we vow to make it heaven."[40] He was nevertheless a serious and ambitious politician and had compiled an impressive reformist record during two terms as Mayor. He lost the
bulk of the Irish vote and most of the German, of course, and less
than 50 percent of the Italians voted for him. Besides being unhappy
with LaGuardia's position on international affairs, many Italians felt
he had been too even-handed, not "ethnic" enough, in awarding political jobs. His victory came largely on the strength of nearly three-
fourths of the Jewish vote.[41]

For all the quarrels between ethnic groups and the displeasure with
aspects of national policy, no group in this time of crisis wished to
be labeled un-American. Although concerned with the welfare of the
mother country, few Germans fell for propaganda of the racist
German–American Bund. "Americans of Germanic extraction do not
want Communism, Nazism or Fascism and they do not want British
imperialism. They want Americanism," the leader of the Steuben Society said.[42] While Italian-Americans at first were much impressed
with Mussolini, they became bewildered and embarrassed by the
hostility that developed between Italy and Roosevelt's government.
They now had to make a choice they would have preferred to avoid.
Still isolationist, most proclaimed themselves loyal to the land of
their residence. The publisher of *Il Progresso,* an Italian-American
newspaper, announced that he was "against any government which
is against the government of the United States."[43] The war thus had
cast its shadow in many places and had exerted pressure in many
ways. Not the least of these was toward an amalgamation of ethnic
groups in New York and other cities into the greater American society.

The changes urban America had begun to experience would continue and grow. The movement to the large cities would continue,
and the most dramatic expansion would be felt in the North and
West. From Mississippi, Georgia, Alabama, and South Carolina,
black and white people would come by the hundreds of thousands,
arriving in greatest number in California, New York, Illinois, and
Michigan. Blacks who moved into Detroit, Chicago, New York, or
Los Angeles went wherever they could find a place. Like the groups
preceding them to urban areas, they probably preferred to live with
people like themselves, and in fact they rarely had a chance to go
anywhere else. Thus the urban population grew by expanding such

black districts as Harlem in New York or Chicago's inner Southside, which already were slums, or by gradual occupation of older dilapidated areas, often in the inner city.

When blacks came in, the whites frequently moved out, or at least wanted to, as soon as they had the money and opportunity. Metropolitan sprawl and movement to the suburbs was in 1941 by no means as common a feature of urban America as it would become, but it had started. In the suburbs people could find less noise, more room, safer and less cluttered streets, and, equally important, status and prestige. A house in the suburbs remained beyond the reach of most city dwellers on the eve of war, and a shift in priorities had markedly slowed construction along the edges, but social and economic forces now under way would lay the foundation for massive changes in a few years to come.

Even the ethnic neighborhoods, once so distinctive and insular, had begun to loosen and change. One New Yorker remembered growing up in the 1920s and 1930s in Brownsville, a 2-square-mile Brooklyn district inhabited by *proste yid*, the "plain Jew," mostly of Russian origin. A Brownsville child rarely saw anyone but Jews and "never really felt that the Jews were anything but an overpowering majority of the human race." As the man recalled: "I don't think my contemporaries and I believed . . . George Washington, Nathan Hale, Tom Mix, Babe Ruth, and Jack Dempsey were actually Jewish, but we never clearly thought of them as anything else."[44] As children of immigrant families grew older, they began to move about, meet people from other groups, and perhaps go to college. "The weakest point of any Italian's personal armor is his pride," a former resident of a Little Italy wrote. "If Tonio, who came over from Italy with Domenick, could produce a college graduate in the person of his son, Pietro, couldn't Domenick do the same with his Guido? And if Giulia could teach in the school around the corner, so could Annina, who had just as much brains and maybe more looks." Italian youth knew little about their fathers' country and cared less, except for the way it affected the United States. Their immediate concern was the draft, and their attitude did not differ much from other Americans': "To some it is an adventure," the same Italian-American wrote, "to others a nuisance; and, to a few, a patriotic duty. Mussolini does not enter the picture."[45]

Whether of German, Italian, Irish, Polish, Jewish, or older Anglo-Saxon stock, before the year was out they all would be on the same side. Millions of urban youth would leave and march down a company street in some camp or training center. Some would not return;

if the war did not end their lives, something or someone they encountered in their travels in this country and abroad would lead them to new homes. Most would come back, either temporarily or to stay, but either way they were not the same people—not after all they had seen and learned. They were now even less willing to live and work as their fathers had done. If they still were sons of Italy or Ireland in some measure, to a greater extent they were American children, and they belonged to themselves.

FIVE

☆

Progress and Poverty in the Countryside

The farmers and people in the countryside could see it more clearly than city folk: America was at a crossroads in 1941. One path headed into the future, and the other showed where the nation had been. Parts of rural America were in the process of forming a different economic structure and a life-style similar to that of the cities, a system grounded in efficiency, specialization, and scientific methods of production and management, but millions of other rural people lived and worked as their ancestors had. Even those people had begun to feel the pull of radio, roads, and automobiles, of government programs and the draft, all of which informed people how far behind they were and made them aware that something better was possible if they were willing to take a risk. As it turned out, more and more individuals were willing to do so, for one of the themes of the year—in truth the expansion of an established theme of recent years—was the movement of people away from the countryside.

They went to the city because circumstances demanded a change, and many who went would have preferred to stay on the land. Some people already had decided to go back, either to live on the periphery of urban areas while keeping a job in town or to try again to make a living in the country, usually at something other than farming. One might return to the country; one rarely returned to farming. Movement out of the cities was not as large as the inward migration, and the gap between the two widened each month. Nonetheless, the United States on the eve of war was much more than a nation of city-dwellers.

Rural America encompassed the bulk of territory, of course, and a good portion of the nation's people. In April 1941 approximately 30.25 million people lived and did their work on farms. Almost as many lived in rural areas without being classified as farmers. Some of them stayed on the outskirts of large towns and cities. Others lived farther out, in a rented house, on a little piece of property they owned, or in one of the almost countless settlements ranging from a few houses to a few hundred—"wide spots in the road" was a popular term—with a general store, a school, probably an auto repair shop, and other services that varied with the size of the village. The fortunate people had steady jobs in town; others tried to eke out a living in such varied activities as trapping, logging and sawing, making moonshine liquor, and work as semiprofessional carpenter, auto mechanics, or salesmen. Some lived on welfare.

Even though not exclusively farmers, in habit and attitude many were rural folk. The government, which identified such people as "rural nonfarm," had counted some 27 million of them in 1940. Together with commercial farm families, they made up 43 percent of the population. Because the Bureau of the Census classified as "urban" anyone living in a town with 2,500 or more people, many others leading a rural life are probably missing from those figures.[1] If all those who in attitude and life-style were comparable to farmers are added in, it develops that rural people in 1941 made up more— although it is impossible to determine how much more—than half the American population. There were also city-dwellers who could easily remember when they had left the countryside to come to town; it had not been long ago in many cases, and they often went back to see their friends and relatives who had stayed home. If the body of prewar America was being formed in the streets and factories, its soul still had deep roots in the land.

How rural people lived and worked varied enormously, partly because modernization had not come evenly to all areas. The long revolution in agriculture, the application of science and technology to farming and rural life, was well advanced in some parts of the country and scarcely noticeable in others. While most marketable goods came from farms using machinery that would be acceptable thirty years later, most people who did farm work had implements much like the tools their grandparents used thirty years earlier. Many aspects of life in the countryside remained little removed from the methods of the nineteenth century.

Nearly all farmers would agree that the most revolutionary instrument of farm work in 1941 was the tractor. It had come to represent for agriculture what the automobile meant to transportation and social change. To outsiders they might all seem alike, those noisy machines. Men who worked tractors had a keen awareness of their peculiarities, how an Allis-Chalmers, for example, differed from the Farmall, the Oliver, the Case, or the Massey-Harris. The John Deere tractor with the "putt-putt" of its two-cylinder engine, the green-painted "poppin' Johnny," was the most distinctive of all. The implement companies had borrowed from the car makers, it seemed, for new machines came from the factories bright and shiny, almost as streamlined as a 1942 Buick or a diesel locomotive. McCormick-Deering's model 1940 even sported fender skirts for the rear wheels.

Many farmers still had to wrestle with older machines—more than one-third were at least ten years old—built purely for functional purposes, with little attention to comfort or fashion. Lightly powered, except for a few large ones, and reeking forever of gasoline, they were made almost entirely of steel. The steering wheel was steel, and the steel or cast-iron seat rested at the end of a huge coil spring or a slab of heavy-gauge steel designed to serve as a spring. The driver returning to the field from lunch (he probably called it dinner) would grab the wheel or sit down and realize immediately how hot the day was. Wise ones used a burlap bag for a cushion and wore gloves, even on the hottest days. The front wheels were steel, and the steel rear wheels had either huge, flat, cleated rims, from 8 inches to more than a foot wide, or a narrow skeletal structure with lugs that protruded like claws all around, designed, of course, to increase traction. The steel wheels and the great weight of the older machines compacted the soil and slowed down everything they did. The metal beasts moved at a snail's pace wherever they went, at work in the field or traveling to the workplace along the road. They could not, or were not supposed to, travel on improved roads; the sign "Tractors with lugs prohibited" was common in many parts of the United States.

The new "all-purpose" machines that had been coming out in large numbers only a half-dozen or so years were almost as revolutionary as the tractor itself. Equipped with pneumatic tires and a higher "road gear," they could travel almost anywhere at good speed. With larger engines, some of them diesels, they could pull multiple plows and larger discs, and it was becoming possible to affix multi-row cultivators, planters, or harvest equipment on the machine itself. Virtually none of the modern field implements—combines, balers, corn pickers—could operate without a tractor to pull it or supply power.

Equipped with modern machinery, the farmer could do wonders. He could plow almost five times as much as a two-horse walking plow and do nine times the work of a plow drawn by a single horse. Rates of improvement in other aspects of farm work were even better.[2] The tractor released for other crops land previously used to grow feed for the now obsolete draft animals. Many a farmer able to shift from horses to machines soon found himself looking around for more soil to till—a pleasing move for him, but a development that, repeated many times over, would have a profound effect on farming in the United States.

Needless to say, not every farmer had managed to acquire a tractor, however much he might have wanted one. Many new machines cost more than a new car, and to put them to full use the buyer also would need the line of attachments designed especially for each make. Before taking that step, the farmer needed to determine that he had funds and enough land to justify the purchase.

Most farmers made do with what they had, which meant that they trudged after or rode behind draft animals. "The most typical scene in the South," a contemporary account stated, "is . . . not a cotton gin or a cotton mill. It is a sharecropper . . . between the handles of a single-stock plow pulled by a mule."[3] The typical farmer in the United States, one might add, although not in all places, made a living walking or riding behind horses or mules. Simple statistics tell the story: Some 6.3 million farms in 1941 contained 1,665,000 tractors, slightly more than one machine for four farms. Several farms had two or more tractors, which left even a higher proportion of farmers—the census suggested approximately 75 percent—without any tractor-drawn equipment. They used horses and mules, more than 14 million of them, and went about their tasks much as farmers had been doing for generations.[4]

Animals thus were tools, and keeping them in good condition accounted for no small part of the farmer's work. Some land had to be reserved for their food; feeding was a regular chore, and they needed health care and protection against weather, especially in winter. The family, particularly the children, frequently felt genuine affection for the horses, gave them all names, and mourned their deaths or the decision to sell them. The death of an animal represented a considerable loss; many farmers who could not afford a doctor for the family did not hesitate to summon the veterinarian when a horse was ailing.

The rhythm of crop production remained the same as ages earlier: Prepare the ground for planting, keep crops cultivated until "laid by," too large for cultivation (some crops, such as wheat, needed no cultivation), then at maturity take them from the field for sale or storage. It began with plowing, of course. The rubber-tired tractor usually pulled two plows (two bottoms), although large machines in the broad, flat fields of the Great Plains or the Midwest pulled more. Most farmers walked behind a plow pulled by a horse, mule, or team. Then followed the task of working plowed soil into plantable condition. Users of draft animals probably started with a spring-tooth harrow, or a skeletal steel platform with spike-like "teeth" pointing into the earth at a designated angle. Tractor drivers used larger versions of the same implements, especially the heavier and more devastating disc—rows of sharp, steel wheels that thrashed and slashed the soil or anything else in its path. Horses and mules trudged at much the same pace, whatever work they did. By the time of final preparation, probably smoothing the surface with a wooden raft-like structure called a drag, the modern tractor would whisk along, to the envy of men who had only plodding draft animals.

Even more striking evidence of the impact of machinery came during harvest. In the autumn, when nights had turned cool, the corn stalks had become crisp and light brown, and the ears had hardened, mechanized farmers started up the tractor and hitched to it (or, in the case of the newest implements, mounted on the tractor itself) the awkward-looking picker, one part of which protruded forward like the neck of a dinosaur. They pulled into the field and with the picker started moving down the rows, making a considerable racket with grinding wheels and whirling belts. The corn seemed to fly from the elevated chute into a wagon trailing behind. If rain held off, the farmer could finish his crop and move on to the fields of a neighbor or relative who had asked to hire the equipment. More than 120,000 pickers plied America's cornfields in 1941, the bulk of them in the Midwest.[5]

As with tractors, however, most growers of corn could not buy or did not have access to a mechanical harvester. People planted corn in every state, often in fields too small for the large machines. Some farmers complained that by smashing the stalks close to the ground, later to be covered with snow, the machines destroyed winter feed for foraging cattle.[6] In many cases the lack of a picker resulted from simple economics. For one reason or another, most farmers had to harvest corn by hand, perhaps by cutting stalks with a long "corn knife" and binding them together in the field. The ears then would be removed and placed in storage, while the remainder became winter feed for animals. The fields of shocked fodder, an agricultural legacy that dated back to colonial America, remained familiar in many parts of the United States.

Most farmers "shucked" or "husked" corn by moving down the rows with team and wagon, grasping the ears one-by-one, stripping off the shuck, and tossing the ears against a high backboard, or "bangboard," constructed on the far side of the wagon. A well-trained team of animals would start and stop with voice signals, and the farmer could continue uninterrupted down the row alongside. "We'd get up at four and drive the horses three miles to shuck corn," a farmer from Kansas recalled. "I'd be out in the field long before the sun was up and hear those ears banging against the high side of the wagon. We tried to get through by Christmas, but shucking in the snow wasn't a bit unusual."[7] Needless to say, harvesting corn was one of the most tedious of farm tasks.

The harvest of hay offered other displeasures. After cutting and allowing the hay to dry, the farmer would use a large, spindly-wheeled sulky rake (or the newer side-delivery machine) to form long rows; he then built little piles (cocks) to be pitched by fork onto the wagon. The haying season seemed always to correspond with the hottest days of summer, in late July and August. One can imagine the sensation of chaff or insects falling on his sunburned, sweaty back and neck at three in the afternoon.

Getting hay onto the wagon represented half the job; the other half involved placing it in storage. Most barns had a huge forklike apparatus that ran along a little track at the top of the barn and extended over the wagon, making it possible to jab the fork (or harpoon) directly into the load of hay underneath. Using a system of rope and pulleys, horses or a tractor would pull bunches of hay into the mow or loft, where another hand would shift the piles around. The least envied hand in any case was the person assigned to distribute hay in the stifling heat and dust-filled air of the loft. Haying season lasted only a few days, which was probably all that saved the loft worker from a serious lung disorder.

Mechanization of the hay harvest led to a larger saving of space than of labor. Most balers stood stationary and still required several hands and much moving of hay. Tractor-drawn pickup balers were the last word in haying. They picked up the hay from a windrow and tied it in rectangular bales to be dropped at the other end. By year's end nearly 25,000 of these machines were available for use.[8] They reduced the need for manpower, but someone still had to heave bales weighing 50 to 70 pounds onto the wagon by grasping the wire that bound them; another person put them in place, and unless the barn had enough space to permit random dumping of bales, some poor fellow still had to fight the heat and dust in the loft, shifting and stacking bales while gasping for fresh air. "Putting up hay" had never been a particularly welcome task of agriculture.

The production of wheat and other small grains was a somewhat different undertaking. Wheat lent itself to agriculture of massive proportion; the larger the field the better, and the larger the operation, the more likely that a machine could be found to do the work. Combines had been a part of the harvest for many years, and they had become steadily larger and more efficient. One found the most machines, and the largest, cutting the broad fields of the Great Plains.

But the combine had not yet replaced the thresher. Country folk could still observe the lumbering threshing machines making their appointed rounds. More than 160,000 still did their work in 1941, only 100,000 fewer than the number of combines.[9] A solitary farmer ordinarily could not finance these expensive contraptions, so several would pool funds to buy one for the community or perhaps to use the services of a custom thresher. Power for the thresher probably came from a conventional, albeit enormous, tractor, but the most excitement came if by chance the machine operated off an old hissing, puffing, smoke-belching steam engine. News that "the threshers are coming" quickened the pulse of many a rural youngster.

Threshing brought together whole families, if not whole communities. It might take as many as a dozen men with wagons and horses or tractors to perform the operation. Wives gathered to visit and help prepare massive amounts of food for the noon meal. Gluttony in such circumstances seemed neither sinful nor inappropriate; it was almost polite, and a compliment to the ladies, to stuff oneself nearly to the point of bursting. The children came too; it would have been cruel to make them miss the threshing. Older ones worked, and while the youngsters asked for something to do, they usually ended up carrying water, playing with one another, and getting in the way.

Wheat threshing rivaled haying in scratchiness, as both produced clouds of dust, chaff, and grain particles. The huge belts whirled and snapped, and the machines seemed almost to shudder, throwing up huge clouds of dust. The men expected the dirt, and the children seemed anxious to get into it. "There was a pride in how dirty one got . . . like being bloodied in combat," one individual recalled. "Even the most fastidious mother and housewife would allow a layer of dirt that would bring a stern word at any other occasion."[10]

No one opposed the use of combines, and farmers turned to the new machines as soon as they could manage to do so. On reflection, however, most probably would agree that the end of threshing meant more than a change in the way one important task was done. "Nothing was quite so romantic," one farmer recalled. A rural expatriate remembered threshing as "a seasonal social event, an observation of the climax of another year, a time to help and share . . . a time to inspect neighbors' barns and livestock and fences and see how things were with them."[11]

Many farmers continued to strive for a homestead that, if it was not fully self-sufficient, supplied much of the family's needs. While giving first priority to crops designed to produce cash income, such as corn, wheat, tobacco, cotton, or soybeans, they performed numerous other tasks to keep the household supplied with needed goods, primarily food. They planted gardens and often kept a few fruit trees, however poorly they might attend them. Livestock had become a "cash crop" to many farmers, but even if they did not have a herd of beef or dairy cattle or a "bunch" of pigs, they probably kept cows for milk and hogs (or cattle) for meat. Approximately three-quarters of the farms kept cows for family use. Butchering served a function not unlike threshing, if on a less grandiose scale— a regular event involving more than one family.

Efforts to maintain self-sufficiency broadened and deepened demands on the rural family. The cows had to be milked, the pigs and chickens fed, whatever the requirements of the growing and harvest seasons. Whenever possible, especially in spring and summer, the farmer liked to turn regular chores over to younger children and to his wife. Except in certain places and in times of urgency, white women did not work the fields. Growing crops other than vegetables and the use of machinery was considered too heavy and complicated for female arms and minds; many women did not drive cars. Black women did do almost everything, although it was a rare black homestead that had an automobile or anything but the simplest tools.

Farmers' wives performed numerous tasks besides cleaning house and cooking meals. Taking care of chickens was "woman's work." "The damn things were probably necessary," was a common male attitude, but "attending to them was generally beneath a man's dignity."[12] Women probably turned the milk separator and used some of the cream to churn butter. They canned fruits and vegetables and made jelly and apple butter. In summer they might take the children into the fields to find wild blackberries, and on the way they would contend with heat, briars, snakes, and chiggers. One defense against chiggers called for covering all parts of the body with clothing—no matter how hot the day—one of the rare circumstances in which many farm women would wear long pants; another method was to tie a kerosene-soaked cord around the ankles. In either case, the medicine seemed almost as objectionable as the malady. A few farm families had turned to newer methods of acquiring and storing food, which might involve customized butchering, buying a quarter or some other fraction of a carcass, and storing it, as well as vegetables, in a commercial frozen food locker. On the eve of the war, however, such jar producers as Mason and Ball continued to do a healthy business.

As the all-purpose tractor had transformed the farms that had them, the coming of electricity produced changes no less revolutionary. "It is the greatest single social benefit yet proposed for the American farmer," a writer exclaimed, the "ushering in" of a "new era in the life of the country man and woman."[13] Electricity eased many chores for the farmer and his wife. It also changed habits and called into question traditional thinking. Previously, it was possible to see some connection between how well one lived and how hard one worked. To those who had electricity and could merely flick a switch, it seemed as if no effort at all was needed, other than the ability to pay the bill.

Unfortunately, most people in the countryside still had to wait for the new era. In 1941 the proportion of electrified farms varied from 70 percent in New England to 10 percent in Mississippi; no more than 35 percent of all the nation's farms had electric lighting, and many nonfarming rural people lacked it as well.[14]

The problem arose partly from low rural income. The acquisition of electricity represented a considerable investment, starting with the need to wire houses built with no prospect of electric power in mind. Then came the purchase of lamps and whatever appliances one could afford. The most useful appliance, a refrigerator, was among the most expensive. A modest-size Coldspot refrigerator from Sears, Roebuck cost approximately $125, a substantial portion of many farmers' cash income for the year. A rural home with electric power often had only lights.

In many areas power lines had not reached close enough to bring electricity into the house. Private power companies operated to make

Far away from the war in Europe Franklin and Eleanor Roosevelt look fit and relaxed at the inauguration, giving no hint of the threatening environment in which his third term—and 1941—began. *National Archives*

But some groups, like the America First Committee, fearing that Roosevelt's foreign policy was edging the country towards intervention, spoke out vigorously in opposition at rallies such as this one, at Madison Square Garden, May 23. From left: Senator Burton K. Wheeler, Charles A. Lindbergh, novelist Kathleen Norris, Norman Thomas. *Wide World*

For most Americans, however, life went on as usual, with more interest in what was happening at home than across the sea. Religion was an important part of social and cultural life. In the countryside it retained many traditional features, including baptism by total immersion, here in process near Morehead, Kentucky. *Library of Congress*

By no means typical of Protestantism, but reflective of its great diversity, snake worshippers were scattered mostly in the upper South. *Courier-Journal & Times, Louisville, KY*

Baseball was still the national pastime, and Joe DiMaggio continued to make headlines. Here he singles in the first inning of a game with the Cleveland Indians at Cleveland, July 16. It was the fifty-sixth straight game in which he got a hit. *Wide World*

In some sections of the country time almost seemed to stand still. Probably an independent operator, this miner in western Pennsylvania still used tools— the carbide lamp, animal-drawn cars—that larger mines had abandoned. *Library of Congress*

Not all of America could acquire expensive, new-fangled machinery. Here farmers thresh wheat at Beerman's ranch in Wyoming in September 1941. Many farmers used combines but many could not yet afford them. *Library of Congress*

The Depression was coming to an end but for the black sharecropper in the rural South, there were few local opportunities for advancement. This farmer plows in Heard County, Georgia. *Library of Congress*

At the bottom of the social and economic ladder, American blacks in the South had lived segregated lives for many years. Separate drinking facilities, like this one in Oklahoma City, were familiar sights. *Library of Congress*

But change was coming to America—black and white. Drawn by industrial jobs in the urban North, rural blacks left the farms in large numbers for life in the big city. This bar on Chicago's Southside in many ways parallels that of whites. *Library of Congress*

Blacks were beginning to earn notoriety and occasionally respect, particularly in the world of sports and entertainment. Here the most famous of all, boxing champion Joe Louis, hits Bill Conn in their heavyweight bout in June. *Wide World*

The automobile quietly was revolutionizing not only where people lived and worked but how they spent their leisure time. Here a couple vacations on the beach in Sarasota, Florida, in January. *Library of Congress*

Shifting patterns of work and play encouraged a more relaxed attitude between the sexes. Such a lessening of social constraints was a necessary condition for the sudden popularity of the big bands. Ballroom dancing was almost a national craze in 1941. This couple "Jitterbugs" in Brooklyn. *Arthur Rothstein,* The Depression Years As Photographed by Arthur Rothstein.

All the towns had local dance bands, giving a community sanction to dance cheek to cheek. Earl Gardner's Orchestra played at Club Hollywood, Kalamazoo, Michigan. *Portage (Michigan) Public Library*

The movies, with their newsreels, infiltrated America's protective cocoon and brought the outside world closer to home. Nearly everyone went to the movies. Black children in Chicago enjoyed white films, like everyone else. *Library of Congress*

No one in Hollywood offered more glamour than the "sweater girl" Lana Turner, whose popularity was a sign of America's more open attitude and appreciation of female sexuality in the midst of a swiftly changing world. *Wide World*

a profit, of course, and they hesitated to string lines through difficult terrain or to remote, sparsely populated areas. Without action by the national government, electricity might never have come to rural America. In the late 1930s, the huge Tennessee Valley Authority began to supply power to towns of the region. After establishment of the Rural Electrification Administration (REA), the government assisted in taking power to the countryside. The project was far from complete when the war began to draw away copper, steel, and other material needed for continued expansion. Most farm people could not get electricity had they been able to afford it.

Americans take electricity as a standard part of life, almost as constant as sun and air. Its absence would be a serious and perplexing business indeed, marking in popular perception a breakup of normal society if not a violation of basic rights. People who had never had electric power experienced no such feelings, and they managed to get along much as their parents had done.

Absence of power did call for a different style of living. The popular kerosene or "coal-oil" lamps gave off enough light for normal activity, but they made reading difficult. "If you turned it too high, it would flame up and start to smoke," one lady remembered. "The chimney would get all black, and your eyes would start to smart. . . . Many of us have these [facial] lines from squinting to read."[15] Better-equipped homes might have a refrigerator or wringer-type washer powered with a small gasoline engine. Most rural homes had no such equipment, so women did laundry by various other means, including the reliable method of using very hot water, Fels Naphtha soap, and a muscle-powered washboard that abused clothes and required women almost literally to "work their fingers to the bone." Nothing surpassed the washboard as a symbol of female servitude and primitive living.

In fact, the entire operation of the laundry was laborious. After washing, women hung the clothes out to dry. Drying in winter, needless to say, presented a considerable problem. Sometimes one could tell that the temperature had dropped below freezing by observing clothes on the line. A pair of trousers could almost stand by itself. In those days before perma-press and wrinkle-free fabrics, nearly everything had to be ironed, and many items needed a substantial coating of starch. There was only one way to do the job: Women had to slide a hot, heavy slab of iron back and forth over the clothes. Heat came from the stove, of course, so the individual had to stand close by and keep two or three irons going. One would be used until the heat gave out while the others were getting ready on the stove.

The pressing results improved in proportion to weight and heat of the iron, which could weigh several pounds. Ironing was hot, heavy work, and many women had burns from grasping a handle the wrong way.

Instead of a refrigerator, many homes had an insulated icebox. The icebox would not keep foods frozen, but not many people had ever heard of frozen food, other than ice cream. It did prevent milk and food from spoiling for a few days (unfortunately, sometimes people learned their produce had gone bad only when they tasted it). The problem with the icebox was keeping it supplied. Some men cut ice from ponds and lakes in winter and stored it in sawdust-lined pits or insulated buildings, to be taken out in summer. Others waited for the iceman to come around or purchased ice at the general store. A 50-pound block of ice might be down to 40 or less by the time it reached home. The cellar helped keep food cool, though not cold, and was most useful for storing root vegetables. Many people made no effort to cool milk or food. There was no way to keep meat more than a couple of days or so. Families made butter regularly, and milk kept coming fresh and warm twice a day.

Among even the best-equipped rural homes only a small portion had a modern system of central heating, most often a coal furnace. A few still used fireplaces, a method in those days considered inefficient and old-fashioned. Most rural homes (and, incidentally, more than one-third of urban residences) relied on stoves. In the kitchen sat a cast-iron wood-burning range made by Home Comfort, Kalamazoo, or some other stove company, which cooked and baked food and gave out marvelous heat in winter, especially with the oven door open. It "dominates the room," a contemporary writer remarked. "On many a farm the countryman prefers to spend the evenings in front of the friendly kitchen stove instead of going into the living room. Feet that have been close to snow all day delight in the toasting warmth of the capacious oven."[16] Unfortunately, the same stove was used for cooking in the summer, and it gave off the same heat. The summertime canning season meant a hot household, especially for the women who did the work. Few rural homes made use of natural "bottled" gas.

The living room or "front room" probably had a wood- and coal-burning heater in one of the various shapes and sizes available. On very cold nights in poorly lighted homes, an overstoked stove might glow with splotches of cheerful red near the bottom of the belly, and the stovepipe was hot enough to ignite wallpaper at a point where the pipe entered the chimney. Bedrooms might have separate stoves, but often they did not, and people had to depend upon body heat and piles of covers. A man recalled from childhood in Michigan that "the upstairs was left to the elements and we slept under all the old blankets we could find. In winter, the frost would form on the inside of windows up there, building up in severe winter to an inch thick."[17] No need to worry about frozen water pipes; there were no pipes.

A house without electricity was almost certain to have no system of running water. In rural areas running water depended upon a powered pump; the alternative to an electric pump was one driven by a gasoline engine, which not many people had managed to aquire. The water supply came either from the ground, through a well driven or dug down to the water table, or from a cistern, a huge brick or cement-lined pit arranged to catch and store rainwater as it ran off the roof. Water was brought to the surface by a hand-operated suction pump or in a bucket raised hand-over-hand or by pulley. For drinking, the water bucket had long been a common feature of rural households. Everyone drank from the same tin or enameled cup or long-handled dipper. A visitor to a village in Missouri found it best not to bring up the issue of sanitation with respect to the water bucket, having discovered that "most people consider an interest in individual drinking vessels (except at mealtime) to be rather comically 'squeamish' or insulting to others who use the objects."[18]

Without running water, a water heater, and a drainage system, taking a bath was a complicated undertaking. It required carrying several buckets of water from the source (which might be outdoors), heating it on the stove, and dipping it all out of the tub afterward. In such circumstances it was understandable that two or three people, even the entire family, might use the same bathwater. Households regularly washed hands and face in an enameled washpan. Men returning from the field might take off the first layer of dirt at the pump outside or at the animals' watering trough. Many people lived their entire lives without taking a shower, and baths, except for the "sponge bath" from a pan, came infrequently, especially for males. "I take a bath once a month, whether I need it or not," men might quip, and in some cases they exaggerated. Through the cold weather, when a dip in a pond or stream was ruled out, a full bath for many males came even less often than that, unless they were courting.

Indoor toilet facilities would have seemed to some rural people a frill and to others even indecent. They were, besides, impossible without running water or a sewage disposal system. The outdoor privy, equipped with the legendary Sears, Roebuck catalog (Montgomery Ward's would do), remained the object of jokes, synonymous with backward country living. The jokes might have had foundation in fact, for while some people kept the structures clean and sturdy (although never, because they regularly had to be moved, made of brick), the outhouse was likely to be the most neglected and abused building on the property. Young men out for a little mischief on Halloween did not give victims choice of "trick or treat," and the trick often involved pushing over the outhouse. Leaky, unpainted, ramshackle, and sometimes doorless, it was an eyesore and a health hazard. For that reason some of the most memorable and useful work of relief agencies of the 1930s had been the construction of new sanitary structures. With concrete foundation, leakproof roof, and smooth, sturdy seat, the WPA or, as many people preferred, the "Roosevelt" toilet represented the ultimate in outdoor privies.

Driving through the countryside often became an adventure for people unfamiliar with an area. While roads of asphalt or concrete connected cities, large towns, and small villages that happened to be near state or national highways, "hardtop" roads remained the exception in rural areas. Small towns in central Michigan "got a mile of pavement," as one person recalled, and then "you were dumped without ceremony back on the dirt and gravel of the local road."[19] Road construction and improvement had been a popular activity of the WPA, the PWA, and other work-relief agencies during the previous decade. Even so, improvement usually entailed occasional grading, smoothing the top, and cleaning out ditches beside dirt roads or laying a bed of crushed stone. By 1941 gravel roads connected most villages.

Nearly half of the nation's mileage had no improvement at all, however, and without regular attention improved roads soon fell into disrepair. The dirt roads and many gravel ones as well might become "washboards," with little gouges spaced at regular intervals, causing such rhythmic battering of the wheels that a speeding vehicle could bounce off course and damage its front end. On summer days, after a dry spell, vehicles raised trailing clouds reminiscent of a dust storm on the Great Plains in miniature, generously coating houses along the road and forcing drivers to keep their windows rolled up. In rainy weather gravel roads splattered automobiles with mud, and dirt roads became impassable. If the spring thaw came too quickly and happened to be accompanied by rain, even thinly coated gravel roads might not hold up. They seemed to have no bottom, and automobiles sank to the axle. As a rule, the farther South one went and the farther West, except for the Pacific Coast states, the worse the roads became.[20]

What rural people did for entertainment varied from place to place, although some practices remained almost universal. Social life for most revolved about family and church. They went to picnics, reunions, and church socials, particularly in summer. Scenes at such conservative gatherings changed little. Older folks chatted in little groups segregated by sex. The men might pitch horseshoes or stand around talking about weather, crops, and the war. A new feature this year might be the appearance of a young man in khaki on leave or pass from camp. He attracted everyone's attention. The men probably asked how "them army fellers" were treating him; the girls thought he looked better—healthier and more confident—than the fellow they had grown up with, the awkward youngster who had gone away several months earlier. The young men who were still civilians might feel a touch of envy at the attention the soldier now received and suspect he was having a life more exciting than theirs.

Baseball was a popular leisure-time activity in summer for people of many ages, partly because it cost little to play and nothing to watch. The closest school probably had a diamond; if not, a reasonably flat pasture could serve as temporary playing field until someone volunteered land for a more permanent facility. Youngsters used one ball until the cover fell off, then bound it up with black or white adhesive tape and played until it became lost in the weeds. Local teams raised the few dollars needed for balls, bats, and catcher's equipment by passing the hat among spectators. Sunday afternoons found one community playing another, a social event that drew people from miles around, many of whom came as much to talk with friends as to see the game. Anyone flying over the great interior would quickly spot how much the baseball diamond made up a part of rural culture.

Professional baseball reached much of rural America via radio. Cincinnati, St. Louis, and Chicago stood on the outer edges of the professional circuit, and broadcasts of their games reached well into the West and South. One of the most popular players had been Jerome "Dizzy" Dean. "Ole Diz," of the Cardinals and later the Cubs, had been not only colorful and an extraordinarily competent pitcher, but also just another farm boy from Arkansas. "Even among the adults baseball was all meaning. It was the link with the outside," one man recalled from boyhood days in Mississippi.[21]

Other social events came with unfailing regularity. Youngsters in the 4-H Club gathered each summer for a grand county exhibition, to show evidence of their work, socialize with peers, and get out of routine duties on the farm. The county fair came in July or August, and families arranged work so as to miss none of it. The fair was for many the highlight of the summer. Many rural people refused to go to dances out of timidity, ignorance (of how to dance), or religious scruples. People who had no such objection might attend a traditional country square dance or the increasingly popular "round" dances. Mountaineers out for adventure went to a sweaty, uninhibited, whisky-sodden version of a square dance called a frolic.

"Goin' to town" had been a custom as long as people had the means to make the trip, usually Saturday afternoon or evening. Not even the busy planting and harvest season interrupted the ritual. "They may come into town a little later," a businessman in Irwin, Iowa, remarked, "but they come."[22] In town the children might go to the movies while parents shopped, chatted, or simply "moseyed around," looking at items they wished they could buy. On warm Saturday evenings in "Elmtown," Illinois, Freedom Street swarmed with town and rural people. "They sit in their cars, on running boards, lean against fenders, walk in droves along the sidewalks," an observer noted. "As friends and acquaintances come by, the latest gossip, scandal, news and jokes are told and retold."[23]

In much of the United States, the traveling road show, or carnival, remained a regular part of activity in warm months. The county fair always included rides and games of the carnival, and at least once (and usually more than once) during the summer a traveling troupe would set up on the edge of a small town and put out the word that it was open for business.

One writer, passing through rural Kentucky, described a setting familiar to many parts of the United States. The show opened outside a little town, and everyone passing by knew that a carnival had arrived. The Ferris Wheel loomed above the trees and anything else in the vicinity, and the familiar grinding music of the merry-go-round drifted across several fields, calling the people to come in, pay ten cents admission, and have some fun. The spectator might first be struck by the people: "a crumbly-looking lot—the carnival people and the visitors too. . . . The young girls' clothes are cheap and tawdy. . . . Some of the men wear pants [that] hang down around their hips as if about ready to fall off." Walking along one came upon a gambling device, one of those wheel games that seemed to offer an opportunity to win something big. "Hur-ry, hur-ry folks," the barker shouted. "Step right up and take a chance. Only a dime, ten cents for a chance to win." The attendant spun the wheel, and someone collected the prize—not one of those impressive items displayed around the tent, but a plaster kewpie doll or a trinket worth a penny or two, probably marked "made in Japan."

Farther down the midway came other sights, other ways to win prizes and spend money. There was the old baseball game, the milk bottle game: "Spill the milk and win a cane. Here you—yes you with the big broad shoulders." The temptress was a seasoned female wearing less than subtle cosmetics, a lady who hoped that bright color and heavy coating would compensate for age and wear. A boy knocked down all the bottles but one. "Mighty good," she shouted. "You're just warming up. Here try again." In another part of the showground, a "hootchie kootchie" dancer squirmed in front of a tent. Clearly there was something exciting inside, so customers, mostly young men, plunked down a coin and went in. Nearby a boy of seven or eight slipped into a shadow and took a leak against a tent pole; three girls looked at one another and giggled. A girl in a tight dress with bright red lips sauntered through the crowd; she gave a boy the eye. They spoke, then disappeared into the night. A few minutes later the girl in the tight dress was back, sauntering among the crowd.[24]

Many people disapproved of the carnival, finding the setting synonymous with chicanery and sinfulness of several sorts. The people who ran it (and many who went) were thought to be seedy, irresponsible seducers, if not outright thieves. And yet the road shows were an inextricable part of rural and small-town America. One could count on their coming every summer.

As a whole, country people lived routine, predictable lives, interrupted on rare occasions by something extraordinary that set the countryside to buzzing. An example was what happened in a village in Missouri, a small town so typical of the southern Midwest that a student who came to study the place called it Plainville. Plainville and the surrounding area came alive over the case of Hobart Proudy, who shot his distant cousin, Mort Proudy, in the "seat of his britches" with a double-barreled shotgun—"gave him both barrels" —for walking on his land. When legal maneuvering produced nothing more than a suspended sentence, Hobart soon found his prize mare dead of gunshot in the field. He blamed Mort, of course, but could prove nothing. "That trouble ain't ended yet," a citizen observed, "Mort and Hobart are telling their boys about it, and they'll finally shoot it out."[25]

While traditional recreation remained alive, new pastimes were finding their way into the behavioral patterns of rural areas. Virtually everyone around Irwin, Iowa, identified the radio, automobile, and movies as forces changing their youth and influencing even some middle-aged people. They pointed to the tractor as most responsible for shortening work and leaving time for other activity. Local residents observed how people lived in the movies—hardly a realistic model, at least in most films of that time—causing them to reexamine their own lives. They heard different dance music on the radio and now sometimes drove 60 miles to Omaha, spent four or five dollars, and reached home not far from the time they should be getting up. In town one faced greater temptation to "spend money . . . smoke, drink, and tell filthy stories."[26]

People who decided to leave the land were reacting most of all to rural economics and conditions that flowed from depressed income. Determining levels of living remained at best an imprecise undertaking for people who did not receive regular pay and who often saw no reason to keep thorough records. "When we know how much it takes to get along," a farmer in Iowa said, "we don't see why we should burden ourselves with keeping books."[27] It was impossible to establish the value of goods consumed from the land, woods, and streams or of the presumed benefits from living with the fresh air and sunshine. By conventional standards of measurement, rural America lagged behind the cities, in several categories far behind. At a time when factory workers and public school teachers, by no means well-paid individuals, earned $1,500 a year, more than one-third of farmers had a net money income of less than $500. Even though these people probably supplied much of their own food, they still ended the year losing, on average, between $50 and $150. Nearly 75 percent of farm families and 70 percent of nonfarming rural dwellers had a net income of less than $1,500.[28]

Rural children received less and generally lower-quality education than their counterparts in the city. Rural youth often quit school as soon as the law allowed, if not earlier. The daughter of a tenant farmer in Illinois explained her unhappiness with going to school in town. "All the kids . . . are broken up into little groups," she said. "They made me feel like I wasn't wanted. About the fourth week, I heard Anne Hogate call me 'that hick.' . . . Pop said if I didn't want to go I didn't have to; so I quit."[29] Most states required attendance until age sixteen, although in Georgia, Louisiana, North Carolina, and Virginia one could quit at fourteen, and some children began the process of dropping out as early as twelve. In 1940 only 25 percent of rural people between the ages twenty-five and twenty-nine had finished high school (in cities it was 48 percent), and more than one-third of farm people had failed to complete grammar school. In South Carolina 14 percent of whites and 27 percent of young Negroes had to sign their Selective Service registration forms with a mark.[30]

The meanness of rural life showed up in other ways, too. Fewer farm homes had telephones than had electric power. Rural areas had approximately half as many doctors per capita as the cities. Nearly half of the babies came into the world with at best the aid of a midwife. The Department of Agriculture calculated that more than one-half of tenant homes and one-fourth of houses occupied by owners had deteriorated beyond repair.[31] At first glance it might appear that rural America constituted one huge slum, and a national disgrace.

The truth was somewhat different. Rural America had many faces. At the top were agricultural corporations, at the bottom the impoverished sharecropper or smallest landowner, with many levels of independent farmer in between. The middle farmers projected what Americans liked to think of farming as being. The top echelon showed the direction in which farming was headed; from the perspective of production, it made the lowest groups virtually superfluous. The worst parts, which were rural slums in all respects and covered embarrassingly large areas, had the effect of obscuring in national statistics places where people lived healthy, well-provided lives.

In California one found some of the most prosperous farmers in the nation. Los Angeles County claimed title to the richest agricultural county in the United States. Coastal farming scarcely resembled agriculture as practiced in much of the country. Only through irrigation had Californians managed to make the valleys bloom. Gasoline, diesel, and electric pumps continued to bring up water from the underground table or aquifers in some places; in others the source was many miles away. A new project had opened in 1940, bringing water from the Colorado River to the Imperial Valley, and work had begun on another project to transport water to the southern part of the long Central Valley.

Imported water combined with warm sun and a long growing season to permit specialization in dozens of items on plots ranging from 10 acres to the enormous agricultural corporations in Southern California. The owners of large establishments usually lived in the city, and workers, more than two-thirds of whom were Mexican, stayed in "Jim-towns," clusters of shacks on the outskirts. Other vegetable fields in the coastal region—25,000 acres in Los Angeles County alone—were in the hands of Japanese. Although these people were efficient and so hard-working as to embody the American work ethic, they received few accolades from their Occidental neighbors. Troubled by the competition, driven by jealousy and racial bias, white growers resented the Japanese farmers in their midst and wished they could do something about them. Their time soon would come.

Traveling east from the coastal region, beyond the deserts of the Southwest and desolate parts of west Texas, one moved into a region known mostly for raising cattle. Wheeled vehicles were commonplace in the cattle country, but the horse still remained an inherent part of the culture. The Westerner's idea of a good time, the novelist Erskine Caldwell observed, was to attend horse and livestock shows or auctions and "sit all day on a sharp rail watching and listening." Caldwell explained that auctions, which might last forty-eight hours, had a precise division of labor, ranging from "boosters" down in the ring, who kept the bidding going, to "agers," who called out approximate ages of animals, and finally to the "sweaters," also called "stewers," who stewed over plugs and culls, hoping to get them for next to nothing in order to resell them to farmers.[32]

East of the cattle country agriculture gradually changed, and standards of living varied a great deal. In the South and in the eastern half of Texas and southern Oklahoma, cotton had caught on as a staple crop. To the north lay an area of few towns, people, or trees: the Great Plains, where people grew wheat on farms that averaged 500 acres. Success depended heavily on the weather, for the farmers had adapted quickly to modern machinery. "Make a killing or go broke" had been the slogan for many years. If wheat farmers did not exactly make a killing in 1941, they did have a good crop year and watched with pleasure as the price moved steadily upward.

Beginning in Iowa and stretching to the eastern part of Ohio, the United States could boast of some of the richest farmland in the world. Known as the Midwest, although most of the land reached farther east than west, or the corn belt, the region could produce almost anything that did not require a long growing season. The people raised much corn, to be sure, and also wheat, oats, cattle, hogs, and many other goods. Residents of the Midwest did not earn as much as farmers in a few other places, but because of greater self-sufficiency and other factors, their standard of living was the highest in rural America. A case in point was the farmer who owned 200 acres of good land in southern Minnesota, in the upper reaches of the corn belt. Although he claimed to clear only approximately $1,000 a year (he did not know precisely), he had a large white house with electricity, refrigerator, and indoor plumbing, and had managed to accumulate a truck, tractor, horses, a 1936 Chevrolet coupe, and a 1937 Chevrolet sedan, all paid for.[33]

Other people in many areas fared far worse. Existence of so many struggling people served to drive down national statistics and make living in the country seem altogether, at first glance, undesirable. Small wonder that large numbers had decided to leave the land and head toward factories in the cities.

One could find pockets of rural poverty in every state and nearly all of the nation's counties. The largest concentration had a northern boundary that began in southern Pennsylvania and stretched southwest north of the Ohio River, across the Mississippi, and into eastern Oklahoma. From that line the area extended south to the Atlantic Ocean and the Gulf of Mexico, encompassing the South and the border states and including the Appalachian and Ozark mountains and parts of the southernmost edge of the Midwest. A population of nearly 40 million lived here in cities, towns, and countryside. Whether in cities or on farms, many lived in poverty. The bulk of the population, more than 60 percent, lived on the land.

People in the hill country of the Ozarks were not in close touch with the Appalachians to the northeast, but the two areas shared a similar culture. Some of the Appalachian mountaineers made their living in coal-mining, of course, and Ozarkers had to live almost entirely off the land. The rest of America learned about mountaineers from mountain music and folklore, reading newspaper articles, and even such comic strips as "Li'l Abner" and "Snuffy Smith." They gathered other impressions from the appearance in 1941 of the successful movie *Sergeant York,* the story of a genuine hillbilly from Tennessee who became the nation's most celebrated hero of World War I. Americans believed that if mountain people lived isolated, backward lives and made little money (although not everyone would call them impoverished), they were a sturdy, independent, innocent folk and a quaint part of America. However they lived, the mountain people must have wanted it that way. After all, when the war ended, did Alvin York not go back to Tennessee?

Stereotypes are always simplistic, but they rarely depart completely from fact. Mountaineers did enjoy aspects of their culture, and most would have been content to live out their lives in the hills, had they found some reason for hope. However robust and self-sufficient their lives might once have been, their problems had grown over the years. Because of mechanization, the mines did not require as many men as a few years earlier, and when not needed underground, people usually turned to the land. Because of overcropping and erosion, the soil of the valleys and hillsides now would grow scarcely anything, although people still tried to farm. Most of the best timber had fallen long ago; some of the game and fur-bearing animals had been hunted or trapped out. As resources diminished, the population had grown. During the decade ending in 1940 the population of Kentucky increased almost 9 percent, large enough in itself; in some eastern counties—Kentucky's hill country—the increase ran as high as 56 percent.[34]

Not surprisingly people in the mountains experienced malnutrition, disease, lack of initiative, and nearly every other symptom of rural poverty. "How many of the children who finished the eighth grade here go on to high school?" a man asked a county superintendent of schools.

"Every one," he replied.

"I can't believe it!"

"None ever finished the eighth grade," he said with a smile.[35]

If mountain men in their idleness could find modest, inexpensive pleasures, such was rarely the case with the mountain woman. On her fell the tasks of keeping food on the table, managing and cleaning a residence that defied cleanliness, and producing another baby almost every year. "Look at that sad-eyed, misshapen woman. How old do you think she is? Forty?" a student of the area explained. "She's barely thirty, and once she was pretty by anybody's standards. Those six dirty-faced, raggedy children playing mountain goat over there on the gob pile are hers. What chance have they got? . . . The boys will grow up to be miners. The girls will blossom at fourteen and fifteen and fade at twenty to twenty-five. Between those years they will marry miners—or become prostitutes."[36]

Officials from government agencies had moved into the hills in the previous few years, planning projects and offering supplies or jobs on relief operations. The WPA had spent $1 million in Knott County,

Kentucky, in 1940 on 25 miles of road, seventeen bridges and via-
ducts, three schoolhouses, one other building, and "274 sanitary privies." Frequently the wages served to perpetuate life at bare subsis-
tence level, and the programs had generated little basic change by
1941, when many had started to dry up.

If problems in the deep South had grown out of circumstances
different from the hill country, they led to similar conditions: depleted soil, overpopulation, listless people carrying all the maladies
associated with abject poverty. The condition had evolved over
many years, starting with collapse of slavery and the plantation system after the Civil War. The sharecrop system and other variations
of tenant farming had proceeded uninterrupted for three-quarters of
a century. Owner and cropper would extract as much as possible
from the land, planting the same crop—in most cases cotton—in the
same place with the same methods year after year, and putting nothing back. The cropper seemed incapable of changing the system, and
the owner, himself in a bind, was unwilling to try. The consequence
had been soil depleted and gullied from erosion, dilapidated buildings, and people impoverished, diseased, and demoralized.

Here and there one found farmers willing to try something different. Some simply gave up and left. "They come off the plantation
'cause they ain't got nothin' to do," one fellow remarked. "They
come to town and they still got nothin' to do."[37] A few shifted to
different products, turning land to pasture and raising dairy cattle.
They had to be able to invest some money and wait a while for divi-
dends, but in time they saw that land with year-round cover did not
wash away as fast and that dairying offered a steadier, though still
small, income. In the Delta and on the other side of the Mississippi
River, more people had managed to acquire tractors and put something back into the land. The more they turned to machines, however, the less they needed tenants or hired help, except at picking
time.

Eleven million people lived in families of tenants or wage workers,
for whom the gross income, according to one "liberal" estimate, was
$250 a year. The people popularized in the writing of William Faulk-
ner and in Erskine Caldwell's *Tobacco Road* and *God's Little Acre*
lived, black or white, in tenant houses of two or three rooms of
rough lumber. The windows had no screens and perhaps no glass.
Feed and flour bags became so popular as clothing—cloth that could

be made into clothing—that companies began selling produce in colored bags with floral or other designs. Meals commonly featured fatback, cornbread, sorghum molasses, an occasional rabbit, squirrel, or catfish, and, later in the summer, vegetables from the garden. A government agent traveling in western North Carolina asked an old man how he had endured the Depression. He had not heard about "any depression," he said; conditions in his part of the country had remained the same almost as long as he could remember.[38]

The New Deal and its numerous programs had come to the South as well as to other parts of the country. Much of Southern agriculture enrolled in subsidized crop limitation programs of the Agriculture Adjustment Act of 1938. Some Southerners received old age assistance; others worked in such relief organizations as the WPA or Civilian Conservation Corps (CCC). One should not belittle those efforts. Anything that allowed an exhausted cotton field to rest or, better yet, to begin a process of replenishment was helpful. Most of the people who received financial assistance could verify their need; anyone could tell by looking at them.

Still, the programs were limited and not always carefully managed. The sums remained small, and the government applied a differential between North and South. If New Yorkers on old age assistance received $25.56 a month and the national average stood at $19.47, old people in South Carolina received $8.24; in Arkansas it was $7.57. Southern workers with the WPA earned slightly more than half the national average.[39] Some subsidies from the AAA unjustly found their way into the hands of landowners. Property retired from cultivation might be land farmed by sharecroppers; a few owners used money from the government to buy tractors, thus displacing more tenants. Other than in the Tennessee Valley, where the government had undertaken a vast program of regional rehabilitation (and even there changes came slowly), the basic condition of Southern agriculture had improved only modestly and in many places not at all. Roosevelt in 1938 had identified the South as the nation's "No. 1 economic problem," and now, in 1941, with the United States entering a new era, it still was.[40]

Backwardness of life and labor in the South coexisted with another agriculture establishment, marked with shiny machinery, scientific methods, and, as America moved toward war, higher earnings. By the end of 1941 cash receipts would total nearly $11.7 billion, better than $2.5 billion more than 1940. Modern growers used commercial fertilizer prepared for each type of soil. Nearly all farmers in Iowa and most in the Midwest had changed to planting hybrid seed corn and by that means alone had improved yield by 15–20 percent. Tractors and machinery, besides advancing speed of work, had eliminated the need to grow feed for horses and mules. In the previous decade it had been possible to shift some 23 million acres from crop and pasture for the animals.[41]

Increased efficiency itself contributed to one of the most persistent and perplexing problems of agriculture. The classical American "farm problem" had not been too little goods but too many, more agricultural produce than could be sold at a satisfactory price—a problem that grew with each advance in the process of production. "The plenty and abundance which technology has made possible is embarrassing us," the Secretary of Agriculture wrote.[42] In the 1930s, when prices had fallen to ridiculous levels, the government began paying farmers to cultivate fewer acres. Now, in 1941, with demand growing on domestic and international markets and the price going up, worry about surplus produce seemed to vanish. The government wanted more production. Could it be that the old farm problem was on the verge of being solved, if only temporarily?

The "farm problem" perhaps, but not the problems of farmers. There were still men who labored over worn-out soil with outdated methods; the other side of the coin was the displacement of workers by better methods, what some people called "eviction by machinery." Solving one problem simply enlarged the other. In the Mississippi Delta twenty-two tractors and thirteen four-row cultivators had pushed 130 tenant families off the land. A farmer in the Red River Valley who had previously worked eleven units of land now could handle twenty-one.[43] Displaced workers had gone to live in nearby towns, some on relief. Even though acres under cultivation had increased since 1940, the number of farms had declined by 57,000, mostly through absorption, one must suspect, into larger operations. Nearly everyone agreed that machinery represented progress and that it was impossible to stand in the way. If the South needed anything, it seemed to be greater efficiency and modern methods. "To talk about simpler times and methods is like talking about unscrambling an egg," the Secretary of Agriculture, himself a former farm boy, wrote. A specialist on rural issues added: "The real question is not: Are we for or against more farm machines? It is: How can we distribute the benefits that more machines in agriculture can confer?"[44]

To many observers the answer seemed obvious enough: Distribute the benefits among fewer people. "I can sum up the problem of the mountains in mighty few words," a man in eastern Kentucky wrote. "There are too many people on too few acres, and mighty rough acres at that."[45] The Department of Agriculture calculated in 1941 that while 12 million workers tried to make a living on the farm, 9 million would be enough to meet current demands. Excess workers thus would have to find something else, no matter how painful the transition might be for themselves and their families. Had the world war and the prospect of American involvement altered the situation? Would more people be needed on the farms after all? Who could say? While forecasts about the long-range future of American agriculture had not changed, needs for the immediate future were impossible to predict.

One trend struck most farmers as objectionable and a cause for future concern. It was natural enough and probably good business for a farmer to increase the size of his holdings. To see land absorbed into a massive agricultural enterprise was another matter altogether. The consolidation movement had already gone a good distance. Scarcely more than 1.5 percent of farmers operated 34 percent of the farmland. Nearly 15 percent of America's farms had become enormous conglomerations, each having 10,000 or more acres. In California 4 percent of the farms contained 66 percent of the total acreage.[46] The large corporation might be the most efficient form of agriculture, but a feeling persisted that farming represented more than economics, that it remained an expression—perhaps exaggerated—of freedom and individualism, that destruction of the individual family farm would represent a blow at the national heart and soul.

Blows to the rural heart and soul would come nevertheless. Farming continued to become more businesslike, even on the family farm. The transition to specialized farming, a change that had been going on for many years, transformed the rural environment and life-style. "One of the first evidences of this meets the eye immediately—the virtual disappearance of the barnyard," a rural scholar noted. Cows, pigs, and vegetable gardens were nowhere to be seen. Flowers had become a luxury. "My husband would plow up that rose garden if I'd let him. He'd plow right up to the bedroom window," a housewife in California remarked. "There is one thing I want you to put down in your book," an "urbanized farmer" told that same scholar. "Farming in this country is a business, it is not a way of life."[47]

The more farmers turned to combines, tractors, and other machines, the less they joined together in threshing or other shared experience. The machines made such community efforts less necessary and played havoc with the tradition of equivalent contribution, of "trading work." One man with a wagon and team of horses contributed much the same amount of labor and equipment as any other. "But a baler costs more, and it wears out," a former work trader explained. "Combines had to be amortized and paid for, and cash came to dominate the transactions. A few men bought tractors with two or three times the work power of others; the exchange was no longer equal."[48] Farmers might bemoan the loss of the cooperative spirit, the cherished values of work and life, but they nonetheless joined the transformation as quickly as they found the means.

Rural folk everywhere found their isolation breaking down, nudged into a national culture. To be sure, the process had advanced farther in some areas than others. In the Northeast, the California coast, and the upper Midwest people could have almost any modern apparatus, if they wanted it, and often they did. They listened to the radio for programs of all sorts, not simply farm broadcasts, and found their purchases guided by advertisements on the air and in magazines. They drove past the local general store to go to a movie or to shop in town; even as they did, they felt a little sad to see the place have to close.

Changes came more slowly to the South, the hill country, and other places, but they still came. The devices of modern culture gradually reached farther into remote areas, helping to bring people out—for a short time at first, and then for longer and longer. While people in the area around Harmony, Georgia, had no desire to change their lives, they could see change going on anyway. Nearly every white family had a car and a radio, and a few had managed to get a tractor. The old practice of visiting on Sunday afternoon had virtually come to an end; it was impossible to find anyone home; "They are all out riding." The population had grown older because most young whites and a few blacks had moved to town. The local white school had only eleven students in grades below high school. It probably soon would have to shut down.[49]

The national government had become a major carrier of change during the years of the Depression. The WPA had built roads, bridges, and schools. The government men might come around to propose a project and perhaps offer a job to the man of the family or supplies to tide the family over. He encountered a much better reception if he came bearing gifts. The gifts rarely came without conditions. "No longer is the education of children, and their subsequent placement in a job, the problem solely of the family and of the community," a scholar of the prewar South wrote. "He who pays the piper will call the tune."[50] To some people the change represented progress and relief—however slow in coming—from ignorance and poverty; others feared they were witnessing the destruction of freedom, independence, and a simpler and probably purer way of life.

While the remarkable circumstances of 1941 had confused the condition of agriculture, they gave some farmers new reason for hope. Higher prices improved the lot of small and middle-size independent operators; the demand for more goods seemed to promise better times to come. A few marginal farmers had discovered a compromise, also made possible by changing conditions: Take a job in town, preferably on a night shift, leaving time in daytime to plant some corn, wheat, or beans, allowing them nominally to "hang on" as farmers. Increasingly these family farm owners took on new concerns. No longer in danger of losing the land, they now worried about keeping the oldest son out of the draft, perhaps, or being able to find (because of shortages) the used truck or piece of equipment they soon would be able to afford. If no one seemed fully capable of interpreting these developments, all would agree they were preferable to conditions in 1931.

Many others who had come to the crossroads in the countryside knew that they would have to take a different path, even if it led them into town. Unlike 1931, they now had—or soon would have—another place to go. In taking that road they only reaffirmed that the direction of agriculture and rural life in the United States was well established, that the future offered little room for a sharecropper walking a furrow behind a plow. It belonged to paved roads, rubber-tired tractors, record-keeping, even time clocks. A student of the Ozarks found the status of life in the hill country, and indeed in much of rural America, comparable to the situation of the stranger—no doubt a government man—who inquired at a mountain cabin about the location of a still. A son of the moonshiner offered to guide the man for twenty-five cents, paid in advance. "I'll pay you when I get back," the man said. "But," the boy replied, "you ain't comin' back."[51]

☆
S I X
☆

Things of the Spirit

As the land had been especially blessed by God, the land praised God in return—so stated one of the most persistent and cherished of American axioms. The United States was a nation of God-fearing, churchgoing people, dedicated to the principles of Christianity. As the country approached the middle of the twentieth century, the people found no reason to challenge that basic assumption. The great issues of the time seemed to confirm an association between nation and religion. Had the United States not been spared the slaughter of world conflict, and did that not seem very much like a sign of divine favor? Each side in the great debate over foreign policy—the one that favored staying out of war and the one that supported resistance to Nazism—saw its position as an expression of moralism. Morality to most Americans meant the same as religion, and being religious meant being Christian.

The United States was a Christian nation, or that is what the people thought. Opinion polls showed that an overwhelming majority believed in God and an afterlife. Most people agreed that churches were necessary, perhaps the most important institution in society, whether they attended or not. "Were it not for them," said an Iowan who had not been to church for five years, "the community would not be a desirable place to live."[1] A foreign student of American culture, Denis Brogan, concluded that organized religion played a larger part in American society than in any other large industrial state. He found that most Americans accepted absolute values, "that they believed . . . things are right or wrong, not merely profitable or pleasant," and the claim that "this is God's country . . . is no mere boaster's boast, but the statement of a sacred truth."[2]

The eve of war nonetheless found churches beset with numerous problems. Evidence from most quarters pointed to stagnation or sluggishness in membership and in attendance at Sunday School and church, particularly in the Protestant denominations—partly a legacy of the Depression, partly a consequence of changing attitudes. Religious leaders found it difficult to appeal to a society steadily becoming urbanized and standardized, a people falling under the influence of radio, the automobile, and other artifacts of modern culture. Division continued between the Christian churches, and while the resultant competition added a measure of vitality to some sects, it led to behavior that was unseemly for people who called themselves followers of Christ. Finally, the international crisis threw American religion, or much of its leadership, into turmoil, raising serious moral questions and adding new reasons for division in Christendom. Religion helped to sustain generous and idealistic features in the American character, but it also served as a sponsor of weakness or meanness. Like the Lord Himself, attitudes moved in mysterious ways.

Church officials did little better than farmers in keeping records, but the best estimates put prewar membership in religious institutions at approximately 65 million. Thus half the population—it might be as meaningful to say *only* half the population—belonged to one of 250,000 churches (or other establishments) in denominations ranging from the Roman Catholic Church, with many million members, to localized Protestant sects, with no more than a dozen or so.[3] These statistics failed to reveal much about the way people practiced their faith or even how many went to a place of worship. Roman Catholics, who established church membership virtually at birth and counted every baby, probably did best in identifying membership and inducing participation in worship services. The statistics offered almost no information about the religious behavior of Jewish people. Americans had difficulty understanding what it meant to be a Jew, and so one simply counted every person of Jewish parentage, falsely suggesting that each was religious and a functioning member of a congregation.

The greatest mystery came in trying to evaluate the Protestants. In the open and individualistic American environment, Protestantism had proliferated in such diverse ways that it was impossible to measure how many Protestants there were or how intensely they practiced their faith. The published numbers did not help much. Many denominations did not establish membership until a later age, often thirteen, and the steadiest churchgoers at times did not appear on official rolls. Many rural churches did not bother to compile a list. Some people were listed as members of a congregation long after they had stopped active participation.

Some Protestants contended that church membership, or even attendance, was not a prerequisite for a Godly life. They were religious, they insisted, even though they did not go to church. One lady in Tennessee decided that she could handle spiritual matters by herself:

> In times back we used to read the Bible pretty much. But seems like you always come across something you can't make out straight. So we just stopped reading it. . . . I guess I got on to the main of it, though. I know that Jesus Christ died to save sinners. And all that me and Calvin have to do is trust in him. . . . We ain't stole and have always told the truth. They's more to it, but I counted them off one day and we is all right. . . . So I ain't bothering about Hell if I never gets inside the door of a Knoxville Church.[4]

When a national poll in November 1940 probed the frequency of church attendance, the answers, as expected, covered a wide range. The most frequent response (18 percent) was "never"; the second highest number answered fifty-two times, or weekly. "Did you go to church last Sunday?" the same pollsters asked; 63 percent said no. Another poll a year later sought to determine if the war had increased interest in religion: 57 percent said no, only 31 percent agreed that it had.[5]

If insecure times—the Depression, and now world conflict—had prompted some people to seek refuge in their faith, they created other conditions detrimental to the practice of organized religion. Collections, which had fallen off in the financially strapped 1930s, had not recovered with improvement of the economic climate. Some churches had to close, and others could afford only a part-time minister, perhaps once a month. Many clergymen discovered that the reward for their work would have to come in ways other than financial. The pastor of an established urban church could expect to live a comfortable middle-class life, little different from many of his parishioners. The Catholic priest, the most stable of the lot, received an average salary of $1,200 and a rectory to boot. With no family to care for, he did not want for the necessities of life.

Most hard-pressed were Protestant ministers who served small urban or rural churches. A Baptist survey revealed in 1941 that rural pastors received annual salaries ranging from $122 to $774.[6] Many ministers had to find a source of supplemental income or, failing that, consider getting out of preaching altogether. A Baptist preacher in Plainville, Missouri, received $10 per month from each of four churches. In between preaching and presiding over funerals and weddings, he spent long hours on the farm. The Methodist minister there sold burial insurance. The preacher at the Holiness Church collected a dollar to five dollars each Sunday morning. He also had a farm but was gone so much with ministerial duties that he could give it little time. Without frequent gifts of hay, food, and household items, he might not have survived.[7]

People who changed residence also had to abandon their place of worship. Finding a new place rarely presented a problem for Catholics, inasmuch as the church was much the same everywhere. The transplanted Protestant might have more of a problem. Followers of formalized churches probably could shift from one denomination to another and notice little difference. A migrant from rural Tennessee, however, accustomed to the homey emotionalism of the little structure down the road, might see a sophisticated urban church as a different world altogether. They were so large, clean, and quiet; he could not begin to match the clothes the townspeople wore, and he would swear they were staring at him as he left at the end of service. He and his family would not return the next Sunday. In time such people might help organize a church to their liking in Detroit, Pittsburgh, or another large city. For the time being they would stay at home. After a long week in the factory and perhaps a hard Saturday night, with no hogs to feed or cows to milk, it felt good to sleep late Sunday morning.

The temptations of popular culture fell heaviest on adolescents, who were more susceptible to something new, more determined to stay in step with peers, more uncomfortable with the restraints commonly associated with dedication to the faith. To teenagers in Morris, Illinois, religion was "comparable in a way to wearing clothes or taking a bath . . . something one has to do to be acceptable in society," a resident sociologist explained. While a few looked at God, the Devil, Heaven, and Hell as real entities and saw life as preparation for the afterlife, religion to most of the high school youth had no content beyond a vague belief in God and a general association with a church. "Most of the kids . . . have no interest in church or what it stands for," complained the Baptist minister.[8] One critic found an explanation in the rules of Protestant churches forbidding drinking, smoking, dancing, going to movies, and "every Sabbath sport but passing the plate," the "chief effect" of which was to persuade the individual "that religion is a system of trivial taboos, having nothing whatever to do with him."[9]

On the whole the Catholic Church had endured the stresses of the time better than Protestantism. By far the largest religious establishment in the United States—because the Protestants were split so many ways—the Roman church had a membership of approximately 23 million, perhaps more. The great source of Catholic growth, immigration from Europe, had largely come to an end, but the practice of infant baptism and church doctrine helped keep numbers at least intact. Church membership was an absolute prerequisite for salvation, and regular attendance was almost as mandatory. Marriage outside the church or—God forbid—a second time was to be avoided almost at all costs. Attendance at Mass, obedience to church rules, and partaking of the sacraments seemed to offer a dependable path to Heaven.

To guide the faithful around the temptations of non-Catholic forces, the church sought to establish institutions of many kinds, starting with education. "Every Catholic child in a Catholic school" had been the ideal for many years. That goal, of course, remained far beyond reach. Denied public funds, private schools had to rely on contributions and tuition from families with children in school. The costs had been too great in many places, and of more than 6.5 million Catholic children of school age, only approximately 40 percent had found a place in a Catholic school.[10] The church tried to reach some of the rest through separate instruction. "Released time" had begun to be an issue for public discussion.

In areas with more people and money, one found the Catholic Youth Organization, the Knights of Columbus—the K of C, a social and service group of Catholic men—and many other groups. The priest did not always say so directly, but the church preferred that Catholics associate with their kind. That was the best way to guard against subversive ideas and above all the specter of mixed marriage, that most feared cause of weakening of the faith. One Catholic official explained that while marriage to a non-Catholic, "carefully protected by the promises," succeeded in many cases, "its 'record' is considerably less satisfying than that of the Catholic marriage. . . . The education of Catholic children in the Catholic faith in a Catholic school amid Catholic surroundings is, as far as human means can go, the best guarantee against defection from the faith."[11]

Catholic schools helped guide youngsters along a carefully marked path to religious adulthood, but in the absence of schools the young Catholic nonetheless had to take each step. It began with baptism, of course, and other ceremonies followed at prescribed intervals, of a fashion little changed from what the parents had gone through. "We learned about God as part of school, or perhaps it is more accurate to say we learned about the church," one person recalled. The youngsters spent weeks in preparation for the solemn and happy ceremony of First Communion, which usually came in first grade. There were the memory lessons, the questions about the faith, with the answers all set down with no equivocation in the Baltimore Catechism from many years earlier. And when they were ready, they began the grand procession; "the girls were all in white, veils and dresses and stockings and shoes, and new white rosaries, their new prayer books. . . . Vestal virgins for Jesus."[12]

A few years afterward came confirmation—more marching down the aisle, more incense, candles, chants, and proclamations. The attraction of Catholic rituals was so powerful that many young men and perhaps most little girls at some point contemplated becoming priests or nuns.

The American church (or, as some people preferred to call it, the Irish church) more closely resembled the organization of fifty years earlier than the institution Catholics would come to know a few decades later. With stained-glass windows, statues, crucifixes, and other ornamentation, with high ceilings and elegant marble columns and communion rails, some as white as freshly fallen snow, there was a sense of mystery about the church of 1941. The priest stood with his back to the people, performing specified tasks as he chanted in Latin; the congregation, some following along in a missal, others pretending to do so, tried to keep pace with what he was doing. Music, also in Latin, came from a choir. During Mass the great hall resounded with all the predictable sounds of ceremony: the sombre chants, the clarion jingle of bells at prescribed moments, the rumble of the congregation standing and kneeling, standing and kneeling, all at the same time. For the faithful who came to worship every Sunday, and some who came each day in between, there was security in these august surroundings and a power that seemed an appropriate reminder of their Almighty.

While far more predictable than Protestants, not all Catholics approached religion the same way. Some individuals, driven by weakness, laziness, intellectual discomfort, or outright rebellion, neglected their holy obligations altogether. The majority of Catholics probably obeyed the rules as a matter of course. They attended Mass on Sunday and the Holy days, went to confession at least once a year, and ate fish or grilled cheese on Friday. If they could feel no evidence of God acting on their daily lives, they were concerned about consequences of straying from the faith. For other Catholics, especially older people, religion manifested through the church represented the only dependable, predictable element of life, and there would have been a great emptiness, a lack of purpose, without it.

A prominent figure in a Catholic community or in any town with a substantial number of Catholics was the priest. "He is an officer of the Roman Catholic government and is responsible to it alone," a student of society in New England observed. Symbols of priestly authority were sprinkled throughout the practices of the church. He was "Father" to all people in the parish and anyone else willing to call him by that title. Other gestures of obedience extended from greeting the bishop (a higher priest) by kissing his ring to the parishioners' humble demeanor when receiving the communion wafer, which only the priest could distribute. In the confessional the priest expected to hear information that might be withheld from parent, mate, legal authorities, or anyone else.

From this lofty position the influence of the clergy could reach far and wide. "This afternoon a woman asked our help for a husband who is unmanageable," a priest in Massachusetts said. "We baptise children, marry them later; we comfort the dying and console the people in grief. And in our confessionals we have the deepest insight into the lives of our people."[13] Acting as arbitrator, lawgiver, guardian, and dispenser of grace and even of financial aid, the priest of the 1940s commanded respect, obedience, and no small measure of power in the secular environment. To many Catholics he was one of the most important—if not *the* most important—people in their lives, certainly of more immediate significance than officials of government. To outsiders, and some insiders as well, he might seem the most pampered and fawned-over individual in the community.

Catholicism remained largely urban and largely the faith of immigrants. Approximately 80 percent of Catholics lived in cities, and the largest congregations, except in rare cases, came from first- or second-generation immigrant families. If the liturgy always came in Latin and the sermon or homily usually in English, the priest might hear confession in Polish, Italian, German, or some other European language. The immigrant centers of the North and Midwest also were centers of Catholic political power. Any description of the culture of America's largest cities, or even the landscape, is impossible without an account of Catholicism and its institutions. Because a community was Italian, it also was Catholic, and because it was Catholic one could make some fairly safe predictions about patterns of life there: the schedule for Sundays and other days of obligation, the expressions of speech, the points of reference. The times of highest merrymaking—the feast days and weddings—and times of deepest sadness led one to the church. Even the greatest sinner probably would want a church wedding, a sanctified funeral, and, if conditions permitted, one last chance at the confessional.

Like many aspects of American society in 1941, the Roman Church was in a state of transition. No longer the target of open sustained attack, as it had been as recently as the 1920s, Catholicism fell short of total acceptance in the non-Catholic populace. Catholicism remained too closely identified with large cities, ethnic minority groups, and, of course, the Roman Papacy to be recognized as merely a different but equally legitimate expression of the community of Christ. The church's hierarchical structure continued to be a source of strength and vulnerability. Centralized authority provided for unity, consistency, power, and confidence, which the growing numbers of American Catholics tended to reinforce. At the same time it discouraged dissent and perhaps fresh ideas and prompted some people to question if such a structure could coexist with American political principles.

If Protestants found the church of Rome to be authoritarian, Catholics might argue that Protestantism had no unity, no discipline, and little organization. Well more than half the nation's church members belonged to Protestant churches, and millions more not counted had some measure of connection to a denomination. By itself the term carried little meaning, encompassing a broad range of the landscape of Christendom, from the most religious of people to those who practiced no worship at all. Young men entering military service found their identification plates—the dog tags—stamped C for Catholic, J for Jew, and P for everyone else. The continued statistical domination of Protestantism was the primary explanation why religious attitudes in the United States were so diverse and so difficult to measure.

As a rule Protestant churches retained the loyalty of female members better than male. For reasons not easy to identify, men strayed from the fold more often than women. It might have been a matter of masculine pride, the refusal to humble oneself before the preacher or anyone else, including God. The fellow knew that if he started going to church the minister would want him to come more often, stop smoking and swearing, take part in the service, and take on an ever escalating scale of responsibility. Whatever the reason, Mother might go to church with the children, leaving Father at home. Once in a while he would go. "My father came to church once a year, on Easter Sunday, looking trapped in his necktie and suit," a man from Mississippi recalled. "He would sit back in the farthest corner of the church in order to make a speedy exit during benediction."[14] By getting out fast, the man could beat the preacher to the door and avoid having to shake hands and exchange the customary forced greetings.

Now and then the minister turned the tables and showed up without warning at the family home. The damned preacher had him cornered, this male who tried to avoid religious people as much as possible muttered to himself. The sight of the minister alighting in front of the house was terrifying, causing wives to dash about picking up papers and hiding ashtrays. The man from Mississippi remembered that his father used to scramble out the back door to hide in the garage or the tall weeds in the back, because he knew that if the preacher ever got you inside, "you would end up on your knees praying, and maybe give five dollars to the new church annex." After a few minutes the little boy would go behind the house, find father in a patch of Johnson grass smoking a cigarette, and say, "Daddy, he's gone."[15]

Church services varied immensely in the broad world of Protestantism. Differences were determined partly by denomination, partly by location and character of congregation. As a rule, the larger the church and the more financially stable its membership, the better the chance that formalized practices of worship would prevail. In established churches in cities and towns—Episcopal, Presbyterian, Congregational, and some Methodist and Baptist—one found an atmosphere not drastically different from a Catholic service. The decorations were simpler and less cluttered than in a Catholic church, especially down by the altar. If there were any odors at all, they were not those from incense or burning candles but the familiar smells of varnish, hardwood floors, and oaken benches. The service was noisier than at a Mass, the congregation more willing to sing, the sermon longer.

A visitor recorded his observation of a neat, middle-class Congregational church in California: "Its services are quiet and orderly; its sermons innocuous admonitions to moral conduct, or intellectualized explanations of the workings of God with man. The sermon is preceded by a fixed ritual, including music by a vested choir, organ accompaniment, and the funeral hush of the carpeted and insulated ediface."[16] These people did not go to church to be challenged or made uncomfortable. Perhaps some individuals found communication with God in that solemn setting and for that attended. Much of the congregation came to do its duty, to pay its dues, to greet peers, and to let those peers and the minister see them in church.

Much of the dynamism in Protestant Christianity came from small churches in the countryside and small towns and in the poverty-plagued districts of large cities. They might call themselves Fundamentalist, Holiness, Pentecostal, or any of dozens of other labels, or nothing at all. These people took their religion seriously, as long as they were involved in it. All took the Bible—their interpretation—literally; all looked to the return of Christ. Although they might disagree as to when, most agreed it would be soon. They believed in a second baptism of the spirit, a conversion that created a new person who manifested Godliness in daily activity as well as in worship.

The central part of worship in such churches, indeed in all of Protestantism, was the sermon. Inasmuch as ministers varied widely in education and experience—many rural preachers had little education and no qualifications for the ministry other than a claim that God had called them—sermons varied a great deal in content, literacy, manner of presentation, and length. The pulpit allowed open expression of the speaker's idiosyncrasies and powers of persuasion; many developed a habit of uttering "uh" or "ah" after every few words. Some preachers or "lay preachers," caught up in their rhetoric and enthusiasm, might go on for two hours or more or until they, and their audience, were thoroughly drained.

The messages in fundamentalist Protestantism remained remarkably uniform. Attending movies was condemned in many churches, a misdeed for which a minister in California recommended two hours of prayer and a scalding bath "to get that filth off." A lay preacher in Missouri attacked divorces, "beer jints," and women "suckin' on a cigarette." People who obeyed the word could expect an afterlife of eternal bliss, beginning, in a dramatization by a streetcar evangelist in a large city, with a first class berth, "plenty of blankets and clean sheets" on "that streamlined train to Heaven."[17]

The highest goal of most Protestant churches was to "win souls to God," that is, persuade the unconverted to accept a new life of worship and Christian behavior. In large, well-established institutions the acknowledgment of faith might involve a simple statement of belief or acceptance of church membership. Fundamentalist sects insisted upon literal application of John 3:7, perhaps the key to much of American Protestant behavior: "Ye must be born again." While conversion might come at any time or in any place, the great drive came during a special season when each church announced the date for its revival.

The revival was a combination of pep rally and recruiting session designed to win converts. It involved nightly services lasting a week or two, longer if the sessions were going well. It might come at any time of year, although most revivals took place between spring and fall, when the weather was good and the roads passable, preferably during a lull in the work schedule. Churches often saw fit to bring in a special preacher, an evangelist noted for an ability to arouse people and win converts. The meeting started with several loud and joyful songs led by a singer who specialized in revivals. Some churches might follow with a testimonial period, when people in the audience proclaimed their joy in being Christian. Then came the sermon, focusing on the sins of man, the impending end of the world as revealed in fulfillment of biblical prophecy, and the agony of living and, above all, dying without accepting Christ. (Although Protestants regarded God and Jesus as separate people, many used the terms interchangeably.)

After the sermon came the invitational, the true reason for the gathering. While the congregation sang an appropriate song, "Softly and Tenderly" (Jesus is Calling), perhaps, or "Almost Persuaded," the evangelist invited—at times pleaded with—sinners to come forward. People who complied might kneel at an altar or a mourner's bench to be joined by sympathetic friends or relatives. The preacher sometimes moved into the audience to work on reluctant people, and members of the congregation might strike out on their own, heading for individuals they knew needed persuasion. The process of conversion did not come easy; it involved much praying, of course, with probably some weeping and confession of wrongdoing. When it was finished, if the person had "come through," there was nothing but smiles and congratulation, shrieks of joy and laughter, or outbursts of sobbing and other activity (depending upon the sect), punctuated with "amens" and "hallelujahs" all around. Another sinner had been born again.

What then happened? "I'm a changed man," a convert in Missouri said. He then listed transgressions from which conversion had delivered him: "(1) gittin' mad at people and wantin' to fight ever'body ever' few minutes; (2) wantin' to tell and listen to them rotten dirty stories they tell in the back room at the garage; (3) needin' tobacco and (4) wantin' to wear a necktie."[18] Another man recalled that conversion produced such "peace and benevolence" that he wanted to embrace the first person he saw in the street, "white or nigger." In some cases conversion produced genuine and lasting change. The convert renounced everything identified as sinful and sought to be dutiful in religious obligation and "Christlike" in daily dealings with people. The attitude remained through life, and death probably came peacefully, with confidence that a reward awaited in Heaven. In other cases conversion seemed more a matter of yielding to a high pitch of emotion. "I could seldom resist," a man said of his experience in the First Methodist Church; "before I turned twelve, I had been 'saved' . . . at least a dozen times."[19] When the revival ended, the evangelist had gone, and the new Christian again faced the problems of life, old temptations might prove irresistible. Some people had to be born again every summer, and somehow conversion never stuck.

Agreement on the goal of eternal life and the need for individual rebirth did not prevent Protestant groups from disagreeing on aspects of worship or Christian behavior. One reader might interpret a Biblical verse differently from another or decide to emphasize a different passage. A member simply might not like the preacher or might take offense at a member of the congregation. When disagreement (or inspiration) became strong enough, people changed churches and sometimes started new sects. There were more than 250 in 1941, all claiming to carry out the true wishes of God. Special application of the word, or application of a special word, led to some interesting expressions of Protestant Christianity.

Baptists, of course, believed that only total immersion or some substantial dampening of the body constituted true baptism. Sprinkling or other token gesture simply would not do. People as a matter of practice did not dunk themselves fully clothed, and so the ceremony could be at least awkward. Baptism in one rural area began with the entire congregation, dressed in Sunday best, traipsing to a nearby pond or stream. The people to be baptized wore white. As the quartet sang "Yes, We'll Gather at the River," the candidates and preacher waded in, probing ahead with a stick to frighten away any snapping turtles that might have occupied the area:

Sister Suke Simpson is first. . . . The preacher places a handkerchief over his fingers and grabs Sister Suke by the nose. . . . The quartet sings louder. Splash! Sister Suke comes up waving her arms and heads for the bank as though she had seen a water moccasin. As she hits the bank she begins to shout, "Glory to God! Praise God! Hallelujah!" Other sisters and a number of brethren join in. Sister Suke tries to shout and leap and keep her dress from clinging between her legs at the same time. The quartet sings crescendo.[20]

The most terrifying manifestation of Holiness Protestantism came from a sect living in the border states and the hill country of the upper South. The activity in the following account took place in Kentucky, although it could easily have been in six or eight other states. The area bore all the markings of poverty: The people were poorly dressed, and the church was made of crude lumber inside and out, with rough wooden benches and posters proclaiming "Jesus is Soon Coming." Heat, when needed, came from a pot-bellied stove in the center, and light came from four kerosene lamps fastened on the front and back walls.

The service began with singing. "I Will Not Be Denied" came first, accompanied by tambourines and dozens of feet patting the coarse floor. Song followed song, sounds rose and fell, monotonous and mystifying; "the emotional effect was terrific," an outsider who had come to observe the session admitted.

Within a short time a general disorder had enveloped the room. A woman screamed in pure ecstasy, "Praise be to God, I'm comin' through." Other men and women jumped to their feet and began to dance, shout, and quiver as the music droned on and the tambourines continued to pound. Suddenly a hush fell over the activity as the preacher glided to a corner and picked up a tattered suitcase; a startling noise came from inside it. As he lifted a 4-foot rattlesnake above his head, the shouting, dancing, and pounding of tambourines burst out anew.

The pandemonium continued several minutes, with each participant free to find an avenue of expression. The snake passed from hand to hand. Some people kissed it, others coiled it around their necks or danced around the bewildered reptile as it lay on the floor. A huge-bosomed woman nursing a baby slid the child to the floor and jumped up to take the rattler, leaving the breast fully exposed. No one seemed to notice. Two men lighted miner's carbide lamps and ran them over their bare arms. Another man turned up a kerosene lamp until the flame ran out of its chimney and lapped around his throat and ears. The smell of sweat and burning hair and flesh became almost sickening, and yet the man's popping eyes, the observer reported, "evinced not pain but hypnotic rapture."

Not even the bite the snake gave the large-breasted woman interrupted proceedings. Ignoring the wound, she rolled on the floor in a heightened state of arousal; others seemed to take inspiration from her behavior. The session continued until each participant had experienced temporary exhaustion or emotional release, some in ways that bore close similarity to a sexual performance. At last the tambourines stopped; amid scattered "Praise Gods" the preacher put the snake back in the suitcase and the people went home.[21]

No less than other sects, the snake-handlers of the hill country found scriptural support for their peculiar form of worship. They pointed to Mark 16: 17–18, which said: "In my name shall they . . . take up serpents. And if they drink any deadly thing, it shall not hurt them; they shall lay hands on the sick, and they shall recover." And in Luke 10: 19 they found: "Behold, I give unto you power to tread on serpents and scorpions, and over all the power of the enemy; and nothing shall by any means hurt you."

So armed, they played with snakes, put flame to flesh, even took poison. Some died, were scarred, or went insane. Many others, so believers claimed, felt nothing at all. They said it was a matter of faith. "We tell 'em if they hain't got th' faith to stand back and not pick up no snakes. They'll eat you up if you don't," one participant explained. "Now onct I seen a man git bit when he was a puttin' a snake in his shirt an' down his britches, an' that snake pert nigh et him up. I guess that was good 'nuf fer him too. The Bible don't say nothin' about puttin snakes down yer britches."[22]

Legislation forbidding snake-handling had no effect. The few people convicted under law spent their time in jail or paid a fine, if they could scrape it up. Believers often tried to turn trials into a religious celebration, complete with hymns, tambourines, and patting feet. In Kentucky, Tennessee, Georgia, Ohio, Virginia, West Virginia, and probably two or three other states, the practice continued to grow with alarming speed. The people claimed to be exercising their constitutional rights, their free expression of religion. "If a feller goes out in the woods and picks up a snake," one believer asked, "is that any business of the law?" "Why, they'll be passin' a law next against speakin' in unknown tongues and against shoutin' and clappin' hands," another complained. "I'll tell you there can't no law make me quit doin' what th' Lord tells me t' do."[23]

Most Protestants wisely avoided the ritual of snake-handling, but many people in rural areas and small towns practiced emotional worship marked by varying forms of noisy exhortation and physical activity.

Nonbelievers argued that conversion often did not last, that within a short time the convert was again engaged in the activities recently renounced with such zeal. Sociologists preferred to explain revivalism in socio-economic terms, pointing out that it succeeded best in rural areas and urban slums, where people had little education and low incomes. Religion offered excitement and release from the stress of life. "Poor people get a sensual or physical thrill and in that there is an attraction," a minister in California commented. "I have had a frank Pentecostal preacher tell me that many of his congregation come to church for just that thrill. . . . Those poor folks get no other thrill out of life."[24]

All such observations carried a measure of truth, for revivalism took in a wide range of religious experience. Fundamentalism, evangelicalism—whatever term one wishes to use—Bible-based, emotionally expressed religion did not encompass as high a proportion of people as it had fifty or one hundred years earlier. It could expect to erode even more as the population moved to the North and West or from country to city, as more economic opportunities opened up, and as Americans faced the draft and other forces impinging on their isolation and past patterns of thought.

But revivalism was a long way from dying as an approach to Christianity in 1941. While largely rural, it had caught on in parts of cities, as people brought it along when they came to town. While weakest in the Northeastern states, it reached nationwide and affected the way millions of people spent their days and nights. Without it Protestantism would have found it impossible to maintain a connection with perhaps a majority of Americans. Religion in the United States would have lost much of its life, vigor, and color.

Most Americans not classified as Christian or as people with a Christian heritage were Jews. Keepers of religious statistics counted every Jew who lived in the area of a Jewish congregation as a member of the faith, which set the number at close to 5 million, nearly half of them in New York City. To contend that all those people practiced their religion came no closer to truth than an assertion that all non-Catholic Christians went to Protestant churches. The rabbis had as much trouble as priests and ministers keeping their charges in line. Jews differed among themselves in ways unsuspected by a detached Christian populace. The Jewish people had not decided on a true meaning of Jewishness. Did being a Jew carry an obligation to observe certain religious practices? Did Jewishness pertain simply to tradition and culture, or birth, or did it mean anything at all? According to a recent account, a Jew might be "a member of one of a dozen ethnic groups, whose skin may be black or white; who speaks Yiddish and reads Hebrew, speaks Hebrew and speaks Yiddish, or who speaks and reads neither; who belongs to one of the three major groups of Judaism, or none; whose place of origin may have been Poland, Africa, Oceania, or Oklahoma."[25] While Jews encountered no barrier to the practice of religion in the United States, they knew that being Jewish in a Gentile environment did not come without difficulty. The more they observed the practice of Judaism or aligned themselves with Jewish causes in international politics, the more they found themselves set apart from the general society, and the more suspicion they aroused in the Christian majority.[26]

A case in point was observation of the Sabbath; Judaism held Saturday to be the day of rest and religious celebration. But, a scholar explained, "the work rhythm of the American week . . . is Christian. Saturday is a work day, the most important day of the week. This rhythm the Jews are powerless to resist. They must accept it or lose out in the competitive race." A group of men in Newburyport, Massachusetts, solved the problem by gaining a virtual monopoly in the scrap metal business, then agreeing to shut down on the Sabbath. The citizens of Newburyport did not object to having their junkyards closed on Saturday. Few Jewish businessmen experienced such favorable conditions. Rather than lose out to Christian competitors, most stayed open.[27]

Determination to observe the faith depended on several factors, including age of the individual, country of origin, and isolation of a Jewish community from the rest of society. The older the person and the farther east the country from which the person (or the family) had immigrated, such as Russia, the more likely he or she was to observe the rules. A few Jews practiced religion almost exactly as they had in the old country. They attended the synagogue regularly. The men wore beards and skullcaps and abstained from smoking, riding, handling money, and making fire on the Sabbath. A girl described the dedication of her orthodox parent: "Last Sukkoth [a minor holiday] it was raining pitchforks, and since on holidays you cannot even carry a handerchief, not to speak of an umbrella, my father couldn't go to the shul [synagogue] without getting soaked to the skin. . . . And he said to me that he felt as if his life had ended."[28]

Younger Jews and immigrants from West European nations for the most part took their religion lightly, if they gave it any attention at all. They worked Saturday as a matter of course and paid no attention to kosher dietary rules. The youngster might skip school on Yom Kippur but did not necessarily go the synagogue. Much like Christians, young Jews found it easier and more fun to do as they wished rather than accept a list of stuffy restraints. Jews, besides, felt the hidden wires of society pulling them toward assimilation and the comfort of acceptance into the greater American culture. The huge impact of the Jewish people on the United States came less in religion than in almost any other area.

The 1940s was a time to try men's souls and a time to reconsider religious attitudes as well. Appeals for unity and evidence that the nation indeed stood for freedom and tolerance had to coexist with the reality of how people felt about each other and suspicions between major religious groups. In large measure the antagonism represented less a spontaneous eruption of feeling than a persistence of issues and suspicion as old as the nation, if not Christianity. In fact, religious prejudice probably had declined over the years, in intensity and perhaps in breadth, yet it had by no means vanished altogether. A strong undercurrent of doubt and suspicion continued to pervade large portions of the population, and issues of the day occasionally pushed those attitudes into open antagonism.

Hostility toward Jews, which reached far back into American history, had not ended in 1941. An older anti-Semitism was being sharpened by the recent growth of American Jewry, its greater visibility in business and government, and the emergence of international issues in which Jews played a central part. One could not talk about the war or Hitler without at some point confronting the "Jewish problem."

It was, of course, impossible to measure racial and religious attitudes. Anti-Semitism—or religious or ethnic prejudice of any sort—was something Americans were not supposed to feel, especially not during the liberalism of the New Deal and not when Hitler was making racial hatred an international calamity. Anti-Semitism had far less obvious consequences than prejudice against black people; it did not prevent many Jews from obtaining prominence in several areas, notably business and entertainment. Nonetheless it did exist.

It is likely that most Americans had at least a suspicion of Jews, although many kept such thoughts to themselves or within a circle of like-minded friends and relatives. The people who did express themselves were bad enough. Such labels as "kike" (a term, incidentally, that originated with the Jews themselves) and racial slurs and jokes remained in the standard repertory of much of the United States. A poll had revealed in 1937 that 51 percent of people with an opinion would not vote for a "well-qualified" Jew for president. In the following year 58 percent believed that persecution of Jews in Europe was either partly or entirely their own fault. In 1939, 20 percent of people with an opinion believed that an anti-Jewish campaign would soon begin in the United States. Among those with an opinion 12 percent replied that they would support such a campaign; 17 percent would be sympathetic. Nearly 32 percent believed that the nation should take steps to prevent Jews from getting too much power in American business. Somewhat later, in July 1942, 44 percent believed that Jews already had too much power in the United States.[29]

The sources of anti–Semitism are fairly easy to identify. An image persisted of Jews as a clannish people, more involved in being Jewish than in being American. They were said to be aggressive, greedy money-grubbers, devious in business dealings and disgustingly— even embarrassingly—successful. Nearly everyone knew what it meant to "Jew down" the price of an item. Few "decent" people found the term objectionable. Most Americans knew no Jews, and the only ones they had heard of were people prominent in business or government (Henry Morgenthau, Jr., was, appropriately, Secretary of the Treasury) or the man who ran the local junkyard, haberdashery, or department store. Whoever heard of a Jew doing "real work," such as farming or standing eight hours on an assembly line? In fact, Jews did all those things, but popular perception placed them elsewhere in the economic system, usually at or near the top. "They are vivid, successful, difficult to fool, frequently aggressive" is how one writer summarized disquieting aspects of the Jewish character. "Gentiles either 'just don't like the Jews' or are definitely afraid of them."[30] The most vociferous anti-Semites warned of a plot by international Jewish bankers to seize control of the world.

Curiously, some of the same people believed that Jews stood in the vanguard of the Communist movement. Karl Marx, of course, had been a Jew, and a recent connection between Jews and Communism had come through Leon Trotsky, the Jewish Bolshevik, who led the Red Army in the Russian Revolution of 1917. One could find a generous sprinkling of Jewish names in any list of known national and international Communists. It made no difference that Trotsky had been expelled from Russian leadership and later, in 1940, brutally assassinated in Mexico. Father Charles Coughlin of surburban Detroit, whose name became almost synonymous with anti-Semitism, had charged in 1938 that Jews had engineered the Russian Revolution, thereby unleashing the threat of world revolution. "The average Jew, the kind we admire and respect, has been placed in jeopardy by his guilty leaders," Father Coughlin added sometime later. "He pays for their Godlessness, their persecution of Christians, their attempts to poison the whole world with communism." To engage this challenge, Coughlin proposed creation of a "Christian Front."[31]

Coughlin and many of his ilk thought it not at all surprising that most Jews supported Roosevelt's policy of resisting Nazism. Critics on the right had long found a connection between Jewish politics and Roosevelt's liberal policies, which they judged to be, if not Communist, at least headed in that direction. "The New Deal is a Jew deal" went a familiar slogan. It is not likely that many individuals believed Roosevelt's true name was Rosenfeld, but some people enjoyed saying so. And now the President's interventionist foreign policy put all the pieces into place. With the United States edging closer each month to involvement in the war, more voices joined the chorus. One of the mildest of those voices would provoke the loudest reaction. Charles Lindbergh did not consider himself anti-Jewish, and his charge that Jews, Britons, and Roosevelt were pushing the nation toward war was no more anti-Semitic than anti-Anglo-Saxon. Nonetheless, the charge gave the movement a respectability it had not previously had. Lindbergh did not gain many new followers with his speech of September 11, 1941, but he did encourage people of his persuasion to identify Jews as part of the problem.

It would be a mistake to characterize prewar anti-Semitism as primarily a religious movement. Most attention focused on the alleged activity of Jews in politics and economics; little public mention was made of—and perhaps little thought given to—the ancient grievance that Jews had been responsible for the death of Jesus. Even so, few Americans could separate religion from what they perceived to be the Jewish character, and the fact that Jews were not Christian helped set them apart from the general populace. Some anti-Semitic leaders came from ranks of the Protestant and Catholic clergy. Gerald L. K. Smith, a preacher in Detroit, had been a notorious Jew-baiter for years. The Reverend Gerald B. Winrod, founder of the Defender Movement, charged that "international Jewry" was responsible for "all the ills of the world." And there was, of course, Father Coughlin, whose publication, *Social Justice,* had insisted by 1941 that the "Jew . . . had no more business in . . . politics and government than had a pig in a China shop."[32] To be sure, many of the clergy took a different view; they blasted their colleagues of the cloth and appealed for tolerance. Nonetheless, in dealings with Jewish brethren, the time before World War II does not stand out as Christianity's finest hour.

For that matter, Christians had some distance to go in dealing with each other. True, the United States did not appear to be on the verge of a religious war. There was nothing to suggest the interfaith hostility of the nineteenth century or even the religious rumbles of the 1920s, when some Protestants stood guard to repulse the Pope's impending move to the United States. Physical attacks of Christian upon Christian were a rarity, nor was the religious press filled with stories of a Papist or a Protestant plot. While religious attitudes had evolved beyond sensationalized threats and groups formed to promote religious conflict, many old fears remained. The parochial press did not hesitate to take jabs at competitors, Catholic or Protestant, raising questions about the legitimacy of their beliefs and casting doubt on their Americanism.

A continuing source of difficulty stemmed from authoritarian structure of the Catholic Church and Protestant perception of the Pope as an anachronistic divine-right monarch. American Catholics, it was said, pledged obedience to a king, and a foreign one in the bargain! Were they Americans first, or Catholics first? Which loyalty had priority? A standard Catholic response, that such a conflict would never arise, left the critics unsatisfied. The Protestants' doubt persisted that the Church, with headquarters in Rome, would ever accept revered American principles of government, notably the separation of church and state. Suspicions about Catholicism bothered even the wife of the President, "not as a matter of faith or religious doctrine," a close friend noted, "but because of its political activities . . . church interference with measures and public activities." Mrs. Roosevelt privately admitted that "if a presidential candidate were a Catholic, she would have to say honestly that it would influence her attitude toward him."[33] Issues that had plagued Al Smith's campaign for the presidency in 1928 had never been put to rest.

Some Catholics added fuel to the controversy. A recent publication, *Catholic Principles of Politics,* written by two priests, struck a reviewer in *Christian Century* as reason for concern. He wrote that the work "will dispel . . . once and for all" the illusion that Catholics had become loyal Americans, far removed from European heritage.

Most disturbing was the contention that the state must recognize the true religion, "the Catholic faith," and protect people from "false religious notions," that is, anything but the Catholic faith. The reviewer called Romanism a "dangerous political creed as well as a false religion," marked with intolerance and fanaticism. Content to enjoy freedom while a minority, Catholics once in control would move to suppress it. "By propagating the Catholic faith," he concluded, "Romanists are no less attempting to undermine American liberties than are nazis or communists."[34]

Some Catholics feared a recurrence of the discrimination that had plagued them during much of the American past. People who believed anti-Catholicism had died in the 1920s "are due for a rude awakening," a writer in *The Catholic World* contended. "The basic hostility of the American public towards Catholicism remains ingrained. . . . I resent the insinuation that the Catholic Church is the natural ally of authoritarianism. . . . The Church has been from her foundation the greatest and truest of democracies."[35] Because the rank and file on both sides paid little attention to such philosophical questions, the contest remained largely a debate, or an exchange of accusations, among clergy and intellectuals of the religious press. Both sides seemed to be speaking up for tolerance, but their perception of tolerance differed, so they continued to go in circles.

Far more Americans experienced doubts of a milder sort, if no less perplexing. Intra-Christian suspicion belonged to the same category as anti-Semitism; at odds with the principles of American democracy, it went mostly unmeasured, unpublished, and often unspoken except in guarded circles. Even so, most people grew up conscious of the differences between Catholicism and Protestantism and aware that, while those differences did not necessarily have to be the source of conflict, they were too fundamental to be casually brushed aside.

Catholics left no doubt about where they stood. A priest or parishioner stated the position without the slightest hesitation or hint of embarrassment: Theirs was the only true church, a claim traceable to that awkward verse in the book of Matthew where Christ presumably commissioned Peter—thereafter identified as the first Pope—to start His church. "Protestantism is rebellion against the authority of Christ. . . . It should not exist," one priest wrote.[36] It was a sin to go to a Protestant church, the clergy reminded its people; if a special event, such as a wedding or funeral, seemed to require entering those forbidden halls, the Catholic first must obtain permission from a priest.

The Archbishop of St. Paul, Minnesota, cautioned his clergy to guard against subversive influence on Catholic children as a result of "necessity, indifference or a pervaded sense of freedom from church discipline." Subversive influences included singing with school choruses or glee clubs in Protestant churches; activity in such non-Catholic organizations as the YMCA, the YWCA, the Hi-Y and the Salvation Army; and attendance at public lectures and forum discussions, unless Catholics "are advised by their pastors of the safety of participation." The Archbishop forbade Catholic students to attend baccalaurate or graduation exercises held in non-Catholic churches. In such cases the students had to receive their diplomas privately.[37]

Protestants could hardly claim that theirs was the one true church, inasmuch as there was not one Protestant church at all, but many. The Bible told them, "Judge not," but Protestants did it anyway. When they looked at Catholicism, it was difficult to see how the Catholics could make it to Heaven. The Catholic worship, the Mass, looked like an exercise in pure ritualism. Fundamentalists could find nothing of reconversion, of being "born again," their prerequisite to salvation. Catholics were forbidden to read the Bible, it was said, lest they might start questioning the priest. Catholics' behavior outside church was even more appalling. Did they not work on Sunday, violating the Sabbath? Did they not smoke, drink like fish, and gamble—practices condoned, if not fostered, by the church itself?

A Mississippian remembered the Catholic church in his town as "ominous . . . a frightening place." Going to church for a funeral, "watching those strange rituals and hearing those solemn litanies," provoked "such terror" that he could hardly stay.[38] The scholar of Plainville learned that Protestant townspeople believed Catholicism to be the most "unchristian" of all religions. As for Christian unity, it seemed far away. The Catholics would need to clean up their behavior and abandon their ridiculous theological arrogance: "When Catholic ecclesiastics learn to stoop and kneel, confess their error and repent like other mortals," *Christian Century* asserted, "the way to complete reunion of Christendom will be open."[39]

The differences between Catholic and Protestant rarely, if ever, produced anything in the way of overt hostility. Catholicism was mostly urban and Protestantism mostly rural, so many people had little contact with individuals of the other faith. The greatest opportunity for tension came when a young Catholic and a young Protestant announced that they wished to marry. A mixed marriage often became a traumatic experience, not so much for the young couple, it seemed, as for their families. Virtually all Christian faiths, and Jews as well, discouraged mixed marriages, as did most parents, whether religious or not. The most troublesome issue involved the status of children who came from the union; in what faith would they be raised? The Roman Catholic Church, unlike most Protestant sects, made official sanction and proper rearing of children articles of faith, a matter of good standing in the church and personal salvation. The Catholic demand for a signed concession from the Protestant partner remained an almost intolerable irritant. Sometimes the parties could not solve the problem and the relationship broke up.

A group of believers that managed to antagonize almost everyone went by the name of Jehovah's Witnesses. The group took its name from an interpretation of Isaiah 43:12—"Ye are my witnesses, saith Jehovah, that I am God"—and Acts 1:8—"Ye shall be witness unto me . . . unto the utter most part of the earth." Witness, then, is what they did, and in the most vigorous way. They placed themselves on street corners ready to talk to passersby and distribute copies of their publication, *Watchtower*. They went from door to door with the same purpose of spreading the word. People unwilling to stop and listen or accept the literature might have it thrust into their hands. Individuals answering the doorbell might encounter a phonograph record blaring in their face. As the Witnesses saw it, the end was so close at hand that no time remained for politeness or timidity.

Hostility arose partly from the aggressive campaigning—the Witnesses, to say the least, were pests—and partly from the message they sought to spread. Their theology came from God, of course, through teachings of the founder, Charles T. "Pastor" Russell, and the leader in 1941, "Judge" J. F. Rutherford. They argued that all religions were wrong and, because they diverted people from the true word of God, were also evil. Although Rutherford assailed Judaism and the Protestants, he reserved his harshest words for the Catholic Church, which he charged with being a political organization that "blasphemes the name of Almighty God, falsely and fraudently represents Him, carries on a racket in the name of Christ, and is the great enemy of God and of the people." Rutherford regarded Catholicism as subversive, "America's Fifth Column," training for the day it could take over the country.[40]

For all their fears of danger for the United States, the Jehovah's Witnesses refused to defend the nation or support its institutions. Members would not vote, hold office, salute the flag, or accept induction into the military forces. Believers could not worship a graven image, they said, and while not absolute pacifists, they could not fight until God gave the order. Insisting that everyone who "witnessed" (and all of them did) was a minister, all young men claimed exemption from the draft. The government denied the clerical exemption, but still the Witnesses would not go.

Not surprisingly, these people came in for insults, ridicule, and even physical assault. They were trying to "make hate a religion," an article in the popular *Saturday Evening Post* charged.[41] Townspeople burned their buildings in some places; in Texas a group of one hundred, which included women, children, and a woman of seventy-eight, were driven like animals several miles down a railroad track to the county line and left to fend for themselves in the intense heat of midday. "To say that they are subversive and a most pernicious menace to the American way of life is a magnificent understatement," a Catholic magazine said.[42] *Christian Century* conceded that they were "peculiarly aggressive, even obnoxious . . . close to disturbing the public peace." Nonetheless the journal deplored the physical abuse, fearing that it smacked of fascism in the United States.[43]

The Witnesses did not enjoy insults or being beaten, of course, and they sometimes sued to have it stopped. But they were not at all discouraged and certainly not willing to change. They knew it would happen, that mistreatment represented a further carrying out of prophecy. After all, had the Bible not warned in II Timothy 3:12 that "all that will live godly in Christ Jesus shall suffer persecution"?

The European war and the growing involvement of the United States presented churchmen with a serious new issue. While ministers understood that the Bible was not an absolutely pacifist document, most agreed that war was fundamentally immoral and justifiable, if ever, only in extreme circumstances. Many men who had been in the ministry in 1917 remembered how they had compromised their principles in World War I and had given support to the American cause. While at the time it had seemed the loyal and possibly the Christian thing to do, looking back with better objectivity led to a different conclusion. They now felt embarrassment and anger, and in the 1930s, when people had come to doubt the wisdom of fighting that first war, many ministers became determined not to repeat that first mistake. Some 13,000 had vowed never to support participation in a future conflict.[44]

As the war took shape in Europe and American opinion and policy gradually changed, some Protestant church people stood by their conviction. They helped organize or joined the Ministers' No War Committee, the Churchmen's Campaign for Peace Through Mediation, and other pacifist or isolationist organizations. *Christian Century,* probably the most influential Protestant periodical, remained to the end a sharp and bitter critic of Roosevelt's foreign policy.

One of the most impressive spokesmen for isolationism in high clerical circles was Harry Emerson Fosdick. A respected Presbyterian minister, Fosdick seemed anxious to cleanse his soul of errors of the past—those tragic days of 1917–18 when he had "twisted and turned," trying to reconcile war and Christianity, speaking against hate while arguing on behalf of slaughtering the Germans. Fosdick now understood the futility of "trying to make that oil and water mix," and he regretted using his Christian ministry "as though holloaing after the dogs of war were the function of the Church of Christ." He had learned from the experience: "Today when I picture Christ in this warring world I can see him in one place only, not arrayed in the panoply of battle on either side, but on his judgment seat, sitting in condemnation of all of us—aggressors, defender, neutral." Fosdick would support war only when the United States was attacked.[45]

Clergymen learned in World War II no less than in struggles of the past that morality lent itself to no single definition. They could follow the path of Fosdick and condemn all—or almost all—wars as a violation of Christ's teaching. Or else they might join countless Christians of earlier times and find war, this war, justifiable on grounds of patriotism or even an exercise in morality, a struggle against evil forces for a world in which Godliness could survive. The more the issues became open to public scrutiny and the United States became involved in the effort against Germany, the more Protestant ministers were willing to align themselves with the forces resisting Hitler. A leading Presbyterian observed that by 1941 most clergy had come to share his belief that aid for Britain constituted aid for the United States. "It is self preservation," he said. [46]

The most articulate rationalization of pro-involvement view came from Reinhold Niebuhr of the Union Theological seminary in New York. Faced with two interpretations of morality, Niebuhr knew which he preferred. German behavior, "fed by a pagan religion of tribal self-glorification," seeks to destroy religion, annihilate the Jewish people, and defy all Christian and humanistic standards of justice, he wrote. "If anyone believes that the peace of such a tyranny is morally more tolerable than war I can only admire and pity the resolute dogmatism which makes such conviction possible."[47] To propagate this point of view and neutralize strength of clerical isolationism Niebuhr introduced in February 1941 a new journal, *Christianity and Crisis*.

It is impossible to know what ministers in thousands of churches were telling their listeners. Many of them preferred to avoid discussing large questions of politics and diplomacy.[48] They probably pointed to war as an example of the world's wickedness and let it go at that. The issue did not involve a simple question of war and peace; nearly all ministers, including Niebuhr, hoped the United States could stay out. The problem was whether or not to support aid to Britain and other measures which, whatever Roosevelt had said, seemed to move the United States toward war. Protestant ministers were split on that issue, and while it is impossible to measure strength on each side, isolationism was stronger in the clergy than in the rest of the population.

The Catholics were also split, though less evenly than Protestants. Most of the Catholic press and probably much of the priesthood favored isolation. Aid to Britain received less support than with Protestants, if only because so many Catholics belonged to Irish, Italian, or German minority groups. A perception persisted in liberal circles of the Catholic Church as a friend of authoritarianism, if not fascism. Critics would point to the structure of church organization, to Catholic support for rightists in the Spanish Civil War, to the Vatican's earlier agreement with Mussolini and purported dealings with Hitler, and to the almost fanatical Catholic hostility toward Soviet communism. The rantings of Father Coughlin and priests who followed him fostered this impression. The Catholic Church, one scholar said, was "the strongest and steadiest force for appeasement in this country."[49]

Catholic spokesmen certainly would deny that the church endorsed fascism or that isolation represented appeasement. They argued that Catholics had no single mind on the war, that such prominent churchmen as Father John Ryan of Catholic University, George Cardinal Mundelein of Chicago, and Archbishop Francis Spellman of New York were strong supporters of the Administration. And if much of the Catholic press endorsed isolation, that position grew out of love for the United States and the Christian ideal of peace, not from support of fascism. "I would not believe [Hitler] if he took the Bible in one hand, the Cross in the other, lifted up his eyes to heaven and swore to God that he was telling the truth," the editor of *Catholic World* wrote. He nonetheless could not agree that this was a war to save civilization and Christianity. Only one factor could change his mind: "The Holy Father . . . will know when this war becomes a crusade. If and when he says, 'God wills it,' I will advocate risking everything."[50]

The Pope never gave the word, of course, and his followers in the United States would march to war anyway. Here was an appropriate commentary on the relationship between religion and politics. While both sides of the great debate over foreign policy invoked religion to bolster their case, the large decisions of government came from other considerations. So it was with the American people. The clergy and religious press articulated, agonized, and argued; the people for the most part made up their minds on different grounds. After all, how many had heard of Harry Fosdick, Reinhold Niebuhr, or John Ryan? How the people stood on such issues as isolation or internationalism, aid to Britain and later Russia depended less on religious affiliation or intensity of involvement—Jews probably to the contrary—than on being Irish, Polish, Italian, or German, followers or opponents of Roosevelt, or simply on an understanding of being an American. War, apparently, was something that belonged to Casear.

Religion in the United States on the eve of war continued to present a mixed picture. While generally endorsing Christianity and Christian principles, many people did not take religion intensely. They attended church either as a matter of course or not at all. America might be called a Christian nation at that juncture, but to say that America was a nation of Christians would be stretching the truth. Those who did pay heed to a faith did so with different levels of dedication, in multifarious ways, the differences marked by identification as Catholic, Protestant, or Jew; variations in the broad world of Protestantism; or conflicts in all three major faiths between traditionalism and agents promoting change.

As is often the case in history, events seemed to be shaping conditions more than people were. Even before war came to the United States, the changes war would bring could be detected: The evolution of attitudes and relationships was accelerated, forcing in a short time the confrontation of issues that otherwise might have taken many years. In a rush to emphasize the treasured values and principles of the United States, tolerance appeared high on the list. Another message common to this time of trouble and challenge, emanating from Washington and carried by radio, newspapers, even the movies, was the need for unity, for America to speak with one voice. While not exactly a petition to tone down one's faith, the appeal for unity at least encouraged rethinking claims to the exclusive possession of the truth. War would not end religious division in the United States, of course, but it did bring Catholic, Protestant, and Jew into a common cause, inducing many people to reexamine their prejudices. Genocidal practices in the regime of Adolf Hitler would magnify the meaning of anti-Semitism in a way previously unimagined. No one would want to be compared with Hitler. Already in 1941 Charles Lindbergh had learned that a charge of anti-Semitism, like anti-Semitism itself, could be a powerful force.

The war was thrusting people together in more direct ways as well. Internal migration of the civilian population mixed people of different religions more than ever before. A bedrock Baptist from Mississippi might work alongside a Polish Catholic in the "Dodge Main" plant in Detroit. Many a young man from Tennessee or Minnesota might come to know his first Jew and, in a surprising number of cases, his first Catholic in the Army, and while the encounter might not always go smoothly, before it had ended each man probably had a more enlightened understanding of the other.

☆

S E V E N

☆

Things of the Flesh

At a time when traditional religious attitudes prevailed in many quarters, Americans continued to face the familiar temptations of the profane world, most notably physical pleasure, now made more appealing and convenient by technical advances and the atmosphere of war. The prewar era, however, did not usher in a revolution in morals and social behavior. That revolution had already taken place in the 1920s, and while the spirit of cultural devilry had given way in the decade or so that followed to a conservative mood, or at least a posture of conservatism, not all the social vestiges of the era of prosperity and Prohibition had vanished. Some people alive in 1941 had been members of the scandalous generation of the Roaring Twenties, and having become forty, say, instead of twenty-five had not caused them to give up all their attitudes of earlier years. These people were more likely to be understanding of the next group of youngsters working their way across the social landscape than their own parents had been of them.

The new generation seemed willing and often eager to carry on quietly the activities its elders had advanced with such fanfare. Many of the forces that had fostered that earlier revolution, far from passing off the stage, had continued to expand as instruments of culture. Even so, there were still strong notions of right and wrong in large parts of the population, the effect of religion and a fundamentalist influence not necessarily measured in church membership. The more the United States came under the grasp of radio, movies, automobiles, mass-circulation media, and the pressures of an unstable world and the more items of culture spread to all sections of the nation, the more Americans had to reconsider a definition of a respectable, moral, and satisfying life. Activity might vary from place to place, from group to group, and certainly with differences in age, but in matters of social behavior much of the United States experienced a split personality, a conflict between what people felt an urge to do and what they felt they should do. It was a society marked with contradiction, gaps in knowledge, and no small measure of deception.

Not surprisingly, much attention focused on the behavior of young people. It was nearly impossible to know what teenagers were doing, now that the automobile had broadened, and made it possible to hide, their field of operation. Asked to explain activity the night before, a youngster might answer "nothin'" or identify such innocent pastime as going to the movies or "messing around"—responses vague enough to avoid the possibility of self-incrimination. Young people had learned long ago that certain information must be kept to oneself or within the clique. Adolescents in hundreds of places behaved much the same as in a small town in Illinois where a "conspiracy of silence" existed and much false representation about social activity. One young lady the Methodist minister believed to be a "paragon of virtue" sang in the choir, taught Sunday School, and never wore cosmetics to church, but at school she was a "smooth number" and a member of five clubs, who went to dances, "smoked, drank . . . and petted heavily." In this town, "young people band together . . . hide their activities from the minister . . . teachers and parents, and go happily with the crowd."[1]

What the adolescents were doing, of course, was seeking pleasure and responding to peer pressure in quest of acceptance and popularity. No one wanted to be called a "droop," "drip," "jerk," "drizzle," or "goon." How much better to be "solid," "classy," "in the swim," or "in the groove."[2] In living two lives, they had discovered what was hardly a new tactic for dealing with parents. Youngsters in 1941 would be neither the first nor the last group to practice deception on their elders. They would play the same games twenty or so years later with their children.

A definition of acceptable behavior depended upon many factors. On the whole, standards were more flexible in the city than in the country or small towns, although some of the wildest activity took place in the back country. Seeking loyalty to religious doctrine and acceptance of moderation and decency as defined by church fathers, the Catholic Church sought to sponsor the social activities of the parishioners. Fundamentalist Protestant sects rejected nearly everything considered recreation, from playing cards to movies to car rides, especially on Sunday. Many people found it difficult to walk that narrow path, and since a first break in discipline seemed to represent a departure from the faith, the offender might as well go all the way. Some of the most notorious sinners were backsliding Protestants.

Smoking and drinking remained for many the prime examples of improper, if not corrupt, behavior. Most Protestant churches roundly condemned both practices. Throwing away cigarettes was often the first act of resolve by a fundamentalist convert. The Catholic attitude seemed to be that smoking and drinking were harmful and needless habits but not in themselves signs of depravity or grave defiance of the church. If Catholics had to smoke or drink, they were supposed to wait until they were old enough, then do so in appropriate circumstances and moderate amounts; such conditions rarely were precisely established. "The Catholic church has never demanded anything but temperance from its people," a priest told his audience. "If you can take a drink and not get drunk, or if you take many drinks and not get drunk it is all right to drink; but if you take one drink and it makes you drunk, you shouldn't drink. . . . The thing to do is to be temperate."[3]

Young people should neither smoke nor drink; nearly everyone gave lip service to that rule. The first known violation often brought the most severe punishment youngsters ever experienced. Parents nonetheless understood that both practices were an inherent part of American culture, and sooner or later young men would probably want to see what they were like. Boys sneaked their first smoke at Lord knows what age, and the first taste of alcohol came not much later. Sometime in their teens they would notice that many of their friends were taking up cigarettes and beer, either as an occasional experiment or as a regular part of the evening's adventure. And of course one could scarcely ignore the magazines, movies, and commercial messages on radio suggesting the camaraderie and feelings of manliness that came from smoking Camels, Lucky Strikes, or Chesterfields, the most popular cigarettes of the day. The boys probably first bought a "cheapie" brand, however, such as Marvels or Twenty Grand for a dime, or Kools, the mentholated cigarette that did not bite the unconditioned tongue and throat so much.

A few young men might have tried making their smokes from a little bag of tobacco and a packet of cigarette papers. "Rolling your own," the cheapest way to smoke, was a special mark of character, the smoker's equivalent of "roughing it." Humphrey Bogart coolly rolled a cigarette in *The Maltese Falcon,* and rugged cowhands in Western movies could turn the trick with one hand. It took some practice, however, and the novice probably spilled more tobacco than he used, trying to pour it on the paper. When he rolled up the cigarette too loosely, more tobacco fell out, and the young man probably stood there with little more than a piece of flimsy paper in his mouth, looking somewhat foolish. Some young people, giving the matter serious thought, decided that they liked neither cigarettes nor identification as a smoker. For others, the date eventually arrived to come out of hiding.

Open drinking took a while longer, if only because of state liquor laws. Most states outlawed drinking before age twenty-one. A few states and many counties continued to prohibit the sale of alcohol, although in most cases the law was a mere fiction. While Mississippi, for example, a dry state, outlawed sale of all alcohol except 3.2 percent beer, people there liked to quip that the only difference with neighboring Tennessee, a wet state, was that in Tennessee one could not buy liquor on Sunday.[4] Others recalled the remark of Will Rogers that "Mississippi will hold faithful and steadfast to prohibition as long as the voters can stagger to the polls."[5]

It would be a mistake to imply that all male adolescents were trying alcohol. A rough survey of a town in Illinois suggested that approximately 40 percent of high school boys drank at some time during the school year, although the proportion for males who dropped out of school was much higher. Many young men doubtless entered their twenties and joined the Army having had little or no contact with liquor. Even so, drinking remained one of the most common, and most commonly denounced, diversions while moving through the teenage years, a sign of rebellion, of trying to grow up, or of conformity with buddies. When the date of accountability, probably the twenty-first birthday, arrived for these people who had been practicing in secret, a fellow knew what to do: "When a boy is able to walk into a tavern, order a 'shot' of whiskey, toss it off, shake a little, belch and say, 'Gimme another,' he has demonstrated to himself and to his associates that he is, indeed, a man among men."[6]

Girls were doing some of the same things. Not many years earlier, only the most daring girl would have tried a cigarette; now, it seemed, girls were smoking and drinking too, right and left. Girls started in much the same manner, and for the same reasons, as boys—secretly at first, as an experiment or because the other kids were doing it. And advertisements had not left out potential female customers. Tobacco companies had come to realize in the 1920s that a huge new market awaited if they could persuade women to smoke. If it could be masculine for the men, why not feminine for women, and sociable, in step with the times, for both sexes? One of the more interesting advertising campaigns rested on implication that smoking could be a beauty aide: "When tempted to overindulge, reach for a Lucky instead," an advertisement of the American Tobacco Company recommended. "Those who keep fit and trim . . . know that Luckies steady their nerves and do not hurt their physical health . . . that Luckies are the favorite cigarette of many prominent athletes who must keep in good shape."[7]

Men still smoked more than women, but the ladies—and girls— seemed to be turning to cigarettes in large numbers. Female smoking represented one of the most conspicuous social trends of the age. Curiously, the people most tempted stood at opposite ends of the social ladder. Low-class females smoked to show open defiance of social convention.

A lady or girl higher up in society who decided to smoke gave the practice a different dimension. For her smoking represented glamour, worldliness, even sophistication, as suggested in an advertisement featuring Lucy Carver Williams, "a member of a distinguished Boston family and, through marriage . . . connected with the Williams family of Rhode Island fame," who testified that she liked Camels. Advertisements for Philip Morris, a slightly more expensive cigarette, for years had featured tiny Johnny Roventini, a former page at the New Yorker Hotel. Always dressed in uniform with pill cap, Johnny appeared on many a printed page, and his familiar "call for Philip Morris" on radio suggested that Philip Morris smokers stayed at exclusive hotels.

Pressure for female smoking was considerable. Most actresses smoked and made a deliberate point of it in advertisements and on the screen. Smoking had become a tool of the acting trade; there were few moods or emotions that could not be made sharper through proper manipulation of a cigarette. Emily Post and others wrote about the etiquette of smoking, explaining proper and refined methods of performing each step of the operation, from lighting up to stubbing the cigarette out. Some health officials suspected that cigarettes might be harmful, many people still considered smoking unladylike, and most Protestant sects proclaimed that it represented the devil at work, but such objections had no effect on girls who wanted to be "in the swim" or sophisticated.[8]

Sales of alcoholic beverages and tobacco continued on a steady rise in 1941. The largest changes came in consumption of beer and cigarettes. Americans drank an average of 1 gallon of "fermented liquor" more than the previous year. They smoked 180 more cigarettes per capita than in 1940 and a remarkable five hundred (twenty-five packs) more than in 1935.[9] People were smoking more, evidently, but a better explanation for the increase is that more people were smoking. Reasons for the changes included greater availability of money to buy the items; a belief (or was it an excuse?), fostered by tobacco and alcohol industries, that smoking and drinking helped one deal with the tension of those troubled times; and relaxation of moral reservations, particularly with women.

Nonalcoholic drugs were another matter. Americans knew little about the remote world of narcotics, and what they knew came mostly from rumor. They had heard correctly that such drugs as opium, morphine, and heroin were addictive and potentially harmful to body and mind. Many people still associated opium with the squalor of a Chinese opium den. They might have heard that people in the entertainment business sought satisfaction of some sort—relaxation, or was it stimulation?—in something called cocaine. Those narcotics seemed to be almost child's play, however, compared with reports about another substance known by many names, among them grifas, grifos, greetas, miggles, mooters, Indian hay, and joy smoke. Most people called it marijuana, or marihuana, and it was the "killer drug."

Information available in 1941 placed marijuana in a special category, a mysterious substance that produced in the user a reaction of almost unimaginable grotesqueness. As one book described it: "Street lights become orangoutangs with eyes of fire. Huge slimy snakes crawl through small cracks in the sidewalk and prehistoric monsters, intent on his destruction, emerge from key holes and pursue him down the street." Having lost all will power, all ability to distinguish between right and wrong, the user was driven to crime, violence, and "revolting immoralities" and finally ended up insane.[10]

Some of the nation's most respected organizations had joined in the assault. The American Medical Association warned that smoking marijuana caused a bloated face, bloodshot eyes, trembling limbs, and eventually "imbecility and death by marasmus (progressive wasting or emaciation)." The journal of the AMA added that while it would be impossible to measure criminal activity—the "thrill murders" and "sex offenses"—that stemmed from marijuana, all "addicts" were prone to "wildest debauchery and sexual crimes." Small wonder that the Bureau of Narcotics called marijuana "the government's most formidable and versatile criminal outlaw."[11]

A frightened and outraged public had risen up against an impending evil. Parents cautioned children, and children probably cautioned each other, about having anything to do with "reefers" or the "dope fiends" who carried them. In New York Mayor LaGuardia appointed a special panel to study use of the drug in his city. By the end of 1941 the commission had not issued a report. Other agencies of government were not as deliberate. Most states outlawed all handling of the drug, and national legislation passed in 1937 imposed a $2,000 fine, five years' imprisonment, or both, for possession of any amount.

For the most part, however, white America had little reason for worry. Use of the drug was confined to a few groups, although within those quarters smoking the "weed" supported a lively underground business. Latin Americans and black people in most Northern cities used marijuana as a recreational drug on the order of alcohol. In Harlem, blacks visited an estimated five hundred "Tea Pads" or smoked a cheaper "sass-frass" on rooftops of tenement buildings. A few whites, both Jewish and gentile boys, knew where to go in the black districts to find inexpensive "tea," "gage," or "shuzzit." The black press in Chicago carried occasional stories of raids on "reefer flats" or "dens" where thrill-seeking "inmates" were said to participate in depraved and uninhibited behavior of many kinds. Most white people probably saw marijuana as a recreation of the colored people and hence beneath their dignity.[12]

There was one outstanding exception: A special association between drugs and entertainers, notably jazz musicians, had long been whispered about. Evidence surfaced in 1941 to give credibility to the rumors. When two members of Charlie Barnet's band died in an auto crash, authorities found marijuana on both men. Police in Detroit arrested a railroad freight checker identified as the nation's leading peddler of marijuana. He had on hand 51 pounds of finely ground "loco weed" that he had been selling for twenty cents a cigarette and $35 for a half-gallon jar. His customers, described but not named, included a film comedian, a singer, bandleaders, and musicians. Military officials had discovered that conscripted musicians had carried the "tea habit" into the Army and at one camp in Georgia were growing the plant in flower pots in front of the barracks.

Such disclosures prompted new efforts to suppress the corruptive practice. "The constant marijuana rumor is no good for us musicians," said Jack Ferentz, president of the musicians' local in Detroit. The publication of that organization added that "some of the so-called 'jazz hounds' who think that their talents show off the best when 'high' should take a trip to Eloise Hospital and see the . . . jibbering idiots who used to think it was fun to be taken out of the world of reality into a false sense of super-being. Now they can't think at all."[13] The union in Detroit voted to expel any member caught smoking marijuana. Government agents had begun milling about the bandstands, taking special note of break time, sniffing the air.

White Americans as a whole remained apart from the underworld of nonalcoholic drugs, protected by lack of accessability and devastating stories in the rumor mill. Most people had never seen a marijuana cigarette, a hard drug, or a "dope" addict, as far as they knew. Cole Porter's reference to cocaine in his popular "I Get a Kick Out of You" had meaning mostly to a few people in the song-writer's line of work.[14]

Millions of people went dancing for recreation. In rural areas square dances were held, and in the hill country frolics (a type of square dance). In cities, small towns, and much of the rest of the nation, dancers moved to the music of the big bands. The music might be slow, intimate, and romantic, like the foxtrot; precise and vigorous, as in a rumba, conga, or some other Latin dance; or almost frantic, as in the Lindy, jitterbug, or boogie woogie. Girls especially appreciated dancing. It was one of the few athletic activities suitable for females in that day and simply great fun. Boys and men danced too, if often with less competence than girls. It was not the most manly form of exercise, but some males took pride in their skill. Others put up with it and stumbled around on the dance floor as the price one had to pay for getting next to the girls.

Still, many people disapproved of the evening out that began at a dance hall or a roadhouse. For some, the dance itself had dubious implications. Dancing brought boy and girl (or man and woman) into close contact, a condition all too intimate and tempting for impressionable youth. Fundamentalists believed in arousing emotions, but that sort of arousal was definitely not what they had in mind. Some dances appeared obscene in themselves, particularly a lively jitterbug, which would include twirling, wriggling, tossing the girl in the air, and a general abandonment of inhibition that showed far too much of the female body. A Lutheran minister voiced the religious argument against dancing succinctly: "When the boy holds a girl in his arms, the Devil takes the place of his soul, and he doesn't see a sweet, clean pure creature in front of him. No, he sees only a scarlet woman there. Dancing makes a boy or girl into a fiend."[15]

A more common objection focused on activity growing out of the dubious setting. Many Protestants considered dance halls absolute dens of iniquity. Others said that dancing might not be so bad, but what else took place at the dance and afterward was unacceptable. With inhibition loosened by dance, the general atmosphere, and— worst of all—probably drink, what happened afterward? Fears of that sort had some grounding in fact. The scholar of Morris, Illinois, found the local dance hall to be the scene of fights and a place where young men would seek (and find) "easy marks." A dancing frolic in the Ozarks usually led to drinking, gunfire, and illicit relations between the sexes.[16] An observer of Kentucky's hill country entered a roadhouse, a "Jenny Barn," to find the jukebox blaring "Tuxedo Junction" and couples dancing a jitterbug "that for sheer carnality would have put Harlemites to shame." Whisky and dance mixed freely in these crude rural structures. Morals were "loose . . . brawls and shootings . . . frequent."[17]

The Catholic Church, a few urban Protestant denominations, many schools, and other social organizations sponsored supervised dances, with varying degrees of success. Denying the moral legitimacy of all dancing, fundamentalist Protestants cut themselves off from control of this popular activity, leaving children to struggle with themselves and their peers. Opponents of dancing seemed to be losing the battle, as the nation experienced almost a craze in 1941, crowding the halls and the dancing schools as well. The Arthur Murray studios alone had nearly 800,000 enrollees.

Other practices struck many people as being at least in poor taste and at worst evidence that society was heading for hell in a wheelbarrow. Movies remained enormously popular, but to some Protestants they belonged to the same category as dance: a corruptive force to be avoided absolutely. The Catholic Church chose to screen all productions and identify films safe for its charges to see. Respectable females of the early 1940s were supposed to refrain from wearing tight sweaters or other form-fitting clothes. The one-piece bathing suit had become a social issue. A poll in 1939 indicated that 63 percent believed it indecent for women to appear on the street in shorts.

Women who showed too much leg risked social repercussions and trouble with the law as well. With temperatures in the nineties in July 1941, women in Redlands, California, reached for the coolest clothing they could find, which in some cases amounted to very little. "There is a difference," the commissioner of police said, "between lewd conduct and a woman's appearance in shorts . . . lewdness and indecency will not be tolerated."[18]

Critics feared that each departure from a perceived—if not carefully defined—social standard, bad enough in itself, might mark a trend toward general moral relaxation. People who argued against dancing, scanty clothing, movies, and even smoking and drinking had a higher concern: that these expressions of moral deterioration would not stop until they had gone all the way. What troubled them most was misbehavior in matters having to do with sex.

Sexual conduct has been among the most sensitive of topics in American culture and for that reason the most difficult to measure. A foreign sociologist of the prewar era found an explanation in the "American Puritan tradition," which, as he saw it, "gives everything connected with sex a higher emotional charge."[19] Puritanism, or whatever conditioned the public attitude toward sex, in the 1940s did not necessarily control private behavior. There is reason to believe that sexual behavior differed from later, more open decades in American history less in amount and variety of activity than in the way the public handled the issue.

People did not talk openly about sex in those days, at least not much, except in uncouth circles and special circumstances. "I have always been hushed up about sex all my life," a lady from Philadelphia confessed in a first painful visit to a marriage counselor.[20] The sociologist in central Illinois quickly determined that if the people in town he had come to study learned he had even a remote interest in sexual behavior, he would have to stop his research immediately. He discovered that the "sex taboo" required that youngsters must not talk about the "forbidden pleasures" except to condemn them, for "to recognize their existence is bad, to condone them is abhorrent to respectable people, and to admit any knowledge of their violation is wicked." When another interviewer asked about contraception in Plainville, Missouri, he was told that "people here don't like to speak about that."[21]

Individuals who defied this unwritten code invited the wrath of an outraged public. Marjorie Myers, a coed at Oberlin College, could testify to that fact. She had written in the local college review that "marriage should not necessarily demand sexual fidelity or constancy" and that "when one ceases to find satisfaction in the other or wishes to exploit the physical attraction they may feel for others, sexual fidelity loses its importance." Those were fighting words for that day. The townspeople protested. Father W. C. O'Laughlin of the Oberlin Catholic Church insisted that the post office ban such "unadulterated filth" from the mails and begin criminal proceedings against writer and publisher. Oberlin, a prestigious liberal arts college, offered Marjorie a choice of leaving school or being confined to her dormitory after 7:15 each evening. The punishment, Oberlin officials said, was not for the writing but because she "necked in the parlor of her dormitory with the odor of beer on her breath."[22]

The conspiracy of silence, of course, was not absolute. A few people either broached the subject in a direct manner or took their children to specialists. Information about sexual topics, as with most aspects of society, continued along an evolutionary path; one could find a more open attitude and more printed material available than a hundred or forty years earlier, although perhaps not as much as during the 1920s. Individuals seeking fuller information could procure manuals on family life and the reproductive process. Professional journals and an occasional popular publication discussed more generalized problems of sexual conduct, usually confining their attention to behavior within marriage. The popularized medical magazine *Hygiene* published in 1941 a frank, illustrated series designed mostly for instruction of young people.

Sex education in public schools had become a topic of debate. A few colleges offered optional courses, although most did not. In ten states, mostly of the Northeast and upper Midwest, public schools provided some form of instruction in courses bearing such titles as Marriage, Health Education, Social Hygiene, and, best of all, "Family Arts."[23] Even in "progressive" states, no one dared call it sex. All other states opposed or refused to support sex education in the schools for various reasons, some of them having to do with the qualification of the instructors.

One teacher who found those objections valid provided interesting information about her profession. Because in most states a woman could not marry and keep her job (and because more than three-fourths of teachers were female) five of six teachers in the United States were unmarried. Of those individuals, one-third admitted unhappiness with single status, a statistic probably designed to suggest that teachers were sexually illiterate, frustrated, or worse. The teacher cited a survey purporting to show that during twelve years of school a student would be likely to have at least two teachers who were "neurotic or downright psychopathic." "Need I point out," she concluded, "what emotional twists our public schools might acquire were they taught the facts of life by random schoolteachers?"[24]

The evolution of attitudes about sex education thus had a good distance to go. Many people still considered writings about sex as nothing but filth; others who rationally might admit the need for better education could find no acceptable avenue of instruction. How could one talk about sex without, well, talking about sex? Learning through the confessional that young men were hearing "profane facts of life" from a doctor in a high school club, a priest in Massachusetts formed a separate club for Catholic boys and ordered them to withdraw from the high school association.[25] Many parents and other responsible people seemed determined that children receive no practical instruction about sexual matters.

Information about the "facts of life" theoretically came in the home. In truth, most parents were so ill prepared or embarrassed that they lapsed into gibberish, neglected the assignment altogether, or passed along misinformtion and prejudices received from their own parents. "I was so scared by what Mother told me Jim might do I did not like the experience at all," one girl remarked after her first date. "I know I was supposed to 'freeze up' . . . and I was so ready to 'freeze up' we walked all the way home without saying much. . . . I was so disappointed in that first date I did not have another for a year." Another fellow remembered his mother's response: "Such things are awful. I endure them only because of your father."[26]

Parents in Plainville and countless other places had no name for sex organs other than "it." For childbirth they concocted several familiar stories. Explaining menstruation was an uncomfortable business for women. They did not even like to say the word, preferring instead that they "felt poorly" or "that way" or simply were sick. Many still called it "the curse." Masturbation fitted into much the same category. Parents talked with considerable embarrassment about "playing with oneself" or "self-abuse," and how it was sinful or would cause pimples, stooped shoulders, blindness, or insanity. The U.S. Naval Academy, somewhat mysteriously, ordered doctors to reject a candidate who showed "evidence of . . . masturbation."[27]

The experience of Russell Baker was not atypical of the way youth learned about sex in the years before World War II. Baker's father had died when he was five, and his mother had little stomach for handling the responsibility. "With her old-fashioned Protestant view of life," he recalled, "sex was not a subject civilized people discussed openly around the house." He lived in dread of the moment she might try. He was spared the experience by the arrival of a distant relative, a handsome, worldy-wise young man called "Uncle Jack." Jack was not really an uncle, but the title stuck.

One day, when he was about eleven, Russell made the mistake of admitting curiosity about the origin of babies. When Russell's mother confessed that she had not got around to that subject, Uncle Jack offered to do the job on the spot. Uncle Jack ordered him upstairs, saying he had something to talk about, "alone."

"I went," Baker remembered. "The awful moment had come at last. I was going to be told the 'facts of life.' That was how everybody referred to sex—'the facts of life.' Nobody ever called it 'sex.' To call it 'sex' was to talk dirty. Upstairs I dropped onto the daybed to await the worst."

Uncle Jack took his time coming up, and when he did arrive he seemed uncomfortable, began walking around, looking everywhere except at Russell. Finally he spoke: "Do you think the Giants can win the pennant this year?"

Delighted with a reprieve from almost certain torture, Russell gave out a "torrent of arcane baseball speculation," which turned into a spirited debate as to the merits of the Yankees and Giants. When they had exhausted the topic of baseball, Uncle Jack knew he had to do his duty. He still looked ill at ease, paced the floor, looked out the window. Finally he turned to face the boy.

"Look here," he said, "you know how babies are made, don't you?"
"Sure," I said.
"Well, that's all there is to it," he said.
"I know that," I said.
"I thought you did," he said.
"Sure," I said.
"Let's go on back downstairs," . . .
"Did you tell him?" my mother asked.
"Everything," Uncle Jack said. . . .
That was my formal sex education.[28]

Youngsters learned about sex any way they could, mostly from peers and experimentation. Terminology had not changed much in recent years. Necking still applied to action that took place above the neck; petting involved enthusiastic probing, short of intercourse, from the neck down—how much and how far down depending upon the people involved, mostly the female. Some people called it "everything but." Sexual relations seemed self-explanatory, although it covered a broad range of activity. Besides the proper terms, the polite words, and strained efforts to avoid using any words at all, a special vocabulary circulated through what one might call the sexual underground, a subsurface channel of communication and social interaction that identified every aspect of activity, from becoming pregnant ("getting knocked up") to contacting venereal disease ("getting a dose"). Many words served to describe practices of intercourse.[29]

Some youngsters heard about sex at a remarkably early age. A researcher of Boston's streetcorner society discovered that children of ten knew all the swear words and had "a good idea of what the word 'lay' means." In Elmtown's lower classes, boys and girls had a "good working knowledge of the facts of life" by age seven or eight, and a few years later an older friend introduced boys to a "new sport." They knew enough to keep this knowledge to themselves, for fear of being called nasty and dirty, or of being punished.[30] Doubtless many youngsters learned about sex more slowly, at a later age; some knew hardly anything at all at the time of marriage. At any rate, the bulk of sexual education for all classes in all areas came from unprofessional sources and in such places as the street corner, the pool hall or local hangout, the barn, the general store, or the family car. Understandably, this education carried much misunderstanding, misinformation, and contradiction.

Women as a rule found intimate relations more mysterious and confusing than did men. Females generally felt less free to talk among themselves than males, so knowledge had to come from daring girls who would talk or the snippets of information Mother let out. Much came from what the boys told, or showed, them. Was sex largely for masculine pleasure, a tool females used to attract and hold a desirable companion? Mother might have left that impression. Many males certainly did not look beyond their own satisfaction. And what about the vernacular of the sexual underground? Were males not trying to "get it"? Were agreeable females not "putting out"? A rumor persisted that it was not supposed to be that way, that sexual relations should be an expression of mutual benefit, but many girls were not sure how satisfaction should come and how much there should be.

Women who had read or sneaked a peak at Ernest Hemingway's new novel, For Whom the Bell Tolls, probably recalled Robert Jordan's account of love-making, when his lover Maria agreed that "the earth moved." Was that the way it was supposed to be? Hemingway in fact had compounded a common perception in this memorable passage. Maria had been more concerned with Robert Jordan's satisfaction than her own, or, rather, her satisfaction came from pleasing her lover. "If I am to be thy woman I should please thee in all ways," she said.[31] Even so, it had been a moving description, and many women surely wondered why their experience had not been as exciting.

Females who by some means had found the way to sexual satisfaction—single ones especially—might find themselves the object of attention, smirks, and gossip. Word had a way of getting around. Men wanted enthusiasm in their lovers, but a female who enjoyed sex a great deal—well, there was something wrong with her. "A girl is not supposed to be a 'lady' if she admits enjoying the physical thrills connected with petting," one person explained.[32] A girl who acquired such a reputation soon discovered how it could affect her social life. Men would stop her on the street or came by her house to offer her a ride. They might arrange a time to call for her (with girls of this sort, one did not have legitimate dates), pick her up, and immediately drive her out of town. Their intentions would quickly become apparent. Boys were expected to "sow wild oats," but not girls. Maybe it was all right for a girl to "shop around," "enjoy life," and "look for Mr. Right," but how was she supposed to do that?

From a superficial glance at society, the girls were doing nothing, and neither were many of the boys, except for the blacks and low-class people who had no morals, or so it was said. On the surface conservative attitudes prevailed. The movies underwent rigorous censorship. Films and radio were cleansed of profanity and the loose and coarse vocabulary that ran through the sexual underground. One had to search long and hard to find copies of such explicit volumes as D. H. Lawrence's *Lady Chatterley's Lover* or Henry Miller's *Tropic of Cancer* and *Tropic of Capricorn,* banned from publication for many years. National polls expressed overwhelming disapproval—more than 80 percent—of premarital sexual activity. The message could not be more clear: Boys and girls should save themselves for wedlock.[33]

People able to probe beneath the veneer of society discovered, as they expected, that while sexual attitudes varied a great deal, much more went on than immediately met the eye. Virtually every researcher who exercised enough patience, tact, and peristence discovered a lively underground activity in the area under investigation. The boys in the Italian slums of Boston spent much of their time talking about and looking for "lays." "The sex taboo is violated by many students," an observer of high school youth in a Midwestern town reported, "but the percentage was not ascertained for even to talk about such things was tabooed." Relying on gossip, rumor, and now and then a confession, he concluded that most student couples from lower social and economic groups who dated steadily were sexually active. That is not to say that only those people engaged in sexual activity; less worried about reputation, they were more willing to talk.[34]

Popular perception identified promiscuity with lower social and economic groups: in the slums and tenements of any large city, dilapidated sections of small towns ("the other side of the tracks"), the impoverished cropped-out parts of the countryside, and black settlements wherever they were. The assumptions often were correct in such places of little money, limited recreation or privacy, and little concern about social convention or tarnished reputation. "In the idleness of the hill country, sex assumes tremendous proportions," a student of the Appalachian region explained. "Sexual intercourse is . . . vital, taken for granted, and indulged in at early age. . . . The virtue of the married man and woman is no more unsullied than that of the unmarried."[35]

The middle and upper classes—the respectable people of society— also experienced a split personality, but it was difficult to spot and nearly impossible to measure. While such individuals had the same temptations as youth in lower economic strata, they all understood the value of a good name. Respectability, after all, allowed them to look down upon others. Religion helped insulate some people from the ravages of sin; with others it increased the agony of indecision. If privileged people strayed, they covered their tracks as much as possible, denied everything, and maintained a posture of absolute righteousness. The investigator in such places as Elmtown could not break through the barrier erected by these people, and he dared not press too far. He could tell from gossip, rumor, and a few factual clues that a good deal was going on, at least with the children of the town's respected citizens.

☆

Pursuit of sexual pleasure (or curiosity) of course carried risks that went beyond conscience, religion, and social pressure. People anxious to reduce those risks could choose among several contraceptive devices and techniques. A national survey of married women published in December 1940 indicated that 17 percent used no birth control; 18 percent tried "simple" methods, such as "safe time" or coitus interruptus (if, indeed, one can call such techniques contraception); and 65 percent used other methods. The "Big Four" included douches, jellies, diaphragms, and condoms but, of course, no pills. As expected, Protestants practiced contraception more than Catholics, and Jews most of all.[36]

The Roman Church, of course, maintained an adamant opposition to birth control. In such states as Massachusetts and Connecticut, Catholics did not hesitate to influence public policy. A law on the books in Massachusetts since 1879 still made it illegal for doctors under any circumstances to give out information about contraception. The church could not have been pleased with results of the recent survey. The 23 percent of Catholics who claimed to reject all contraception of course would receive high marks; on the other hand, 43 percent admitted to using the most popular "artificial" methods. Church officials probably also wondered about that 34 percent who used "simple" methods.[37] Which simple methods? The only practice consistent with church doctrine involved efforts to identify the "safe time" in the female cycle, the "rhythm method" sanctioned by the Pope in 1930, also called "Vatican Roulette."

Unmarried couples who engaged in sexual activity probably used a male contraceptive, if anything. Known by such names as condoms, prophylactics, safes—most people called them rubbers—these devices were available at drugstores, in the pharmaceutical area, hidden behind the counter, and at places well known in the sexual underground. Single girls had less access to contraceptives than males, and few would have procured them had they been available. Only the men's restrooms at gasoline stations had vending machines that for the proper coin tumbled out a little package marked "Sold for prevention of disease only," which symbolized the deception of the age. Buying contraceptives at the drugstore was embarrassing enough for men; for women it was virtually unthinkable, and for one to do so would have reddened the face of many a pharmacist who guarded them.

After all, advance preparation would be a confession of premeditation, and few girls were willing to admit—even to themselves—that they planned to have illicit intercourse. To be swept away by music, mood, excitement, or even alcohol was one thing; to proceed calmly and deliberately to the sex act was something else. "No nice girl will go up to a man's room," a member of Boston's street society said. "If you take her out in the car, that's all right. If she goes up to your room with you, she's really a bum." The investigator correctly concluded that "even the most promiscuous like to maintain the pretense that they do it seldom and never in such a premeditated fashion."[38] A woman's determination to protect an image of herself doubtless constituted a cause of premarital pregnancy. If the fellow did not bring along a means of protection, the couple took their chances.

Illicit union at times did lead to pregnancy, of course, and then the wayward girl might encounter responses ranging from pained acquiescence to threats and proclamations of calamity. Location, social standing, and religion had much to do with the reaction of family and friends. Most black communities looked upon illegitimacy as too bad, maybe shameful, but the sort of thing that happens. White people in the hill country reacted much the same way: "[V]ery little stigma is attached either to the girl or to her illegitimate offspring.[39] With much of white America, illegitimacy was an absolute disgrace, so steps were quickly initiated to soften the blow or hide the fact altogether. The logical solution was marriage, in which case local gossips could start counting. Many young men acceded to wedlock, either because they wanted to or felt they should. Reluctant fellows might feel a nudge.

In some cases the parents of the girl in trouble did considerable nudging. The sociologist in Morris, Illinois, had an opportunity to observe an episode that demonstrated that the day of the shotgun wedding had not passed. It began when a "mildly hysterical" country girl named Martha walked into the office of the prosecuting attorney, her ankle-high men's shoes soaked, her legs covered with mud and coal dust. The story unfolded that she was pregnant and had told her family. A great deal of expostulation and hand-wringing had failed to produce a decision on a course of action—until, that is, the father came home for lunch. He knew exactly what he wanted. "When I come home, if you aren't married, I'll kill you both," he screamed, and for emphasis gathered up his shotgun and a box of shells as he went back to work.

That warning started Martha on her 7-mile trek on foot to town, arriving in an understandably excited state of mind. She wanted justice. Agreeing that the time for action had come, the prosecuting attorney sent a deputy sheriff in search of the person identified as the guilty party. A young fellow soon pulled up in a truck. He admitted that he had "been with her a few times." "I'll marry her," he said, "but I won't live with her. The kid isn't mine."

"When do you intend to marry Martha?"

"Now's as good a time as any. I gotta deliver that load yet tonight, so let's get goin' . . . the old man means business."

Martha, her newly established fiancé, the prosecuting attorney, deputy sheriff, and resident scholar then trooped as a party to the clerk's office for a license, and from there to the office of the judge. After a short ceremony the judge solemnly announced: "Young lady, you are a married woman now."

Martha grinned.

"Is that all?" asked the boy. "Can I go now?"

Told that the ceremonies were over, he turned, put on a grimy cap, and bolted for the door.

He pulled away in the truck.

Martha started walking back home.[40]

Statistics seemed to verify the popular belief that promiscuity was a malady of society's lowest classes. The Bureau of Census reported more than 83,000 illegitimate births in 1941, approximately 41 for each 1,000. For white people the rate was 19 per 1,000; for non-whites, 174.4. Nearly 50,000 illegitimate children were nonwhite, mostly black. For the most part, the highest rates for whites came in states with low income: West Virginia, Virginia, New Mexico, Maine, and Vermont.[41] The numbers probably would have been much higher had all births out of wedlock found their way into the record books.

Nonetheless, government statistics did much better at measuring illegitimacy than sexual activity. The higher a person was on the social and economic ladder, the more determined he or she—or, just as likely, the family—would be to hide mistakes. Such people probably made better use of contraception in the first place. An unmarried mother might come from the other side of the tracks and the father from a better neighborhood. People in Plainville began to gossip when an upper-class boy dated a "lower-element" girl, because "everybody knows what he's after." "For an upper-class girl to have a date with a lower-class boy would be inconceivable." A researcher in Elmtown detected "a strong tendency for young . . . males to exploit lower class females sexually."[42] While rumors persisted, the young man often managed to escape culpability. No one kept statistics on "unmarried fathers." Middle-class parents might send a pregnant daughter out of town to a relative or a special home; at least she dropped from sight and returned fresh and slim several months later. They might find an abortionist. One estimate set abortions at 500,000 a year, all of them illegal, performed usually by "borderline M.D.s."[43]

The standard treatment for impending illegitimacy was marriage, usually to the father of the child, although other noble young men sometimes volunteered, perhaps because they mistakenly believed they were responsible, perhaps out of genuine affection for the girl in trouble. Martha's child would be born legitimate, as would all children of mothers married before the time of delivery. The number of cases of induced wedlock, of course, could not be determined. The scholar in Morris pursued the time-honored practice of month-counting in cases of ninety recent marriages. In 55 percent he found little question that the gossip had been true; in 12 percent a baby was born eight to nine months after the wedding, so judgment had to be inconclusive; a third group of fourteen couples left the state and could not be monitored, but when they returned for a visit, lo and behold, eleven couples had a child with them. The evidence seemed clear in 20 percent of the cases that marriage had come before conception.[44]

By the eve of World War II, sexual activity had started to become an object of professional curiosity. Known to few people, and not with the unanimous approval of colleagues, a small number of professional researchers were trying quietly and tactfully to pry the lid off this forbidden topic as a part of an inquiry into communities or specific social groups. One ground-breaking investigation focused exclusively on the sexual behavior of the American people. The project had begun in 1938, when Indiana University offered for the first time an undergraduate course on marriage. The man who became coordinator was a middle-aged, conservative-looking (and living) professor of biology, Alfred T. Kinsey, known in narrow academic circles as an expert on the gall wasp. As Kinsey delved into sexual aspects of marriage, a new field of academic and human concern began to unfold. He came to realize that there had been much less professional examination of human sexual activity than, let us say, that of gall wasps. Teaching logically led to conferences with students, and in short order Kinsey began recording "sex histories" of people who agreed to participate in face-to-face interviews.

News soon circulated on the campus and around the small southern Indiana town of Bloomington. "Grapevine" publicity produced an upsurge of enrollment in the course on marriage. Kinsey believed the students came not because of potentially "racy" subject matter but out of genuine intellectual curiosity and a desire to remedy their abysmal ignorance about an important aspect of their lives. Other people on campus and in town had doubts; a professor of bacteriology complained that the slides Kinsey used were "even stimulating to me." Members of the local clergy protested the teaching of such matters to Bloomington's youth. Many people wondered about what went on behind the closed office door of the stodgy Alfred Kinsey when a pretty coed came in and started discussing explicit aspects of sex.[45]

Pressure from many quarters, mostly the clergy, caused Kinsey to resign from the course in September 1940. The move, which doubtless came with regret, had the result of leaving more time for what had become Kinsey's major interest: case studies of human sexual behavior. He collected a small staff, continued recording "sex histories," and eventually established the Institute for Sex Research at Indiana University. Although willing to take interviews almost anywhere he could get them, he sought samples of people in many age groups and from different levels of society. Several fraternities and a few sororities at Indiana volunteered the cooperation of their full membership. Kinsey traveled to cities in the Midwest and the East. "Have been to Halloween parties, taverns, clubs, etc., which would be unbelievable if realized by the rest of the world," he wrote. "Always they have been most considerate and cooperative, decent, understanding and cordial in their reception. Why has no one cracked this before?"[46] By the end of 1941 Kinsey had histories of 2,535 individuals. By 1947 there would be 12,214. Kinsey published the results of his long study in two massive, scholarly, highly controversial books: *Sexual Behavior in the Human Male* (1948) and *Sexual Behavior in the Human Female* (1953).

Those volumes presented not an account of activity in the 1940s or any given year, but a description of sexual behavior during the lives of people surveyed between 1938 and 1947 (in the case of females research continued to the early 1950s). The "Kinsey Report," so intimately associated with the postwar era—the late 1940s and the 1950s—largely dealt with activity from an earlier period. While Kinsey made no claim to having described the sexual behavior of all Americans, he hoped that his findings contained a representative account of activity in the United States. Whatever the shortcomings of the Kinsey report, no fuller description of sexual activity on the eve of World War II exists.

Kinsey discovered no revolution but a steady exploitation of sexual outlets under way at least since the 1920s. The generation that followed World War I had expanded sexual behavior substantially, and the succeeding generation had maintained the pattern. If there had been a change at all in the 1930s and early 1940s, it was to step up the pace of activity.[47] If people in 1941 had learned the extent and variety of practices in their society, they would have been at least as shocked as the Americans first exposed to the reports in 1948 and 1953, and no less willing to accept them.

A few samples tell the story: Kinsey reported that nearly 50 percent of all females who married experienced premarital intercourse.[48] In the case of males the proportion ranged from 67 percent of men who went to college to 98 percent of men who had finished only eighth grade. Thus, in relation to the rest of society, the colleges were not—as popularly perceived—dens of iniquity after all. By age forty, approximately 26 percent of married women admitted extramarital relations; 40 percent of men with high school or college education had been unfaithful to their wives. Roughly 62 percent of females and well over 90 percent of males at some time had had masturbatory experience. Nearly everyone, male and female, petted before marriage. The volumes also described a variety of sexual experience that struck many readers as absolutely unbelievable.[49]

Kinsey presented his findings in dry, scholarly language and filled his pages with formulas, charts, and graphs. Some readers might have concluded, much to their surprise, that a book about sex could be almost dull. Nonetheless, it was a sensational publication, and the significance for life in America approaching mid-century, including 1941, shone through. Kinsey's volumes suggested that in sexual behavior people during the 1940s did almost everything that later generations would think of, and they did it practically as often. But from the way they acted, one could never tell.

It is not likely, however, that they approached the activity in the same fashion as individuals in a later era who experienced less inhibition and pressure for restraint. People in 1941 felt the pull of conscience, church, and family, the need to avoid standing in open violation of social convention. If they yielded to temptation, many still believed their behavior was wrong or at least did not want others to know about it. The scholar of Elmtown's youth, doing research at the same time as Kinsey, explained that American culture had resolved the contradiction over sex through a "clandestine complex" that enabled people to release tensions secretly and at the same time maintain public dignity and a good name. That is, they did one thing and said another, but not, the scholar concluded, "without compromising the mores and creating serious personal and social problems."[50]

☆

The split personality—the conflict between social standards and social behavior—was not made better by prevailing attitudes toward divorce. The Catholic Church loudly attacked divorce, especially if followed by remarriage, as a deadly serious offense. One could confess other sins; it was hardly satisfactory to confess divorce. While Protestant churches did not make divorce a cause for damnation, they disapproved of the breakup of marriage. Much of the middle and upper classes looked upon divorce as a disgrace and clear evidence of personal failure; it could be a cause for dismissal from a job, an occasion of financial disaster, and a humiliation for the families of the people involved.

Many people continued to look at divorce as a plaything of the frivolous and unprincipled—the movie stars, for example, and rich people who had nothing better to do. Americans smiled at the mention of Reno, Nevada, immediately recognizing the place wealthy women went for a "quickie" divorce. They laughed at the antics of Tommy Manville, a playboy who seemed to be perpetually getting into or out of a marriage. Tommy took his fifth bride in 1941, a twenty-two-year-old showgirl he had met four days earlier. "We're glad we waited until we were sure," the groom remarked. Before the year was out, only seventeen days after the wedding, Mrs. Manville had arrived in Reno. "We were tempermently unsuited for each other," she said.[51]

The trends, even for divorce, gave many people reason for concern. Dissolution of a marriage was becoming more common and in some places easier to obtain. Most states still demanded a residency requirement of one year; it was five in Massachusetts, and in South Carolina, which had no divorce law, one evidently had to wait forever. Other states, in an obvious attempt to attract the divorce business, softened demands on applicants. Idaho matched Nevada's forty-two-day residency requirement; in Wyoming it was sixty, in Florida ninety.

Grounds also were changing. All states continued to respect the most common causes: adultery, desertion, and alcoholism. In Maryland evidence that a wife had been "unchaste" before marriage and in Virginia proof that the lady had been a prostitute could set a man free. Florida now honored "a violent and ungovernable temper" and "extreme cruelty" as grounds for divorce—causes so vague as to permit the citation of almost any offense. Miami had passed Reno as the nation's capital of divorce.[52] Americans ended 293,000 marriages in 1941, a rate of 2.2 per 1,000 population. While the statistic was not nearly as high as it would later become (in 1978 it would be 5.2) and represented only approximately one divorce for every six marriages, the trend since the early 1930s had been steadily upward.[53]

Even people who objected to divorce in principle probably would concede that certain circumstances warranted bringing a marriage to an end, as in the case of Mrs. Mae Katt of Chicago, a gray-haired forty-eight-year-old "with the husky build of the champion bowler she is." Suspecting her husband of unfaithfulness, Mrs. Katt hid in the trunk of his car. The philanderer drove not to work, but to pick up another woman, and proceeded to ride around from 8:30 to 1:00 A.M., and Mae was able to hear every word they spoke. "What made me the maddest," she complained, "was that every time the woman mentioned me, she'd call me 'old Nuts and Bolts'—and then they'd both laugh." Mrs. Katt, who weighed 191 pounds, sued her husband after spending four days recovering from carbon monoxide poisoning. She won her case: a divorce and $15 a week alimony.[54]

Women experienced the split personality, the entanglement of moral restrictions and the impulse toward social adventurism, even more than men. Women were held more strictly accountable to traditional standards of morality and at the same time were urged by forces of temptation—usually by men—to give them up. Society continued to accept the notion that young men would do all they could to encourage their dates toward intimacy, and it was up to the girl to say no. Advertisers tried to pull women every which way, depending upon what companies had to sell. It might be toward behavior traditionally considered part of the man's world, such as smoking and driving cars. As a rule, however, the popular media operated within a framework of stereotypes, accentuating distinction between the sexes.

Problems of recent years had not encouraged the concept of equality of the sexes. The nation had not had enough jobs for men, let alone women, in the 1930s, and a working female with a working husband was keeping a breadwinner out of a job. She should be at home; her place was there anyway, especially if she had children. National polls of the 1930s repeatedly reflected this mood. The public approved of women's serving on juries but disapproved (by 2–1 margin) of a woman's holding high government office. In 1939, 67 percent approved a bill (introduced in Illinois) that would prohibit women from working in business and industry if her husband made more than $1,600 a year, and 56 percent supported (31 percent opposed) a measure in Wisconsin to bar from state and local government the wives of men earning more than $1,000. A poll in Detroit in July 1941 showed that 61 percent believed a married female teacher should resign or be fired.[55] Unlike some towns in Michigan and many in other states, the Detroit school system did not release women who married while on the job. It did refuse to hire married women.

In several ways the conditions of 1941 were serving to strengthen traditional views of sex roles. Reviving an image of men as soldiers, the bearers of the most stringent and dangerous burdens, fed the notion of women as helpers, with a special duty to support the warriors. The draft had introduced new dimensions to social relationships, causing some to break up with the departure of the male and providing others a new rationale (or excuse) for heightened sexual activity. Others moved abruptly into marriage. A young wife who went to work, or stayed at her job, bore the risk of jeopardizing her husband's deferment, which in most cases was based on dependency. The most common consequence of the year's events probably was confusion, although it became clearer each month that the old pattern of social relationships could not last.

If 1941 was not a time of activism or of a substantial feminist movement, changes in the status of females continued to filter into American culture, because of either evolution in social behavior or new conditions emerging from a world at war. Some women worked outside the home, of course, because they wished to or had to support themselves. Females made up 25 percent of the work force. The small feminist movement that had survived the Depression continued to press for women's rights. The National Federation of Business and Professional Women's Clubs endorsed, as it had many times before, the Equal Rights Amendment, then languishing in Congress. The movement continued to suffer from the division that had been a plague since the 1920s. Many professional women opposed all legislation that distinguished between the sexes. Others, such as the anthropologist Margaret Mead, believed that some women needed special protection of laws regulating female labor.[56]

Women agreed that the new conditions opened new opportunity and that in the industry growing out of military rebuilding women should have a place "not as a woman, but as a citizen and a human being." "We do not expect to see . . . a boxer in a knitting factory, nor a woman on a tractor," the head of the Federation said, "we expect those controlling the program to use common sense in the discernment of individual fitness for jobs." Here and there evidence that females were moving into new areas appeared. Consolidated Aircraft announced in July a program to train four hundred women for light machine and assembly work. For the most part, employers remained hesitant to depart from traditional notions of female frailty in the industrial workplace, fearful of unleashing multiple unknown forces.[57] The large transformation in employment of women would start in 1942; then came the deluge. The coming of war would promote, as one scholar said, "a greater change in women's economic status than a half century of feminist rhetoric and agitation."[58]

Meanwhile other changes continued to seep through. The growing popularity of pants, or slacks, as convenient if not attractive female attire also carried symbolic meaning. If men refused to accept responsibility for living clean lives, women—or some women—demanded an equal right to be sinners. Indulgence in the social vices might seem a dubious way of promoting the Constitution and Declaration of Independence, but smoking, drinking, premarital sex, and extramarital sex were areas where equal treatment for all citizens had plainly been neglected. Females undertook those activities partly because they wished to and partly because men were doing them, although an equally persuasive explanation probably was that the men wanted them to. While American manhood continued to endorse in theory the principle of feminine purity and to protect a special "man's world," male beneficiaries of adventurous female behavior did not mind at all when their companions joined them in "a little fun."

To say that 1941 came at the end of a period of social conservatism does not mean the United States had reverted to a time before the ascendancy of conservative attitudes. A nation never returns to an older era. Changes had become so absorbed into the culture that they ceased to merit the attention received when they were introduced. Necking in automobiles and other adventurous activity—so novel and scandalous in the 1920s—remained commonplace with youth in 1941. One did not find in that year the daring, illegal drinking of the 1920s, when all drinking was illegal and much of it daring, but there was drinking nonetheless, and the pace was picking up. Consumption of cigarettes per capita had approximately doubled from the 1920s. If women seemed to be more traditionally oriented, and if most of them seemed prepared to accept identification as the "weaker" sex, they were doing more of the things that men were doing. Absolute equality might not have been an announced goal—most women would have denied it was a desirable goal—but in an increasing number of cases masculine behavior provided the standard women sought. Females were on the edge of a virtual revolution in dealing with work. In social attitudes the year 1941 had markings of a time that had passed and an age that was to come. It was the time in between.

Another America

Of the forces affecting outlook, income, and general character of life in the United States, nothing was more important than color. From most points of view it was best to be white in prewar America. While a white skin offered no consistent guide to thought and behavior and no guarantee of success and prestige, being something other than white substantially lessened one's chances for developing individual capabilities and living a life of comfort and respect. For nonwhite people, and most conspicuously for black Americans, 1941 belonged more to the past than to the future. In social and economic relationship to the whole of society, in the perception and treatment by the white majority, the status of blacks had changed only slightly, if at all, in recent decades. The most meaningful commentary on black people in the United States involved not how far Negroes had come but how far they had to go.

And yet, if one looked closely and correctly interpreted developments in that time of transition, it might be possible to see signs of the future. The war had created a new situation to which black people, ever so slowly in some cases, were beginning to respond. All the forces instrumental to change in years to come—movement out of the South, the need for manpower in military and civilian industries, a recognized connection between wartime objectives and civil rights, black activism, and, by no means least important, an awakening of interest on the part of the national government—were to put in an appearance before the year was out. The year 1941 was not a time of revolution in civil rights, but seeds of revolt were being planted.

By government definition, "nonwhites" fell into only a few categories. Approximately 70,000 people of Chinese descent lived in the Chinatowns of a few large cities, notably San Francisco; 130,000 Japanese-Americans lived in the United States, mostly on the Pacific Coast, the bulk of them in California; there were approximately 335,000 "native Americans," or Indians. The government in 1940 had counted 377,433 Mexican-Americans in the United States. There were of course many more, perhaps ten times as many, and while the government considered people of Mexican origin white, their circumstances fitted the category of nonwhite.[1]

Each of those groups struggled to survive in white America. The Japanese, largely by their own efforts, did best; the Mexicans and Chinese also persisted, if on a lower social and economic level. American Indians, largely isolated on reservations in the West and plagued with almost every possible social and economic malady, barely survived. If generally insignificant in numbers, these racial minority groups had made and would continue to make huge contributions to American culture. They also were a reminder that when it came to race, the United States in truth was not a melting pot.

There was, of course, a better reminder. In nearly all circumstances a mention of nonwhites, a minority group, or a race problem referred to the status of black people. Blacks constituted easily the most numerous and visible racial minority group, and the most embarrassing challenge to America's perception of itself. In an estimated nonwhite population of 13,671,000 (not counting Mexicans), nearly 13 million were black, just short of 10 percent of the population. While Indians and people of Asian ancestry were largely isolated and segregated, Negroes could be found nearly everywhere in the South. In the North it seemed almost impossible to travel to a large city or anywhere by train or bus without seeing evidence of this distinctive feature of the social landscape. Blacks held many service jobs in the cities: elevator operators, maids or janitors, the "Red Cap" porters or pullman attendants on the trains. One rarely saw a black bus driver, but Negroes were almost always in evidence around bus stations and railroad terminals, waiting for transport, doing the menial work, or trying to hustle a few pennies by shining shoes or performing other personal service.

Whether they lived in the North or the South, black people stood at the bottom of the social and economic ladder. In Wasco, California, for example, where only a small number lived, Negroes ranked far below Japanese, some of whom were not eligible for citizenship, and beneath Mexicans, some of whom had entered the country illegally. Black people usually worked at unskilled, menial, low-paying jobs, and many kinds of work were out of reach for them. Professional athletics, an area that in time would provide a path to distinction and financial success, remained mostly closed off. Boxing had started to open up—Joe Louis was an obvious example, and young "Sugar" Ray Robinson was about to become one—but baseball, the most prestigious and popular sport, kept them out absolutely.

Evidence to document black economic and social depression was everywhere. Blacks had less education than whites; a remarkably large number had finished not a single year. Black people lived mostly in shacks in rural areas or worn-out, poorly maintained tenements in cities, at least three-fourths of which lacked significant plumbing. The infant mortality rate was nearly double that of whites and the maternal death rate more than double. Negroes had substantially higher rates of crime for all but a few upscale offenses, such as counterfeiting. More than half the people executed in 1941 were black. Blacks could expect to live an average of twelve years less than whites. A contemporary scholar concluded in 1941 that in every aspect of economic measurement blacks stood many times worse off than whites, and "comfort, home ownership, job security, and the enjoyment of finer things of life are absolutely out of the realm of possibility of the majority of Negro families."[2]

There were, as always, exceptions to the rule. Each black community needed teachers, doctors, shopkeepers, and professional people, who acquired a higher standard of living. A few people in the North worked in the same places—in the auto factories, for example—as white employees. A decent proportion of those better-paid people finished high school and probably insisted that their children get a diploma. One black person out of a hundred even had graduated from college. Black men were making a mark in literature and the arts and in academic fields, especially sociology. Still, the upper and middle classes had only a minimal statistical effect on the general quality of Negro life. They were, according to one black writer, "like single fishes that leap and flash for a split second above the surface of the sea—are but fleeting exceptions to that vast tragic school that swims below in the depths, against the current, silently and heavily struggling against the waves."[3]

The years of the New Deal had produced spotty evidence of change. A small number of blacks found better jobs, a good portion of them with the government. The largest change probably came from incorporation of many black people into various government relief programs, such as aid for the aged, the disabled, and dependent children. By the spring of 1941, 16 percent of workers for the WPA were black. No one was likely, however, to equate relief with racial progress; it did not mean an end to poverty. The Northern states gave higher relief payments than the Southern states, where most blacks lived; the Southern states paid higher benefits to whites than to blacks. The black Mississippian who qualified for old-age assistance could count on $84 for the year.[4]

A foreign scholar then engaged in a massive study of the problem would identify what he called an "American dilemma" as a conflict between the "American Creed," the widespread endorsement of high moral and political principles, and the reality of how whites went about their dealings with black people.[5] To put it in much simpler terms: the Americans did not "practice what they preached," not when it came to blacks. If virtually all people realized that black people lived in poverty and were objects of prejudice and discrimination, they blamed the condition at least partly on the blacks themselves. They understood as well that such problems stood outside the mainstream of life in the United States. Politicians in the North saw nothing to gain from addressing the issue of race, except in the most general way. Politicians in the South dared not advocate any change in the status of the race. Other problems, such as the war, the economy, and the draft, seemed more important. The injustice suffered by the black people was, in the popular perception, an old and complex problem that related mostly to the backward Southern states. It was best not to dwell on such matters. Civil rights as pertaining to racial conditions was an issue whose time had not come.

A presumption of black inferiority manifested itself in the myriad images, stereotypes, and terms of reference that made up white perception of the black. The first clue to a white person's attitude was what he or she chose to call members of this large minority group. The terms most accepted on both sides, used commonly in formal discourse and the public media, were "Negro" and "colored." Everyone, of course, was familiar with "nigger." Most white people and—curiously—nearly all black people used the word at some time. Its use by whites was invariably construed as contemptuous, and black people took offense when they heard it from a white. "Nigger" was a coarse word, and many whites who refrained from its use were concerned more with their own dignity than with that of black people. Other derogatory labels, such as "darky," "spade," "dinge,"

and "shine," all alluded to black people's appearance. To be called "black" would strike many Negroes as a definite insult.

In the North all the labels circulated, from the most insulting to those meant to convey honor and respect. The choice of terms in the South constituted part of the racial code of conduct. Addressing black people by Mr. or Mrs. was forbidden, except in unusual circumstances—a rule followed in newspapers—so Southern whites might refer to a black man by his first name, if they knew it, or by "Jack" or "George." Use of "professor" or "perfesser" seemed sufficiently ambiguous, as did "uncle" or "auntie." Every Southern black man at some time was "boy," even if he was ninety. "Nigger," the most common term, might be inappropriate for Southern whites who had no desire to offend, whereas "Negro" sounded too much like Yankee speech. A cross between the two, "niggra," became for such whites an acceptable compromise.[6]

A special literature had grown out of the separate place of the black in society. "Nigger" jokes dealt with several themes, chiefly ignorance, irresponsibility, and superstition. Figures of speech like "sweatin' like a nigger at an election" were popular. Rural youth played with a variety of slingshot identified as a "niggerkiller." Little rhymes and jingles, handed down over the years, remained much a part of culture in the United States. They were repeated automatically, with no thought of their implications:

> Eenie, meenie, minie, moe,
> catch a nigger by the toe.
> If he hollers make him pay
> fifty dollars every day.

Stereotypes characterized blacks as irresponsible, if not degenerate, in social behavior, highlighted by a notorious sexual laxity that rates of illegitimacy and veneral disease appeared to substantiate. Like anything having to do with sex, this information mostly circulated through society's undercurrents, in ways intended to ridicule. Reports told of the strong skill and sexual capacity of Negro women, the "tigress" myth. Males reportedly possessed a virtually irrepressible sexual urge. Stories from the underground, which often seeped to the surface, credited all black males with remarkable credentials. Talking to the "boys" at the barber shop, a farmer in Texas compared a rattlesnake he recently had killed to the sex organ of "ole Joe Louis."[7] A researcher encountered many people in the South, including several physicians, who held "absurd ideas about the anatomical characteristics of the Negro people."[8] Popular accounts blamed all interracial sexual activity on instigation by the black, and a belief persisted that blacks of either sex would go to considerable lengths to obtain a white partner.

The most grievous violation of prevailing mores had to do with relationships between white women and black men. The danger of such contact constituted for white people the most serious manifestation of the problem of race, occupying the first rank in what Gunnar Myrdal called the "order of discriminations" in the United States. According to whites, such relationships almost never occurred voluntarily, unless the woman was "white trash" eager to flout social convention or earn a great deal of money. In the North, the sight of a white woman and a black man walking together along the street would provoke at least a second look or a disapproving glance, even from, as one scholar put it, "a liberal-minded Northerner of cosmopolitan culture and a minimum of conventional blinds." The white woman probably faced such social ostracism that she either tried to keep the relationship secret from white peers or gave up on the white community and threw in her lot with the blacks. Such interracial contacts in most cases involved "sexual experimentation in bohemian and radical circles" or white prostitutes who catered to Negro men.[9]

In the South, that form of racial mixing was downright dangerous—for the white female and particularly for her black consort. The relationship had to be kept in secrecy as absolute as possible. A white woman discovered in such a situation (if her participation was unquestionably voluntary) was looked upon as abnormal, ostracized, and run out of town. Her black partner, at the least, would be whipped and ordered to leave. If he realized that he had been found out, he might have already skipped the area. For the most part, Southerners contended that no white woman would have anything to do with a black man, so any such contact had to be explained as a result of black aggression. Every black male thus became a potential rapist. The female could save herself by charging the black with assault. "It's God, woman and country with us and no niggers are going to touch our women," a policeman in Georgia said.[10] Interracial marriage was not only socially unthinkable; it was illegal throughout the South, in Indiana, and in all but five states west of the Mississippi River, thirty states in all.

In the recent past, the black man's punishment for sexual advance (or for being accused of it) on a Southern white woman had been prompt and predictable: death, usually by lynching. That method of private or "mob justice" no longer seemed fashionable by 1941. The government listed only four cases of lynching that year, all of them, incidentally, of black males. Doubtless there were other cases— lynching was not the sort of activity that one rushed to report— but the practice clearly was falling into disuse. A national campaign to outlaw lynching had gained considerable strength, although Congress had not been willing to act. The decline did not necessarily mean a change in attitude toward sexual aggression by Negro men. More acceptable alternatives now included shooting the accused man on the spot or working through the legal system, secure in the knowledge that Southern juries would not fail to convict and order quick execution of black defendants accused of a sexual crime.

Other stereotypes pervaded American society, extending to all aspects of life, including entertainment. Listeners laughed at such black radio characters as "Beulah" or "Birdie" on the Gildersleeve show or "Geranium" with Judy Canova. Good-natured, strong, and in many ways admirable, these ladies also were maids, servants to white people. Cartoons and films projected blacks with large lips and enormous eyes, easily frightened, easily satisfied, on the order of the youngster "Buckwheat" in the popular *Our Gang* comedy series. "To the movie addict," a student of the business wrote, "Negroes are lazy, light-hearted mortals who tap dance on the slightest provocation and are prone to burst into spirituals during a thunderstorm."[11] Lincoln Monroe Perry, better known as "Stepin Fetchit," at some time played all the authorized Negro roles.

On the screen black men kept their distance from white women. One black writer pointed out the implications of the film industry's code of conduct: "Nobody protests when Dorothy Lamour or Joan Crawford caresses a monkey, or ape, or kisses a horse on the neck." In *King Kong* a gorilla picked the clothes off a white woman. "But if in the place of a brute a human with a black skin perchance is substituted," the writer continued, "then all of the flames and fires of hatred and prejudice will be aroused and the conflagration which is destroying the souls of men will be unloosed upon its mission of murder and infamy."[12]

Eddie Anderson, Jack Benny's valet "Rochester," succeeded by projecting familiar images. Rochester liked pork chops, watermelon, grits, everything associated with the black man's appetite. He was as lazy and irresponsible as he could get away with being—not above occasional bouts with the bottle, cavorting with ladies (the black ladies, that is), or carrying a razor. Black people accepted Eddie Anderson's role on radio with little worry about racial insult; they enjoyed his sassiness and his clever manipulation of the boss, perhaps the most they could hope for in that age. While Rochester remained the most popular black entertainer, he also was the carrier of a social message: Success for blacks must come in prescribed circumstances, virtually never in competition with whites.

At times, white people insisted upon portraying blacks themselves, making it possible to fashion Negroes exactly as they wanted. Nearly every town or school put on minstrel shows, with whites appearing as blacks, singing traditional music and performing skits that projected Negroes as slow-moving, superstitious simpletons. There were dozens of "Rastus" stories. Al Jolson's rendition of "Mammy," with blackened face and exaggerated eyes and lips, remained one of the most familiar performances in the country. Millions of people listened to Freeman Gosden and Charles Correll, both white, performing as blacks in *Amos 'n' Andy,* the radio program that purported to project black life in Harlem, with subliterate dialogue and the lackadaisical pursuit of simple pleasures and absurd ambitions, as expressed in such "representative" people as Lightnin', Sapphire, Kingfish, and, of course, Amos and Andy. The following discussion between George "Kingfish" Stevens, the shiftless loafer, and his shrewish wife Sapphire projected many racial stereotypes:

SAPPHIRE: George Stevens, I done made up my mind that I'm gonna have a husband that dresses good, knows nice people, and is got a steady job.

KINGFISH: Sapphire, you mean to say that you is gonna leave me?

SAPPHIRE: George, I know why you're a no-good bum. It's on account of your association with Andy Brown. Why don't you meet a nicer class of men?

KINGFISH: Well, I ain't got da opportunity to meet 'em, they's all workin'.

SAPPHIRE: Well, that Andy Brown is the cause of it all. What has he ever accomplished?

KINGFISH: Well, yesterday he had a run of thirteen balls in da side pocket without leanin' on da table.

SAPPHIRE: Now, that's exactly what I mean: Andy hangin' around a pool table all day. Why don't he go to a cultured place like a public library?

KINGFISH: They ain't got no pool table there.[13]

Eliciting humor from real or imagined aspects of Negro life did not by itself constitute an injustice. White society also produced its funnymen, self-ridicule, and silly people. Stereotypes served to characterize many groups of people other than Negroes. As a rule, however, white society could manage balance and proportion in describing itself. There was no pretension that ethnic or occupational shortcomings represented the whole person or the group. In the case of blacks, the unfavorable image was virtually all that existed. For many millions of Northern and Western whites, racial imagery kept alive perceptions about a people with whom they had little or no contact. Many—probably most—white people grew up convinced that a lower position for blacks was part of the natural order. The stereotype perpetuated a condition that the stereotype had helped create. Prejudice had helped depress blacks in the first place, and now low standards of income, education, health, and morality reinforced the view that black people were inferior. Myrdal wrote that "white prejudice and Negro standards . . . mutually cause each other."[14]

The public perception, then, was that the black man's world was in no small measure what he made it, and for all its shortcomings, it offered special rewards. However distasteful the urban slums of the North and rural slums of the South might appear to whites, those conditions suited the black man's temperament. In the catchy "I Got Plenty O' Nuthin'," written in 1935 for *Porgy and Bess,* George and Ira Gershwin had made poverty in Negro life appear altogether charming and enviable.[15]

If whites lived with a dilemma, a consequence of their treatment of blacks, Negroes had a different "American dilemma" growing out of an urge to emulate a society that had done so much to suppress them. What had evolved was behavior so racially distinctive as to constitute, in some thinking, a separate culture. Ever the black nationalist, the novelist Richard Wright saw his people seeking a society apart from the whites. "We . . . developed a secret life and language of our own," he wrote. Black people built different speech through voice inflection, honeyed drawls, and hurried pronunciation, assigning words new meanings: "We polished our new words, caressed them, gave them new shape and color, a new order and tempo, until . . . they became our words, our language."[16] Some whites agreed that black people had become distinctively different in personal relationships, in attitudes toward work and pleasure, and in aspirations and goals.

In most respects however, black society constituted less a separate culture than a modification of white society, the changes directly or indirectly attributable to the depressed status of this large minority group. If some American music, such as jazz, grew out of the black experience, Negro musicians also drew heavily from the whites. If big band swing music was a white invention, some of the "biggest" big bands were black. Denied access to professional baseball, blacks developed parallel leagues, played in the same parks, and often used comparable names: New York Black Yankees. Negroes went to the white man's movies, wore suits, ties, and dresses (indeed, they often outdid whites in contemporary fashion), hoped for the day when they could own a car, and worshiped the same God in churches as similar to the white establishments as a shortage of funds would allow them to be. If it is possible to speak of a black subculture, or two subcultures, both were modifications or contorted imitations of the society that surrounded them. "American Negro culture is not something independent of general American culture," Gunnar Myrdal wrote. "It is a distorted development, or a pathological condition, of the general American culture."[17]

Most black people did not like the idea of being black. Not that they openly expressed a desire to be white; a "white nigger," the person light enough to "pass," carried little honor in black culture. Most communities had tendencies toward being "partial to color," or "color struck," that is, they disapproved of dark skin, kinky hair, and pronounced Negroid features. "I prefer a light person for a sweetheart or a wife," a young fellow in Chicago explained. "They are more affectionate . . . attractive, more intelligent." "Black is the very worst color you can be," a girl in the South said. "I really think colored people are worse to black people than white people are.[18] Negro publications carried advertisements for Nix Liquid Bleach Lotion or Nadionola Bleaching Cream, which promised to turn "dark unattractive skin to a lighter, lovelier shade . . . that men openly admire, women secretly envy."[19] The object was to be not white, but brown. "Light brown is the best," Sarah Tuck from North Carolina said.[20] Chicago's blacks truly were not black, so one could surmise from the title of their part of the city; they called it Bronzeville. Heavyweight champion Joe Louis was the "Brown Bomber."

To improve their appearance and, indeed, to resemble whites more closely, blacks performed various cosmetic operations. James Baldwin remembered "mercilessly" scrubbing his skin and "attacking" his head with Vaseline, combs, and hard brushes because "it was shameful to have 'nappy' hair."[21] The best prospect for change came in hair-straightening, an elaborate operation known in some circles as a "conk." Malcolm X, the charismatic black nationalist during the

1960s, recalled a much different phase of his life in 1940–41, when he acquired his first conk in Boston, administered by his friend Shorty. Following Shorty's instruction, Malcolm purchased the prescribed supplies: Vaseline, two combs, a pair of gloves, two eggs, two medium-size white potatoes, and a can of Red Devil lye. "Going to lay on that first conk?" the man at the store asked. "Right," said young Malcolm, a broad grin on his face.

Shorty mixed and stirred the concoction. "Never use a metal spoon. The lye will turn it black," he cautioned in words that scarcely could have been comforting. "It's going to burn when I comb it in—it burns bad. But the longer you can stand it, the straighter the hair." Shorty began to work the solution in, and suddenly, Malcolm explained, "my head caught fire. . . . My eyes watered; my nose was running. I bolted to the washbasin . . . cursing Shorty with every name I could think of." Shorty tried to calm him down: "You get used to it before long."

Glancing in the mirror, Malcolm observed a transformation that "after a lifetime of kinks" was "staggering."

> On top of my head was this thick, smooth sheen of shining red hair—real red—as straight as any white man's. . . . I vowed that I'd never again be without a conk. . . . I had joined that multitude of Negro men and women in America . . . brainwashed into believing that black people are "inferior"—and white people "superior"—that they will even violate and mutilate their God-created bodies to try to look "pretty" by white standards.[22]

When black people went the other way, when they modified white behavior or created new forms, they often endorsed and perpetuated images and stereotypes that whites associated with the Negro. What whites might see as raucous, brazen behavior, blacks looked upon as spontaneous, relaxed, and expressive of genuine emotion. "This race has the greatest of the gifts of God, laughter," wrote W. E. B. Du-Bois. "It dances and sings; it is humble . . . it loves women. It is frankly, baldly, deliciously human in an artifical and hypocritical land."[23]

Malcolm X made a similar observation watching dances while working as shoeshine boy at the Roseland Ballroom in Boston. The white people danced mechanically: "left, one, two; right, three, four . . . as though somebody had wound them up." When on rare occasion the blacks had the place to themselves, a different scene unfolded before young Malcolm's eyes: "They'd jampack that ballroom, the black girls in wayout silk and satin dresses and shoes, the men sharp in their zoot suits and crazy conks, and everybody grinning and greased and gassed . . . flinging high and wide, improvising steps and movements," until one couple after another, exhausted and drenched in sweat, stumbled off the floor.[24]

Richard Wright explained such behavior as a consequence of oppression. Because whites had shut them out of art, education, and other avenues of expression, black people found outlets in new "violent forms of dance," speech, and "wild, raw music." In the process of escaping oppression blacks created a new culture, making "the principle streets of our Black Belts—Lenox Avenue, Beale Street, State Street, South Street, Second Street, Auburn Avenue—famous the world over."[25]

Black spokesmen agreed that their people were more sensual and less inhibited in love and sexual relations. They explained the difference in the black ability to relax, the willingness to be open, honest, and "human." "We . . . frankly want the bodies of our mates and conjure no blush to our bronze cheeks when we own it," DuBois wrote.[26] Malcolm X conceded that black men sought out white females, especially blondes. When white girls attended Negro dances in Boston, "a lot of black girls nearly got run over by some of those Negro men scrambling to get at those women." Malcolm's blonde companion was for him "a status symbol of the first order."[27]

Blacks made no effort to challenge white people's stories about the special sexual competence of black men. They widely believed that most women secretly wanted black lovers and that many white women actively sought them out. As a boy in Lansing, Malcolm watched white girls cross the bridge that separated the Polish neighborhood from the black area. "Lansing's white women . . . were famous for chasing Negro men," he recalled. Malcolm's friend Shorty boasted that he "had a few" before leaving Lansing—"them Polack chicks that used to come over the bridge." "Here," in Boston, he continued, "they're mostly Italians and Irish. But it . . . ain't no different nowhere—there's nothing they love better than a black stud."[28]

No effort to resolve the black people's dilemma had proved effective. Stressing "blackness" only served to reinforce racial ideas that seemed to justify subjugation. Besides, a thriving and truly separate black culture was not possible within the American environment. Efforts to imitate whites verified notions of white superiority while creating self-doubt and much frustration. The whites clearly did not want black people to be truly a part of their society. Different people would follow different paths, of course, but the collective black personality in 1941 remained split: part African, part American, each providing small measures of satisfaction, the two together failing to bear robust fruit.

Black American society on the eve of World War II was predominately Southern. Approximately 10 million of the nearly 13 million black people in the United States, more than 75 percent, lived in the deep South or the border states. Negroes made up slightly more than one-fourth of the Southern population, although in the state of Mississippi they were almost half, and in some counties they formed a majority. In an area bound by tradition and habit that considered its blacks necessary and their continued subjugation just as necessary, relations between the races changed slowly. What had evolved— what continued to prevail in 1941—was the Jim Crow system, discriminatory racial practices and segregation enforced by law and sustained by a political structure in which black people had no part.

Separation in the South extended to most areas. Seventeen Southern and border states maintained dual school systems. There were separate churches, restaurants, theaters, waiting rooms, and drinking fountains. Buses or streetcars might have movable signs designating areas "For White People" or "The Colored Race." In the absense of instructions it was understood that whites should be seated from front to rear and blacks from the back forward. In no case must a black person sit forward of a white. As a rule the farther north one traveled the less pronounced segregation became. In Baltimore whites and blacks used the same waiting rooms in bus stations. Many department stores maintained separate elevators for blacks and whites, although some places might have only one. The availability of toilet facilities at gasoline stations remained a problem for patrons unfamiliar with the area. Could black people use the rest room? Were there separate facilities for blacks? Every new stop was an occasion for speculation and often embarrassment.[29]

What was not prescribed by statute was ruled by an etiquette of race relations that extended to nearly every social custom. Whites were not supposed to eat with blacks, invite them for a social visit, or shake hands with them. The black must not for any reason approach a white man's house by the front door. An expatriate white Mississippian recalled a time as a child when he had become seriously ill. Because no white doctors were available, the family called in a Negro physician, who proceeded to save the young man's life. "Which door did he come in?" the man asked years later. "I declare," said his grandmother, pausing to remember. "I believe he came around back."[30]

The consequences of Jim Crowism, of course, went beyond the psychological impact of separation. As a rule, coaches, waiting rooms, and schools, all facilities set aside for the blacks, were old, ill equipped, and poorly maintained. It could have been, as one observer claimed, that Negro education had made "tremendous strides" in recent decades, as witness an enrollment surpassing 45,000 in such black colleges as Fisk, Tuskegee, and Hampton Institute. But those strides had come from a starting point of nothing at all in the way of education for Negroes. Despite much recent discussion of the need to improve, if not equalize, educational standards, Negro education remained distinctly inferior to a white system that ranked among the lowest in the land. Less than 30 percent of Negro teachers had four years of college training; in the case of whites it was approximately 53 percent. White teachers in 1940 earned $1,193 in Louisiana; their black counterparts received $504. Black teachers in Mississippi could count on $235 for a year's work. More than 54 percent of black Alabamans had less than five years of school; nearly 14 percent failed to finish one year.[31]

A student of race relations in the South could "hardly believe his eyes and ears" as he observed the primitive buildings; the lack of equipment; the untrained, poorly paid teachers; and the "bottomless ignorance of the students" in one-room Negro schools. He described a rural setting not far from Atlanta where students ranged in age from six to seventeen. The teacher, a frightened, sickly girl of about twenty, said she had been to high school. No student knew who was President of the United States; none had heard of such black leaders as Walter White or W. E. B. DuBois. One young man knew about Booker T. Washington: He was "a big white man." While several students could identify Joe Louis and Ella Fitzgerald, only one had heard of the Constitution of the United States; it was, he said, a newspaper in Atlanta. Gunnar Myrdal added that a good portion of rural black schools were "at, or near, this cultural level."[32]

Another researcher calculated that 60 percent of Negro schools had only a single teacher and that 230 counties in fifteen Southern states provided no high school for black students. "I sincerely wish we could do better educationally for our young Negroes," Senator Theodore Bilbo of Mississippi said, "But . . . the Negro in the balmy

Southland, 'perpetuates' at so rapid a rate that our public school systems are constantly faced with new problems in providing schooling."[33]

The entire social and legal structure rested upon a political system also firmly in the hands of the whites. Black people could not change what they had not created; they had no political power. The whites would not let them vote. Of more than 3 million adult blacks in eight states of the deep South, perhaps 80,000 to 90,000 managed to participate in the election of 1940. The methods of disfranchisement remained almost as varied as they had been for a half-century. While the poll tax had already been abolished in North Carolina, Louisiana, and Florida, a literacy requirement, which could use trick questions or compel answers to difficult questions, remained popular. Negroes nearly always failed the test. The black person seeking to register might learn that the forms "had run out" or that he should go to another place, or wait for the registration board. In addition to those standard methods, one nearly always could find members of the courthouse gang or other husky whites willing to greet the black man who showed signs of seeking the vote. Usually, "What do you want here, nigger?" would be enough.[34]

If the system seemed cruel to outsiders, to most Southerners it was simply the way things were or an expression of divine will. "I don't think God meant for a superior race like the whites to blend with an inferior race and become mediocre," a Southern physician said. A Mississippian later able to manage better objectivity explained that as a young man he never questioned or tried to understand his relations with local blacks. "The broader reality was that the Negroes in the town were there," he wrote; "they were ours, to do with as we wished."[35]

Black people responded to these conditions in different ways. Nearly all resented white arrogance and the subjugation of their people. "Maybe all white people ain't alike," Essie Mae Jones said, "but I don't like none of them." Most intolerable were the poor whites—the rednecks, crackers, wool hats, swamp rats—who thought being mean to Negroes gave them status. In the words of one black man: "These old peckerwoods—clay eaters—ain't got a thing but a lot of tobacco to go in their jaws. . . . They think they are better than the Negroes around here. That's the thing that makes me sick."[36] A few Southern blacks developed hatred almost too intense to be restrained. Rebellion, however, came at great risk and was almost certain to bring punishment. Such blacks probably would soon leave the South.

Most Negroes acquiesced in a system they could not change or effectively challenge. "Papa told me how to get along with white people," a girl in North Carolina recalled. "He say, 'Don't raise your voice but talk quiet like. . . . Let them have their way.'" Mary Hopkins said that when she rode the bus, "I jes' go on to the back. That's the place they got for us. You don't never get in trouble like that."[37] Some Negroes would flatter a white man by calling him "judge," "colonel," or "lawyer." Another stratagem involved clowning, playing the fool, jiving (jibing), appearing ignorant. A Negro driver who ran a red light told the policeman that he had seen white folks going on green and thought the red was for coloreds. As much as possible, Southern black people handled racial discrimination by avoidance, lessening its impact by reducing contact. Middle- and upper-class people acquired cars as quickly as possible, if only to avoid the humiliation of travel on public transport. "The farther they is from me," one fellow said, "the better I like it."[38] Segregation, it turned out, could work both ways.

Separation represented only one feature of a society designed to maintain a sharp distinction between the races. An equally significant expression had to do with economics. The most common form of economic activity for Southern blacks, of course, was agriculture. No generalization can serve to describe the status of all Negro farmers. Some—in Virginia approximately 60 percent—owned their land; a few earned reasonably comfortable incomes, several hundred dollars a year. The large majority of black people in agriculture continued to be impoverished, landless wage hands, sharecroppers, or engaged in some variation of tenant farming. In no group in the United States was poverty more widespread or blatant.

Black farmers experienced the problems familiar to Southern agriculture while gaining few of the benefits that recent changes, such as mechanization, had brought to some farms. The cycle began in spring, when the cropper renewed an oral agreement with the owner of the land. In return for the use of 10 or 15 acres and an advance for supplies, the tenant promised one-half the crop. From that point he had to contend with the forces of nature: soil that probably was depleted, the boll weevil, the unpredictability of weather. When those had passed, he still had to deal with the lord of the land. The landowner kept the books, and the cropper had to accept his statistics. Black people had a little poem to fit the occasion:

A naught's a naught,
five's a figger;
all for the white man;
none for the nigger.[39]

To clear several hundred dollars was virtually unheard of for a tenant; in the area around Harmony, Georgia, the average cash income was $150. Approximately one-third of Harmony's croppers ended the year in the hole.[40]

Understandably, no comfortable living emerged from such an income. Finding food often became a pressing problem. The staple provisions were fat hog meat, coarsely ground cornmeal, and sorghum molasses. The best-provisioned months came after settlement time, from October to Christmas (assuming there was a settlement), when the family might have a little money and some goods stored from summer, and from March to July, after the advance for the new crop. The times of skimpiest rations came during January to March and July to October. During those months families of sharecroppers found food wherever they could. Much of the time they simply had to "strap it"—tighten their belts.

Ladies' Home Journal, in one of its series of articles, "How America Lives," focused on the plight of a black family in Warren County, Mississippi. The man and wife each had brought children into a second marriage, and so sixteen people now lived in a three-room shack. They slept in four beds. The walls had no decoration other than newspapers. The fireplace filled the house with smoke, but the family was used to that, and in summer the smoke helped keep out mosquitoes and other flying varmints. The father hoped to make $50 from the year's cotton crop and perhaps pick up an odd day of work, for 90 cents, during the winter months.[41]

Even that miserable existence had been put in jeopardy by the forces of change. Mechanization arrived slowly in the Southern states, but it eventually did come, particularly to the trans-Mississippi area. Tractors and machine-drawn implements, such as the mechanical picker, pushed blacks and whites off the farm. Government programs had not been as useful as New Deal reformers had hoped. As much as he would have preferred to stay, the Southern black felt compelled to leave the land.

By 1941 the typical Southern black was an urban dweller. No more than 45 percent still lived on farms; the rest had come to town, marking the character of nearly every community. In Yazoo City, Mississippi, for example, where black people made up approximately half the population, they could be seen everywhere on the town's sidewalks or riding slowly along the streets in wagons pulled by draft animals. Black men cut the grass and did janitorial work for whites, and women came around to the back of the house to pick up the week's wash. On Saturday the main streets overflowed with black people talking and laughing on the corners or going in and out of the cafés that would let them in. "Their shouts and gestures and the loud blare of their music were so much a part of those Saturdays," a former resident remarked, "that if all of them had suddenly disappeared the town would have seemed unbearably ghostly and bereft."[42]

The vast majority of black people did not find urban life a great deal better than what they had left behind. The small professional and middle classes that could manage better conditions led conservative lives and in many ways imitated their white counterparts. They could not, however, escape the consequences of the South's social system. A black lawyer, doctor, or professor from a school such as Tuskegee Institute in Alabama, probably received a measure of respect from the white people who dealt with him regularly, but the lowest "peckerwood" could call him "boy," "nigger," or anything he chose. And if he rode the bus he had to go to the rear. Every town had at least one Negro district that went by an appropriate name: Niggertown, Smoketown, Darkytown, Cabbage Patch, Little Africa. Invariably they were the worst parts of town, near the railroad tracks or the dirty industrial areas. The buildings were old and in need of repair; few had an indoor toilet—at least one that worked—and even fewer had a bath. The owner lived somewhere else, and the only time he showed up was to collect the rent.

Work, if any could be found, usually consisted of the dirtiest, hardest, lowest-paying jobs available, work that reinforced the black people's subordinate status. One apparent advantage of moving to town was that it opened an opportunity for female employment as maid, cook, nanny, or some other type of domestic servant. In many cases the female was the only person who could find work, a fact that did no good for the ego of the male or the solidarity of the family. The family also found itself faced with stresses customarily associated with city life—the attractions of crime, vice, and loose living in general. Whether they lived in town or on the farm, they were still black, the South was still the South, and it seemed that it would stay that way forever. Could they do anything about it?

Well, they could go north. "I've never been there, but I like it from the way they describe it," a young man in Mississippi remarked. "You wouldn't have to work like you do here, and you have more freedom. . . . I know I'd like Detroit, and I'd like to go now."[43] They could still hear that little song that had been circulating in the South for several years:

> *I'm going to Detroit, get myself a good job,*
> *Tried to stay around here with the starvation mob.*
> *I'm goin' to get a job, up there in Mr. Ford's place.*
> *Stop these eatless days from starin' me in the face.*[44]

And so they headed north, as black people had been doing since at least the time of World War I. The traffic had never stopped, although it varied from year to year, and the start of another war soon would cause the pace to quicken. "Going to New York," a man recalled, "was good-bye to the cotton fields, good-bye to 'Massa Charlie,' good-bye to the chain gang, and, most of all, good-bye to those sunup-to-sundown working hours." In the North they would live in a house with electricity, running water, and all the latest conveniences. As they planned the trip they broke out the old spirituals, such as "Jesus Take My Hand" and "Hallelujah, I'm on My Way to the Promised Land."[45]

The trip north by train was strange and probably an unnerving experience for people leaving the home county for the first time, and an equally large shock awaited once the traveler reached the destination, where he expected to live perhaps the rest of his life. One city dweller explained the revelation as follows: "It seems that Cousin Willie in his lying haste had neglected to tell the folks down home about one of the most important aspects of the promised land: it was a slum ghetto . . . a dirty, stinky, uncared-for closet-size section of a great city."[46] Virtually all the 3 million Northern blacks lived in separate sections of a town or city that had taken a special name. Most black people in New York lived in Harlem; in Detroit many went to a place called, with some lack of precision, Paradise Valley. What Chicago's whites referred to as the Negro, or nigger, district comprised a 7-square-mile area on the inner South Side stretching from 31st Street to just beyond Cottage Grove, and from Lake Michigan to the railroad tracks across State Street. Residents called it Bronzeville.

Moving north changed the character of Negro life; whether it improved the quality was debatable. In the North, blacks usually could vote and could receive a somewhat reasonable trial if they had to go to court. In theory they could go anywhere they wanted, shop at any store; no one demanded that they go to a separate coach or to the back of the bus. In fact, black people who bothered to vote probably chose between white candidates; there was one Negro congressman in 1941 and no more than a handful of black state legislators. The idea of a black mayor for Chicago, Detroit, or Gary, Indiana, would have seemed preposterous. Proprietors of stores and restaurants often discouraged black patronage by rudeness, overcharging, or slow service. The best places, besides, were too expensive. There were no Jim Crow laws, and some black children went to racially mixed schools, but others attended classes filled mostly or entirely with other blacks. Even the schools intended for Negroes bore the names of white people. Gary had Roosevelt High School, and at the other end of the state Evansville's black school was Lincoln. Crispus Attucks in Indianapolis, named after a black hero, was an exception.

The key to the black people's status in the North was economics. Of course, instrumental in determining economic status was white prejudice, the application of stereotypes and all that followed. Black people lived in slum districts partly because they could not afford to go elsewhere. It was logical that they trade at stores in the neighborhood and go to the closest schools. People who worked in Northern cities made more money than in the South, but fewer people worked. Unemployment for black males stood between 20 and 25 percent in most cities, sometimes more. When they did find work it probably was in the traditional service occupations or the dirtiest jobs in industry. Henry Ford, with his much-acclaimed generosity toward blacks, liked to put Negroes in such places as the foundry. Black women realized that little less—perhaps no less—than in the South, Northerners wanted them mostly as cooks or maids. "Before the soreness of the cotton fields had left Mama's back," Claude Brown wrote, "her knees were getting sore from scrubbing 'Goldberg's' floor. Nevertheless, she was better off. She had gone from the fire into the frying pan."[47]

Malcolm X received an introduction to urban society as a shoeshine boy at the Roseland. His predecessor on the job, a man named Freddie, had hit on his "big" number, quit work, and said he planned to buy a Cadillac. Beforehand, however, he showed Malcolm the tricks of the trade, such as how to make the shine rag pop like a firecracker. "Dig that action?" he asked. . . . "It's a jive noise, that's all. Cats tip better, they figure you're knocking yourself out." An enterprising young man could provide service of many kinds—"they'll come asking you for rubbers . . . for liquor, some will want reefers. But you don't need to have nothing but rubbers . . . until you can dig who's a cop. You can make ten, twelve dollars a dance for yourself, if you work things right," Freddie said. "The main thing you got to remember is that everything in the world is a hustle."[48]

With only rare exceptions black residential areas in the urban North were dirty, noisy cities within a city, places of widespread poverty where much of the population was unemployed or underemployed and the people lived in filthy tenements with plumbing that might or might not work. In Chicago they called such places "kitchenettes." "What they do is this," wrote Richard Wright. "They take, say, a seven room apartment which rents for $50 a month to whites, cut it up into seven small apartments, of one room each; they install one small gas stove and one small sink in each room . . . rent these kitchenettes to us at the rate of, say, $6 a week." Thus the same space for which whites had paid $50 a month cost black people $42 a week. Five or six people often lived in a single kitchenette. Malcolm found similar places in Harlem, "rat-trap" apartments "crawling with everything you could mention that was illegal and immoral."[49]

The ghetto understandably was a seedbed for crime. Black people, with less than 10 percent of the population in 1940, had nearly 23 percent of all arrests. Blacks were almost three times as likely to commit crimes—or at least to be arrested—as whites.[50] The underworld in the black ghetto probably began with a numbers operation—it was called "policy" in most cities—which was illegal but hardly ever prosecuted. Because of its enormous popularity, and thanks to bribery, "policy" went on unchallenged unless by chance "the heat was on." Nearly everyone played the game as much as they could afford, hoping for that "day of jubilee" when their number would hit.

The black slums had more than their share of murder, rape, and often serious crime, as well as, of course, prostitution and a lively drug traffic. Businessmen in Harlem had come to worry about a loss of white patronage due to a recent rash of robberies, most of them at the hands of innovative teenage boys. One new technique was to throw a man to the ground, pull off his trousers, and run with them; another involved "putting an arm around a victim's neck, a knee in his back, and robbing him," which the youngsters called "mugging."[51]

The most visible citizens of the ghetto were often people involved in the rackets, who seemed always to be hanging around (apparently they never had to work), with sharp clothes, classy cars, bankrolls readily flashed, and colorful names. At the proper places in Harlem, for example, one might run into a character called "Dollarbill." Dollarbill liked to show his "Kansas City roll," which looked like a stack of hundred-dollar bills. The boys suspected that he had a hundred-dollar bill on the outside, a twenty on the inside and fifty ones in between. Even accounting for deception, it was a lot of money. "Cadillac" Drake had a string of the "stringiest, scrawniest, black and white prostitutes in Harlem." Friends joked that Cadillac's girls did not make enough to feed themselves, let alone him. "Bad-looking women work harder," he always said. There was also "Sammy the Pimp," "Jumpsteady" the burglar, and a man called "Few Clothes," once the slickest pickpocket in Harlem but now sidelined with arthritis. Unfortunately those individuals often were the most envied and imitated people, a visible proof of Freddie's admonition to Malcolm that everything in the world was "a hustle."[52]

Sin, crime, and vice in the ghetto existed side by side with religion. Chicago had approximately the same number of churches as "policy" stations, and every city's black district had numerous storefront operations labeled Baptist, Methodist, Mt. Zion, and African Colored. The minister might compete with kings of vice for the title of the community's best-known citizen. Perhaps half the 250,000–300,000 people in Bronzeville had been converted, although many became backsliders. The basic approach was fundamentalist Protestantism, accented with moods, sounds, and gestures that had evolved through the black man's Christianity. The music might be the best in Christendom.

One step removed from the churches and a standard part of black urban culture were the faith healers, spiritualists, palm readers, and crystal ball gazers. Every ghetto had dozens if not hundreds of those subtle hucksters, all providing multiple services for a price. Madam Williams, for example, offered black Chicagoans advice on "life, love, health, domestic and financial conditions." Nearly all dealt in "gigs"—helping clients pick numbers for the daily game; Madam Williams boasted of eleven hits in three days. Professor Edward Loew charged one cent to three dollars for gigs based on the "science of the Zodiac." Doctor Pryor had his Japo Oriental Company on the first floor and King Solomon's Temple of Religious Science in the basement. The Temple taught "The Fellowship of God and the Brotherhood of Man," while the Japo Company sold such items as Sacred and Lucky Powders, John the Conquerer Oil, and Dr. Pryor's Holy Floor Wash and House Spray Oil, the latter guaranteed to "rent houses, draw crowds and eliminate the evil works of the Devil." Dr. Pryor's talents also included giving out gigs.[53]

Every black ghetto had an entertainment area with pool rooms, bars, dance halls, and the like, the most elaborate being Harlem and Chicago's South Side, the two largest black urban populations. Bronzeville's nightclubs and bars featured "shake" dancers, expert "mixologists," jukeboxes playing such music as "Doggin' Around," "Truckin' Little Woman," "Franklin D. Roosevelt Jones," and "Brown Gal." On the right days in summer, one could go out to Comiskey Park and watch the American Giants play baseball. If the Kansas City Monarchs happened to be in town, spectators had an opportunity to see "the greatest pitcher of all time," Satchel Paige. If moviegoers could see only white man's films, blacks at least could give them a different twist, if only in advertising. Thus, "Gone With the Wind" starred Hattie McDaniel and Butterfly McQueen; another poster billed Rochester as "The Man Who Made Jack Benny Famous."[54] Bronzeville had received a special blessing when Joe Louis married Marva Trotter, a local girl. The union frequently brought the champion to town; to black America nothing compared with a visit by Joe Louis.

Except for Marva and Joe, Harlem had as many attractions as, and more people than, Bronzeville. There were the Black Yankees, the Globetrotters, and many people famous in entertainment: Billy Eckstine, Billie Holiday, Ella Fitzgerald, Count Basie, the Mills Brothers, the Ink Spots, and many others. Even such lofty titles as "Duke" and "Count" or leading bands that were among the most prestigious in America could not ensure the privileges afforded to much more modest whites. Black entertainers knew the rules, so when they came to town they usually stayed at the Theresa Hotel and "hung out" at the bar of the Braddock Hotel near the backstage entrance to the Apollo Theater.

For all the grievous shortcomings the ghetto continued to offer its attractions, especially for black youth recently removed from the listless, dead-end culture of the South. If one could look beyond the dirt and the shabby tenements and learn to maneuver through (or with) the crime and the racketeers, one might appreciate the bright lights, the excitement, the security and familiarity of a black culture. Having seen Roxbury, the middle-class "snooty-black neighborhood" of Boston, where people were "breaking their backs trying to imitate white people" Malcolm X felt more at home in the slum, among folks who were "not putting on airs." He was "completely entranced" by the "hip cats" with straight hair who squired "cool chicks," some of them white, in a black Buick or Cadillac with broad white-sidewall tires, men who knew all the "jive talk." "Skin me, daddy-o," they would say, or "my man!! . . . Gimme some skin."

Though still neutral, America began to prepare for war. The draft brought young men from different backgrounds and sections of the country together for the first time, subjecting them to often strange situations in new surroundings. These men are undergoing induction at Fort Slocum, New York. *Arthur Rothstein,* The Depression Years As Photographed by Arthur Rothstein

Factories began to gear up for military production. Refashioning industry for defense barely had started at Willow Run, Michigan. Holes in the ground marked the spot where Henry Ford's massive B24 bomber plant would soon stand. *State of Michigan Historical Collections*

Defense production gave new power to the "enfant terrible" of the labor movement, John L. Lewis (left), who taunted the president and threatened to paralyze the war effort. Head of the United Mine Workers, he speaks with colleagues Philip Murray and Thomas Kennedy. *United Mine Workers*

The greater labor needs, increased production, and the promise of big money led to much industrial strife. Here women support the men striking at the Ford plant in April. *The Archives of Labor and Urban Affairs, Wayne State University*

Defense production eventually took priority over automobiles in 1941. An M3 comes down the line at the Chrysler Tank Arsenal near Detroit. *The Archives of Labor and Urban Affairs, Wayne State University*

Industrial establishments all across the country joined in preparation for war. The Navy yard at Charleston, South Carolina, gets ready to launch two destroyers, the *Tillman* and the *Beatty*. *Library of Congress*

The change-over in production proceeded steadily but slowly. New equipment was slow to find its way to the new army. These "Big Ears" were a poor substitute for radar. *National Archives*

The arrival in 1941 of the M3 Medium tanks, here in action near Lake Charles, Louisiana, might have startled small town America, but it was welcomed by the GI's engaged in military maneuvers. *National Archives*

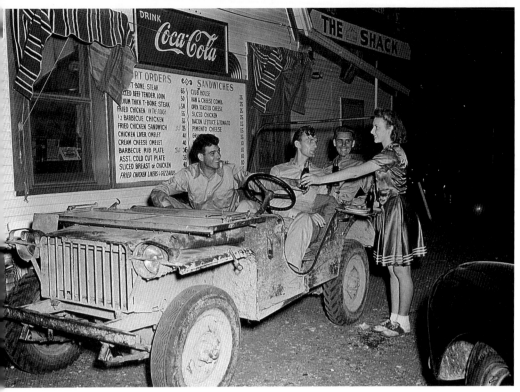

The new GI's might have felt uncomfortable away from home, but wearing the uniform carried its rewards, ranging from the smile of a pretty carhop in Arkansas to getting one's picture taken. *National Archives*

The demands of the defense industry accelerated the population shift from rural to urban America. Towns that experienced a defense boom often paid a price in crowded conditions and a disrupted way of life, as revealed in this scene at the Electric Boat Works at Groton, Conn. *Library of Congress*

Conditions for defense workers were often crowded and uncomfortable because of a housing shortage, as illustrated by this attic apartment of a defense worker in Erie, Pennsylvania. *Library of Congress*

Financial and economic transactions concerning the war effort centered in cities like New York which, in 1941, was still able to absorb the growth of activity such transactions engendered. Here, the El track and a street in lower Manhattan in December. *Library of Congress*

America could no longer hover on the brink of war after the attack on these battleships at Pearl Harbor that fateful Sunday morning. *National Archives*

Once committed to war, Americans rallied behind Roosevelt. Fiorello LaGuardia addresses a "Defend America" rally, at Madison Square Garden, December 15, 1941. *Wide World*

The die is cast. President Roosevelt signs the Declaration of War, December 8, 1941.
National Archives

Within a remarkably short time Malcolm had managed to imitate the model. Dressed in a "Cab Calloway" suit with 4-inch-brimmed pearl gray hat, with fire-red conk, half high on alcohol or reefers or both, he inspired people to stand and watch him pass. "New York was heaven to me" he said as he moved down from Boston, "and Harlem was Seventh heaven."[55]

A few people might have felt the same ecstasy as Malcolm; for far more people, and in time for Malcolm, a sobering realism would set in. On balance, moving north probably enhanced freedom and expanded the black man's options. Blacks breathed more freely than in the South, if only polluted air. Moving north did not produce true emancipation and certainly not racial equality. Segregation was of a different sort; it was neither enforced by law nor as rigid and all-pervasive as in the South. But for the most part it was still segregation. And there remained the dirt, the crowding, the unemployment and poverty, the lure of drugs and crime. How was it possible to avoid those social traps? What was left to do after making the move north? As Claude Brown said, "where does one run to when he's already in the promised land?"[56]

And still they continued to come—from the South to the North and soon, following a new path, from South to West, mostly California. The black migration represented part of a general population movement inspired by hope for work growing out of the war boom; in fact, Negroes responded more slowly to shifting national currents than whites. By the end of 1941, black people would start to leave in larger numbers, however, beginning the largest migration during one decade in the history of the trek out of the South.

The status of black people in 1941, like many aspects of American society, was affected more by the identification of problems than by the finding of solutions. Those Negroes who moved north or west looking for work, as well as the black people already in the North who visited employment offices, mostly encountered disappointment. Much of the growth in military production called for skilled workers, positions for which few black people could qualify. It was an old story, part of the cycle in which one racial problem fed another. For unskilled work, industries found a surplus of white labor, either as a legacy of the Depression or because of migration following much the same path as black people's. More white people moved than blacks. And of course the stereotypes came into play, the perception of the black as lazy, unreliable, and suitable, if he was to be hired at all, for only certain jobs.

Most firms preferred to not interject the issue of race into employment practices: It was safer to abide by traditional habits and simpler to hide in that vague domain called "company policy." "While we are in complete sympathy with the Negro, it is against company policy to employ them as aircraft workers or mechanics . . . regardless of their training," the President of North American Aviation said. "There will be some jobs as janitors for Negroes."[57] Vultee Aircraft in Nashville took a similar view: "We do not now believe it advisable to include colored people with our regular working force. We may, at a later date . . . add some colored people in minor capacities as porters and cleaners." None of Vultee's 6,000 workers in 1941 were black; Douglas Aircraft had ten blacks out of 33,000 workers; Boeing had three—two porters and a cook. Martin Aircraft in Baltimore, Colt Firearms in Hartford, and General Motors and White Motors in Cleveland employed none.[58]

Black men also experienced difficulty with military service. At a time when many whites searched for a way to avoid induction into the Army, some blacks complained that they could not get in. For many young males the Army offered more in food, housing, pay, and status than they could obtain in civilian life. More than 1.8 million registered the first year, a number larger than the black proportion of the population. Only thirty-three were classified as conscientious objectors. Over 16 percent of the people who volunteered were black. While the Department of War announced that blacks would constitute the same proportion of the Army as in the population, about 10 percent, it became clear that the number fell far short. In some areas Negroes had difficulty meeting military standards. Blacks made up nearly 60 percent of the people rejected because of illiteracy—12 percent signed their names with an X—and in some areas showed special susceptibility to venereal disease. More than 63 percent of black registrants were rejected for physical, mental, or educational disability.[59]

Also important were a general prejudice against black people and doubt about the reliability of the black soldier. Negroes served on draft boards of the Northern states and in three states of the South and border area. In most of the South black membership on the boards was out of the question. "Some white boys might refuse to let Negroes examine them and that would cause trouble," the Governor of Tennessee said. Besides, he added, "this is a white man's country."[60] During the first year, nearly 92,000 Negroes came into the Army through the selective service system, slightly more than 10 percent of the number inducted. Approximately 30,000 had been passed over in the induction process, and Negroes made up less than 6 percent of the Army in 1941.

Once in uniform, the black soldier did not leave all problems of civilian society behind. He served and trained in a segregated unit. He probably took commands from a white officer. The Regular Army had only three black officers when the buildup began, and while the call-up of the reserves and National Guard brought in several more, there were not enough to go around. Black units probably ended up in a remote part of camp and were slow to receive suitable equipment.

The black soldier discovered that being an agent of the United States, wearing the nation's uniform, carried no special privileges. Most camps were in the South, and many Southerners who lived near the camps were anxious to demonstrate that nothing had changed in race relations. Putting on a uniform gave the black man no right to be "uppity." Conflicts between white and black soldiers or between black soldiers and white townspeople took place frequently. In August, state policemen in Arkansas pushed a detail of black soldiers off the highway. A white officer who protested was slapped and called a "nigger lover." An incident in Louisiana in September 1941 ended in a pitched battle between black soldiers and white military police.[61] Which race was to blame for starting such incidents differed from place to place, but they left the impression—valid or not—that the consequence of a black-and-white Army had been racial trouble.

Other branches of the armed services avoided racial conflicts. The Navy and Marines filled their ranks by enlistment, which allowed them to discriminate however they wished. They chose to exclude black men, except as messmen. Admiral Chester W. Nimitz explained that experience had shown "that men of the colored race, if enlisted in any other branch than the messman branch and promoted to the position of petty officer cannot maintain discipline among men of the white race over whom they may be placed by reason of their rating. . . . Teamwork, harmony and ship efficiency are seriously handicapped." The Secretary of the Navy argued that putting blacks in the Navy would be "like putting them in hell."[62]

Thus, white America approached the international crisis for the most part as if nothing had changed—or needed to change—in relations between the races. If the leadership spotted a contradiction between this position and the moral case for a war against fascism, it preferred not to dwell on it. Negroes, as one person had put it, were there for whites to use or to ignore as they saw fit.

More than ever before, black people refused to accept the reasoning of white leaders. More and more blacks were starting to speak out. In such individuals as Walter White, Roy Wilkins, the writers Langston Hughes and Richard Wright, and several others a Negro leadership had emerged, known to a growing number of people and exerting increasing influence among whites in positions of power. The black press, which now included more than two hundred publications of all kinds, insisted on treating the war differently from the coverage in white newspapers. The black press did not write much about Dunkirk or Ribbentrop or the war in Russia; they did deal with the growth of the military industries in the United States and the character of an expanding American military force. Writers wanted to know if white leaders meant what they said in justifying the struggle against Germany.

Many blacks spotted the contradiction between avowed American principles, the large objectives of the world war, and their own status in American society. A lady from Chicago asked the question perhaps most relevant to the time: "Why must our men fight and die for their country when it won't even give them a job that they are fitted for?"[63] Canada Lee, star of the stage adaptation of *Native Son,* announced that he would rather fight such people as Governor Eugene Talmadge of Georgia than Hitler. Richard Wright, who later would abandon the United States, almost supported Japan out of hope that "the Japanese will assume the leadership of the 'darker races.'"[64]

The bulk of black petitioners remained patriotic. Most newspapers in the black communities of large cities and most black spokesmen expressed a desire to support the United States. All demanded a change in social, economic, and military policies that would permit black people full participation in the huge changes then underway. What did the Negro want? "We are elevator boys, janitors, red caps, maids—a race in uniform," Langston Hughes complained. Negroes wanted "the things any self-respecting citizen of the United States desires." "Our immediate concern is employment," the Chicago *Defender* said. "We want work so that we can eat, pay our rent, patronize our businesses."[65] The black press also demanded a halt to segregation in the Army and society in general and an end to the exclusiveness of other military forces. In broadest terms, black people wanted equality and integration, or an elimination of the "dilemma" identified by Gunnar Myrdal.

President Roosevelt was not unsympathetic to appeals from the black community. While he probably believed that black people were inferior, he knew they deserved much better treatment. His Administration had provided more economic benefits than any other. Even now he had special black advisers, called the "Black Cabinet," including such people as Robert Weaver and William Hastie, who offered recommendations on issues concerning Negroes. Roosevelt, who above all was practical and interested in results, feared that disturbance of the racial *status quo* would interfere with plans for national economic and military rejuvenation. A biographer of the President wrote: "The general policy of the administration, if it had one, was separate but equal—in military, in civilian agencies, and—by exhortation—in defense industries, but the separation often thwarted the equality."[66] Problems of the black population remained far from the top of Roosevelt's list of priorities.

So the thing to do was change his priorities, a small number of black leaders decided, having perceived the significance of the changing times. "For five months we were given the runaround," one said. "It was only then that . . . several . . . of us planned the March." The march was a proposed demonstration of at least ten thousand black people in Washington, D.C., on July 1, 1941. The idea had originated with A. Philip Randolph, head of the Brotherhood of Sleeping Car Porters, and was endorsed by Walter White and other black spokesmen, and eventually by nearly all of the Negro press. While Randolph hoped to improve the morale of, and respect for, his people and "shake up official Washington," the immediate goals were jobs in defense factories and integration of the military forces.[67]

News of the project brought no pleasure to Roosevelt. He considered the demonstration a vexing diversion from the central thrust of putting the Lend-Lease Act into force and organizing the nation for the struggle against fascism. He wanted unity, an indication of dedication and single-mindedness from all groups during this time of crisis. A march by blacks not only destroyed that image but would cause resentment and perhaps provoke hostile action from white people. Washington, after all, was segregated and in nearly all respects a Southern city.

Even so, he could not ignore the threat. Roosevelt met with White and Randolph, hoping to persuade them to cancel the demonstration. What did Negroes want? he asked. They wanted an order abolishing discrimination in the armed forces and in industry producing military equipment. It will not work, Secretary Knox and other military leaders present at the gathering said. Racial mixing in the military, especially aboard ship, would be catastrophic. Would it be possible to take a first step, perhaps put Negro bands on battleships? Roosevelt wondered. To black leaders that proposal looked like tokenism, subterfuge, and an evasion of the problem. The meeting broke up with nothing settled. The march was still on, and some black people had begun to talk of a massive turnout, a gathering of 50,000 or even 100,000.[68]

As the time for the march drew near, Roosevelt made one last effort to head it off. He sent his wife Eleanor and Mayor LaGuardia, both popular with the nation's black people, into another consultation with leaders of the march. "You know where I stand," Mrs. Roosevelt said, and LaGuardia also reminded the Negroes of his sympathy for civil rights. Both warned that the demonstration was a mistake and might cause serious trouble, if for no other reason than because most of Washington's police were white Southerners. Evidently provoked, the black leaders then threatened a second march—on New York City. "What for?" the Little Flower cried out. "What have I done?" The meeting did produce a compromise. Roosevelt would issue an executive order of sorts, and the leaders agreed to cancel the demonstration.[69]

Roosevelt put out the order—No. 8802—on June 25, one week before the march was to have taken place. The black leaders had settled for half a loaf, at best. The directive did not cover military operations, and provisions pertaining to civilian matters lacked clarity. Employers and labor unions doing business in national defense, with the national government, were forbidden to discriminate because of race, color, creed, or national origin. A new Fair Employment Practices Committee would supervise the order. Blacks differed in their assessment of the measure, but many considered it an important first step. One leader, Mary McLeod Bethune, called it "a refreshing shower in a thirsty land."[70] A black newspaper, somewhat carried away, announced its belief "that the day when we shall gain full rights, privileges and opportunities of American citizenship is now not far distant."[71]

It would take time to determine if Roosevelt's action would be significant. The President appointed two blacks and three whites to the FEPC. Mark Etheridge, publisher of the Louisville *Courier-Journal,* a liberal but also probably a segregationist, became chairman. Blacks were disappointed; they had wanted LaGuardia. The first hearings did not come until the end of October. Meanwhile occasional signs of hope had started to surface: The Army announced the opening of a training base for the first black pilots at Tuskegee Institute. Graduates—the first class had thirteen members—would become part of the 99th Pursuit Squadron. It was still segregation, but on a more prestigious level. A few firms decided that they might need to take a new look at hiring practices, no doubt a consequence of subtle prods from Administration officials determined to have concrete evidence of movement. Such companies as Republic Aviation, Curtiss-Wright, Grumman Aircraft, and North American announced plans to hire Negroes. United States Cartridge in Tennessee said it would take on three thousand.[72]

Other signs suggested that in important areas change had to wait for another day. The Army remained segregated; the Navy was still all white. The government in truth had no civil rights policy and was not anxious to establish one. Roosevelt knew there was justice in the black man's cause, yet he hoped Negroes would wait a while longer and allow him to concentrate on Hitler. Perhaps later, sometime in the future, it would be possible to address these issues. The policy that did exist belonged to the states, the most important aspects of which were negative measures in the South designed to ensure that black people would remain citizens of another America. What had been true at the start of the year remained true at the end: The most meaningful observation about black people in the United States in 1941 was not how far they had come but how far they had to go.

And yet, beneath the segregation and discrimination, beyond the stereotypes and popular perceptions about race, careful observers might detect stirrings of unrest. A framework for the future had started to take shape. The movement north continued, and it did not take long to see that north of the Ohio or in the Pacific states, the black man became different. Slowly the factory doors would open wider, less because of a reformist spirit or action by the FEPC than out of a need for labor. As it turned out, the Army would want a large number of black men, and even the Navy would decide to take a few; service in the military forces provided blacks with unassailable grounds for demanding, if not equality, at least a great deal more than they were getting. The war had already laid open the contradiction between American principles—the "Four Freedoms," for example, as proclaimed by Roosevelt—and the status of black people in the United States.

The Negroes showed signs of abandoning their behavior of the past; some of them were shedding docility, listening to their spokesmen, and acting as if the Constitution applied to them. Richard Wright least of all could hide an impatience. "We are the new tide," he wrote. "We stand at the crossroads. . . . Men are moving. And we shall be with them."[73] The march on Washington had amounted to a threat of a large movement of black people to improve the position of the average black citizen. Something, at last, had attracted Washington's attention. Who could forget how the white leaders had squirmed, bargained, and even yielded when faced with a genuine threat? The black people would not forget, as the Chicago *Defender* observed: "A. Philip Randolph . . . opened the eyes of the President and demonstrated to the doubting Thomases among us, that only mass action can pry open the iron doors that have been erected against America's black minority."[74]

Joe DiMaggio, Joe Louis, Joe Palooka . . .

If 1941 was a time of work, with more jobs to be had and more work to do, it was also a time for more play. Americans participated increasingly in familiar popular pastimes. The starting point was popular culture of the 1930s, broadened in appeal and modified in noticeable ways by a new age that had started to engulf the United States. An increase in personal pressure, a highly charged international environment, and the uncertainty of America's future produced new incentives for seeking relaxation—for "getting a little fun out of life" while one still had the chance.

Leisure activities that had been popular for years tended to be inexpensive. Americans in large numbers continued to play checkers, dominoes, Chinese checkers, and all sorts of card games and to work crossword and jigsaw puzzles, especially in winter. They hunted, fished, and attended church and community gatherings, especially in summer. Visits to family or friends, while at times more an obligation than a source of pleasure, remained one of the most common social outlets in the United States. Often the most expensive part was transport, further indication of how life had come to revolve about the car. The automobile represented recreation in itself; a family drive for pleasure had become so commonplace that the term "Sunday driver" took on special meaning. People in their teens and early twenties drove the car to skating rinks, for roller-skating had become a national mania; in the car they cavorted with the gang, cruised the streets, and parked on country roads. For the young, the car was much more than a means of travel.

An improving economy brought other entertainment within reach of more people; with money to spend on pleasure, they showed increased interest in most kinds of commercial entertainment. Popular culture did not necessarily mirror behavior at that time but did show glimpses of it. From motion pictures one could conclude that while sex was a considerable force, in the 1940s it was not talked about directly. Radio suggested that black people were different, much different, from whites. While no generalization can encompass something as diverse as professional entertainment, much of it exposed its audience to an idealistic concept of life, sustained white middle-class values, and gave an uplifting, most often happy, ending to its stories, even though it might come through violent means.

The mere existence of a growing, glamorous, incomparably publicized entertainment business constituted a social force. Most people could scarcely help but be influenced by the situations and characters of popular entertainment, and many wished to *be* the characters—to become performers. How many black boys tried boxing because of Joe Louis? How many white boys wanted to play center field, or some position, because of Joe DiMaggio? How many girls wanted to act because Joan Crawford acted, to smoke a cigarette because actresses smoked, to sing because Judy Garland sang? While the entertainment media represented only one force—or one category of forces—shaping people and character, in no other nation did it do so much to mark standards, aspiration, and national image or to show the world and Americans themselves what America wanted.

Travelers on the entertainment circuit in New York City might have found it difficult to believe that a war was going on or that the Depression had not ended. As befitting that bustling international metropolis—the capital, in many ways, of the world—New York had something for every taste. No less than in years past, American theater in 1941 began in the big city. A survey of plays produced for Broadway ranged from Shakespeare, performed by Helen Hayes and Maurice Evans, to such farcical comedy as *Arsenic and Old Lace,* with Boris Karloff. Contrary to speculation that it would never end, the stage adaptation of Erskine Caldwell's earthy novel *Tobacco Road* closed in June after running seven and one-half years and more than three thousand performances.

For the most part Broadway theater offered escapist entertainment, much music and comedy, with an occasional drama. The Olson and Johnson musical, *Hellzapoppin,* with Happy Feldon and Jay C. Flippin in lead roles, still drew good audiences, as did *Lady in the Dark* and *My Sister Eileen. Panama Hattie,* with music written by

Cole Porter, entered a second year, providing a first starring role for Ethel Merman. The opening of Richard Wright's *Native Son* had caused much excitement. The book's social commentary had provoked much controversy, of course, and the director, young Orson Welles, was one of the "hottest" names in entertainment. The show closed in June after fourteen weeks, heavily in the red. Inevitably, perhaps, politics and war made an appearance on stage with the production in April of Lillian Hellman's *Watch on the Rhine*. It was still doing well at the end of the year. In truth, Broadway was having only a mediocre year. A survey of the 1940–41 season, which ended in May, showed twelve "hits," four "moderate hits," and forty-five shows that would have to be classified as failures.[1]

The Broadway stage nevertheless continued to have a large impact on American culture. It glamorized an important art form and did much to determine what kind of live entertainment would be seen in other cities. Some shows in fact did better on the road than in New York. Broadway was a training ground, a reservoir of talent for other entertainment. The live stage remained a sounding board—albeit an expensive one—for the film industry, and with a few exceptions a successful Broadway show eventually would make it to the screen. In 1941 Hollywood producers paid $175,000 for the rights to *Arsenic and Old Lace* and an astonishing $285,000 for *Lady in the Dark*. The New York stage attracted some of the most creative talent, and popular music often had its introduction on Broadway. For *Pal Joey,* performed by Gene Kelly and June Havoc, Richard Rodgers and Lorenz Hart produced such tunes as "I Could Write a Book," "Bewitched, Bothered and Bewildered," and "The Lady is a Tramp"— all destined to remain popular long after the musical had closed.

New York, of course, had much more than Broadway. The popular bands moved around, but one could find a larger number for a longer time in New York than anywhere else. Benny Goodman liked to perform at the New Yorker Hotel; Glenn Miller spent long stretches at the Pennsylvania, Eddy Duchin at the Waldorf, and Harry James at the Lincoln; Guy Lombardo, even then the "king of corn," rarely left the Roosevelt. For opera nothing in the United States could match the New York Metropolitan. Featuring such performers as Lily Pons, Lawrence Tibbitt, John Charles Thomas, and Risë Stevens, the Met had a fine season, ending with a net loss of only $14,000. New York also offered nightclubs of every description, professional and amateur sports, and for those few individuals—perhaps four thousand—who had been adventurous enough to buy a receiving set, some interesting television shows.[2]

Even though New York continued its reign as America's premier cultural center, it did not reflect the tastes and behavior of all the people. Some entertainment in New York was truly national; some would have to be classified as elitist. The most prestigious stage shows cost $3.30 or $4.40, more money than the "typical" person could ordinarily afford. For all Broadway's impact on popular culture, most people would rather go to a movie. Many Americans did not enjoy opera, and if they did they could not afford a ticket. A concert by a top performer—Nelson Eddy, the most expensive, received $4,000–4,500 a night—might cost seven dollars. Expense of entertainment varied with the kind of activity, of course, and with location. In Greenwich Village anyone "not an arrogant spendthrift or an out-and-out drunk" could get by on five dollars, but nightclubs on the Upper East Side, with cover charge and seventy-five-cent drinks, would cost at least twenty.[3] Most people—for that matter most New Yorkers—had to be content with entertainment far more modest than stage productions or nightclubs.

While radio might not have been, as one scholar claimed, the most important "cultural medium . . . since the invention of printing," by 1941 it provided almost universal entertainment for the United States. After the original purchase, radio came virtually free, unless one happened to have a set that operated on batteries. Some 57 million radios served 29 million homes in 1941; nearly 14 million sets were sold during the year. More than 85 percent of the people had radio.[4]

Radio in the 1940s represented what television would later become: a vast and varied avenue for information and entertainment (but mostly entertainment) pitched to the perceived tastes of many kinds of audiences. The broadcast day began with a hodgepodge of short programs offering news, farm information, and weather, along with audience-participation shows with music and light comedy, such as Don McNeil's *Breakfast Club*. Then the stations moved into the meat of daytime entertainment. The short sketches or serials started between 10:00 and 10:30 and would continue, but not without interruption, until approximately 5:30 P.M. The object of derision from almost their introduction, these shows had attracted such collective labels as "washboard weepies" and "sudsers," but most people came to call them "soap operas." Not every program had a soap manufacturer as sponsor, but many did. Proctor & Gamble, a company that spent nearly $11 million a year on radio advertising—far more than any other firm—sponsored no fewer than sixteen daytime dramas at the same time. The programs were popular and economical. Each edition of top-notch evening entertainment, such as Jack Benny's show, might cost as much as $17,500. A soap opera could be produced for $1,500–$2,500.

Promoters of such shows understood, of course, that most women did not work outside the home, so soap operas on radio, even more than later versions on television, catered to the female taste. Women often had the lead roles; male characters were kindly grandfathers or handsome young bachelors, vulnerable before stronger women. In a quarter-hour (a few shows ran longer) the listener could stay abreast of the tribulations of Helen Trent, Judy and Jane, Our Gal Sunday, Betty and Bob, Young Dr. Malone, Young Widder Brown, and John's Other Wife, or discover what followed when *Portia Faces Life* or *When a Girl Marries*. Fifteen minutes rarely afforded time to solve a problem (the sketch probably received only eleven), so the story ran at snail's pace, through countless twists and turns, often consuming weeks before reaching a conclusion. The daytime dramas seemed to say that women experienced restlessness and maybe even an urge for a little scandal, but not enough to do anything about it. The year before America went to war, some sixty shows filled the airwaves, encompassing 85 percent of daytime broadcasting.[5]

If the children had to yield to Mother at one time, they probably won out at another. By 5:00 or 5:30, the female listener who sustained the soap opera had begun to turn her attention elsewhere, and while she could work while listening to the radio, distractions made it less satisfying. The children were probably home, and in the short days of winter they asserted their claim on the radio. They could choose from a group of programs targeted specially at the preadolescent mind, mostly male: Mandrake, Jack Armstrong (the all-American boy), Captain Midnight, Tom Mix and his Straightshooters, or, in early evening, The Lone Ranger.

The heroes of radio were agents of justice, honor, and truth, generally middle-class values. They spent their time chasing hoodlums and watching over the morals of the community. Radio's bad men of that age usually practiced conventional villainy. Robbery was the most popular crime, followed by murder. The customary motivation was greed. Occasionally a more creative criminal—a demented professor, perhaps—devised a plot to control or destroy the world. Hitler had brought such schemes within the realm of plausibility. Some heroes were humans who used their talents with exquisite wisdom and efficiency, invariably acting "in the nick of time." Others had extraordinary, superhuman, capability, and it probably was inevitable that one would be called Superman.

One of the most unusual talents belonged to a character called the Shadow, the protagonist of a half-hour program broadcast at 5:30 Sunday, Eastern Time. The Shadow, every youngster knew, was in reality Lamont Cranston, "wealthy young man about town who, years ago in the Orient, learned the hypnotic power to cloud men's minds so that they could not see him." The ability to become invisible must have opened some interesting opportunities for this hero of radio, but of course the Shadow would use his power only for noble purposes. "Who knows what evil lurks in the heart of men?" Listeners had the answer: "The Shadow knows." Each episode ended in much the same fashion: The villain might be in the act of a crime or gloating over a recent evil deed. Suddenly, a chuckle or a command burst out of thin air (the listener needed to imagine the Shadow "appearing" invisible). "Who said that?" the startled hoodlum might shout. "Where did that voice come from?" At that point listeners knew that lawlessness had been "foiled again." If Cranston's relationship with Margo Lane, his faithful "friend and companion," remained something of a mystery, even more so than the association of Superman with Lois Lane, followers of the Shadow accepted Margo as part of the show, with no suspicion that the relationship was anything they could not describe to Mother.

After an hour or so devoted to news, sports, and weather, usually around 6:00–7:30, radio took up evening entertainment. Families able to afford only one set might now encounter the greatest chance for conflict. Radio at that time provided the widest choice in programming: a fairly even split among variety, drama, and audience-participation programs (mostly quiz shows). Miscellaneous programs dealt with news, public affairs, and popular or classical music. The most successful music show, *Your Hit Parade,* closely identified with its sponsor, Lucky Strike cigarettes, presented each week's ten most popular songs.[6]

In drama, the *Lux Radio Theatre* was a clear favorite. Introduced by the film director Cecil B. DeMille, the program used top-name actors to re-create some of the most successful current movies. Crime and mystery drama included *Suspense, Inner Sanctum, I Love a Mystery, Lights Out,* and a show called *Big Town,* featuring Edward G. Robinson. The crime shows, while longer and more sophisticated than programs broadcast in late afternoon, showed the same moral markings. "This program praises the police. . . . Crime does not pay except as fiction," proclaimed an announcer for *Gangbusters,* a program that burst on the air at 9:00 Friday evening to the clatter of machine guns, police sirens, and other sounds of violence. Another show, marked with "horrifying physical assaults [and] weird unhappy noises," billed *Mr. District Attorney* as "champion of the people, guardian of our fundamental rights." Inspired by Thomas E. Dewey of New York, the DA had no name; the program was, in the assessment of *Time,* the "most popular Whodunit on the air."[7]

It was almost inevitable that at some time the family radio would come to rest on one or more of the evening's variety shows. While nearly all programs offered comedy and at least a touch of music, formats varied in accordance with the talents of the star. Bing Crosby featured much singing on the *Kraft Music Hall.* Red Skelton provided slapstick, simplicity, and overstatement in his standard characters, "Deadeye," "Clem Kadiddlehopper," and the "mean widdle kid." Edgar Bergen could be as harsh and insulting as he wished, speaking through his dummy, Charlie McCarthy. Bergen's *Chase & Sanborn Show* added the comedy team of Bud Abbott and Lou Costello in 1941, partly to exploit the sudden success of Abbott and Costello in films and partly to create a standing "feud" between Charlie and Costello. Jack Benny's program had several continuing characters: Rochester, singer Dennis Day, and Phil Harris, the alcoholic band leader (and his silent drinking buddy, Frank Remley). The most persistent theme was Benny's purported cheapness. Listeners knew about the antique Maxwell automobile he still drove, the deep subterreanean vault where he kept his loot, and his agony over whether to buy metal- or plastic-tipped shoelaces as a Christmas present.

Different surveys produced different results, although a poll of listeners credited Bob Hope with having the most popular show in 1941, followed by Benny and Fibber McGee and Molly. Despite a marked decline in the previous five years, variety programs continued to dominate. They made few intellectual demands on listeners and permitted a momentary respite from serious matters, no small considerations at a time when radio had to deal more and more with such names as Churchill, Tojo, and Hitler.

Critics continued to bemoan what radio did with its time, the failure to utilize this important means of communication to advance art and education. If they found encouragement in a few shows—the remarkable popularity of the NBC Symphony Orchestra, for example, and an occasional drama or public interest presentation—much of radio's offerings were deemed tasteless, dulling to the senses, and not at all broadening to the mind, the sort of criticism later made of television.

The critics knew the reason: In the United States radio was a business, part of the capitalist system, not an instrument of government or a part of the structure of education. Radio was organized primarily to make money. Some 750 commercial stations, 527 of which belonged to one of four national networks (Mutual, CBS, NBC Red, and NBC Blue), competed for advertising accounts. Radio avoided controversy and refrained from knowingly offending any group that could retaliate by turning off its broadcasts or boycotting its advertisers. The individuals who ran radio and advertising proceeded on the assumption that people tuned in to feel better, not to be challenged. Any stimulation that took place was likely to be other than intellectual.

Radio nonetheless was part of the culture and was educational in ways not necessarily planned: a molder of practices and reflector of attitudes and of an era. If programming suggested that people kept sexual attitudes mostly to themselves, one might conclude by the same measurement that violence was rampant and not necessarily immoral. Drama on radio thrived on violence. World War II was radio's war, and radio was as much a part of the war as any new weapon—a machine to describe a conflict fought with machines, a means of instant communication during a time when developments came instantaneously, a means of mass communication in a war that encompassed entire national populations. Radio did much to prepare Americans for what would soon be their war, and in the end it did function as an instrument of government policy.

Radio, of course, made demands on listener and performer unlike those of television, which would supersede it. The need to create a mental picture solely through sound called for special techniques. Use of sound effects, a separate art, helped a great deal. A narrator might set the scene. The Shadow needed Margo or someone to whom he could explain his predicament. Another person could not always be present, however, so heroes of radio developed a strange habit of muttering to themselves. "Great Scott!" Superman exclaimed as he whisked through the air. "The bridge is rocking like a pendulum—if I can get down underneath it—down on the piers— quick—it's going—matter of seconds—down—down."[8] The Lone Ranger often talked to his horse when Tonto was not around, and Silver seemed to understand. The listener understood as well. By requiring the use of imagination, radio encouraged listeners to create scene, mood, and sensation, which the mind's eye often could make more convincing and impressive than, say, a camera image. Given a chance to do so, however, people would take to what they could see. Individuals who observed the passing of radio's golden age knew that in the transition something had been lost.

If people wished to get away from radio, out of the house and into town, chances are good that they went to the movies. Motion pictures remained one of the least expensive—an average of 25–30 cents per ticket—and most available means of entertainment. Even so, the industry began the year beset with numerous problems. The salaries of some performers and executives seemed ridiculously high, and the more actors earned the more temperamental they became. War threatened to eliminate much of the European market, which in past years had provided the margin of profit. Attendance in the first half of the year was disappointing. Exhibitors could not understand why economic improvement had not spilled over to their business. Could it be that people were too busy or too tired? Had the war put them "in the blue mood and not interested in entertainment"? Some people blamed competition from traveling carnivals and professional baseball. A few critics suggested that the trouble ran deeper: The lush years of films had run out, and the industry stood on verge of collapse.[9]

Shortly after midyear, however, the slump came to an end, and people began returning to theaters in large numbers. If a single movie could be credited with the turnaround, it would probably be the film biography of Sergeant Alvin York, the celebrated hero of World War I. A native of the hills of Tennessee, York had consented to the production with reservations; Gary Cooper must play the lead, he demanded, and no "oomphy girl" could portray his sweetheart. Those were not crippling restrictions. No city slicker himself, Cooper fitted so effortlessly into the role of the honest, clumsy hillbilly that he easily won an Academy Award for the performance. Young Joan Leslie was pleasantly stimulating without being exactly "oomphy." In all, the cast (which included Walter Brennan) was excellent, the story timely and moving.

Although it was about war, *Sergeant York* was barely a war movie. It devoted little time to military action—too little, in the view of some critics. It dealt nearly as much with York's original pacifism as with his astonishing military feats. "Sergeant York does not glorify war, does not horn in on World War II," one review noted.[10] Still, the film, which opened in July, could not help but arouse national pride and lead many an observer to conclude, with Alvin York himself, that objection to war might be less compelling than the need to fight. More people went to see *Sergeant York* than any other film in the last half of 1941, and reviewers were virtually unanimous in its praise.

For the student of popular trends, another film was more revealing than *Sergeant York. Buck Privates,* featuring the new comedy team of Bud Abbott and Lou Costello, sought to exploit interest in America's new Army, and yet not cause audiences to take it, or the war, seriously. With a cast that included the Andrews Sisters, a popular singing trio, the movie employed slapstick, musical comedy, and the sort of trivial treatment some of the print media had given to military concerns. "If . . . 'Buck Privates' can be considered any criterion," one reviewer wrote, "a draftee's life is just a jitterbug paradise, where comedians enliven the humdrum of work at camp, and hostesses . . . pep up the boys with patriotic songs and boogie-woogie, strictly eight-to-the-bar."[11]

Expected to have gross receipts of $1 million, five times the cost of production, the movie was significant in several ways. It established Abbott, the straight man, and the fat, bouncy Costello as the "hottest comics in town," much in demand for radio as well as film. Before the year ended they had appeared in no fewer than five movies. The film's success encouraged production of "the pratfall, pie-throwing, blank-cartridge pistol shooting type of physical comedy," particularly with military themes. Abbott and Costello would follow with *In the Navy* and *Keep 'Em Flying;* Bob Hope did well in *Caught in the Draft;* Stan Laurel and Oliver Hardy came out with *Great Guns.* Before the year's end Jimmy Durante, Jackie Gleason and other comedians appeared in movies of approximately the same character, requiring hardly any reflection about the world situation on the audiences' part.

One type of movie in which interest seemed to remain constant was the Western. Every producer reserved some funds for Western films, and one studio, Republic, devoted approximately half its production schedule to movies about the old West. Westerns came in two grades. Top-level productions might star almost any of the best-known performers and were aimed at the standard-price evening audience. Examples in 1941 included *Western Union,* from a book by Zane Grey, with Robert Young, Randolph Scott, and Dean Jagger, and *They Died with Their Boots On,* another account of the "last stand" of George Custer, with Errol Flynn and Olivia De Haviland, two of the most prominent names in the industry. Far more common were lower-grade, low-budget, black-and-white productions designed to attract youngsters from five or six years old up and young minds of any age.

The B (or was it C?) Western usually came as part of a double-feature package that might also include a crime or suspense feature, cartoon, serial, and newsreel. For ten cents, children were getting their money's worth. The shows invariably came on Saturday, usually starting in early afternoon and running well into evening. Adults as a rule tried to avoid the theater on those days, if they could trust the kids to go alone, for the building was noisy, the aisles were filled with rubbish and moving bodies, and objects occasionally flew through the air.

The Saturday Westerns maintained remarkable uniformity in characters. The lead was a vigorous, neatly tailored, serious-minded individual with a loyal, erratic "sidekick" to provide comedy and occasionally help the hero out of a tight spot. Roy Rogers had George "Gabby" Hayes, Hopalong Cassidy had Andy Clyde as "California," Tim Holt rode with "Lasses" White, and Johnny Mack Brown with Fuzzy Knight. The rotund Smiley Burnette not only added comedy to Gene Autry's movies but made the star, whose body had expanded along with his career, look trim by comparison. Autry, who ranked first in popularity, sang in his movies, as did Rogers (no. 3) and Tex Ritter (no. 10). William Boyd as Hopalong Cassidy (no. 2) probably could not carry a tune, and other members of the Western top ten did not sing.[12]

The plots of B Westerns showed equal consistency. Although usually not lawmen, the heroes appointed themselves responsible for maintaining the peace. Occasionally the hero had to be called in to put down the law; nothing could be more threatening than a sheriff gone bad. The heroes never smoked or drank; they shot to wound or, even better, to disarm, not to kill. They kept an appropriate distance from women. Horses were much revered and pampered; the rules of the day forbade showing an animal out of breath or sweating. The dialogue seemed never to change. "I'll give you one hour to get out of town," the hero might say, or, "Bill, you and Slim go thataway. Me and Sam'll take the short cut and head 'em off."[13] Indians had been receiving more respectful treatment in recent years; scheming businessmen and bankers now made better villains. Republic used the same supporting actors so frequently that crooks became almost as familiar as heroes. Such "bit" performers as Roy Barcroft died or went to jail almost every Saturday. The "big" Westerns no less than Saturday "cheapies" drew a pronounced distinction between right and wrong. What listeners had heard on radio drama, they saw repeated on the screen.

Not all movies carried the moral tone of low-grade Westerns. The potential for conflict over the content of films always existed, in view of the industry's goal to sell as many movies to as many people as possible. Of one point the film producers—the eight major companies—were certain: If there had to be rules, they should make them themselves. The industry had created the Motion Picture Producers and Distributors of America, headed by Will Hays, a Presbyterian from Indiana. The man in charge of enforcing the production code during the 1930s and early 1940s was Joseph I. Breen, a Roman Catholic. The movies called for almost as much use of the imagination as radio, for under Breen's virtual dictatorship the Hays Committee imposed a stringent censorship. Toilets were not to be shown on the screen. If a couple sat on the edge of a bed to kiss, the female's feet could not leave the floor. Language had to be clean. It had taken extraordinary leniency to allow Clark Gable to utter "I don't give a damn" in *Gone With the Wind* in 1939. Nudity, of course, was out of the question.

With recent changes in fashion—the popularity of women's slacks, shorts, and form-fitting bathing suits—and a new group of "glamour girls" who featured body as much as face (and more than talent), some producers believed the time had come for liberalization of the rules. Breen did not agree, and early in 1941 he lectured the film industry about its tendency to emphasize women's breasts, either by putting them in low-cut dresses or in "sweater shots" that clearly and conspicuously outlined the bosom. "All such shots are in direct violation of the Production Code" and will not be tolerated, he wrote. "Intimate parts" of the body must be fully covered, of course, and they cannot be "clearly and unmistakably outlined by the garment."[14]

Breen resigned his post in late spring to take another job, and at approximately the same time Hays was spending several weeks in the hospital with pneumonia. The controversy that followed stemmed partly from some filmmakers' belief that times indeed had changed, partly from the supervising committee's temporary gap in leadership. As more controversial material slipped into movies, other organizations undertook responsibility for evaluating content. The sharpest vigilance came from the Roman Catholic Church; the church's Legion of Decency for years had applied a system for ranking films, taking special exception, as one publication remarked, to "sweater girls" and "Veronica Lake closeups."[15] Most films rated B, "objectionable in part," a Catholic magazine explained, "offend through a cheap and perverted attitude toward the sacred human faculty of sex."[16] The most severe judgment, a rating of C, "condemned," was tantamount to an order for boycott by Catholics who cared for their immortal souls.

Denied authority to deal with sexual themes openly, directors sought to reach the same subjects through subterfuge and intimation, encouraging viewers to find in the dialog whatever meaning their principles would allow. Their intentions did not escape the Catholic magazine *America*. In a recent movie titled *They Ride by Night,* a truck driver in a beanery made reference to a "classy chassis" and "head lights." "Only the naive would suppose he is talking about an automobile instead of the waitress, Ann Sheridan (advertised as the Oomph girl by her studio)," *America* charged. The reviewer commented that "some writers have not yet learned that some things belong behind a screen, not on it." The magazine recommended production of more films on the order of *Rebecca,* and *Knute Rockne, All-American,* the schmaltzy biography of a Notre Dame football coach in which Ronald Reagan appeared as the ill-fated player George Gipp.[17]

The church reacted with outrage to the appearance in the fall of *Two-Faced Woman.* In that comedy, starring Greta Garbo and Melvyn Douglas, a wife masqueraded as her twin sister, and the husband, misled by the deception, made enthusiastic love to a lady he believed was not his wife. Although both remained fully clothed, of course, and the film contained no shots of sexual action and no four-letter words (to depart from those standards would have been shocking indeed), the plot was preoccupied with sexual activity. "There's a double-entendre to nearly everything that is said between the two," one reviewer explained, "and nearly everything is said." Even *Variety* remarked that "how some of the lines of dialogue elude the scissors is . . . a mystery."[18]

The Catholic Church could not have agreed more. The Legion of Decency marked the film with a ringing C, and church officials in several cities gave it special attention. Archbishop Francis J. Spellman denounced the film in a letter read at Masses throughout New York as "a danger to public morality." Word went around among Catholics, especially where youngsters gathered, that *Two-Faced Woman* would start a person on a beeline to hell. The priests wanted their charges to repeat the oath that they would not watch such filthy material; some absolutely forbade it as best they could. Most Catholics probably complied with the warnings and admonitions, but they also wondered what the commotion was about. In some cities, such as Philadelphia, the film now attracted larger audiences than before the outcry.[19] The producer of the film, Metro-Goldwyn-Mayer, preferred not to have the sort of publicity *Two-Faced Woman* had caused. Catholics, after all, were supposed to boycott not only the movie but also theaters that showed the movie, a fact that could adversely affect the huge Loew's theater conglomerate, of which M-G-M was a part. The studio recalled the film, made changes, and rereleased it at the end of the year. The Legion of Decency changed the rating to B, "objectionable in part."

That episode, along with threats of censorship by officials in several states, caused producers to reevaluate other films already finished or in production. Howard Hughes, for example, decided to delay release of *The Outlaw,* a Western much different from the sort that featured Roy Rogers or Gene Autry. *Variety* reported concern about "bosom shots of Jane Russell, buxom 19-year-old newcomer who is starred." In truth, a movement to suppress the film had started with Hughes's publicity agent, Russell Birdwell, who spotted an opportunity to publicize for later use a movie that could offer little beyond titillation.[20]

The world war, of course, was too promising a reservoir of stories to ignore, so several films appearing between 1939 and 1941 related to the politics of the era. Most of the early "war movies" dealt with either the war in Europe and the character of the adversaries or aspects of the American rearmament program, in works ranging from the Abbott and Costello comedies to the more serious *I Wanted Wings* and *Dive Bomber. International Squadron* with Ronald Reagan, *A Yank in the R.A.F.* with Tyrone Power, and *Action in the North Atlantic* with Humphrey Bogart, were among the few that brought together activity in the United States and Europe. On the whole the movies applauded the new Army and rearmament as necessary, exciting, and frequently funny. They drew clear distinctions between the adversaries in the European war: the gallant British and the arrogant, brutal Germans. Japan was scarcely noticed. The film industry thus reflected the state of opinion in the United States; it remained consistent with the policies of the Roosevelt Administration.

That was a problem, of course: Hollywood and Roosevelt were going too much in the same direction, and opponents of Roosevelt's course could find a partial explanation for its popularity in the support given to the President by Hollywood, with its enormous potential for influence. Rather than using the war to sell movies (which was probably what they were doing), moviemakers were said to be using movies to sell the war to the American people. Most isolationists probably agreed with the charge, and a small group of senators started to take note of Hollywood's treatment of the war.

The most vehement objection came from Senator Gerald P. Nye of North Dakota. After listing several "propaganda" films, including *Sergeant York* and Charlie Chaplin's *The Great Dictator,* Nye invited his colleagues to "see who is doing this." He proceeded to read a list of executives in the film industry: Harry and Jack Cohn of Columbia, Louis B. Mayer and Sam Goldwyn of M-G-M, Joseph Schenck, Darryl Zanuck, Arthur Loew, Sam Katz, David Bernstein, Murray Silverstone, and several others. Nye did not directly issue a charge of Jewish war-mongering (as Lindbergh soon would do), but his list conspicuously omitted "Gentile-sounding" names. "Hollywood is a raging inferno of war fever," the Senator continued. "The place swarms with refugees and British actors. In Hollywood they call it the army of occupation." Nye explained that profit for the industry came from foreign distribution, now confined mostly to Britain. If the British lost the war, the margin of profit also would be lost. "Are you ready to send your boys to die in Europe to make the world safe for this industry and its financial backers?" he asked.[21] A special Senate subcommittee, which included several prominent isolationists, then proceeded with hearings on war-mongering within the movie industry.

The hearings provoked some of the liveliest verbiage of late summer—in the committee room and in the press. Producers hired Wendell Willkie as counsel, denied the existence of an interventionist conspiracy, and charged the subcommittee with anti-Semitism and an attempt to stifle free speech. "If anti-Semitism exists in America," Nye answered, "the Jews have themselves to blame." He reiterated that "those primarily responsible for the propaganda pictures are born abroad."[22] If the episode hinted at latent prejudice in American life, it also reflected national feelings about foreign policy. The film industry attracted many allies. Mayor LaGuardia, for example, approved the movies' treatment of the war. "Films can do all sorts of camera tricks but the scenarist isn't alive who can show anything good in the Hitler regime," he said. "You can't make a gentleman out of a Nazi."[23] Some isolationists and at least one member of the subcommittee, uncomfortable with the charge of censorship and anti-Semitism, began to have doubts about continuing the proceedings. Chairman D. Worth Clark of Idaho did not officially disband the subcommittee, but it stopped meeting in October, leaving its status in a state of suspension. Feeling vindicated by events, the film industry now believed itself safe to produce more war movies.

Sprinkled among the year's comedies and war films came a few memorable movies. Warner Brothers revived an effort to film a story written several years earlier by Dashiel Hammett. After experimentation with *Dangerous Female, Satan Met a Lady,* and *The Gent from Frisco,* the studio wisely decided to retain the original title, *The Maltese Falcon.* George Raft turned down the lead role, as did such other "tough guys" as Edward G. Robinson and John Garfield. Humphrey Bogart finally snapped it up. The *Falcon* would become a virtual classic and would establish a standard by which to measure other detective stories. Here one could find all the "tough-guy" jargon of the age: a pistol was a "heater"; characters might "take it on the lam," "hit the hay," look for a "fall guy." Bogart, a lesser Hollywood "heavy" noted mostly for a becoming sneer, made the character Sam Spade famous, and vice versa.[24]

Probably the most significant production of the year was *Citizen Kane,* a film that was all but stamped the personal property of Orson Welles. At age twenty-six Welles co-authored the screen play, produced and directed the movie, and played the title role. Based loosely on the career of the publisher Willam Randolph Hearst, the film pioneered the practice of shooting against the light and at bizarre angles, overlapping conversations, and many other new techniques. "It is . . . brilliant, unreeled in method and effects that sparkle with originality and invention," one review said.[25] Many ordinary customers nonetheless found *Citizen Kane* strange and difficult to follow.

The most successful performers included the giants of Hollywood's golden age. Mickey Rooney, who turned twenty-one, showed the greatest box office strength, followed by Clark Gable. A list of the most popular stars included Spencer Tracy, Gary Cooper, Bette Davis, James Cagney, Judy Garland, and also Abbott and Costello, Bob Hope, and Gene Autry. One actress not on the list seemed different from others. "If there be one star in Hollywood who merits a picture of strength and beauty it is Ingrid Bergman," one columnist wrote.[26] Striking in beauty, talent, and unspoiled demeanor, the Swedish actress had not quite hit her stride. Perhaps it would soon come, for rumor placed her first in line to be Maria in the film to be made from Hemingway's *For Whom the Bell Tolls.*

Leading newcomers stood out more for their appearance than for their talent. Veronica Lake, for example, wore her blonde hair in the fashion of an English sheep dog. Sometimes she covered the left eye, sometimes the right, but almost never could she see out of both. "I did it so I'd be noticed in the mobs of girls who surrounded me," she confessed.[27] Other newcomers included Gene Tierney, Maureen O'Hara, Martha Scott, Dean Jagger, Broderick Crawford, Mary Martin, and Richard Whorf. Some would go on to long careers; none would establish an identity comparable to Gable, Bogart, or Cooper—people already established in the business.

The war giveth and the war taketh away; in the case of the movies it was mostly the former. International politics created new subjects for treatment on film; it helped provide funds and incentives for people to go to the movies. NBC and CBS were spending $1.5 million to $2 million a year on television; informed people identified television as potentially one of the most important industries in the country and a powerful competitor for the entertainment business. There was general agreement, however, that the flowering of the exciting new medium would have to wait for the end of the war period, when there would be no problem with scarce materials or strategic equipment.

The war helped extend the golden age of Hollywood through 1941 and a short time beyond. All studios made money that year; Warner Brothers nearly doubled its profits, and Loew's Incorporated (M-G-M) cleared almost five times the amount of 1940. Estimates of weekly attendance at theaters varied; some ran as high as 85 million. Receipts totaled more than $800 million, the largest recreation expenditure for the American people unless one counted money spent on all kinds of publications. The United States remained the pacemaker and giant of the film industry. The most successful European performers, Greta Garbo, Charles Boyer, Ingrid Bergman, and many others, eventually found their way across the Atlantic, for, as a foreign observer noted, "it is only in America that the full possibility of fame is attained."[28] Approximately 65 percent of the world's films came from the United States, and in the United States approximately 90 percent came out of Hollywood or its environs. The movie industry paid some of the highest salaries in the land and continued to be the nation's most glamorous business.

Film performers were almost universally envied, and the impact of the industry remained enormous. A visitor to the United States found films to be "incomparably the most effective medium of expressing and influencing the American way of life."[29] With the possible exception of radio, nothing did as much to promote the standardization of speech and dress, encouraging people to think and act all in the same way. *Photoplay* and other fan magazines had monthly circulations ranging from 250,000 to 500,000. *Harpers,* by contrast, sold approximately 100,000, the *New Republic* less than 30,000. The daily press nationwide followed the careers and, as much as possible, the personal lives of performers. A survey in March discovered that most reader interest was not in the war or national or world events, but in New York gossip columns, the little sections that reported trivia about personalities in the entertainment business.[30] Men called to military service kept personal collections of pinups, as they were called, usually publicity photos of Betty Grable, Lana Turner, and other glamorous ladies of film.

With such interest, adulation, glamour, and purported wealth, it was small wonder that many American young people—particularly girls—spent years with no objective other than getting their "big break" in the movies. The story of Lana Turner, the "sweater girl" and one of the prettiest females in movies, was legendary. She had gone to Hollywood with her mother looking for an honest way to make a living and was "discovered" by Billy Wilkerson sitting at a soda fountain. "Lana didn't have to act," one writer said of her talents, "she just walked along wearing a tight-fitting sweater."[31] Lana turned twenty in 1941 and appeared that year with Clark Gable in *Honky Tonk;* the road seemed to point in no direction but up. One might add that she had started along in another direction: marriage and divorce. A four-month marriage to the bandleader Artie Shaw had ended. More were to come.

Nearly everywhere one could find girls awaiting their time. Sarah Tuck, a black thirteen-year-old in North Carolina who liked Shirley Temple, wanted "to be a show girl and sing and dance."[32] Two-thirds of the girls answering a survey in New York wished to become actresses. The scholar in Elmtown, Illinois, found several people waiting for stardom. One girl, working as a maid, had seen an advertisement about a school of drama designed to lead to "a Hollywood career." "If I can go there," she said, "I can be an actress, and oh, boy!" Another girl compared herself to Joan Crawford because "she usta work in a restaurant too." A third young lady, a "cross-eyed seventeen-year-old . . . known for her 'B.O.,' poor clothes, dirty skin," was fired from three jobs because she sang all the time. At last the truth came out: She was practicing for a career as a "torch singer." A girl from South Dakota made national news because she had the "exquisite temerity" to turn down a movie contract.[33]

There was the additional problem of taking movies too seriously, of being unable to separate fact from what unfolded on the screen.

Virtually no one accused producers of being realistic in those days. Forever fearful of driving away the audience, filmmakers refrained from confronting the less pleasant truths of life and human relationships. Good stood miles apart from bad, and it was easy to tell the difference; the truth always came out in the end. Romance was overpowering and everlasting; at least the film never lasted long enough to suggest anything different. "In the moral lexicon of Hollywood," one observer put it, "honesty is always rewarded, evil is always punished, and crime—in an exquisite reflection of the pragmatic emphases of our world—does not pay."[34] If the film industry remained a "dream factory," the war gave no reason to expect anything different. The movies produced thus far indicated that war films offered realism only to the extent that sometimes the truth happened to coincide with Hollywood's preconceived notions.

Going to the movies was largely escapism. The movie house offered a needed respite, and most people who went would find a way to distinguish between truth and fantasy, although they might do so with some regret. The war, which one might have expected to provide a powerful stimulus to reality-testing, instead became for many the supreme expression of idealism, a real-life enactment of cinema's theme that the "right" forces inevitably win out. For individuals who treated movies as something other than fantasy—a genuine learning experience, for example, or a true reflection of life—discovering the truth became more painful than it should have been. Some people doubtless wasted too much time waiting to be "discovered" or measuring situations and people, including themselves, by models found on the screen.

The impact of Hollywood went beyond the United States. In that day before globalization of military power, what had been regarded as Americanization in foreign nations came largely from movies. In its depiction of coarseness and cruelty no less than in projecting glamour and endless opportunity, Hollywood misled foreign audiences more than it did people at home. The chief constable in a suburb of Liverpool, for example, reported "the pernicious and growing habit of . . . youths to use Americanisms, with nasal accompaniment, in order to appear, in their own vernacular, tough guys." "Lay off, cop," a young hoodlum shouted as he was being searched; "'oh-yeahs' are frequent in answer to charges," the officer continued, "and we are . . . threatened to be 'bumped off.'"[35]

☆

In popular music, the year 1941 stood squarely in the era of the big band. Named after their leaders, these organizations comprised ten to fifteen musicians playing largely brass and wind instruments, along with piano, drums, and possibly a guitar. As they grew larger, some groups later added strings, mostly violins. Although each big band sought its own distinguishing sound (or a more famous band's), many performed in a style that had become known as swing. It was the age of swing.

Swing had emerged from the musical ferment of the early 1930s as an effort to move away from sorrowful blues and sentimental ballads and to put life into music. The label was perhaps traceable to a record of Duke Ellington, "It Don't Mean a Thing if It Ain't Got That Swing." Swing grew out of jazz, and many people believed it was essentially the same. "They've poured a little gravy over it," Louis Armstrong said. "No matter how you slice it, it's still the same music."[36] But to most it sounded smoother, more melodic, and less spontaneous than jazz. When those qualities increased and traces of jazz diminished, swing gave way to "sweet" music—soothing, slower, more conservative tempos, played by the same musicians on most of the same instruments. Swing music was for fast dancing, the Lindy or jitterbug. Sweet music was meant for romantic, slow, foxtrot dancing. As a rule, people did not dance to authentic jazz. Jazz hounds preferred to concentrate on listening, tapping their feet, and moving their hands and shoulders in time with the beat. Dancing would break their concentration.

All bands played swing, and some tried jazz, but listeners could not agree on which label to apply to each organization. One fact was clear: The era began with Benny Goodman. "His was the band that sparked the whole big band scene," a participant recalled.[37] Goodman was the "King of Swing." Gene Krupa, Duke Ellington, Charlie Barnet, and others also played "hot" or "solid" music for energetic dancing. The conventional rhythms of Dick Jurgens, Jan Garber, and Guy Lombardo classified their bands as sweet. "Hepcats" of the day scorned their sounds for failing to be "in the groove"; they called it "mickey mouse" music. While encouraged to "swing and sway," Sammy Kaye's listeners probably heard mostly sweet songs at his public appearances or on his radio program, *Sunday Serenade*. More difficult to classify were Glenn Miller, Tommy and Jimmy Dorsey, Harry James, and several others. "There are those who think Miller nauseous sweet, overarranged and lacking in change of style, but they are obviously eccentrics and to be shunned on campus," a reviewer from UCLA wrote. The term "sweet-swing" seemed to be an acceptable compromise for bands like Miller's.[38]

In the era of big bands, the bands dominated popular music. Only a few vocalists—Bing Crosby, Kate Smith, and the Andrews Sisters, for example—could carry a concert or sell a record on their own. Most popular singers belonged to one band or another: Dick Haymes was with Harry James, and Ray Eberle with Glenn Miller. Peggy Lee joined Benny Goodman in August, when Helen Forrest quit. Tommy Dorsey used Connie Haynes, Jo Stafford, the Pied Pipers, and Frank Sinatra. Singing for Jimmy Dorsey, Bob Eberly and Helen O'Connell were perhaps the most popular and attractive vocalists on the circuit. A singer might help make a song distinctive— Tommy Dorsey's popular "I'll Be Seeing You," for example, clearly bore the mark of Sinatra—but in 1941 the singers were supposed to complement the band and enhance the reputation of the leader. The chance for a separate identity would have to come later. At least sixty or seventy dance bands were nationally known; *Variety* listed the itineraries of more than three hundred. Hundreds more whose reputation did not extend beyond their local areas played the same sort of sweet and swing music.

Much of the tone for popular music was set by the handful of bands that could reach a mass audience. Ordinarily radio would have been one of the best ways to do so, but a conflict with song publishers over royalties kept most popular music off the air until the fall; not until October 30 could Bing Crosby sing his theme song, "Blue of the Night," on the *Kraft Music Hall.* Still, several bands had radio shows they wanted to keep, even if they could play only music from the public domain. It was not easy to make convincing swing music out of "London Bridge Is Falling Down," but the bands tried.

Music also circulated through the sale of sheet music, largely to the benefit of the composer and lyricist, and through records, which in 1941 were breakable 78-RPM platters with one song on each side. A record was customarily identified with the recording "artist," probably a band. The record industry had a banner year in 1941 with sales of approximately 100 million, as against 70 million a year earlier.[39]

Producers of popular music also made use of a system of 300,000–400,000 coin machines in places ranging from plush urban cocktail lounges to seedy taverns and noisy frame roadhouses. "The gaudy jukebox," one report said, "is the social hub for a half-score million young Americans." They put a nickel (a quarter for six songs) in a brightly lighted Wurlitzer or Capehart machine and waited for music to come out "solid," with a "boggie-woogie" beat, perhaps, and proceeded to listen or "cut a rug."[40] The somewhat disreputable environment ascribed to "juke joints," and even that grating term, did not diminish the coin machine as an instrument of culture that promoted the music business. Jukeboxes brought in nearly $90 million a year; operators spent $10 million on records.

Finally, the bands sought to sell themselves through personal appearances, ranging from one-night stands to long-term commitments at such famous nightspots as the Cocoanut Grove in Los Angeles. For the listener, the live performance was the biggest treat of all. "This was it!" a follower of the business explained. "To stand in front of one of your favorite swing bands . . . with the trumpets and trombones blasting away right at you and the saxes supporting them and the rhythm section letting loose with those clear, crisp swinging beats—it all added up to one of the real thrills in life."[41] The audience often responded by stamping feet, screaming, shouting, and dancing in the aisles. Nationally known bands probably spent the winter playing at hotels in large cities.

The most popular songs of the year included "Daddy" by Sammy Kaye, "I Don't Want to Set the World on Fire" (Inkspots), Glenn Miller's "Chattanooga Choo-Choo" and "Elmer's Tune," and "This Love of Mine" by Tommy Dorsey. Jimmy Dorsey's recording of "Maria Elena" and "Green Eyes" sold nearly a million copies. Partly because of the conflict over royalties on radio, classical compositions took on new life as popular music. Tchaikovsky's Piano Concerto in B-Flat Minor, relabeled "Piano Concerto" or "Tonight We Love," became familiar as the sound of Freddy Martin. The bands, of course, continued to play the songs that had made their reputation. Bunny Berigan had to play "I Can't Get Started With You" or "Marie" on his trumpet wherever he went; Harry James kept repeating "Ciribirbin" and "You Made Me Love You." Listeners of Glenn Miller were disappointed if they did not hear "In the Mood," "Pennsylvania 6–5000," "I Got a Gal in Kalamazoo," and others. Latin beats—the rumba and conga—enlivened and diversified all dance music. Near the end of the year, the pensive "White Cliffs of Dover," showing sentimental longing for peaceful times, rose rapidly in popularity. Mostly, however, people liked songs with lively rhythm.

Judging from their popularity in 1941, it might have appeared that the big bands would go on forever. The music was varied, appealed to all age groups, and seemed suited to the needs of the day. For genuine physical and emotional release, nothing surpassed a good jitterbug. Those who looked closely, however, might have seen signs of trouble. As the bands grew larger, they became more expensive. Glenn Miller carried seventeen musicians and six singers in a total troupe of thirty. Tommy Dorsey's group expanded to thirty-five. Kay Kyser had the most profitable band (he earned $1 million in 1940) because he exploited films, radio, records, and appearances—and because he used only fourteen musicians and instrumentalists and two singers, almost every one of whom had a second job.[42]

The band circuit was rigorous, confining, and not conducive to a full and healthful life. Travel fatigue and auto and bus accidents were occupational hazards. A member of the Dorsey band complained that Tommy "either had a reserve tank built in or he had no bladder at all"—he never wanted to stop the bus. Sinatra recalled that life on tour involved rotating between five places: "the bus, your hotel room, the greasy-spoon restaurant, the dressing room (if any) and the bandstand. Then back on the bus to the next night's gig, maybe four hundred miles away or more."[43] Some people could not handle such a schedule. Bunny Berigan, for example, developed a drinking problem; he died in 1942 at age thirty-three. Military service had started to erode musical groups. It was possible to detect restlessness among the performers. Doris Day, barely eighteen years old, "retired" and left the band of Les Brown in 1941. Jo Stafford of the Pied Pipers decided to get married, as did Helen O'Connell; they later would return as individual performers. Frank Sinatra contemplated leaving Dorsey to strike out on his own. The singers, who were products of the big band, were on the verge of taking over.

None of that could discourage the people who danced and snapped their fingers to the sounds of 1941. It was their music, and the next generation would have to find something else. The big bands were a way of expressing their tastes, even their age. Swing music did not start with the war, but the rapid, almost frantic pace so fitted the moods and needs of the era that it came to be identified as the music of the war—and of the year before war came to the United States.

The second most popular music in the United States went by various names: hill music, music from "down home" or "back home," folk music, country, or Western. Probably the most recognizable designation was "hillbilly." Country music received no attention from professional publications, such as *Variety* or *Metronome,* unless it was derision. Makers of popular music and most listeners considered such entertainment lacking in sophistication, taste, and artistry, contributing nothing in the way of content or sound. To admit enjoying hillbilly music was in many circles tantamount to confession of musical illiteracy, if not general backwardness. Country music nonetheless had become a national phenomenon, reaching millions of people, all rural areas of the United States, and many industrial centers. It was impossible to consider entertainment in the United States and the musical tastes of the American people without taking songs of the countryside into account.

The original hillbilly music came out of the uplands of the Southeast. It took little preparation, few people, and virtually no money to form a string band or hillbilly group—two or three people would do—and south of the Ohio River such organizations outnumbered standard dance bands. They had been singing in the hills as long as folks could remember, individually and in groups, and with some measure of organization. In Pikeville, Kentucky, for example, people assembled every June for a "singin' gatherin'." Sounds coming from those amateur performances tended to be monotone, nasal, and loud. "Most of the singers don't know a half-note from a question mark," a man who had come to observe remarked, "so without a natural harmony, the only variation between voices is in quality—and quantity. Volume is most important." The music nonetheless satisfied the people who attended. At a time when the visitor to Pikeville was prepared to pronounce mountain music uniformly bad, a lady turned to him from across the aisle to remark: "They really can sing, can't they?"[44]

Country music had moved some distance toward professionalism. Building on pioneering efforts of Jimmy Rogers and the Carter family, equipped with guitar, fiddle, and perhaps banjo or autoharp, entertainers wailed their songs of love, tragedy, and almost anything else pertaining to "real life," as they liked to say. Such old songs as "Barbara (Barbry) Allen" mixed with "Red River Valley" or other more recent ballads. A "foot-stompin'" hoedown might follow a hymn learned in a Protestant church. Country music long had been popular on radio, beginning in the 1920s with WSB in Atlanta, and dozens of stations had regular "barn dances" or programs designed for a rural audience. From Nashville radio station WSM carried each Saturday night the *Prince Albert Grand Ole Opry*. On the stage of that show in 1941 one could hear such promising young performers as Bill Monroe, Minnie Pearl, and the Opry's first singing star, Roy Acuff. Ernest Tubb, although a successful country singer, would not receive the call to the Opry until 1942, when he brought down the house with "I'm Walking the Floor over You."

At the start of the 1940s Chicago was a more important center of country music than Nashville, and a program originating in that city, the *National Barn Dance,* overshadowed the *Grand Ole Opry.* Beamed every Saturday night over powerful station WLS, the show reached millions of Americans in the Midwest and beyond. Its performers, Red Foley, George Gobel, the Hoosier Hot Shots, Prairie Ramblers, and Lulu Belle and Scotty, were well known in much of the United States.[45]

As the people moved west, country music went along and then was modified to fit the local environment. Texas surely produced more entertainers than Tennessee or Kentucky. Hollywood seemed on the verge of replacing Chicago as the center of country music. Western songs were different from the music of the hill country, but the instruments were the same and some performers felt comfortable with either. Gene Autry, one of the most successful singers in the United States, earlier had performed with the *National Barn Dance.* Several of his songs, such as "The Last Roundup" and "Be Honest With Me," clearly cowboy songs of the Southwest, carried familiar country themes of sorrow, death, and tarnished romance.

Commercialization of country music added to its strength as a maker and reflector of culture. No less than "sweet" and "swing" songs, rural music offered entertainment, relaxation, and release from tension; a hoedown or mountain frolic could be as vigorous as a jitterbug. Country musicians could claim that they played swing long before it became fashionable in ballrooms (a hoedown was a type of swing), and yet the connection became official when Bob Wills and his Texas Playboys began turning out "country swing." Country music helped establish a separate rural identity. Associated with the gingham dress, jeans, and overalls, said to be "genuine" and "human," it expressed a rural point of view, even rural pride. And if by chance the people could not make it on the farm and had to move to the city, their music would be one of the few sources of comfort they could take with them into the strange world.

If country music was taken by other parts of society to be a badge of backwardness, the performers and listeners were doing quite a bit to bring that judgment on themselves. They played into the hands of their detractors, and with apparent relish. "Hillbilly" performers saw country entertainment as an antidote for a society—and a music—that had become urban, overcivilized, and false. Their comedy, and sometimes the music, stressed lack of sophistication and the local vernacular. They took pride in presenting themselves as country bumpkins in dress and demeanor. What they considered unpretentious, "down-to-earth" behavior looked to others like glorification of ignorance and illiteracy.

The growth of glamorous forms of entertainment did not cause Americans to give up old habits. The money spent on all types of literature surpassed the investment in radio or movies, and in those days a small sum would buy a great deal. A newspaper cost a few pennies a week, perhaps twenty or thirty; most magazines sold for ten or fifteen cents. The standard hardcover book cost two or three dollars. By waiting a few months it might be possible to acquire a bestseller at almost no cost. The paperback revolution had begun in the United States with the introduction of Pocket Books, a firm that offered softcover reprints of selected popular works for a quarter. Pocket Books published 10 million volumes in 1941 and expected to do more the next year.

The year did not stand out for the production of good fiction. F. Scott Fitzgerald died in January, and his final manuscript, *The Last Tycoon,* finished by another author, appeared in print near the end of the year. Some people found the event symbolic of the passing of an era. In truth Fitzgerald belonged to an age that had passed earlier, and so it was with the man. Hemingway remarked that he had "died inside himself" at age thirty or thirty-five, and *The Last Tycoon* had "that deadness, the one quality about which nothing can be done in writing . . . like seeing an old baseball pitcher with nothing left in his arm coming out and working with his intelligence for a few innings before he is knocked out of the box."[46]

Writers seemed to be marking time. Many had moved away from social activism, the intense liberalism or radicalism of the 1930s, and had not yet become absorbed in the war. Perhaps—as with Fitzgerald—they were awaiting their successors. At the peak of his career, Hemingway was basking in the success of *For Whom the Bell Tolls,* his story about the Spanish Civil War. Royalties and proceeds from the sale of movie rights (rumored to be $150,000) might have left him a wealthy man, except for an expensive life-style, the costs of previous wives, and a graduated income tax now beginning to soar under the pressure of military expenditures. "If anyone asks the children what their father did in Mr. Rooseveldts [sic] war," he angrily wrote a former wife, "they can say 'He paid for it.'"[47]

If the war came slowly to novelists, producers of nonfiction were dealing with little else. Charges leveled at the film industry easily could have focused on the print media, for nearly all books about the war carried a clear ideological message. Francis Hackett explained *What Mein Kampf Means to America.* Douglas Miller warned *You Can't Do Business with Hitler*—"which is to the effect," one reviewer wrote, "there'll be no business and no you." William L. Shirer's *Berlin Diary* was, of course, distinctly and authoritatively anti-Nazi. Released in June, it sold more than 550,000 copies by the end of December and would be the publishing sensation of the year, surpassing everything in fiction. Several books treated aspects of the new Army, and such prominent Americans as Archibald MacLeish and Stephen Vincent Benet felt moved to publish views about world politics. One could tell from the titles in nonfiction that these were extraordinary times.[48]

The status of periodical publication—magazines and journals— gave hints as to the state of the reading public. Americans liked their material light, lively, compressed, and illustrated, preferably in color. The great success story continued to be *Reader's Digest,* which by 1941 had a circulation of 4 million, an eightfold increase in a decade. Originally a publication of reprints, its pages now included many original articles. Whether original or reprinted, all essays were relevant to life and could be read in a few minutes; many carried a clear moral message.

Because it offered more than one magazine, the empire of Henry Luce probably topped the field of periodical publication. *Time* sold at a rate of nearly 1 million a week because it gave easily read coverage of events of the day. *Life, Time's* pictorial brother, now had a circulation of approximately 3 million. Readers of the two magazines (and *Fortune* as well) had to accept the twist given the news by Mr. Luce—he was almost the magazine counterpart of Robert Mc-Cormick—but when carefully done, the reader might never notice the slant. The success of *Life* and *Time* had prompted imitators in *Look* and *Newsweek.* For sheer bulk the most practical purchase in magazines was the popular *Saturday Evening Post.* Weekly issues ranging from 80 to 130 large pages of fiction, nonfiction, pictures, and humor could be had for "5 cents the copy." Small wonder that nearly 3.3 million copies sold each week. Editors of the *Post* and its imitator *Collier's* did not worry much about price. Their profits came from advertising, and the *Post's* pages were full of it.[49]

Seeking to discover reading taste in Wasco, California, a scholar found the following publications at a newsstand: fourteen adventure and detective titles, fourteen "love-story" magazines, and eleven movie magazines, nearly all published in pulp. The dealer also carried eighty comic book titles, of which he sold, in this small town, six hundred copies a month.[50]

One of the most revealing developments, in fact, was the enormously large readership for comics. The comics came in two forms. The so-called comic books were really little magazines 10 × 7 inches and sixty-four pages long—a spinoff of older pulp magazines that came of age in 1938 with publication of *Action Comics,* featuring Superman. Publishers offered 128 titles in 1941, and although overpriced at 10 cents, at least 10 million sold each month. Virtually every newspaper carried comic strips in black-and-white on a single page during the week and in a special section of several colored pages in Sunday editions. Many characters came out in both comic magazines and newspapers. Superman, for example, appeared in two magazines and 230 newspapers, with an estimated combined circulation of 25 million.[51] The number of readers could never be determined, but it certainly reached many millions. Youngsters often traded "comic books" with friends or resold them for two or three cents and purchased others secondhand for a nickel, so readership would be much larger than the number of original sales. Comics represented the most common literature for children and might have been the most frequent reading material for Americans in general.

The popularity of comics had become, understandably, a cause of concern. In the first place, it suggested shallowness of thought and reading habits, of course, if indeed one could regard comics as reading material. They essentially offered picture stories, and one could scarcely expand a vocabulary from bursts of speech in the balloons that carried words of the characters. In the second place, the comics, or "funnies," in many cases were not funny. One critic complained that "that colorful and carefree world . . . of slapstick and innocent jokes has all but disappeared . . . shouted down and blotted out" by such characters as the Phantom, Dick Tracy, and Flash Gordon. *Time* complained that comics exposed children to "an overseasoned, indigestible, nerve-shattering, eye-ruining diet of non-comic murder, torture, kidnapping, sex-baiting."[52]

In truth, comics reflected some of the contradictions that permeated American society. While far too many comic books and "funnies" in the newspapers were far too violent and in other ways objectionable for children, they existed alongside Donald Duck, Blondie, and the Katzenjammer Kids, comics designed as family entertainment or for the innocent mind. Comics laden with violence usually carried a moral message, the idea expressed in movies and on radio: Crime does not pay. Crooks were crooks in those days, and no one saw any need to inquire into the causes of their maladjustment. That would only confuse the issue and spoil the fun. They were simply bad people, and the heroes of the comics—either such superpeople as Superman and his latecomer rival, Captain Marvel, or the talented mortals—felt fully justified in using violence to suppress evil ways.

The same diverse mixture existed with respect to sex. No display of sexual activity appeared, of course, and the hero often demonstrated prudish moral principles. But plenty of female flesh could be seen on Wonder Woman; Sheena, Queen of the Jungle, in a leopard-skin suit; and Velveet in her off-the-shoulder blouse. In the seemingly innocent "Li'l Abner" by Al Capp, Daisy Mae had one of the skimpiest costumes in the funnies. Persons who preferred men as sex objects could find much to interest them in the comics.

For some creators the purpose seemed clear enough: to succeed in the market place through the tactic of shock or thrill. Mixed in with the suggestive and the crime-fighting strips were the innocent comics, the genuine "funnies." A key point in child development might have been traced had it been possible to notice when a youngster turned first to "Terry and the Pirates" instead of Donald Duck.

One of the most popular comics, "Joe Palooka," the creature of Ham Fisher, was almost never funny and only modestly violent. The strip was attractive partly because it was clearly drawn; the characters almost jumped at the viewer, especially in the large, colored Sunday edition. The settings were uncluttered, the sentences short and simple, the plots uncomplicated. The strip thrived also through exhortation to moral principle. Joe Palooka, a sort of an urbanized Alvin York, represented salt-of-the earth, solid Americanism. His popularity indicated that in a world of turmoil the simple values still offered much attraction to people in the United States, an expression of idealism and of the rewards one might expect from remaining true to the faith.

In Ham Fisher's comic the differences between good and evil became obvious at a glance. Joe, the heavyweight boxing champion, was tall and blonde, with umblemished skin and not an ounce of fat. Palooka might be strong and clean, but he was no Clark Gable or Robert Taylor. His looks were boyish but in no way handsome; he was a "plain" Joe. His opponent, in the ring or in life, usually wore a heavy beard that no amount of shaving could cause to disappear (in terminology of that day, a "five o'clock shadow"), had much ugly body hair and a mean, devious expression. Speech helped distinguish hero from villain. Joe in fact butchered the language by chopping off words, running them together, and breaking the rules of grammar. Sloppy English evidently helped identify him as a "common" American, by implication an honest one. The use of proper English struck some people as "putting on airs," British-sounding, and almost un-American. At least Joe spoke clean language; his most vulgar expostuation was "Tch, Tch." His adversaries used the slang of the day, such words as "bum," which aligned them with the underworld. And how they cursed! No periodical would print actual profanity or obscenity, of course, and so swearing came out as a stream of exclamation marks, asterisks, and other symbols from the top row of the typewriter. The reader could fill in whatever words he chose. With lines of contrast so clearly drawn, a conflict could end only one way.

The strip expressed the racial attitudes common to the era. Black people were not important to the series; their subjugation was taken for granted. All Palooka's opponents in the ring were white. The only black on the scene was "Smokey," Joe's trainer, who fitted the stereotype of the humble, affectionate, loyal servant with kinky hair, huge lips, and "Negro" speech. "Wheah at Mah Boy?" he said. "Ah'm burstin' wide open—ah cain't stan' dis suspents. Wheah at Mah Boy?" There is no evidence that anyone challenged this characterization.

Joe was a supreme patriot, which in 1941 meant to Fisher hostility toward Germany and obedience to government policy. Enlisting in late 1940, Joe carried his customary naïve, honest simplicity into the Army. He refused promotion to corporal because he wished to remain "just plain Joe." He nearly lost an exhibition match to a hairy beast from a different unit named Ruffy Balonki. When Joe stopped to salute generals who entered the arena—even though saluting with a boxing glove looked slightly awkward—Ruffy belted him. Off duty from Fort Dix, he was at a skating rink when a friend happened to collide with a huge man. "Look vere you go or I mebbe schmear you und your loussy uniform," the big man shouted. The accent tipped off the merits of the case, of course, and the intruder had insulted the United States Army to boot. Joe and his friend proceeded to overpower four or five hoodlums, and when it came out at the police station that the villains were from "that bund outfit [the German-American Bund] we've had trouble with," the judge congratulated Joe "on the fine job you did to those vermin."

Joe maintained a romantic relationship with a pretty, but not glamorous, working girl, a simple American commoner named Ann Howe. Readers assumed the couple would eventually marry, but duty came first. Meanwhile, Joe gave off not the slightest hint of interest in premarital physical pleasures. Nothing beyond expected displays of affection happened between the two. His girl picked him up at camp one time, and when Joe asked "D'you know some place we kin park an'—an' talk?" Ann knew he had nothing more in mind than conversation.

"Don't look for escape in the current funnies," a critic warned in 1941. "Stick to the saner world of war and horror on the front pages."[53] He could not have meant Joe Palooka. The strip had inspired a movie in the 1930s, and Rodgers and Hart were planning a musical for Broadway about "Private Palooka." Fisher received tributes from such groups as the Mormon Youth Rally in Salt Lake City, which proclaimed Joe "the symbol of American youth." Joe Palooka showed not how people behaved in 1941—or ever—but how many Americans believed life, in the face of devilish troubles and temptations, should be lived.[54]

In professional sports, baseball remained the foremost attraction, capable of arousing interest of between one-third and one-half of the population. The games of most major league teams were broadcast on radio, and in some cities several stations carried the same games. Only the New York Giants and Yankees, clubs that could not reach an agreement with sponsors, did not have radio coverage. The home games came live from the ballpark, of course, and if the station carried games on the road—some did not, and others omitted Sunday games—the broadcast originated in a studio, where announcers "recreated" the action from brief descriptions received on a teletype machine. Baseball dominated sports coverage in the newspapers the year round. At World Series time in the fall, it seemed everyone became a fan. The Series of 1941, a special case because both teams were from New York, even interrupted activity on the Stock Exchange. Nothing seemed more typically American than baseball at a time when people took pride in stressing native culture. The sport had found its way into the vocabulary: Everyone knew what it meant to "get to first base." Nine of the ten largest news stories of the year in the Associated Press related to the war. The other one had to do with the pennant race in the National League.[55]

The year was much better than average for baseball, although one could not tell at the time if it represented the end of an age (which, mostly because of the war, would be the case), or the middle of a longer era. It was a time of such innovative general managers as Branch Rickey of St. Louis and Larry MacPhail of Brooklyn, and a time of personalized ownership: the Wrigleys and Comiskeys in Chicago, Horace Stoneham of the Giants, "Spike" Briggs of Detroit, Tom Yawkey in Boston, and Connie Mack, who remained synonymous with the Philadelphia Athletics.

The ballparks offered much in the way of character and individuality. Many were small, such as the "crackerboxes" at Wrigley Field in Chicago and Sportsman's Park in St. Louis, home of both the Cardinals and the Browns. At Crosley Field in Cincinnati, fans sat on the outfield grass on opening day. Larger parks included Briggs Stadium in Detroit, the legendary Yankee Stadium, which would hold 72,000, and Cleveland's massive Municipal Stadium, with more than 80,000 seats. The Giants' home in New York had features of both. Distances to the outfield fence at the foul lines were short; on windy days a pop fly down the line could devastate a pitcher's morale. The spacious middle part of the park made it difficult at times to find the centerfielder. The Polo Grounds surely was better designed for horses than for ballplayers. While rumors circulated about new sites—California with its growing population certainly deserved major league baseball—transportation could present a problem until air travel became better developed and more fully trusted. The war fairly well settled the issue of expansion, or changing cities, for the immediate future. Except on radio, the big leagues did not extend farther south or west than St. Louis.

To boost attendance, several clubs had recently turned to playing games at night. By 1941, only Chicago and Boston in the National League and Detroit, Boston, and New York in the American League did not have lights. Night baseball had come to stay, not to the satisfaction of all participants. Many players believed that it interrupted their routine and perhaps shortened careers. They agreed with Phil Wrigley, owner of the Cubs, that the game belonged in warm summer sunshine. "Would you play night baseball?" a writer asked Bob Uhle of the Tigers. "I'd play a banjo if they asked me to," he said. "But night baseball is tough." "Schoolboy" Rowe was more direct: "[T]hey can have it."[56] League policy forbade scheduling more than seven home games under the lights.

The year produced its share of interesting and significant developments. Boston's National League club changed its name to the Braves, considered more manly than the Bees or an earlier name, the Doves, and a substantial improvement over the original name, the Boston Bean Eaters. Hank Greenberg, powerful hitter of the Detroit Tigers, was the highest-paid player and one of the first to be drafted. His salary went from $55,000 a year to $21 a month. Greenberg's popularity in Detroit, breaking through religious and ethnic barriers, showed that athletics could serve as an instrument of social change. A sportswriter remarked that because of baseball this "Manhattan Jewish boy [had] made good without going into the ready-to-wear line."[57]

It was a year of bright and promising young men. Bob Feller signed for $20,000 at age twenty-two. Lou Boudreau, at twenty-four, became Cleveland's manager and remained the team's shortstop. A rookie, Harold (Pete) Reiser of Brooklyn, won the National League batting title with an average of .343. Other prominent newcomers included Hal Newhouser, Phil Rizzuto, Gerald Priddy, Peewee Reese, and Lou Novikoff, the "mad Russian," who performed poorly after moving from Los Angeles up to the Chicago Cubs.

The season had started sadly with news in June that Lou Gehrig had died just short of his thirty-eighth birthday, barely old enough to retire. The "iron man" of the New York Yankees, the clean-up batter behind Babe Ruth in the Yankees' frightening lineup, Gehrig had nearly all Ruth's talents and none of the Babe's rowdy personal habits. "I never knew a fellow who lived a cleaner life," Ruth remarked, with no particular tone of envy. "I think the boy hustled too much for his own good."[58] The fatal ailment (amyotropic lateral sclerosis) was difficult to understand and nearly impossible to pronounce. People were content ever after to call it "Lou Gehrig's disease." Preparation began immediately for a movie, and the *Sporting News* encouraged fans to suggest a performer to play the lead. Most votes went to John Humphries, a pitcher for the Chicago White Sox, who looked like Gehrig. Other names included Eddie Albert, Spencer Tracy, Gary Cooper (who would get the part), Jimmy Foxx of the Red Sox, the manager Charlie Grimm, John Wayne, Ronald Reagan, and Johnny Mack Brown.[59] All sports enthusiasts admired and respected Gehrig; they all mourned his passing, realizing that a classic Yankee era at last had ended.

Now a new regime had come to take its place. Yankee dominance seemed as firmly established as in the previous generation, and some of the players as imposing. The best of the lot, Joe DiMaggio, hit safely in his fifty-sixth consecutive game in 1941, a record destined to stand perhaps forever. Handsome, generously talented, and almost as likable as Gehrig, the "Yankee Clipper" had demonstrated even better than Greenberg that a member of a former restricted minority group could leave the ethnic neighborhood and move among the most honored agents of American culture. He was so smooth and cool in the way he looked and talked, if it were not for his name no one could tell he was Italian. Why, the children worshiped him the same way they would an American. A history class in Cincinnati placed him ahead of Lincoln and Washington in popularity and significance. He even had inspired a song, "Joltin' Joe DiMaggio," which made a showing on the charts.

DiMaggio won the Most Valuable Player award in the American League even though he was probably not the league's best batter. That distinction would have to go to Ted Williams of the Boston Red Sox. Williams hit thirty-seven home runs; he went six for eight on the last day of the season (a doubleheader) to finish batting .406, the last person to reach the lofty mark of .400 for many years.

As compared with a later era, attendance at major league parks appeared small. Only one club, Brooklyn, drew more than a million fans; several had less than half that amount. The St. Louis Browns attracted barely 175,000 spectators for the entire year. Even so, expectation was lower in that time, and the total attendance of more than 10 million came close to being the most ever recorded. Had not the American League race been so one-sided, the two leagues combined might have set a record. The Yankees, with DiMaggio and such talented players as Charlie Keller, Tommy Henrich, Joe Gordon, Phil Rizzuto, and many others, clinched the title on September 4, earliest in history, their fifth pennant in six years.

The contest in the National League partly offset a lackluster American League race. From April through September the St. Louis Cardinals and Brooklyn Dodgers staged what the New York *Times* called "perhaps the greatest season-long two-club flag race in the history of the National League."[60] The contest attracted the attention of nearly everyone. President Roosevelt remarked that 1941 looked like "Brooklyn's year." "I want St. Louis to win," Senator Harry Truman of Missouri wrote. "We can't let a bunch of Kike trolley dodgers slander our biggest town."[61] The race was not decided until the last week.

The Dodger victory introduced a new dimension to the World Series, for Brooklyn was unique in the baseball circuit, if not in the United States. Stories abounded about the people who came to Ebbets Field. Many people still remembered Big Abe with the foghorn voice; Apple Annie, the little lady with such uncouth remarks for the other team; and the swarthy little fellow in seat thirteen who had a single expletive: "ya bum ya." Sportwriters named him "The Spirit of Brooklyn." Diversity was what one found among the people who supported Brooklyn's baseball team. Early in the 1941 season a serious composer, Russell Bennett, had written *A Symphony in D for the Dodgers* in four movements, which was broadcast May 16 on the Mutual Radio Network. Folks at Ebbetts Field felt more comfortable with the music of a group of volunteer rooters, the "Symphoney," which paraded the aisles between innings to serenade the audience. The most memorable piece was "Three Blind Mice," played each day as the umpires appeared on the field.

If spectators criticized the home team, it was out of affection and a wish to spur them on, for Brooklyn's fans were nothing if not loyal. Three years earlier a Dodger supporter, Robert Joyce, a mail carrier, had killed two followers of the New York Giants (Giant fans were special enemies) for calling the Dodgers bums. Only the year before a Dodger rooter, Frankie Gernano, who was on parole, dashed on the field to assault an umpire for a bad call, even though the official, the husky George Magerkurth, was twice Frankie's size.

"The truth is, probably," one reporter decided, "that the Dodger fan's love for his team is, like all great loves, born out of suffering." The Dodgers had not always been a challenging, alert team. They were known at one time as the Headless Horsemen of Ebbetts Field. Who could forget the time when Babe Herman's pants caught fire on the field because the Babe had neglected to put out his cigar before sticking it in his pocket? The Dodger fan "suffered when Hack Wilson got to arguing with a man in the stands and a fly ball came and hit him on the head. He suffered when three of his heroes came sliding into the same base at the same time. He suffered when his absent-minded darlings batted out of turn."[62] Those days had passed, however, and now with such players as Billy Herman, "Cookie" Lavagetto, Joe Medwick, Hugh Casey, Kirby Higbe, Dolph Camilli, Reese, and Reiser, the Dodgers had become magnificent.

For any city to claim a pennant was reason for celebration, and for Brooklyn to win, after twenty years of losing, it became almost a catastrophe for New York City. Perhaps 1 million marched in a victory celebration down Flatbush Avenue, at which time players "were admiringly mauled and pummeled and kissed by exuberant rooters. . . . Police were trampled, women fainted, baby buggies were overturned . . . automobile tops caved in." A frightened visitor from Britain asked if he had happened onto a revolution.[63]

Brooklyn's victory also seemed to promote an ideal matchup for the World Series, pitting the aristocracy of baseball, the rich and arrogant Yankees, against the team of the factory worker (or the unemployed), the Jews and Italians and other minority groups, of the quarrelsome manager Leo Durocher, and, according to imagery of Willard Mullin's cartoons in the *Sporting News,* the Brooklyn bum. For all the excitement at its beginning, the Series of 1941 developed into a disappointing, one-sided contest. For years to come no Dodger fan could forget the pivotal fourth game, when, with two out in the ninth inning and the Dodgers ahead, Brooklyn's catcher, Mickey Owen, failed to catch a third strike on Tommy Henrich. Nearly everyone would agree that Hugh Casey had thrown the ball badly and that if Henrich had not swung he would have walked; Durocher called it a "wild pitch." Even so, Owen would acquire the label of "goat" and a distinction that would mark his career as a baseball player. New York went on to win the game. The Series, instead of being tied at two games apiece, then stood at three-to-one in favor of the Yankees. They ended it the next day.

For followers of the Dodgers it had been a devastating blow, far more crushing personally than the darkness then clouding America's international politics. Throughout Brooklyn people crowded into bars in search of something to ease the pain. "Their swagger gone," a sportswriter reported, "Brooklyn fans looking dog tired, dirty and even pathetic kept repeating 'wait'll next year.'"[64]

In other sports, 1941 was a year of mixed development. While the greater availability of money heightened public interest in professional and amateur activity, apprehension mounted as to the impact of war on each sport. Except in rare cases, the effect was minimal. Early in the year the Boston Bruins took the Stanley Cup in hockey, defeating the Detroit Red Wings in four games. At approximately the same time Notre Dame University announced that young Frank Leahy of Boston College had replaced Elmer Laydon as football coach. Rumor had it that in hiring Leahy, who had played for Knute Rockne, Notre Dame had beaten out Purdue, Louisiana State, and the Detroit Lions. Later in the year Leahy's first Irish team would finish third in a poll for the Associated Press. Duke, designated to play Oregon State in the Rose Bowl game, came in second. Minnesota, with a record of 8-0 under coach Bernie Bierman, was picked as the nation's best college football team. Mauri Rose earned the pole position for the race on Memorial Day at Indianapolis at a speed of nearly 129 mph, then won the race driving relief after his car had stopped. By winning the Belmont Stakes in June "without even mussing his hair," Whirlaway captured the triple crown of racing and the title "horse of the year" en route to one of the most prestigious reputations in the history of the sport. Bobby Riggs won the singles championship for men in the United States Open in tennis; for obvious reasons, no tournament took place at Wimbledon.

In professional football, the Chicago Bears stood above all other teams. The season started in customary fashion with last year's winner, the Bears, playing an "all-star" game at Soldier Field. Chicago won 37–13 over a college team that included Tom Harmon and Forest Evashevski, both from the University of Michigan. The brightest spot for the collegians was probably the performance of speedy Jackie Robinson of UCLA. The Bears went on to tie Green Bay for the Western Division title with a record of 10–1 (they beat each other); Chicago then defeated the Packers in a playoff and, led by Sid Luckman and George McAfee, captured the league championship, outclassing the other division winners, the New York Giants, 35–9. Were the Bears, the team that the year before had beaten Washington 73–0, the greatest football squad in history, as some people claimed? Having set eight league records in 1941 (including most yards penalized), they could at least still claim to be "Monsters of the Midway."

Basketball on the college level was rapidly catching on as a spectator sport. It was the day of finesse rather than power, of the two-hand set shot, of free throws scooped from between the knees, of speedy, shifty, almost clever players. Nat Holman, coach of City College of New York, said that the "backbone of great teams" were men 5 feet, 10 inches tall, weighing about 170 pounds, "fast and rangy." Holman's "dream team" would have three such people and two big fellows, "say 6 feet 2 or 3."[65] Occasionally a considerably taller player could be found. West Texas State boasted of a center 6 feet 10 inches who spent most of his time hanging around the basket to swat down opponents' shots. Even though goaltending was no more against the rules than in hockey, many people believed that basketball should be more than a mere test of size. They looked upon the gangly giants as freaks and probably a corruption of this game of skill.

The game was changing and, as some people saw it, being corrupted in other ways. Some observers detected a disturbing tendency to dispense with planning and organization, and simply to dash down the floor and fire at the basket, sometimes without stopping to get set. Critics—mostly from Eastern colleges, which favored deliberate play—saw that style as chaos. Midwesterners called it the "fast break." If such behavior removed some of the artistry from the sport, it seemed to satisfy spectators. Surveying one night's games, a writer found an average score of 45–34—"almost two points a minute," he noted with astonishment. "That means action and plenty of it."[66]

At season's end two teams could claim the mythical national title. Wisconsin, having replaced Indiana as champion of the Big Ten Conference, won the NCAA tournament by beating Washington State. In a contest at least as prestigious as the NCAA crown, Long Island University, coached by Claire Bee, won the National Invitational Tournament in New York City.

For the greatest intensity in sports, one would need to go to the high school games. Football and basketball absorbed the energy of thousands of young men each fall and winter; they attracted the interest of millions of parents and fans. The system probably was best developed in the Midwest. Segregation robbed Southern schools of much competent talent; black schools in the South could not afford organized sports. Streetcorner basketball, the full development of black urban talent, remained a few years away in Northern cities. Basketball (for that matter, nearly all sports activity) was mostly for white people. Midwestern people took their high school sports seriously. In Indiana, where attendance at basketball games far surpassed all other states, it seemed that every school that enrolled at least five males had a team. For an important tournament in Kokomo, fans started to line up at 5:30 P.M. to buy tickets that were to go on sale the next morning. The crowd grew so large and impatient that officials were rousted from bed to open the windows at 4:00 A.M. The tickets lasted thirty minutes. It was not uncommon for the basketball structure to accommodate more people than the population of the town, let alone the school, and no less than thirty gymnasiums in Indiana seated from 3,000 to 8,000.[67]

In small Midwestern towns sports teams represented the community. "Business, professional and working men . . . demand . . . winning teams," an observer of the system in Illinois noted. "The Board pays the maximum to the coach and expects him to 'deliver the goods.'" Feelings understandably ran high in those contests, on all levels of participation. By the time one basketball game in Illinois ended, the referee had ejected two players of one team and had called technical fouls on the coach, the fans, and the Superintendent of Schools.[68]

The most impressive sports story of the year was not the World

Series or even the Dodger victory in the National League, but the remarkable performance of the heavyweight boxing champion, Joe Louis. Louis's fights became national social events causing friends to gather around the nearest radio or the radio with the clearest reception. Some 50 million people listened, an audience larger than any other offering on radio, save perhaps an important address by the President, could claim. If that statistic sounds high, it might be helpful to note that boxing was a popular old sport showing signs of revitalization after years of corruption and mediocre competitors. On radio the fights cost nothing, no small consideration in a nation still struggling with economic woes; they were spaced close enough to promote continuous interest, and far enough apart to avoid boredom and to permit enthusiasm to build. The key to the phenomenon was Louis himself. Showing a remarkable combination of speed, grace, and power, probably superior to Dempsey, Tunney, or any previous competitor, he was a black man who had come to dominate a part of the white man's world.

Black people had never seen anything like it. "For one Negro who rejoices in the scientific achievement of Dr. George W. Carver or the artistic and athletic achievements of Mr. Paul Robeson," a foreign observer noted, "there are a score whose hearts are lifted up at the thought of Mr. Joe Louis, the 'brown bomber.'"[69] The black press gloated with each victory over a succession of white opponents. "Every time you knock a guy out, I feel bigger and bigger," an open letter to the *Defender,* Chicago's main newspaper for blacks, said. "My daddy says you have given us colored boys a lot of faith and courage in ourselves. . . . My teacher . . . said you are the only Champion we have. And she said Negroes need more heroes whose characters have not been blotted by scandal and slander." Benefiting from mass communication, especially radio, news about Louis traveled from Harlem to Bronzeville, from the slums of Memphis to the miserable shacks of Mississippi; he had become the first black national hero, the individual who did more than any other to boost his people's morale since Negroes had arrived on the North American continent. "There is but ONE Joe Louis," a black columnist declared; "none was before him; none will come after."[70]

To some whites Louis was a black man who had made it through work and determination, the sort of progress others could achieve if only they would put forth the effort. Whites probably indulged in self-congratulation over what Louis's success said about a society that would let a black man make it to the top. Louis, besides, was the right kind of black person, unlike that other boxer, Jack Johnson, who years earlier had swaggered about, taunting the whites. Louis scrupulously observed the color line: no white women for him, or so it seemed. In truth, he did cross over. "My God," he later recalled, "the women, the starlets, white and black, came jumping at me. I didn't resist one pretty girl who had a sparkle in her eye." Louis was wise enough to keep such matters quiet. He had "a nice thing going" with the Norwegian actress and skater Sonja Henie, which they kept "under cover."[71]

Whites could follow Louis's exploits secure in the notion that he represented no challenge to their basic characterization of race, which admitted that, after all, Negroes were capable of possessing special "physical" attributes. Otherwise, Louis was all black: Humble and barely literate—he had quit school in fifth grade—the champion spoke with a drawl and terrible diction, was clean and honest enough to make the game respectable, and was irresponsible enough with money and personal affairs to meet the white man's stereotype of the black. A marital dispute with his wife, Marva, in 1941 received national publicity. She sued for divorce, publicized the charges, and then withdrew them. Most black people were chagrined; many whites shrugged off the affair as the sort of behavior one could expect from a "nigger."

It is not easy to say how many listened to the fights to cheer the champion and how many to hear him put in his place. Doubtless many white people were dazzled by this splendid athlete and hoped to see his talents receive a just reward. Sportswriters had touted the second match with the German boxer Max Schmeling in 1938 as a test of Hitler's claims of racial superiority and perhaps a contest between democracy and fascism. Louis dutifully won for the United States and for democracy in devastating fashion; people were not sure about the racial implication. Other whites thought more or less along the same lines as the neighbors of a Texan who recalled that whenever Louis fought, farmers and their sons gathered around an old battery-powered radio "in the unifying prayer that some 'white hope' would whip old Joe's black ass for us."[72]

Russell Baker remembered hearing those fights of Joe Louis, and how people in the white community at Lombard Street in Baltimore listened to the sounds coming over the radio. There was the ring announcer, shouting at the top of his voice: "In this corner—weighing 197 pounds [he fought best at 202]—the Brown Bomber from Detroit." Then came the great roar from the crowd, the clang of the bell, and the voice of Clem McCarthy; in short order it would be over. Down on dismal Lemmon Street, where black people lived, the clapping, cheering, and general celebration began almost immediately. Out on Lombard, however, the domain of the whites, one felt the "silence of a tomb. . . . While uptown Baltimore debated war and the future of civilization, the men of Lombard Street sat on their stoops in shirtsleeves, puffed their pipes, and pondered a cruel theological question: . . . why had God permitted Joe Louis to become the heavyweight champion of the world?"[73]

But listen they all did, and it was quite a show. Louis began the year meeting approximately one challenger each month—the "Bum-of-the-Month Club," as sportswriters called the brawlers pushed into the ring by promoters hastening to act while the market flourished. A contender might astonish the fans with his ability to absorb punishment, might temporarily appear to threaten Louis's supremacy, or might bring something novel to the spectacle. "Two Ton" Tony Galento had trained for his bout in 1939 by drinking huge amounts of beer, apparently expecting that at 235 pounds sheer bulk would allow him to win. Now Lou Nova was boasting of a "cosmic punch." "My new application of cosmos to prize fighting will prove the most sensational step forward in the history of pugilism," he announced. "Gosh," said his manager, "I don't know what he's talking about."[74] Whatever it was, it did not work, for Nova, no less than all the others, fell before the champion.

The one genuine contest came in June, when Louis took on Billy Conn. The twenty-three-year-old son of a steelmaker, weighing only 174 pounds, Conn showed finesse and stamina in outboxing Louis; the champion looked helpless and bewildered as he sat with hanging head at the end of the twelfth round. "You losing, chappie," Jack Blackburn, his trainer, told him. "You gotta' knock this guy out, or you lose." Then, overconfident and careless, Conn attempted to overpower his opponent, who outweighed him by at least 25 pounds. Louis knocked him out in the thirteenth. "I ain't near the fighter I used to be," Louis said shortly afterward. "My reflexes are too slow. By the time I throw my fist Conn is going away and I can't hit him solid."[75] Though tired and obviously stale, Louis won all his fights in 1941 and by the end of the year had defended his title nineteen times. At age twenty-seven he seemed likely to be champion for several years to come.

☆

The great problem of 1941—in sports as in everything else—was to figure out what was to come. Times certainly seemed to be changing, but which way? The high times of the 'twenties, those lively and optimistic times, now seemed so distant a memory as to make one wonder if they ever existed. The Depression of the 'thirties, by no means a distant memory, seemed at last to be fading away, as everyone hoped it would, but there was no guarantee the next era would be better.

It was the war that was changing things. The war was everywhere—the movies, the songs, even the terminology of sports. One saw it in a summary of the match between Louis and Conn: "A speedy light cruiser of the ring failed to withstand the heavy firing of the greatest dreadnought of modern boxing."[76] *Sporting News,* the publication devoted exclusively to baseball, had started to deal with the draft, introducing a regular column to review the status of players in the conscription program. How far would the process go? How much would war affect sports and the entertainment business? Military service could devastate an athletic career and seriously change the fortunes of a team. Yet, in a society purporting to be democratic, what else could one do? People in entertainment did not want to appear to be asking for special privileges, to be dodging the draft. Morrie Arnovich, a baseball player for New York, took a bridge from his mouth to prove the Army had rejected him because of bad teeth. As a Giant, he said, he particularly disliked being called a dodger.[77] Greenberg had gone, and so had the pitcher Hugh Mulcahy of Philadelphia. Fred Hutchinson had joined the Navy. Rumors circulated about Feller, Williams, and other prominent athletes.

What was to come of the class of '41, the young athletes—or, for that matter, anyone—who graduated in the spring? How could anyone make plans when the future seemed so uncertain? Could Brooklyn anticipate playing New York the next year, a chance to atone for the humiliation so fresh in the minds of fans? Would there be a World Series in 1942? When would Conn fight a much-deserved and anticipated rematch with Louis? Louis was not sure, but in September he received a hint of his future, and the future of his nation, when the draft board classified him 1-A.

TEN

"Hell, This Isn't a Pinochle Party We're Having— It's War!"

The days were getting shorter now, and the states farthest north might have had a frost or two. Winter was on the way. On the farms that meant the usual tasks of harvest season: picking cotton, shoveling corn, and other hard work limited only by the hours of daylight available at that time of year—a merciful limitation in many cases, although farmers probably wished the days lasted longer. The weather was unusually wet in the fall of 1941, and some ears of corn had started to sprout before they could be taken from the field. Still, it would be a large harvest, and farmers could take comfort in the knowledge that demand was high and the prices were going up.

In much of the United States it was the most beautiful time of year. Nature displayed its brightest colors every autumn, of course, and occasionally the right combination of sunshine, moisture, and temperature produced an especially brilliant spectacle. The year 1941 seemed such a time to a British visitor who happened to be traveling the countryside in New England when valleys, ravines, and mountains wore every shade from scarlet to russet gold. "It was, though we knew it not," he later would write, "the last autumn in America before a war which maybe will last through many falls and will bring to the people of the United States, inevitably, great agony of soul, enormous tragedy, the death of youth, the tears of women." The setting of war seemed—and indeed was—a world removed from this masterpiece of nature in the American Northeast. Here, with blue

265

sky, sunshine, and huge white clouds floating as if sails on a ship, one found only "peace and loveliness, exquisite beyond words to describe, almost beyond the range of art to depict. . . . The maples have turned vivid red, their foliage ranging like tattered tapestry woven into the colours of other trees by innumerable gradations of delicate tones which no mediaeval needlewoman ever worked upon her frame."[1]

City people might have found it increasingly difficult to get to the countryside in the fall of 1941. More and more firms were turning to production of war goods, and the government seemed in considerable haste to have them made. People with jobs often found themselves required to work Saturday (or part of it), sometimes even Sunday. It did not leave much of a life with the family, but a weekly income approaching $40 or more helped make the long hours tolerable. Other members of the family, except possibly the wife, did not miss family togetherness much anyway. They were moving steadily into separate avenues of work and social activity.

If life was becoming more complex, the complexity came disguised in attractive packages. Life had not been easy during the Depression, but it had been fairly simple. Now, with work getting better, life was still difficult and no longer simple. The lure of more wages from longer hours was too attractive to pass up, and the worker usually had no choice anyway. With higher income came higher expectation: a better place to live if one could find it, more appliances, higher utility bills, more meat and less macaroni and cheese, a car for those who did not own one, a better car for those who did. Whoever could not pay cash for such purchases—and few people could—would buy them "on time," on "the Morris Plan," or by some other system of installment buying. With the resulting enlarged commitment, the consumer had to work as many hours as possible.

There was another catch. Millions of people experienced for the first time—double the number of 1940—a special obligation: an income tax and a separate deduction for Social Security. Even the President remarked that after paying taxes he had difficulty making ends meet.[2] There was no cause for complaint. A higher tax, after all, probably resulted from higher income. Most workers probably realized they should seize the opportunity while it existed. Even so, people who remembered what they had had to do to get by in the 1930s might have been surprised to find they were not enjoying these good times more.

People still unemployed or underemployed continued to experience the same idleness, possibly a day or two at some odd job, and the same dullness of spirit. Unemployment had dropped to less than 6.5 percent by October, heartening for the government and followers of economic news, but many people were still struggling without jobs or with jobs that paid little. Many deprived people lived in rural areas, of course, scratching the soil of marginal or worn-out farms. Even though this year might bring them a few more dollars in cash or even a doubling of income—from $100 per year, say, to $200— they still lived in poverty. Friends, relatives, or relief agencies could usually provide something to eat, so there was little chance of starvation, but the food was always the same, and a lot more than food was needed to be truly alive. The children needed dental work and other medical care; the radio needed batteries or tubes or something (anyway it would not work); the car had a leaky radiator, perhaps, or tires worn bald or laden with boots. Worst of all, at least for the man of the family, was a feeling of worthlessness and failure. Could it be that time had come to give up on the home place (however agonizing the thought of leaving might be), throw everything in the car, say your prayers, and start out for that city, so distant and mysterious, where companies were said to be hiring anyone who presented themselves for work?

Traveling the Atlantic Coast one could see signs of the time. Seaports bustled with rows of merchantmen loading crates of goods— munitions probably, although it was impossible to know the contents of those huge boxes. On some days New York looked like an invasion site, so many vessels came in to gather supplies to take back to Europe. Some of the ships took on partially dismantled airplanes, which, being too large for the hold, stood in full view on the deck. The destination of those vessels was not hard to guess: Britain, mostly, although a few had begun to risk the long, perilous voyage to Russia.

Looking to sea, many people doubtless thought about German submarines waiting, like a wild animal in ambush, for a suitable victim. They could not be seen, but they were out there. Hitler did not intend to permit unrestricted supply of his enemy, of course, and in much the same fashion as in World War I, Germany had sent U-boats to lie along Atlantic traffic lanes from the British Isles to the United States. Congress had unwittingly simplified the German task by ordering American ships out of the trade in contraband. The purpose had been to enhance the safety of ships and to ensure neutrality for the United States. The result was that submarine commanders were free to operate with little danger of striking an American vessel and precipitating the sort of incident that had brought the United States to war in 1917.

Submarines had plentiful targets, and the effect on British shipping had been devastating. They had taken to operating in groups—wolf-packs, they were called—which would wait for cargo vessels to lumber into range, then would strike. One convoy lost twenty-two ships in a single night. Occasionally a submarine slipped close to the American coast and sank a tanker. At night the sky would show a deep, dark red glow from the burning oil, a sight as beautiful as it was alarming. American ships would not be able to carry war goods to Europe until Congress lifted the ban in November, so the miserable seamen seeking to escape that fiery hell were probably British and not American. That thought offered little comfort to people who observed the expanding conflict on the Atlantic. They could see that the war was getting close.

Only a casual reading of newspapers (which was all some people gave them even now) indicated that the situation had worsened considerably since the start of the year. Flattered and sobered by appeals from Winston Churchill, and fortified with the Lend-Lease Act and public opinion polls indicating that at least two-thirds of the people approved his policies, Roosevelt had sent his men searching the nation for military supplies to send abroad. At the end of June the focus of war news had shifted to the gigantic struggle that began when Germany attacked Russia. The Russo-German conflict was a turning point in World War II and prompted a new phase in the debate over foreign policy.

Isolationists contended that any rationale for Roosevelt's policy had now vanished. With Germany preoccupied on an eastern front, Britain's desperate plight had gone away. The Atlantic Ocean was in no danger of falling to a hostile power. The character of the Germans' enemies had changed, and surely the United States did not contemplate alignment with the Russia of communism, the dictatorship of Joseph Stalin, guilty in recent memory of bloody purges and brutal collectivization of farms. The United States had no stake in a conflict in which the combatants were equally evil or, as *Time* described them, "like two vast prehistoric monsters lifting themselves out of the swamp, half-blind and savage."[3] A Catholic journal commented: "To defend democracy with the help of Stalin would be like calling in Jesse James or John Dillinger to maintain law and order."[4] The United States was advised to stand off and watch, even to enjoy the spectacle. "The best thing that could happen," Hamilton Fish, an isolationist Representative from New York, said, "would be to have the Nazis and Communists fight it out and destroy each other."[5]

Roosevelt had a different assessment of the situation. Within a short time he revealed his conclusion that whatever objection Americans might have to communism and whatever charges one might make about the regime of Joseph Stalin, the threat to the United States and to the world came from Germany. Russia would receive help from the United States.

Like other moves in foreign policy, the people approved the government's decision. A survey indicated that if they had to make a choice, Americans by 72 to 4 percent supported Russia rather than Germany. They nonetheless expected Germany to win.[6] Most people were thus endorsing a position that only months before would have been unthinkable; indeed, less than a year earlier Americans had supported Finland in a conflict with the Soviet Union. The new attitude partly reflected the intensity of feeling about Hitler and fascism— anything, apparently, was better than the Nazis. It represented less a softening of feeling toward communism than a need during those tumultuous times to trust and follow the President.

During the latter half of the year, however, a different perception of the Soviet Union slowly began to surface. The government started to emphasize practical issues, common Russian–American objectives, rather than ideological differences. The press looked for evidence of Soviet success on the massive eastern front. Americans had never been hostile to the Russian people, and now and then it was possible to hear a favorable remark about the Soviet government, usually to the effect that time and experience had caused the Communists to change. An American journalist, Ralph Ingersoll, reported a highly successful interview with the Soviet leader. "I was enormously impressed by the man," he wrote. "I was impressed by the . . . thoroughness with which he knew his own mind and the rapidity and intelligence with which he expressed it." Drew Pearson reported that Averell Harriman, a railroad magnate, a dabbler in diplomacy and Democratic politics, and certainly a capitalist, had called Stalin a "great guy."[7]

A former Ambassador to the Soviet Union offered more words of encouragement. Joseph E. Davies's memoir, *Mission to Moscow,* went to press in October and appeared in bookstores at the end of the year. "The Russia of Lenin and Trotsky—the Russia of the Bolshevik Revolution—no longer exists," Davies wrote. In its place had developed state socialism "operating on capitalist principles and steadily and irresistibly swinging to the right." Soviet leaders wished only to create a society where men could live as equals, governed by principle, dedicated to peace. "They are fighting our fight now against Hitlerism," Davies concluded, and "should receive every possible help as speedily . . . as we can stand."[8]

The most practical reason for supporting Russia, of course, had to do with the course of the war. "If Germany routs the Russian army quickly," one observer noted, "or keeps Leningrad in a state of siege this winter and immobilized the Russian air force, we must realize that she can't be defeated except after a decade of war or war conditions. So we must pull for Russia with might and main."[9] Discomfort from alignment with the Soviet Union became more superfluous with each day's news from the Russian front. The Nazi war machine charged across eastern Poland and across the Ukraine, overwhelming hundreds of towns, hundreds of thousands of men, heading toward Leningrad, Moscow, and Stalingrad. The closer the Communists came to total collapse—in ordinary circumstances not an unwelcome development—the greater loomed the power and the greed of the mighty *Wehrmacht*. Many Americans found themselves looking for even the smallest Russian victory, if only as a sign that the Germans were not invincible.

As the country moved through the long days of summer and into the fall, the debate over foreign policy raged in full fury, corresponding with blistering temperatures in the East and Midwest. The rallies, parades, name-calling, scuffles, and skirmishes continued. A piece by Carl Sandburg in August showed that nothing but the intensity of the debate had changed: "The Fight for Freedom Committee utters its desperate cry that we must now . . . declare war on Nazi Germany while the Committee to Defend America says use convoys." The America First Committee mounted a campaign "aimed straight at terrorizing every father, mother or sweetheart," warning that draftees would be "butchered by crazy galoots running the government."[10]

Convinced more fully in August than in March that the world faced collapse, interventionists scarcely could find ways to put the problem in perspective. How could they make it understood that this was not merely "another war," another European squabble, and that the future of the United States, not to mention the world, hung in balance? They wrote to Congressmen, signed petitions, and published handbills, pamphlets, ads in newspapers, and even books. They spoke on radio and at rallies, participated in parades, and tried to discredit such opponents as Nye, Wheeler, and especially Lindbergh. Taken together, the maneuvers constituted an extent of private activism perhaps unprecedented in American foreign policy.

Isolationists responded with equal forcefulness. If the United States faced a crisis, a leader of the America First Committee charged, it was "manufactured by war-minded members of President Roosevelt's cabinet and shrieking interventionist groups." "If I were to name the leading war makers in the United States," Representative Fish, from Roosevelt's district in New York State, said, "I would place Secretary Stimson at the top of the list. Then there would be Secretary Knox, Secretaries Ickes and Wickard, and Field Marshal Harry Hopkins."[11]

The President's family had come in for a share of criticism. Opponents had never liked the President's wife. Eleanor Roosevelt was not a beautiful woman, which perhaps made hostility easier. Her high-pitched "upper New Yorkish" voice commanded admiration only from people who enjoyed what she had to say—more of the un-American, European flavor that enemies found in the Roosevelt presidency. Probably more liberal than her husband, she was much too active and outspoken for people with a conventional view of womanhood. In the campaign of 1940 Republicans somewhat cruelly had distributed buttons reading "We Don't Want Eleanor Either."

Ever watchful for evidence of preferential treatment for the first family, critics mocked "I wanna be a captain too," on learning that a son, chubby Elliott Roosevelt, who at first glance looked like anything but a warrior, had received a commission in the Army Air Corps. Later a second son seemed to have benefited from having a President as father. The Chicago *Tribune* informed readers that Captain James Roosevelt, "titular member of . . . the marines," had received a desk job in Washington and was making plans to "move with his bride into a spacious little home of 14 rooms in nearby Maryland."[12]

The sharpest jabs, of course, were directed at the President. Isolationists continued to accuse him of deception, lying, seeking unlimited power, and planning to take the United States to war. Representative Claire Hoffman of Michigan explained the President's foreign policy—as did many of Roosevelt's critics—in terms of the failure of the New Deal. When it appeared that the United States was on verge of a new depression, Hoffman explained, Roosevelt moved "to distract the people's attention . . . by fabricating a national emergency, due, he said, to a threat of the invasion of this country by Hitler."[13]

The isolationists had to be content with demonstrations, charges, and warnings. Even though they occasionally showed impressive strength in Congress (the measure to extend the term of draftees, as mentioned, passed in the House in August by only one vote), in each case they failed. In the final analysis they did not have the votes. Whatever one might think of it, the show belonged to Roosevelt.

The President's performance was purposeful, although not altogether open and honest. At some time during the year, probably in spring or early summer, he had decided that assisting Germany's enemies was not enough, and nothing short of American intervention could assure the defeat of Hitler and fascism. Roosevelt would not voice that conclusion openly, however, for fear the people would not accept it. "Why doesn't the President come to Congress and ask for a declaration of war?" Wheeler asked. "That is the honest thing to do and that is the decent thing to do."[14] Roosevelt had his reasons for doing otherwise. He feared that Congress might not pass a simple declaration of war. Even if it did, he would have to deal with a sharply divided American population. Ever a careful reader of public opinion, Roosevelt interpreted polls to mean that he should proceed with caution.

Evidence continued to suggest that while most people had come to accept the possibility of intervention, and more were prepared to accept bolder risks in foreign policy, the bulk of the population still wanted to stay out. Should the United States go to war "now" with Germany and Italy? Gallup pollsters asked at the end of June; 76 percent said no. Many Americans continued to have difficulty finding a connection between events across the sea and their own safety and welfare. Europe, after all, was still far away. "They don't even know what democracy is," a member of Roosevelt's government complained. They "are . . . more interested in movies and radio and baseball and automobiles."[15]

Returning home after witnessing months of chaos in Europe, Eric Sevareid could scarcely believe what he encountered. Afire with hostility toward the regime of Hitler, he began giving lectures, and the more he tried the more frustrated he became. "I knew the answer," he said. "I was sure I knew it as I had never been sure of anything in my life." The people came in large numbers, listened to this man they had heard on the radio, gave him generous applause, and then went away apparently unchanged. He detected distrust on many faces and could hear women already chatting about weather or the price of goods or the problems of getting good kitchen help. Time after time a man would come up at the end, pat his arm, and say: "Now let's . . . have a little drink with some friends of mine, and suppose you give us the real low-down." "They could not believe that I had already told them all I knew," the newsman lamented.[16]

A British author who had come to observe American opinion, Philip Gibbs, encountered some of the same attitudes. "I believe that England is fighting our battles," a lady from Massachusetts told him. "And yet when you ask me directly about sending our boys overseas . . . something in my very soul stops short of that." Watching crowds stream along New York's streets on a sunny day in September, or later joining jovial passengers aboard a "superluxury streamline train" traveling across the Midwest, Gibbs saw no hint that somewhere else a great war was going on.[17]

"What was the President to do?" Sevareid asked, "Was he to withhold action until a clear majority of his countrymen had made up their minds, and so risk arriving too late . . . ? Was it his duty to lead or to follow his people?" The hesitation in public opinion, a continuation of the great dilemma, created a special problem for a President determined to participate in the destruction of Nazism. The President decided to lead cautiously while giving the impression that he was not leading at all, another Rooseveltian exercise in indirect action. He would try to keep subtle pressure on the Germans while making sure that Germany would appear responsible if hostilities developed. "I am not willing to fire the first shot," he said to a group of confidants. A member of the Cabinet noted that "he is . . . waiting for the Germans to create an 'incident.'"[18]

Roosevelt did move to widen the opportunity for Germany to create an incident. He had responded to submarine warfare by designating a huge part of the Atlantic Ocean as a "New World Neutrality Patrol Belt"—a step to enhance the security of the Western Hemisphere, he explained. American ships were going to "patrol" the western Atlantic. The Secretary of War noted that Roosevelt "kept reverting to the fact" that the vessels were going to "watch for any aggressor and to report that to America." Stimson knew what Roosevelt truly had in mind: "[Y]ou are not going to report the presence of the German Fleet to the Americas. You are going to report it to the British Fleet," he reminded the President. "I wanted him to be honest with himself."[19]

The President remained so enigmatic as to be maddening to friend and foe alike. Just when he appeared to have decided on action, with a goal clearly in mind, he reversed course or muddled the situation with meaningless words or vague generalities. Early in August he suddenly left town. Reports said that he had gone fishing along the Northeastern Seaboard, seeking relief from the terrible heat in Washington. For several days the press received little information.

In the second week of August the story broke: The President had been to a conference with the Prime Minister of Great Britain at a place called Placentia Bay off the coast of Newfoundland. Roosevelt and Churchill, the press reported, had agreed to a remarkable document called the Atlantic Charter, which was aimed at the "final destruction of Nazi tyranny." It was a startling piece of news. Or was it? Details were sketchy and unclear. At a press conference aboard the presidential yacht *Potomac,* Roosevelt remained characteristically coy and puzzling. What did you talk about with Churchill? reporters asked. How will the Atlantic Charter be implemented? What does it mean? "Interchange of views, that's all. Nothing else," he said. Was the United States closer to entering the war? "I should say, no."[20]

Although the people did not know what Roosevelt had said to Churchill, or even that there had been a meeting until after it had ended, it took no expert to see the direction events were taking. On the President's command, American warships had gone far out to sea. He persisted in calling the action a patrol, while critics charged that Roosevelt had instituted a convoy, a virtual act of war against Germany. The distinction was probably lost on many people. Americans might not have known that their destroyers were in fact searching for submarines and in other ways assisting the British Navy to protect precious cargo ships. Anyone who listened to news broadcasts understood that the vessels operated in the same waters as German submarines and that, if only because of accident, a clash was easily possible.

It happened the first week of September, about the time of year when a few leaves had started to change color in Maine and on the upper peninsula of Michigan. Parts of the Army had begun to move south for the huge war games in Louisiana. New Yorkers rejoiced that the Yankees had clinched the pennant the day before, and in another part of town fans watched to see if the Dodgers could hold up through the last three weeks in the National League. German armies had begun a siege of Leningrad and seemed likely to reach Moscow before the dead of winter set in. Hitler had more important matters on his mind than relations with the United States. Roosevelt probably welcomed the trouble at sea more than the German dictator did. Churchill was no doubt delighted to hear that an American destroyer, the *Greer,* had had an armed—albeit bloodless—encounter with a German U-boat. The vessels had fired at each other. Roosevelt had his incident.

But it was not quite a reason for war. The President's reaction suggested that he was ready for conflict, although no more willing than in previous weeks to ask directly for a declaration of war. Embellishing the facts somewhat, he put the blame squarely on the Germans. The attack was, he said, "piracy legally and morally." "We have sought no shooting war with Hitler," the President continued. "But when you see a rattlesnake poised to strike, you do not wait until he has struck before you crush him." He then announced orders for the Navy to shoot on sight, to engage any submarine encountered on the open sea. The objective of the speech, according to the Chicago *Tribune,* was to frighten the people into war. The "hidden purpose" was to make this "artificial crisis serve . . . as an excuse to impose new totalitarian restraints upon the American people. His aim is a dictatorship which will mean the destruction of the republic."[21]

Although not anxious for war with the United States—at least not yet—Hitler did not permit Roosevelt's order to halt his submarine campaign. German and American vessels continued to maneuver in the same waters, looking for each other. Americans therefore were not surprised with the news a month later that a torpedo had torn a huge hole in the side of another destroyer, the *Kearny,* causing the death of eleven American sailors. "History has recorded who fired the first shot," the President said. "Americans have cleared our decks and taken our battle stations."[22] He said no more, however, and declined to ask for war again on October 30, when a submarine sank the warship *Reuben James,* killing more than a hundred Americans. So it was in the fall, and so it would continue the rest of the year: Germany and the United States were apparently following a deliberately hostile course, and more clashes on the high seas were inevitable. The two nations might not have been officially at war as December began, but at least they were shooting at each other.

News from the area of the Pacific was equally grim. Eclipsed for many months by the European war, events in Asia took a deadly serious turn the latter half of 1941, and almost before anyone had noticed, the United States had a second crisis on its hands. Few Americans could explain how it had happened. The gist of the problem seemed to be (the details were in fact a great deal more complex)

that Japan wished to seize vast amounts of territory, particularly in China, and the United States refused to give its assent. Japanese efforts to define and justify its program—the need to establish, as the government in Tokyo explained, the "Greater East Asia Co-prosperity Sphere"—sounded like nothing more than Oriental gibberish designed to embellish crass and greedy imperialism. Because American policy had amounted to little more than denunciation, not backed up with lavish assistance to Japan's enemies, the Japanese seemed to have far less reason than Germany for irritation with the United States. Most Americans, including several isolationists, approved of or accepted in silence the government's policy in the East, thinking it morally correct, inexpensive, and almost risk-free.

In spite of warnings from such people as Walter Lippmann, who contended that Japan constituted a substantial potential enemy, Americans continued to regard Japan with confident derision. They had trouble seeing the Japanese as anything but aggressive little people trying to play with the "big boys." The feeling persisted that Japan's alliance with Germany, signed in September 1940, had left the Japanese subservient and willing to imitate and obey their powerful white ally. An editorial cartoon in the Los Angeles *Times* showed a Japanese soldier speaking in a telephone booth. "Adolph, Hello!" the soldier said. "What I Do Next?"[23] A joke that circulated during the summer had the Japanese government sending a cable to Berlin: "We are starting an anti-Semitic movement; please send us some Jews." If war were to start with Japan, would the United States win or lose? a poll in November asked; 93 percent picked the Americans (1 percent said Japan would win) and, more revealing, only 35 percent believed the winning would be difficult.[24]

Relations went steadily downhill in the latter half of 1941. While continuing to control much of eastern China, Japan began in July a daring new thrust into French Indochina. Roosevelt froze Japanese assets in the United States, which placed a severe strain on Japan's stockpiles of vital war material, particularly oil. Japanese leaders now faced difficulty any way they turned. Either diplomacy would have to eliminate the barriers to trade erected by the Americans, or Japan would have to seize sources of materials, which would probably bring on war with the United States. The Japanese moved in both directions at the same time. The government created a war cabinet, with General Hideki Tojo as Premier, and proceeded with plans for an attack. The economic restrictions, Tojo charged, amounted to "little less than . . . armed warfare."[25]

Meanwhile discussions in Washington became so frequent and so urgent that the names of the Japanese negotiators—Ambassador Kichisaburo Nomura and Saburo Kurusu—difficult as they were to pronounce, grew familiar to all Americans who followed the news. Ambassador Nomura was the big one, about 6 feet tall, in his late sixties. Kurusu, the special envoy, liked to trumpet his knowledge of American culture. Married to an American, he announced on arrival in November: "I hope to break through the line and make a touchdown." He barely came up to the shoulders of Cordell Hull, and it was suspected that in Kurusu's case—perhaps with all Japanese—size was deceiving. Kurusu had signed the devious treaty with Germany, and Hull would later report a belief that "from the start . . . he was deceitful."[26] A citizen could scarcely look at a newspaper or newsreel without seeing those curious men with eyeglasses, huge double-breasted overcoats, and their interminable bows and smiles. To the beleaguered Japanese diplomats, who did not know what their government planned for the United States, their behavior was simply good manners and proper diplomacy; to Americans it came to represent two-faced trickery, apparently a national characteristic of the Japanese.

The result was diplomatic deadlock: The Japanese would not abandon expansion, and the United States refused to accept the movement or to restore trade privileges. Japanese leaders concluded that there could be no dealing with the Americans short of war. The string had run out, and all apparent signs—the behavior of Japanese officials in the United States (they had begun to burn code equipment), reports of movements of ships and troops in Asia, and bellicose pronouncements on Tokyo radio—indicated that hell was soon going to break loose in the Far East.

Despite those ominous signs, the United States was not prepared for the war that was to come. The armament factories, so conspicuous a part of social and economic life, had absorbed by December only 10-15 percent of the work force. The Army had grown to 1.6 million after more than a year of conscription, but compared with other large nations it remained small, incompletely trained, and ill-equipped; stories continued to circulate about dissatisfaction among the draftees. The people divided sharply, though not evenly, on the issues of isolationism and Roosevelt. Labor's wars with management, and with itself, had not yet ended, and as late as December 7 the nation did not know if coal would be mined for stoves and furnaces, factories and steam locomotives. There was much national activity, but no widely accepted national purpose and dreadfully little effort to deal with problems springing from the activity.

Few people now believed that the United States could avoid war much longer. Roosevelt had admitted at Thanksgiving time that the United States might be at war by Thanksgiving a year later, but most people who followed national events assumed that America's first enemy would be Germany. While news from the Pacific was worrisome and a foretaste of dismal times ahead, it did not seem to carry the danger of immediate conflict. To be sure, a few individuals had a different view. Walter Lippmann's column "Today and Tomorrow" insisted on December 6 that the United States faced "a head-on collision with Japan." Much more common was the attitude of Dwight Eisenhower. "I . . . had no idea that battle would be precipitated by the Japanese," he reminisced. "If we got into war—and with each passing week I became more and more sure we could not stay out—I felt sure the Nazis would provoke it."[27] The object of Japanese diplomacy, in tune it seemed with national character, was to stall for time, to maneuver, to hide the facts, and to gain territorial objectives while avoiding provoking the Americans. Most people continued to assume that Japan lacked the means and the will to risk a direct assault upon the United States.

Thus the air attack on that sunny Sunday in Hawaii came to the American people, as to the battleships lying idle below, as a bolt out of the blue. The state of knowledge in the United States made the assault appear fully unwarranted, much more so than an attack by Germany would have been, an act of "unspeakable treachery." Most Americans felt anger at the attack on Pearl Harbor, but Cordell Hull had the rare pleasure of expressing himself to the enemy, in the persons of Nomura and Kurusu when they appeared at his office shortly after the news had reached Washington. People about the State Department tried to discover what the Secretary of State had said behind the closed door. One report had it that he had shouted "Scoundrels!" in his best Tennessee dialect, and then "Piss Ants!"[28] Not all the words might have been understandable to Admiral Nomura, who spoke English poorly anyway, but the Secretary's tone was unmistakable.

In the morning they were at peace, going to church, sleeping late, reading the paper, listening to the radio—the things Americans usually did on Sunday—and in the afternoon they were in a war, heading into a new role in world affairs that would last perhaps as long as the nation. The enemy came shortly before eight in the morning to Hawaii, and reports arrived in the nation's capital at approximately 2:00 P.M. on a cold, windy Sunday afternoon. Radio began broadcasting the news at 2:25 in the East, and earlier by the clock, of course, in the successive time zones to the west. The first people to get the word were those who happened to be listening to the radio. In New York, a hurried voice broke into the broadcast of a professional football game when the Brooklyn Dodgers had the ball on the 45 yard line of the New York Giants: "Japanese bombs have fallen on Hawaii and the Philippine Islands. Keep tuned to this station for further details. We now return you to the Polo Grounds."[29]

At Fort Leonard Wood, Missouri, draftees were lounging around after the noon meal, which was always large on Sunday. Some were sleeping, others were reading comic books. One soldier had a small "blary" portable radio tuned to a program of popular music. Readers looked up when the announcer told about the bombing, and the sleeping men were awakened. After a few minutes of tense silence, a soldier made a dirty remark that broke the spell. No one became excited, and most discussion concerned the possibility that furloughs planned for Christmas now would be canceled. One fellow remarked that "there wasn't any use" saving for a trip home, so he and a few buddies began an impromptu crap game.[30]

For many people the news, whenever they heard it, needed interpretation. Millions of people knew nothing about a place called Pearl Harbor and had no idea what to make of the information that Japan had bombed it. It was not part of the United States, as far as they knew; besides, exchanging shots for several weeks had not brought war with the Germans. Efforts at explanation probably left details still fuzzy, but one fact became clear: Whatever their reason for acting, the Japanese meant to have a war, and however much Americans might have wished a different outcome, the great dilemma had been resolved in a resounding fashion.

"It has come," one man noted in his diary. "The terrible things that have harassed all the rest of the world, the horrible things that have ended certainty and peace for so many, many millions—all that now has come to us. . . . I cannot describe the effect."[31] It was a time of mixed feelings if ever a time had been. Probably the most common private emotion was sadness. The sadness at reports filtering through about the disaster at Pearl would have been deeper had the full extent of losses in lives and machinery been known. But the sadness came also from the realization that raising the new Army had been no symbolic gesture. Millions of sons, husbands, and brothers would not stop with basic training and playing "war games." They would leave the country to kill and be killed. Deep, sobering thoughts surely entered the minds of everyone who understood what had taken place.

Many isolationists experienced gnawing anger that under Roosevelt's leadership the nation had reached this point of no return. They had seen it coming, had tried to turn the ship of state, and now here it was. Senator Nye spontaneously remarked that the government "had done its utmost to provoke a quarrel with Japan."[32] *Christian Century* called the war "an unnecessary necessity," and "Bertie" McCormick at the *Tribune* gave an equally auspicious pledge to support "our country Right or Wrong." As a rule it was not a time for criticism of policy. The people did not like that kind of talk and would not stand for it. The President's critics knew that they would have to follow and assist the person they disliked so much, thereby contributing to his power and popularity. They still believed they were right, that Roosevelt was a notorious liar; they knew as well that they now would have to pay him tribute.

For the most part the nation put its best face forward, displaying not fear or defeatism, but determination, confidence, and even exuberance. Interventionists and members of the Roosevelt Administration had good reason for satisfaction. The long period of uncertainty and indecision had passed; the nation had a single, easily identifiable objective. In one government office employees sent out for coffee and sandwiches and joked about Japanese aircraft. Everyone felt "a sense of excitement, of adventure, and of relief." Eric Sevareid already felt like a winner. While he suspected that a "stunned and anxious nation" slept badly the night of the attack, Sevareid had "a feeling of enormous relief; the feeling that we had won even before the fight began, had survived, even before the onslaught." He "slept like a baby."[33]

Men in uniform now took on special significance. They were the people who would absorb the blows, endure hardship, and protect the nation—heroes even before they had done anything. They enjoyed the attention and were determined to show themselves equal to the task. Servicemen in Times Square seemed happy that Japan had gone to war. "We can whip them in no time," they remarked. The folk singer Woody Guthrie observed a similar attitude in sailors making the rounds of cheap bars in Los Angeles. One man said something about wanting a "close crack at them Jap bastards." Spirits rose with each round of drinks, and another sailor, surveying the situation, decided that life could not be much better. "Well, men," he said while raising a glass of beer donated by the bartender, "I

. . . got a good uniform on. Got a free glass of beer. Got some real honest music. Got a great big war to fight. I'm satisfied. I'm ready. So here's to beatin' th' Japs." Girls sitting in booths got up, smiled, and volunteered to dance with servicemen in the crowd. A guitar-player joined in: "by God, we gotta treat our soldiers and sailors like earls and dukes from here on out."[34]

There was, indeed, a certain exhilaration about it all, an excitement fashioned by danger, by the magnitude of challenge, by a conviction that the United States had entered the war blameless, with the noblest of objectives. Joe Palooka could have no more perfect plot. "Dirty little Japs" ranked with "little yellow bastards" as the most common expletive. "How terrible for the Japanese—it's mass suicide," a lady in Chicago said. A reporter explained that "people seem to believe . . . that Japan has only two bathtubs in the Navy, no money, no oil and all Japanese fliers are so cross-eyed they couldn't hit Lake Michigan with a bomb. . . . We have God and everybody on our side, and boy, watch us go."[35] Russell Baker recalled that at age sixteen he could hardly believe the news that came over his small radio in Baltimore—"nothing more than a few specks on the map, a country whose products were synonymous with junk, a pipsqueak country on the far side of the earth—it was grotesque that such a country would take on mighty America."[36] Hearing the news in Dallas, an audience watching *Sergeant York* broke into "thunderous applause."

The United States had an opportunity to show its vigor and power in the grandest fashion, to do for the world what the world could not do for itself. A well-known journalist, Jonathan Daniels, virtually burst with the pride and excitement of the moment: "Fear at such a time? It is the hour for elation . . . when a man can fight for what America has always meant—an audacious, adventurous seeking for a decent earth. . . . We are alive—rudely awakened. That is not basis for fear but sign that our destiny survives. We are men again in America."[37]

In that heady atmosphere the government did its duty. Roosevelt took only ten minutes to deliver his speech on Monday, December 8; after talking about the day "that will live in infamy," he asked for declaration of war against Japan. Congress went to work. The gangly, gray-haired John McCormack wanted to suspend the rules and pass the measure at once. Joe Martin, the House minority leader, wanted to make a speech. The Democrats yelled "vote, vote, vote," but more Congressmen—mostly Republicans—insisted on speaking. Jeanette Rankin of Montana jumped to her feet and tried to object.

"Sit down, sister," John M. Dingell of Michigan said. Charles A. Eaton of New Jersey, who did not need a microphone, boomed out that we must "kill this accursed monster of tyranny and slavery." Speaker Sam Rayburn ordered a roll call. When Congresswoman Rankin again tried to interrupt, she was thrust aside abruptly by Speaker Rayburn. They all voted "aye," of course, all but Mrs. Rankin, who said "no" with a weak smile. Republicans wanted Rankin to change her mind and make the vote unanimous. She refused. But 338 to 1 was not bad.[38]

The Senate would do better. Even the reporter joined the spirit of the times in his account of the action in the upper chamber: "Little squint-eyed Gerald P. Nye, who has been the darling of the American Quislings, intimate of Charles A. Lindbergh. He couldn't muster the guts for a No. He voted Aye. Robert M. LaFollette Jr. voted Aye. Venerable old George W. Norris of Nebraska . . . voted Aye 82— to nothing, a complete shutout of America First, a route [sic] of isolationism."[39] Going to war had taken less than an hour.

For a while the rush to unity overshadowed all other moods. Newspapers and magazines blossomed with expressions of support from people of many levels of society. All talk of dissatisfaction among the troops vanished immediately. "Our citizen soldiers are fighting mad now and they go about their duties with a new spirit," one report stated.[40] Bishops of the Methodist and Catholic churches endorsed the war effort; more and more churchmen began to follow the reasoning of Reinhold Niebuhr. Most conspicuous among America's newest warriors were people who had been outspoken opponents of foreign policy. Virtually every isolationist critic of the President came forward to place himself before the altar of patriotism: Senators Robert A. Taft and Arthur Vandenberg, who advised "licking the hell out of them in twenty minutes," Charles Lindbergh and John L. Lewis. Representative Fish offered what he probably considered the fullest measure of devotion. He planned to volunteer as an officer in a combat unit, "preferably with colored troops," he said. "There is no sacrifice too great . . . to help annihilate these war-mad Japanese devils."[41]

The entertainment business joined the movement with a great burst of enthusiasm. The film industry canceled the Academy Award ceremonies, offered its services to the government, and even began building air raid shelters in the studios. Producers planned new war movies, although they now seemed inclined to make serious films and leave behind the tomfoolery displayed in *Buck Privates*. The songwriters' union asked for an "all out" effort for patriotic music.

Not about to let the public mood pass them by, the writers were already at work. Within days song titles circulated by the dozens. Many were silly and blatantly racist. Examples included "You're a Sap, Mr. Jap," "The Japs Haven't Got A Chinaman's Chance," and "When Those Little Yellow Bellies Meet the Cohens and the Kelleys." The best chance of success was accorded to "We Did it Before and We'll Do it Again."[42]

More men rushed to volunteer than the military services could handle on short notice, and many had to be turned away. Their chance would come soon. Even the most impressive civilian job, be it senator, mayor, movie star, or chairman of the board, now seemed insignificant beside a military title, and it appeared that everyone in politics or with political connection wished to don a uniform and get into action, many demanding rank and positions for which they could show little qualification. Representative Lyndon Johnson, a man with no military experience, served a short term as lieutenant commander in the Navy until Roosevelt called him back to the government. Older politicos, some in very high places, were distressed to learn that their day for military glory had passed. Fiorello LaGuardia of New York, who already had two jobs, lived out the war frustrated that the Department of War would not make him a general. Perhaps no politician received more abrupt deflation than Harry S. Truman of Missouri, who had asked General George Marshall for appointment as a colonel of artillery. "Senator," the plain-spoken chief of staff said, "you're too damned old."[43]

The start of war sparked a new interest in the enemy, particularly efforts to understand the Japanese character and what had driven them to such foolhardy action. *Sporting News* added a new angle to the popular conclusion that Japanese aggression had grown out of a feeling of inferiority, a "runt's complex." The Japanese had always been "feeble hitters," the "bible" of baseball explained. "It was always a sore spot with this cocky race that their batsmen were outclassed by the stronger, more powerful American sluggers." Indeed, Japan could never have committed such a "vicious, infamous deed" if the spirit of baseball "had penetrated their yellow hides."[44] Perhaps the Los Angeles *Times* best revealed how the ebullient anger of the day carried over to identification of the Japanese as brutal, treacherous, and almost subhuman. "It was the act of a mad dog," an editorial in the *Times* said, "a gangster's parody of every principle of international honor . . . the self-signed death sentence of a murderous savage."[45]

One of the most persistent, and insulting, interpretations of enemy behavior was that the Japanese were dupes of the Germans, and the more intelligent Europeans were planning policy and pushing the gullible Japanese into action. LaGuardia charged that "Nazi thugs and gangsters" had "masterminded" the attack at Pearl Harbor. Roosevelt passed along an unconfirmed report that some of the aircraft attacking Hawaii bore the Nazi insignia. The Fight for Freedom organization purchased a full-page ad in the New York *Times* to remind readers of where the greatest danger lay. "Berlin prompted this attack," the message ran. "Berlin is the meaning of this attack. . . . Berlin is the world enemy and world danger."[46]

Concern emerged in many quarters that the United States, driven by a desire for revenge, might forget that Germany, after all, represented the most powerful foe. Roosevelt had not asked for war against Germany on December 8, and much uncertainty remained as to how to proceed. As it developed, Hitler lifted the President out of his predicament. He went to war with the United States. Foreign Minister von Ribbentrop summoned the American representative, Leland Morris, to his office on December 11. He read Morris a dispatch and then screamed *"Ihr Präsident hat diesen Kreig gewollt; jetzt hat er ihn"*—Your President has wanted this war; now he has it.[47]

The first days of war demonstrated that for all their enthusiasm the Americans had no experience with living in a war zone and found the idea of an enemy attack novel and at the same time confusing. A genuine fear of air raid, sabotage, or hostile action of some sort permeated the United States through the rest of December. Military and civil authorities had swung into action with hasty, often impromptu measures to mobilize the nation's defense. The FBI placed suspicious individuals in custody; the Army began fortification of coastal areas, and armed guards took up positions at bridges, power stations, and defense factories. The White House took numerous precautions, including placing anti-aircraft guns on the roof. New York mobilized more than 60,000 air raid wardens, and cities far in the interior began work on some system for spotting and identifying aircraft. Newspapers and magazines published pictures of enemy planes and instructions on what to do when they were spotted. Mayor LaGuardia, the Director of Civil Defense, urged the people, somewhat mysteriously, to "stand firm against air attacks."[48]

The greatest danger, and greatest confusion, existed on the West

Coast, the area most vulnerable to attack from the Japanese. The first fright developed the night of December 8, following which the Army reported that two squadrons of aircraft "crossed the coast line west of San Jose . . . , reconnoitered the San Francisco Bay area and other sections of California." The fact that the planes had neglected to drop bombs, fire shots, or do anything warlike seemed unimportant. "The planes came from a carrier," General John L. DeWitt, military commander in the area, announced. When some people, puzzled by the strange enemy behavior, questioned that information, DeWitt became agitated:

> Death and destruction are likely to come to this city at any moment. You people do not seem to realize we are at war. So get this: last night there were planes over this community. They were enemy planes. I mean Japanese planes. Why bombs were not dropped, I do not know. It might have been better if some bombs had been dropped to awaken this city.[49]

Help was on the way for California. Faithful to his duty, Director LaGuardia flew "through fog and rain" from Washington with his assistant, Mrs. F. D. Roosevelt, in tow. Arriving in California, the chunky mayor announced: "I don't know how long I'll be out here. I have a city of my own to take care of too, you know." Many people found it difficult to take the "Little Flower" seriously, even in those troubled times. He was so short and round, so full of fight and fire—his resemblance to the comedian Lou Costello did not help—so enthusiastic in his desire to serve. While he was speaking in Los Angeles, news arrived that New York was having an air raid alarm. Did the Mayor wish to speak to his aides by phone? "No," he said, "just tell them to follow instructions heretofore given." With that remark the audience broke into applause, appreciating what had to be a case of enlightened planning and efficient handling of an emergency.[50] New York, apparently, was ready for anything that might come.

In truth, civil defense went no better in the Mayor's city than on the West Coast. New Yorkers were no better than San Franciscans in dealing with an air raid. Two warnings swept the East Coast on December 9; people could not agree if they were rehearsals, a genuine threat, or the result of a "phony" tip that enemy bombers were on the way. No one seemed to know what was happening. In any event, the sirens went off at 1:30 and again at 2:04 in the afternoon. Fighter planes took to the air; aircraft spotters manned their posts; schoolchildren were sent home; police cars dashed through the streets with sirens screaming.

New Yorkers scarcely acted as if their city was under seige. Instead of seeking a place of safety, many people came out to see what all the noise was about. Others grumbled about the interruption of routine. "Times Square immediately adopted a 'so what' attitude and went right on reading news bulletins," the *Times* reported. At the corner of Clinton and Grand in Brooklyn, a man who called himself Yussel the Pretzel-Peddler argued for five minutes with an Irish policeman. Yussel had a basket of fresh pretzels to sell and refused to get off the street. Another policeman "almost lost his mind" arguing with two busloads of people. He insisted they get out and take shelter, but "not a passenger would budge." The policeman had to settle for getting the buses out of sight. "What was I to do?" he asked in frustration, "use my gun on them?" How did he feel about his city's performance? a reporter asked LaGuardia, who by this time had moved on to Seattle. "Humiliated," the Little Flower answered.[51]

For several days the West Coast continued to experience genuine fear of attack, a popular confusion fed by countless rumors. One report had the Japanese fleet exactly 164 miles away from Monterey; another placed thirty-four ships between San Francisco and Los Angeles. Other reports warned of periscopes, ship sinkings, and aircraft not far off the coast. Those were strange feelings for people unaccustomed to living within a war zone. Some individuals refused to allow so small a matter as an air raid to prevent them from going about their business or driving their cars, even when it was pitch dark. Thus, the "weird" blackout of December 12 produced in San Francisco a strange mixture of noises: cars crashing, people shouting and cursing, sirens wailing, and dogs howling all over town.

In truth, of course, the Japanese had neither the intent nor means to launch an assault on the continental United States. At the time the Army was placing sandbags around strategic buildings, manning anti-aircraft batteries, and scanning the darkened sky, and while Californians hurried about collecting candles and blackout shades, the nearest enemy forces were 5,000 miles away. But the people did not know what the Japanese had in mind; few individuals understood the logistical requirement for an attack on the United States, and those who knew the range of ships and planes had been dumbfounded by the attack at Pearl Harbor, a target thought beyond the reach of Japan's war machines. "Since Honolulu was bombed and a freighter loaded with lumber was sunk 1,300 miles off the West Coast," one journalist explained, "there has been no scoffing . . . at any report, regardless of its origin or likelihood."[52]

The source of the reports could not have been more impressive, for people presumably privy to the fullest knowledge and expert on such matters—such ranking officials as LaGuardia and General De-Witt—were the most excited purveyors of alarmist information. Had there been no fear and no reason to believe the enemy might attack American soil, the government might have found reason to create an atmosphere of danger. In a way it did. While it is not correct to say that authorities deliberately fabricated stories of hostile activity, they made little effort to allay popular fear, preferring to seize upon the turmoil to press for unity of effort.

If alarmism produced fear, it also produced excitement, and many people found the first weeks of war to be a time of high drama and suspense unlike anything they had ever encountered. They now belonged to one huge national team, were Uncle Sam's players, engaged in an undeniably worthy cause. The excitement became all the more satisfying when danger passed without incident, without mass destruction. All the air raid alerts were either rehearsals or false alarms. A few dented fenders, some injuries, and even a small number of accidental deaths were tolerable consequences, elementary battle casualties in a way, part of the mystery of a darkened city in time of war. "It's thrilling," a lady said after a blackout in Los Angeles. "It's like we've been reading about. They should have done this before."[53]

In the same city, a "woman's page" writer apparently decided that inasmuch as one had to put up with this business of war—the blackouts and inconvenience and such—one might as well make the most of it. In a short space the author revealed a great deal about the atmosphere of the day and attitudes of the age:

> We know you've already put a flashlight beside your bed, arranged the radio at arm's reach, put your easiest-to-put-on clothes closest at hand. And now we're all going to have the merriest American Christmas of them all, thankful that we have a lot of handsome Army, Navy and Air Corps fighters to protect us.
>
> Just so all of you women can do your share in the emergency, we think you ought to be dressed right. So we've found this little number we call the "blackout dress" because it is completely black except for the alluringly feminine jeweled pink buttons fastening down the front.
>
> This dress . . . does much for your figure, 24 hours around the clock. No need for us women to get so hysterical we forget that the woman's job consists of being charming for the stronger sex.

For many Americans, the admonition of LaGuardia in Los Angeles seemed appropriate: "Hell, this isn't a pinochle party we're having," he said, "it's war."[54]

For one group of Americans war produced a special problem. Jeanne Wakatsuki, a seven-year-old resident of Ocean Park, California, suspected something was wrong shortly after her father departed with a small fleet of fishing boats. Instead of disappearing over the horizon as usual, the boats turned around and headed back toward the base at Terminal Island. "What is Pearl Harbor?" Jeanne's sister-in-law, Chizu, asked her mother. "What is Pearl Harbor?" Mama yelled to the man who had brought the news. He simply kept running, shouting to people along the docks. When Papa Wakatsuki returned to shore, he set about destroying papers and other items, even burning the beautiful flag with the red ball in the center he had brought to California thirty-five years earlier. Jeanne did not understand what it meant, nor did she understand why two weeks later mysterious men in trench coats and fedora hats—looking much like George Raft, Humphrey Bogart, or other people from the movies—took Papa away. She would not see him for nearly a year.[55]

Jeanne's father, of course, had run afoul a dubious manifestation of the patriotic spirit sweeping the United States in the first weeks of war: the blatant racism expressed by many public officials and cocky superpatriots and suggested in the titles of hastily composed patriotic songs. Racial hatred was a product of the circumstances, but, perhaps like all racism, it was incapable of making distinctions and rested on an assumption of group guilt. Some people blamed all Japanese for the treacherous attack on Hawaii, and whether they lived in Tokyo or on the West Coast of the United States made no difference. Woody Guthrie encountered this attitude in sleazy bars in Los Angeles a day or two after war had started. One civilian customer was clearly frustrated at the ease with which young men in uniform were attracting attention. A double shot of hard liquor and a glass of beer helped put him in a military spirit. He announced to assembled customers that while he could not serve in the Army or Navy, he was prepared to "beat th' livin' hell outta ever' Goddam Jap in this town!"[56]

Japanese-Americans had the great misfortune of being in the wrong place at the wrong time. While only 130,000 lived in the continental United States, more than 90,000 resided in California, an area sprinkled with naval bases, shipyards, and aircraft factories, the part of the United States thought most vulnerable to attack. Most Americans were familiar with the name Quisling, the infamous betrayer of Norway; the Spanish Civil War of 1936–39 had produced the term "fifth column," which related to subversion, a threat from inside the home country. And here, for God's sake, the United States had thousands of the enemy living in its midst. All Japanese-Americans immediately became potential "fifth-columnists," if not outright hostile combatants.

Fear and anger helped give credence to rumors spreading throughout the area: The Japanese were poisoning food, signaling the enemy (Wakatsuki's boat had a short-wave radio), picking out strategic targets, and planning sabotage or even an armed uprising. No matter that two-thirds of these people—the second generation Japanese, the so-called Nisei, mostly people in their teens and early twenties—had American citizenship and a large majority were loyal to the United States. No one bothered to establish guilt or ask what they thought. What mattered most was that they were of Japanese origin, and because they were Japanese they could not be true, trustworthy Americans.

No decision had been made on the status of Japanese-Americans as the year came to an end, but the future scarcely looked promising to these people. The Wakatsukis began to notice disapproving glances, to hear insulting remarks, and to sense hostility from the local white populace. Friends and relatives seemed troubled and guarded. Many were hesitant to venture far beyond the neighborhood. Momentum had started to build toward decisive action, a policy that would be considered one of the great mistakes of the war, perhaps a first crack in the armor of principle and noble purpose with which the nation had enveloped itself. Papa Wakatsuki would not return home for a long time after agents took him away, and home would take on new meaning. In time he would be joined in exile—in special internment camps—by Jeanne, her family, and virtually all other Japanese-Americans in the United States. For those people more than most, the year 1941 marked a beginning and an end.

The last year of peace had turned into the first days of war, and until the end of the year, at least, it was not a good war for the United States. The Germans continued to hammer at Moscow, and the fate of the Russian nation still seemed in doubt. The Japanese advanced almost at will in the Far East. Americans took inspiration in a detachment of 379 Marines who had put up dogged resistance at the tiny outpost on Wake Island. Even so, Wake fell on December 23, and enemy forces had landed on the Philippine island of Luzon, pushing toward the capital city, Manila. Although Roosevelt had promised help for General Douglas MacArthur and his army of American and Filipino troops, knowledgeable men knew that the Philippine Islands, America's largest foreign territory, was doomed.

The United States began to look and sound like a country at war. The novelty and excitement of entering the conflict had started to wear off, and the reality of the dreadful undertaking set in. The Office of Price Administration announced rationing of tires the last week of December; production of automobiles would soon have to stop. Americans without new cars? What better indication that this truly was war! Roosevelt ordered a seven-day week for all defense industries as soon as the factories could put the people to work. Soldiers drafted for twelve and then thirty months faced a second extension, lasting God knows how long—the "duration" had become a new catchword. Far more men, millions more, were destined to be called to the colors. Many families had the most prosperous, though probably not the merriest, Christmas in many years; many tried to make the most of it. Some men would not make it home for Christmas. Their units suddenly had had their orders changed. Eleanor Roosevelt wept as James and Elliott departed for new military assignments. It was hard, she said, and then wept again as she told a friend about the occasion.[57] If Mrs. Roosevelt was nothing less than the nation's first lady, she was nothing more than a mother of boys who might be killed.

The British Prime Minister had rushed to the United States almost as fast, it might have seemed, as the Japanese had gone to Hawaii. He wanted to be on hand when the Americans, who in truth had two wars to fight, made their plans, to be sure they put the right one first. There he was, the cocky old bulldog, the wily old bastard, with puffy pink cheeks and a large cigar clamped in his mouth, sitting with the President as reporters crowded around the desk. He acted almost as if he belonged in Washington. Maybe he did. He appeared again on Christmas Eve to offer good wishes for the holiday season and to give Americans permission to have a happy Christmas. "Let the children have their night of fun and laughter," he said. "Let us grown-ups share to the full our unstinted pleasures," and then "turn . . . to the stern tasks and formidable years that lie before us."[58]

Churchill was good at that sort of thing. Some people felt flattered that the British leader chose to spend Christmas with them. Former isolationists probably looked upon the Prime Minister's appearance with the President as altogether appropriate, a bitter reminder of the struggle of previous months and of the fact that they had lost.

Americans said farewell to 1941, and many of them did so with considerable relief. "What a year it has been—war, strikes, everything uncertain, one has never known what is going to happen next," one lady said.[59] They said goodbye to that year marked with high unemployment and with elements of society that characterized the America of another age: the fights of Joe Louis, two white teams playing the World Series, horses and mules in the fields, Packards and Studebakers on the highway, hot days without air-conditioning, swing music in sweaty ballrooms, blaring juke boxes in smoky, smelly roadhouses, and, if one had the money, traveling from Chicago to New York on the Twentieth Century Limited. Roosevelt belonged to that age; he almost seemed to take it over. For Americans "1941 will be recalled as the year of indecision, a year of furious preparedness, a year of sadness, a year that ended with total unity and single-mindedness of purpose," the Los Angeles *Times* mused. "A great struggle has begun. The world moves on."[60]

The United States was moving as well. The observer seeking to understand direction and reason would find that the last year before the war was shaped both by familiar forces of an era and by new factors emerging from the troubled present. Economic need had always been such a force, especially in a time still marked with scars of depression. Because of economic need, people moved, mostly to cities; economic need caused government to become larger and more involved in people's lives, changes that the population for the most part endorsed or accepted out of resignation. Americans might not like to admit it, but they were becoming less individualistic, less willing to accept responsibility for their fate, more inclined to look to Washington for help. The tractor, automobile, radio, and movies continued to be powerful agents of culture; all affected work goals and aspirations, all stood as yardsticks as well as shapers of behavior, of what it meant to be an American.

Now a new force had come forward. It was the war that made 1941 most distinctly different, marking the year as a time of transition showing two faces of America. Conditions of the year showed that war—this war—left its mark in many ways, as both a suppressant and an activator of change, a force for holding in place the old as well as for bringing in the new.

By reordering national priorities, war indeed can function as a conservative force. People who had to get along with oil-fueled aladdin lamps in 1941 probably still used them in 1945, unless by chance they had moved to town. Not many farmers could get electricity because of the war; virtually no one would be able to get a car. It was clear in 1941 that the war was delaying the expansion of civilian flight and propping up travel by rail; it held back the development of television to benefit of a traditional concept of Hollywood. It held in place some famous old firms, such as Packard, that otherwise probably soon would have gone under.

More conspicuous and in the end more meaningful was war as an agent of change. Who could fail to notice the changes in radio, movies, and other familiar instruments of culture, as well as the speeding up of older movements, such as the growth of cities, legitimizing as never before expansion of power in the national government? It would be difficult to find a new social force more powerful than the Army, or military forces in general. While the people directly involved in 1941 would be small—approximately 1 million inductees—some effect extended through friends and relatives to many more, and in months to come the number would multiply considerably.

The Army brought some changes that were anything but subtle: a new home for the conscripts, new duties, the jolting regimentation of military life. The soldiers received better food and medical care, for most the first experience with anything resembling a comprehensive medical program. While not as easy to measure, the effect on attitudes also had to be considerable. These largely provincial young men received an education: They would learn about the United States and eventually the world, about themselves and men from other states, other religions, and other ethnic groups. Although virtually every serviceperson expressed a desire to return to what he or she had left, most would discover that in many important ways it was impossible to go back to the old life. Whether Polish, Irish, a Jew from the Bronx, or a poor white from upper Tennessee, the Army dressed its recruits alike, gave them the same rules and food, demanded virtually the same behavior from each, and in that way acted as a powerful instrument of assimilation.

Heterogeneity nonetheless remained one of the strongest distinguishing national characteristics. At first glance, in fact, it appeared that the war made internal division worse. The conflict between isolationism and supporters of Roosevelt represented the most conspicuous aspect of national affairs in 1941, and trouble between management and labor, partly a consequence of war, probably ranked second. The war made black people more acutely aware of inequality and almost sparked the first mass civil rights demonstration. Religious affiliation and ethnic identity helped determine one's position on the war in Europe. Wartime issues made many Americans more aware than ever of Jews and made Jews more aware of themselves.

And yet the war created another mood that tended to hover like a cloud above the general populace, coexisting with continuing conflict between individual groups. Calamitous events abroad promoted the idea of America as haven and protector, a special place indeed. The attitude encouraged a search for common principles and created a need to appear loyal and patriotic, giving concrete meaning to a common American identity. Felt most intensely by ethnic minority groups—people whose loyalty might be in question—the mood called for blunting the effects of being Catholic or German or Jewish in favor of being American. What had existed most of the year as steady pressure burst at year's end into a ringing demand. At no time in their history did Americans feel greater obligation and desire to support their government than on December 8, 1941. If prewar America remained more a salad bowl than a melting pot, because of the war the salad was being covered with a heavy dressing.

The great venture that the United States began in 1941 would not stop with the defeat of Germany or Japan, not in a lifetime or in several lifetimes. When the men came back at the end of the war, other men would replace them abroad. The commitment of the United States remained on the other side, on several other sides. That was perhaps the greatest change of all. The men might come back, but the United States did not. The role of leadership in world affairs, taken with however much reluctance in 1941, would not vanish in 1945; the country would not find a way to put it down. If Americans during 1941 were debating whether or not to become involved in politics of the world, after 1941 the question was not whether, but how much and where the involvement would end.

Were they special people—these people of 1941, the generation of the 1930s and 1940s—or did they only live in a special time? This generation that had experienced America's greatest Depression would fight its largest war. They could tell that their time on earth was not easy, and to call it challenging would not be enough, but the full significance of the age would be discerned only by looking

In 1945, the United States inherited the earth.

back from years in the future. It was better to look back after the troubles had passed. There had been problems and mistakes, to be sure, and attitudes that other generations might never understand. With the passage of time it would be possible to overlook the petty quarrels and selfish attitudes, and with more time—in light of how it all ended—it might be possible to forget they had happened. At least they had done the big things right. For the most part, those people would like what they saw in retrospect—what it said about their ability to struggle, suffer, persevere, pick the right cause, and fight the good fight. The issues seemed so clear from a distance, the cause so just, the battles so well fought. Maybe they were special people after all.

If Americans in the future would have some difficulty adjusting to a new position, finding a realistic path, and accepting the notion that America could be capable of poor judgment or even error, it was of course partly because they faced a world, and a scope of responsibility, far more complex than what they could look back upon in the months before Pearl Harbor. It might also have been because of the way that last year had turned out. If they had been so right this time, could they ever be wrong? Never in American history have large national and individual questions been answered with such force and clarity as in 1941.

Notes

☆

One. The Great Dilemma

1. This description comes generally from *Time*, January 6, 1941, 9–10.

2. *Life*, February 24, 1941, 4.

3. Edward Bliss, Jr., ed., *In Search of Light: The Broadcasts of Edward R. Murrow 1938–1961* (New York, 1967), 35–36. See also Erik Barnouw, *A History of Broadcasting in the United States, Vol. II. 1933 to 1953: The Golden Web* (New York, 1968), 140–42.

4. Eric Sevareid, *Not So Wild A Dream,* (New York, 1946, 1976), 178.

5. *Life*, February 10, 1941, 52–54; *Time*, April 28, 1941, 54–55.

6. Henry Misselwitz, "American Baseball Conquers Japan," *Living Age*, May 1940, 222–25.

7. Halett Abend, "Yes, the Japanese Can Fly," *Saturday Evening Post*, April 19, 1941, 29.

8. Lucien Zacharoff, "Japanese Air Power," *Aviation*, September 1941, 48–49, 146, 148, 150.

9. Harold E. Fay, "The Emperor Who Plays God," *Christian Century*, August 28, 1940, 1049–51. See also "God, Emperor, High Priest," *New York Times Magazine*, November 23, 1941.

10. *Time*, February 24, 1941, 79; *Life*, December 30, 1940, 18–19.

11. William L. Shirer, *Berlin Diary* (New York, 1941), 137.

12. Nashville *Tennessean*, October 31, 1941.

13. Shirer, *Berlin Diary*, 53.

14. Douglas Miller, "Why Germans Act as They Do," *New York Times Magazine*, August 31, 1941. See also Douglas Miller, *You Can't Do Business with Hitler* (Boston, 1941).

15. Letter to the editor from Howard Mason, *Life*, March 24, 1941, 6.

16. Joseph E. Davies, *Mission To Moscow* (New York, c. 1941; Pocket Books edition, 1943), 452; "What We Must Defend," *New Republic*, February 17, 1941, 227.

17. Russell Baker, *Growing Up* (New York, 1982), 197. For opinion polls see "American Opinion About the War," *Harper's Magazine*, April

1941, 549–52, and Hadley Cantril, *Public Opinion 1935–1946* (Princeton, N.J., 1951), 966–78.

18. Philip Gibbs, *America Speaks* (Garden City, N.Y., 1942), 14.

19. *Time,* January 6, 1941, 9–10.

20. Robert E. Sherwood, *Roosevelt and Hopkins: An Intimate History* (New York, 1948), 191.

21. *Time,* January 6, 1941, 9–10.

22. Arthur Krock, "Will We Stay Out?" *New York Times Magazine,* January 12, 1941, 3.

23. Erskine Caldwell and Margaret Bourke-White, *Say, is this the U.S.A.* (New York, 1941), 3, 74.

24. Cited in Sherwood, *Roosevelt and Hopkins,* 166.

25. Herbert Agar of Louisville *Courier Journal,* cited in New York *Times,* January 13, 1941.

26. Stephen Vincent Benet, "Six of Us Talking," in Stephen Vincent Benet *et al., Zero Hour: A Summons to the Free* (New York, 1940), 5.

27. Archibald MacLeish, *The American Cause* (New York, 1941), 6–7.

28. Gibbs, *America Speaks,* 31.

29. Baker, *Growing Up,* 141–42.

30. August 25, 1941, 65.

31. New York *Times,* January 4 and March 1, 1941; Detroit *Free Press,* January 26, 1941.

32. Speech of September 7, 1940, cited in Rex Stout, ed., *The Illustrious Dunderheads* (New York, 1942), 71.

33. Cited in Sherwood, *Roosevelt and Hopkins* (note 20 above), 166.

34. Cited in James MacGregor Burns, *Roosevelt: The Soldier of Freedom* (New York, 1970), 46.

35. Lawrence Hunt, *A Letter to the American People* (New York, 1941), 7.

36. Mark Lincoln Chadwin, *The Warhawks: American Interventionists Before Pearl Harbor* (New York, 1970), 210; Wayne S. Cole, *Charles A. Lindbergh and the Battle Against American Intervention in World War II* (New York, 1974), 171–73.

37. James T. Patterson, *Mr. Republican: A Biography of Robert A. Taft* (Boston, 1972), 244, 243.

38. New York *Times,* January 13, 1941; for a detailed discussion of the controversy over the lend-lease proposal, see Warren F. Kimball, *The Most Unsordid Act: Lend-Lease, 1939–1941* (Baltimore, 1969).

39. Both proposals in Kimball, *Most Unsordid Act,* 186–87, 205–6.

40. Hunt, *Letter to American People,* 43–44.

41. Arthur H. Vandenberg, Jr., *The Private Papers of Senator Vandenberg* (Boston, 1952), 10.

42. Henry Luce, "The American Century," *Life,* February 19, 1941, 61–65. See also W. A. Swanberg, *Luce and His Empire* (New York, 1972), 180–83.

43. Oswald Garrison Villard, "Are We to Rule the World?" *Christian Century,* March 26, 1941, 422.

44. Burns, *Roosevelt,* 129.

45. "Ground Plan for a Post-War World," *New Republic,* February 10, 1941, 169.

46. William Allen White, *The Autobiography of William Allen White* (New York, 1946), 642.

47. From a newspaper essay of April 13, 1941. Reprinted in Carl Sandburg, *Home Front Memo* (New York, 1942), 53.

Two. Building the New American Army

1. *Life,* March 31, 1941. For an evaluation of the Navy, see Los Angeles *Times,* May 5, 1941.

2. Robert Dallek, *Franklin D. Roosevelt and American Foreign Policy 1932–1945* (New York, 1979), 249.

3. *Time,* September 16, 1940; Rex Stout, *The Illustrious Dunderheads* (New York, 1942), 184. See also William L. Langer and S. Everett Gleason, *The Challenge to Isolation,* 2 vols. (New York, 1952), II: 680–82.

4. Director of Selective Service, *Selective Service in Peacetime: First Report of the Director of Selective Service, 1940–41* (Washington, D.C., 1942), 323–25.

5. Los Angeles *Times,* June 29, 1941. For conscription practices, see also Detroit *Free Press,* March 9, 1941, and Burton Lindheim, "Draft Board Drama," *New York Times Magazine,* May 18, 1941, 6, 31. For marriage statistics, see Bureau of the Census, *Historical Statistics of the United States, Colonial Times to 1957* (Washington, 1960), 22, and J. Frederick Dewhurst & Associates, *America's Needs and Resources* (New York, 1947), 33.

6. Mentor L. Williams, "American Humor and National Security," *Michigan Alumnus Quarterly Review,* April 26, 1941, 261.

7. Meyer Berger, "Luck O' The Army," *New York Times Magazine,* December 8, 1940, 8.

8. "This Man's Army," *New Republic,* September 23, 1940, 406; Dorothy Dunbar Bromley, "They're in the Army Now," *New Republic,* January 6, 1941, 13.

9. William F. Ogburn, "Effects of the Draft on the Rest of Us," *New York Times Magazine,* February 23, 1941, 3, 26.

10. The Infantry Journal, *The Soldier's Handbook* (New York, 1941), 224–25.

11. *Your Year in the Army: What Every Soldier Should Know* (New York, 1940), 45.

12. Donald E. Houston, *Hell On Wheels: The 2nd Armored Division* (San Rafael, Calif., 1977), 50.

13. *Life,* April 21, 1941, 86.

14. Peter Chamberlain and Chris Ellis, *AFV (Armoured Fighting Vehicles of the World) 11: M3 Medium Lee/Grant* (Berkshire, England), 5 and *idem, Pictorial History of Tanks of the World 1915–1945* (Harrisburg, Pa., 1972), 195–96, 202–3.

15. Martin Blumenson, *The Patton Papers 1940–1945* (Boston, 1974), 43; Patton to Terry de la Mesa Allen, September 30, 1940, in *ibid.,* 13.

16. Marion Hargrove, *See Here Private Hargrove* (New York, 1942), 118; Samuel T. Williamson, "The Jeeps Have a Word for It," *New York Times Magazine,* October 5, 1941, 4, 21.

17. Meyer Berger, "The American Soldier—One Year After," *New York Times Magazine,* November 23, 1941, 30, and *idem,* "Uncle Sam, Chef," *New York Times Magazine,* June 15, 1941, 10–11, 16.

18. Forrest C. Pogue, *George C. Marshall: Ordeal and Hope* (New York, 1966), 116.

19. Edgar Snow, "They Don't Want to Play Soldier," *Saturday Evening Post,* October 25, 1941, 14; Chicago *Tribune,* August 19, 1941; *Reader's Digest,* November 1941, 112–14.

20. Samuel A. Stouffer, *The American Soldier: Adjustment During Army Life,* 2 vols. (Princeton, N.J., 1949), I: 78.

21. Alden Stevens, "Morale in the Camps," *Graphic Survey,* October 1941, 515.

22. Stouffer, *The American Soldier,* I: 55, 59–62.

23. *Variety,* May 14, 1941.

24. Chicago *Tribune,* July 8, 1941.

25. Detroit *Free Press,* June 8, 1941.

26. Stevens, "Morale in the Camps," 516.

27. Detroit *Free Press,* March 12, 1941.

28. *Life,* October 13, 1941, 128; *Reader's Digest,* December 1941, 14–17.

29. Harry Benjamin, "Morals Versus Morale in Wartime," in Benjamin Robinson, ed., *Morals in Wartime* (New York, 1943), 185, 190–91.

30. "What About Army Vice?" *Christian Century,* March 26, 1941, 414.

31. Henry L. Stimson and McGeorge Bundy, *On Active Service: In Peace and War* (New York, 1947), 379.

32. Harold Lavine, "Why the Army Gripes," *Nation,* August 30, 1941, 179–80.

33. Henry McLemore, "The Lighter Side," Los Angeles *Times,* June 25, 1941. For a discussion of rules set down in the *Umpire Manual,* see unpublished manuscript by Christopher R. Gabel, "The U.S. Army G.H.Q. Maneuvers of 1941," 83–85.

34. Blumenson, *Patton Papers* (note 15 above), 38; see also Nashville *Tennessean,* September 21, 1941.

35. Major Bell I. Wiley and Captain William P. Govan, *The Army Ground Forces: History of the Second Army* (Washington, D.C., 1946), 28–29.

36. Gabel, "U.S. Army Maneuvers," 83–84, 216, 283; see also *Time,* September 22, 1941, 32.

37. Dwight D. Eisenhower, *Crusade in Europe* (New York, 1948), 12; see also Eisenhower's letter to Patton, September 17, 1940, in Blumenson, *Patton Papers,* 14.

38. Eric Sevareid, *Not So Wild a Dream* (New York, 1946), 203; Berger, "American Soldier—One Year After" (note 17 above), 3–4.

39. For reports on these developments, see *Time,* November 3, 1941; Detroit *Free Press,* April 25, June 5, 1941; Los Angeles *Times,* June 29, 1941; and Chamberlain and Ellis, *AFV: M3 Medium* (note 14 above).

40. Pendleton Herring, *The Impact of War: Our American Democracy Under Arms* (New York, 1941), 20.

41. Berger, "American Soldier—One Year After," 30.

Three. Spurts and Sputters in the Economy

1. Bureau of the Census, *Historical Statistics of the United States, Colonial Times to 1957* (Washington, D.C., 1960), 92–94, 122–23.

2. Chicago *Tribune,* August 3, 1941; Irmus Johnson, "Something Really Just as Good," Nashville *Tennessean,* September 21, 1941.

3. Chicago *Tribune,* July 3 and August 22, 1941; Webb Waldron, "Two Million Unemployed Through 'Priorities,'" *Reader's Digest,* October 1941, 137–40.

4. Donald M. Nelson, *Arsenal of Democracy: The Story of American War Production* (New York, 1946), 113–14. Another official, Leon Henderson, decided that the best time to talk to Roosevelt was during lunch. He watched closely to see when the President's mouth was full

of food, then "let fire." "Leon, what's the matter with you?" Roosevelt remarked one day. "You aren't eating." John Gunther, *Roosevelt in Retrospect* (New York, 1950), 55.

5. James M. Burns, *Roosevelt: The Soldier of Freedom* (New York, 1970), 52–53; Nelson, *Arsenal of Democracy,* 127–28.

6. *Time,* April 28, 1941, 13; Burns, *Roosevelt,* 119.

7. Bureau of the Census, *Historical Statistics,* 99; Joel Seidman, *American Labor from Defense to Reconversion* (Chicago, 1953), 28–29.

8. Irving Bernstein, *Turbulent Years: A History of the American Worker 1933–1941* (Boston, 1970), 734–36. Comparative statistics appear regularly in the trade publication *Automotive Industries.*

9. Bernstein, *Turbulent Years,* 738–39.

10. Keith Sward, *The Legend of Henry Ford* (New York, 1948), 370.

11. Detroit *Free Press,* February 11, 1941.

12. *Ibid.,* January 5 and March 5 and 9, 1941.

13. Chicago *Defender,* January 4, April 19, 1941; see also August Meier and Elliott Rudwick, *Black Detroit and the Rise of the U.A.W.* (New York, 1979), 85.

14. Detroit *Free Press,* April 2, 1941.

15. *Ibid.,* April 3 and 6, 1941.

16. *Ibid.,* May 23, 1941.

17. Bernstein, *Turbulent Years,* 747. The contract appears in Detroit *Free Press,* June 21, 1941.

18. Bernstein, *Turbulent Years,* 750–51.

19. John Day, *Bloody Ground* (Garden City, N.Y., 1941), 316–17.

20. Words and music by Merle Travis. Copyright © 1947 by Hill & Range Songs, Inc., Elvis Presley Music, Inc., Gladys Music, Inc., and Noma Music, Inc. Rights administered by Hill & Range Songs, Inc., New York.

21. Saul Alinsky, *John L. Lewis: An Unauthorized Biography* (New York, 1949), 5.

22. For methods of mining, see Bureau of the Census, *Historical Statistics* (note 1 above), 356; Alinsky, *John L. Lewis,* 3–13; and McAlister Coleman, *Men and Coal* (Toronto, 1943), 3–24, 279–90.

23. Day, *Bloody Ground,* 319–20; Bureau of the Census, *Historical Statistics,* 372.

24. Day, *Bloody Ground,* 319.

25. Bureau of the Census, *Historical Statistics,* 93, 358; the contract, the Appalachian Joint Wage Agreement, appears in Coleman, *Men and Coal,* 312–30.

26. Arthur M. Schlesinger, Jr., *The Coming of the New Deal* (Boston, 1958), 137–38.

27. Day, *Bloody Ground*, 316.

28. Herman P. Miller, *Rich Man, Poor Man* (New York, 1964), 57.

29. Day, *Bloody Ground*, 295.

30. New York *Times*, April 2, 3, and 16, 1941; Day, *Bloody Ground*, 287–90; *Coal Age*, May 1941, 77–80.

31. Detroit *Free Press*, May 22, 1941.

32. *Coal Age*, June 1941, 36, and July 1941, 71.

33. Bernstein, *Turbulent Years* (note 8 above), 754–66.

34. Seidman, *American Labor* (note 7 above), 64–65; Nashville *Tennessean*, November 17, 1941.

35. Nashville *Tennessean*, November 4, 1941.

36. *Ibid.*, November 23, 1941.

37. Polls in 1941 showed that more than 70 percent of people questioned considered many union leaders racketeers, 75 percent believed they had too much power, and 61 percent thought many union leaders were Communists. For these and other public surveys, see Hadley Cantril, *Public Opinion 1935–1946* (Princeton, N.J., 1951), 396–97, 821, 872, 875.

38. Los Angeles *Times*, June 6, 1941.

39. *Ibid.*, June 10, 1941.

40. *Ibid.*, December 10, 1941; see also *ibid.*, December 7, 1941.

41. Seidman, *American Labor*, 44.

42. Nelson, *Arsenal of Democracy* (note 4 above), 139.

43. For economic statistics see *Variety*, March 5, 1941; Chicago *Tribune*, August 3, 1941; Bureau of the Census, *Historical Statistics*, (note 7 above), 97, 164, 166, 208–10; and *The Economic Reports of the President, January 1948, January 1947, July 1947* (New York, 1948), 105, 153.

44. National Resources Planning Board, *Security, Work, and Relief Policies* (Washington, D.C., 1942), 597.

45. Milton F. Wells, "Whose Standard of Living?" *Christian Century*, August 21, 1940, 1027–29.

46. Chicago *Tribune*, August 13, 1941. See also Bureau of the Census, *Historical Statistics*, 165; J. Frederick Dewhurst & Associates, *America's Needs and Resources* (New York, 1947), 65; and James T. Patterson, *America's Struggle Against Poverty 1900–1980* (Cambridge, Mass., 1981), 79–80.

47. Director of Selective Service, *Selective Service in Peacetime: First Re-*

port of the Director of Selective Service, 1940–41 (Washington, D.C., 1942), 211–13; Nashville Tennessean, September 21, 1941; Nathan Sinai, "Physical Fitness and the Draft," Harper's Magazine, October 1941, 546–52.

48. "Food Is Also Power," Fortune, August 1941, 102–4; Burns, Roosevelt (note 5 above), 53–54.

49. Philip Gibbs, America Speaks (Garden City, N.Y., 1942), 21.

50. Chicago Tribune, September 7, 1941; Nashville Tennessean, October 1, 1941.

51. These advertisements appeared in Life, March 3, 1941, 20; Time, February 24, 1941, 51; and New York Times Magazine, November 23, 1941.

52. Los Angeles Times, December 7, 1941.

53. Statistics on registration of all new cars appeared regularly in the trade publication Automotive Industries. See, for example, the editions of April 1, 1941, 394, and November 15, 1941, 50.

54. Day, Bloody Ground (note 19 above), 204.

55. "Your Used Car—Did You Buy Safety or Disaster?" The American Weekly, a part of Nashville Tennessean, December 7, 1941, 13.

56. August Hollingshead, Elmtown's Youth: The Impact of Social Classes on Adolescents (New York, 1949), 397–98.

57. Detroit Free Press, March 26, 1941.

58. Elliot V. Bell, "Planned Economy and/or Democracy," New York Times Magazine, November 23, 1941, 5.

59. National Resources Planning Board, Security, Work, and Relief Policies, 490. This report, not released until 1942, was prepared in 1941.

60. Bell, "Planned Economy," 19, 21.

Four. On the Road and Into Town

1. Bureau of the Census, Historical Statistics of the United States, Colonial Times to 1957 (Washington, D.C., 1960), 8–9; idem, Sixteenth Census of the United States: 1940, Population, Volume III, Characteristics of the Population (Washington, D.C., 1943), 19.

2. Bureau of the Census, Historical Statistics, 12–13.

3. Bureau of the Census, Vital Statistics of the United States, 1942, Part I (Washington, D.C., 1944), 33; J. Frederick Dewhurst & Associates, America's Needs and Resources (New York, 1947); Department of Health, Education and Welfare, Vital Statistics Rates in the United States 1940–1960 (Washington, D.C., 1968), 798–99.

4. Walter Goldschmidt, As You Sow (New York, 1947), 73.

5. Statistics on travel appear in Bureau of the Census, *Historical Statistics,* 467, and Encyclopaedia Britannica, Inc., *1942 Britannica Book of the Year* (Chicago, 1942), 132, 234, 448.

6. Council of State Governments, *The Book of the States, 1941–1942* (Chicago, 1941), 173.

7. Erskine Caldwell and Margaret Bourke-White, *Say, is this the U.S.A.* (New York, 1941), 10–11.

8. Detroit *Free Press,* March 9, 1941; see also Arthur D. Dubin, *Some Classic Trains* (Milwaukee, 1964).

9. Bureau of the Census, *Historical Statistics,* 430.

10. Population statistics appear in Bureau of the Census, *Characteristics of Population,* 108, 156; Richard Polenberg, *One Nation Divisible: Class, Race and Ethnicity in the United States Since 1938* (New York, 1980), 34–36; and E. P. Hutchinson, *Immigrants and Their Children, 1850–1950* (New York, 1956), 6–7.

11. James West (Carl Withers), *Plainville, U.S.A.* (New York, 1945), 55.

12. August Hollingshead, *Elmstown's Youth* (New York, 1949), 192–93.

13. *Ibid.,* 159.

14. Dewhurst & Associates, *America's Needs and Resources* (note 3 above), 416.

15. Cited in *ibid.,* 413–14.

16. J. C. Furnas, *How America Lives* (New York, 1941), 179–84.

17. Polenberg, *One Nation Divisible,* 19; Dewhurst & Associates, *America's Needs and Resources,* 413–14.

18. Dean Acheson, *Present at the Creation* (New York, 1969), 16; Robert E. Sherwood, *Roosevelt and Hopkins: An Intimate History* (New York, 1948), 295.

19. See Los Angeles *Times,* May 20, 1941, and Bureau of the Census, *Historical Statistics* (note 1 above), 462.

20. Chicago *Tribune,* July 2 and August 13, 1941; see also William D. Middleton, *The Time of the Trolley* (Milwaukee, 1967), and E. E. Kearns, "The Popular Trolley Coach," *American City,* August 1941, 93–94.

21. Clark Craig, "Cape Cod Gets a War Boom," *Harper's Magazine,* March 1941, 369–72.

22. *Ibid.,* 373–74.

23. Lowell Clucas, "Defense Comes to Our Town," *Saturday Evening Post,* March 15, 1941, 12–13, 98–102, and "In Bridgeport's War Factories," *Fortune,* September 1941, 158. See also New York *Times,* January 16, 1941, for an account of York, Pennsylvania; James E. Zachary, "When a Defense Boom Hits a Defenseless Village," *American City,* October

1941, 47–49, for Charlestown, Indiana; Frank J. Taylor, "Blitz-Boom," *Saturday Evening Post,* July 19, 1941, 14–15, for San Diego; "Portrait of a Defense Town," *Parade,* September 21, 1941, 24–25, for East Hartford, Connecticut; and Blair Bolles, "The Great Defense Migration," *Harper's Magazine,* October 1941, 460–67.

24. Chicago *Tribune,* August 9, 1941.

25. "Wash. the No. 1 Boom Town of America," *Variety,* March 12, 1941.

26. Alden Stevens, "Washington—Blight on Democracy," *Harper's Magazine,* December 1941, 50–58. See also Bernard Weisberger, ed., *The WPA Guide to America* (New York, 1985), 136.

27. Los Angeles *Times,* May 2 and 3, 1941.

28. *Ibid.,* July 12, 1941.

29. For descriptions of Los Angeles, see Otis Ferguson, "To the Promissory Land," *The New Republic,* July 14, 1941, 49–52, and "To The Promissory Land II," August 4, 1941, 150–53.

30. Philip Gibbs, *America Speaks* (Garden City, N.Y., 1942), 166.

31. Jack Alexander, "The Duke of Chicago," *Saturday Evening Post,* July 19, 1941, 10–11.

32. *Time,* February 24, 1941, 48.

33. Alexander, "Duke of Chicago," 70.

34. Mark Lincoln Chadwin, *The Warhawks: American Interventionists Before Pearl Harbor* (New York, 1970), 212; Chicago *Tribune,* August 15 and 19, 1941.

35. Cited in Leo C. Rosten, *Hollywood: The Movie Colony, The Movie Makers* (New York, 1941), 191.

36. *Life,* April 14, 1941, 93.

37. Marie Di Mario, "Little Italys," *Common Ground,* Winter 1941, 23.

38. *Ibid.,* 21–22.

39. Ronald H. Bayor, *Neighbors in Conflict: The Irish, Germans, Jews and Italians of New York City, 1929–1941* (Baltimore, 1978), 17–20.

40. Nashville *Tennessean,* October 5, 1941.

41. Bayor, *Neighbors in Conflict,* 52–55.

42. Chadwin, *The Warhawks,* 10.

43. Bayor, *Neighbors in Conflict,* 120; see also John P. Diggins, *Mussolini and Fascism: The View From America* (Princeton, 1972), 349–51.

44. William Poster, "'Twas a Dark Night in Brownsville," in Wilson Smith, ed., *Cities of our Past and Present* (New York, 1964), 217.

45. Di Mario, "Little Italys," 24–26.

Five. Progress and Poverty in the Countryside

1. Population statistics appear in Bureau of the Census, *Historical Statistics of the United States, Colonial Times to 1957* (Washington, D.C., 1960), 9, 47.

2. Department of Agriculture, *Agricultural Statistics 1943* (Washington, D.C., 1943), 425.

3. Arthur F. Raper and Ira De A. Reid, *Sharecroppers All* (Chapel Hill, N.C., 1941), 145.

4. Bureau of the Census, *Historical Statistics,* 284, 289.

5. *Ibid,* 284.

6. So said farmers near Irwin, Iowa. Edwin O. Moe and Carl G. Taylor, *Culture of a Contemporary Rural Community: Irwin, Iowa.* U.S. Department of Agriculture, Bureau of Agricultural Economics, Rural Life Studies No. 5 (Washington, D.C., 1942), 38–39.

7. Grant Heilman, ed., *Farm Town: A Memoir of the 1930s* (Brattleboro, Vt., 1974), 35–36.

8. Department of Agriculture, *Agricultural Statistics 1943,* 425.

9. *Ibid.*

10. Curtis Stadtfeld, *From the Land and Back* (New York, 1972), 162.

11. Heilman, *Farm Town,* 23; Stadtfeld, *From the Land and Back,* 160.

12. Stadtfeld, *From the Land and Back,* 25.

13. Letter from Kermit C. Cooke, *Rural America,* March 1941, 11.

14. Department of Agriculture, *Agricultural Statistics 1943,* 471; Bureau of the Census, *Sixteenth Census of the United States: 1940, Agriculture, Volume III, General Report* (Washington, D.C., 1943), 544–51.

15. Robert A. Caro, *The Years of Lyndon Johnson: The Path to Power* (New York, 1981; Vintage ed., 1983), 512.

16. Haydn S. Pearson, *Country Flavor* (New York, 1945), 93. A survey of facilities in rural America can be found in J. Frederick Dewhurst & Associates, *America's Needs and Resources* (New York, 1947), 143–44.

17. Stadtfeld, *From the Land and Back,* 40.

18. James West (Carl Withers), *Plainville, U.S.A.* (New York, 1945), 32–33.

19. Stadtfeld, *From the Land and Back,* 143.

20. For a summary of the condition of roads see Dewhurst & Associates, *America's Needs and Resources,* 229–30.

21. Willie Morris, *North Toward Home* (Boston, 1967), 104.

22. Moe and Taylor, *Irwin, Iowa* (note 6 above), 42.

23. August Hollingshead, *Elmtown's Youth* (New York, 1949), 109; see also Waller Wynne, *Culture of a Contemporary Rural Community: Harmony, Georgia.* U.S. Department of Agriculture, Bureau of Agricultural Economics, Rural Life Studies No. 6 (Washington, D.C., 1943), 43–45.

24. John Day, *Bloody Ground* (Garden City, N.Y., 1941), 253–54.

25. West, *Plainville,* 96–97.

26. Moe and Taylor, *Irwin, Iowa,* 50.

27. *Ibid.,* 44.

28. Department of Agriculture, *Agricultural Statistics 1943,* 418–19; Dewhurst & Associates, *America's Needs and Resources,* 69.

29. Hollingshead, *Elmtown's Youth,* 343.

30. Walter W. Wilcox, *The Farmer in the Second World War* (*c.* 1947; republished, New York, 1973), 17; Director of Selective Service, *Selective Service in Peacetime: First Report of the Director of Selective Service, 1940–41* (Washington, D.C., 1942), 402.

31. David Edgar Lindstrom, *American Rural Life* (New York, 1948), 137; Wilcox, *Farmer in Second World War,* 17.

32. Erskine Caldwell and Margaret Bourke-White, *Say, is this the U.S.A.* (New York, 1941), 114.

33. J. C. Furnas, *How America Lives* (New York, 1941), 161–75; Lindstrom, *American Rural Life,* 131.

34. Day, *Bloody Ground,* 318–19, 323.

35. *Ibid.,* 49.

36. *Ibid.,* 320.

37. Dorothea Lange and Paul Schuster Taylor, *An American Exodus* (New York, 1939), 34.

38. Raper and Reid, *Sharecroppers All* (note 3 above), 53, 164, 218.

39. National Resources Planning Board, *Security, Work, and Relief Policies* (Washington, D.C., 1942), 64, 196–98; Raper and Reid, *Sharecroppers All,* 234–35.

40. Samuel I. Rosenman, ed., *The Public Papers and Addresses of Franklin D. Roosevelt,* 13 vols. (New York, 1938–50), 7: 421.

41. Bureau of the Census, *Historical Statistics* (note 1 above), 283; Wilcox, *Farmer in Second World War,* 10–11.

42. Claude R. Wickard, "The Future of the Farm," *New Republic,* February 3, 1941, 139.

43. Lange and Taylor, *American Exodus,* 25; Edgar Schmiedeler, "Will History Repeat Itself in Agriculture?" *Rural Sociology,* December 1941, 295–97. See also Dale Kramer, "Eviction by Machinery," *Nation,* April 21, 1941, 497–99.

44. Wickard, "The Future of the Farm," 139; Bureau of the Census, *Historical Statistics,* 278; Paul S. Taylor, "Goodbye to the Homestead Farm," *Harper's,* May 1941, 597.

45. Day, *Bloody Ground,* 321.

46. Schmiedeler, "Will History Repeat Itself?" 295–97; Walter Goldschmidt, *As You Sow* (New York, 1947), 13.

47. Goldschmidt, *As You Sow,* 22, 28.

48. Stadtfeld, *From the Land and Back* (note 10 above), 170.

49. Wynne, *Harmony, Georgia* (note 23 above), 43.

50. Raper and Reid, *Sharecroppers All,* 139–40.

51. Otto Ernest Rayburn, *Ozark Country* (New York, 1941), 343–45.

Six. Things of the Spirit

1. Edwin O. Moe and Carl G. Taylor, *Culture of a Contemporary Rural Community: Irwin, Iowa* (Washington, 1942), 61.

2. D. W. Brogan, *U.S.A.: An Outline of the Country, Its People and Institutions* (London, 1941), 69.

3. J. Frederick Dewhurst & Associates, *America's Needs and Resources: A Twentieth Century Fund Survey* (New York, 1947), 326–27.

4. Tom E. Terrill and Jerrold Hirsch, eds., *Such as Us: Southern Voices of the Thirties* (New York, 1979), 127.

5. Hadley Cantril, *Public Opinion 1935–1946* (Princeton, 1951), 699, 1152. See also Clifton E. Olmstead, *History of Religion in the United States* (Englewood Cliffs, N.J., 1960), 563–64, and Hornell Hart, "Religion," *American Journal of Sociology,* May 1942, 888–97.

6. Douglas Ensminger, "The Rural Church and Religion," in Carl C. Taylor, *et al.,* eds., *Rural Life in the United States* (New York, 1949), 118–19.

7. James West (Carl Withers), *Plainville, U.S.A.* (New York, 1945), 149.

8. August Hollingshead, *Elmtown's Youth* (New York, 1949), 243–45, 256.

9. Channing Pollock, "Why I Don't Go to Church," *Reader's Digest,* October 1940, 74–75.

10. Josephine Quirk, "Calling on All the Laity to Save Neglected Children," *America: A Catholic Review of the Week,* December 6, 1941, 231.

11. Brother Gerald J. Schnepp, S. M., "Three Mixed Marriage Questions Answered," *Catholic World,* November 1942, 207.

12. Curtis Stadtfeld, *From the Land and Back* (New York, 1972), 136–37.

13. W. Lloyd Warner and Leo Srole, *The Social Systems of American Ethnic Groups* (New Haven, 1945), 171–73.

14. Willie Morris, *North Toward Home* (Boston, 1967), 47.

15. *Ibid.*

16. Walter Goldschmidt, *As You Sow* (New York, 1947), 125.

17. *Ibid.*, 128; West, *Plainville*, 153–54; Erskine Caldwell and Margaret Bourke-White, *Say, is this the U.S.A.* (New York, 1941), 42–44.

18. West, *Plainville*, 159.

19. Morris, *North Toward Home*, 38, 39.

20. John Day, *Bloody Ground* (Garden City, N.Y., 1941), 102–3.

21. *Ibid.*, 2–5.

22. *Ibid.*, 11–12.

23. *Ibid.*, 13; see also "Snake Revivals Recur in South," *Christian Century*, September 4, 1940, 1087.

24. Goldschmidt, *As You Sow*, 139.

25. Guild's Committee for Federal Writers' Publication, Inc., *New York Panorama* (New York, 1938), 85.

26. See Charles C. Alexander, *Nationalism in American Thought, 1930–1945* (New York, 1969), 155–56; Nathan Glazer and Daniel Patrick Moynihan, *Beyond the Melting Pot: The Negroes, Puerto Ricans, Jews, Italians, and Irish of New York City* (Cambridge, 1963), 137–43.

27. Warner and Srole, *Social Systems of Ethnic Groups* (note 13 above), 200.

28. *Ibid.*, 196.

29. Hadley Cantril, *Public Opinion 1935–1946* (Princeton, 1951), 381–82; see also "The Jewish Problem in America," *Atlantic Monthly*, June 1941, 699–706, and July 1941, 68–76.

30. Katherine Hayden Salter, "The Gentile Problem," *Christian Century*, August 28, 1940, 1052; Cantril, *Public Opinion*, 382.

31. Charles J. Tull, *Father Coughlin and the New Deal* (Syracuse, 1963), 211.

32. Roy and Alma Tozier, "The Battle of the Bible Belt," *New Republic*, March 10, 1941, 334–36; Tull, *Father Coughlin*, 229.

33. Joseph P. Lash, *Eleanor Roosevelt: A Friend's Memoir* (Garden City, N.Y., 1964), 242; see also Harold Bosley, "Is a Religious Storm Brewing?" *Christian Century*, July 31, 1940, 949–49.

34. Cyril C. Richardson, "Catholics and Religious Tolerance," *Christian Century*, November 6, 1940, 1373–74.

35. Michael F. Moloney, "What of Our Heritage?" *Catholic World*, May 1941, 187, 189.

36. Leslie Rumble, M.S.C., "Are American Catholics Growing Soft and Satisfied?" *America: A Catholic Review of the Week,* January 4, 1941, 343–44.

37. Letter of Archbishop John G. Murray, reproduced in *Christian Century,* May 22, 1941, 659.

38. Morris, *North Toward Home* (note 14 above), 41.

39. West, *Plainville* (note 7 above), 145; Walter Marshall Horton, "What Is Protestantism?" *Christian Century,* December 11, 1940, 1551.

40. H. C. McGinnis, "Rutherford and His Witnesses Find You Catholics a Bad Lot," *America: A Catholic Review of the Week,* February 15, 1941, 512.

41. Stanley High, "Armageddon, Inc.: Jehovah's Witnesses Make Hate a Religion," *Saturday Evening Post,* September 14, 1940, 18–19, 52–53, 58.

42. H. C. McGinnis, "Russell, Then Rutherford, Spawn Jehovah's Witnesses," *America: A Catholic Review of the Week,* February 8, 1941, 481.

43. John Haynes Holmes, "The Case of Jehovah's Witnesses," *Christian Century,* July 17, 1940, 896–98.

44. Alexander, *Nationalism in American Thought* (note 26 above), 170–71; Olmstead, *History of Religion* (note 5 above), 565–66.

45. *Christian Century,* January 22, 1941, 115–18.

46. "The Church and the War," *Time,* February 3, 1941, 35–36.

47. *Christian Century,* December 18, 1940, 1578–80; *Time,* February 3, 1941, 36.

48. In a poll taken on November 13, 1941, 55 percent of the people questioned believed that priests and preachers should not discuss American intervention from the pulpit; 34 percent believed they should. Cantril, *Public Opinion* (note 5 above), 790.

49. Mark Lincoln Chadwin, *The Warhawks: American Interventionists Before Pearl Harbor* (New York, 1970), 147.

50. "Where We Stand on the War," *Catholic World,* April 1941, 4. See also *America: A Catholic Review of the Week,* October 25, 1941, 71, and George Q. Flynn, *Roosevelt and Romanism: Catholics and American Diplomacy, 1937–1945* (Westport, Conn., 1976), 70–71, 86.

Seven. Things of the Flesh

1. August B. Hollingshead, *Elmtown's Youth* (New York, 1949), 256, 166. This study of Morris, Illinois, a town of 6,200, came from research conducted on youth aged 13–19 from May 1941 to December 1942.

2. Anita Brenner, "High School Youth—Not Flaming, but Realistic," *New York Times Magazine,* October 26, 1941, 10–11, 23.

3. W. Lloyd Warner and Leo Srole, *The Social Systems of American Ethnic Groups* (New Haven, 1945), 174.

4. Willie Morris, *North Toward Home* (Boston, 1967), 54; see also Council of State Governments, *The Book of the States 1941–1942* (Chicago, 1941), 384–85.

5. Gunnar Myrdal, *An American Dilemma: The Negro Problem and Modern American Democracy,* 2 vols. (New York, *c.* 1944; Harper Torchbook edition, 1969), I: 457–58.

6. Hollingshead, *Elmtown's Youth,* 316–17, 408.

7. Robert Sobel, *They Satisfy: The Cigarette in American Life* (New York, 1978), 101.

8. Sobel, *They Satisfy,* 118–19; Emily Post, "The Etiquette of Smoking," *Good Housekeeping,* September 1940, 37; *Life,* February 17, 1941, 38–41.

9. J. Frederick Dewhurst & Associates, *America's Needs and Resources* (New York, 1947), 94–95. Surveys on these topics were sketchy and probably not very reliable. In a poll of 1939 only 39 percent answered that they did not smoke. In 1944, 29 percent of men and 64 percent of women said they did not smoke. Asked in 1939 if they drank alcohol, 58 percent said yes—70 percent of men and 45 percent of women. "Do you agree," another poll in 1939 asked, "that liquor is what usually causes the downfall of girls?" 46.2 percent said yes. See Hadley Cantril, *Public Opinion 1935–1946* (Princeton, N.J., 1951), 419–20, 789.

10. Cited in Larry Sloman, *Reefer Madness: The History of Marijuana in America* (Indianapolis, 1979), 108. See also David Solomon, *The Marihuana Papers* (Indianapolis, 1966), 24, and George Randall McCormack, "Marihuana," *Hygeia,* October 1937, 898.

11. S. R. Winters, "Marihuana," *Hygeia,* October 1940, 885–87.

12. For example, see the Chicago *Defender,* October 11 and 25, 1941, and Allen Geller and Maxwell Boas, *The Drug Beat* (New York, 1969), 26–27.

13. *Variety,* August 29 and March 26, 1941; Sloman, *Reefer Madness,* 137.

14. "I Get A Kick out of You," © 1934, Harms, Incorporated, New York.

15. Hollingshead, *Elmtown's Youth,* 263.

16. *Ibid.,* 404, 420, 423; Otto Ernest Rayburn, *Ozark Country* (New York, 1941), 111.

17. John Day, *Bloody Ground* (Garden City, N.Y., 1941), 144.

18. Cantril, *Public Opinion,* 117; Los Angeles *Times,* July 24, 1941.

19. Myrdal, *American Dilemma* (note 5 above), I: 60.

20. Emily Hartshorne Mudd, "Sex Education for the Married Couple," *Hygeia,* August 1941, 602.

21. Hollingshead, *Elmtown's Youth,* 238, 288–89; James West, *Plainville, U.S.A.* (New York, 1945), 166.

22. Detroit *Free Press,* March 30, 1941; *Life,* April 14, 1941, 40.

23. John Newton Baker, "Where Will Your Children Learn About Sex?" *Hygeia,* April 1941, 346–50.

24. Ann L. Crockett, "Should Schools Teach Sex?" *Reader's Digest,* November 1940, 37.

25. Warner and Srole, *Social Systems of Ethnic Groups* (note 3 above), 173.

26. Hollingshead, *Elmtown's Youth,* 224; Mudd, "Sex Education for the Married Couple," 603.

27. West, *Plainville,* 191–94; Alfred C. Kinsey, *et al., Sexual Behavior in the Human Male* (Philadelphia, 1948), 513.

28. Russell Baker, *Growing Up* (New York, 1982), 131–32.

29. See, for example, William Foote Whyte, "A Slum Sex Code," *American Journal of Sociology,* July 1943, 24–41; West, *Plainville,* 166.

30. Whyte, "A Slum Sex Code," 25; Hollingshead, *Elmtown's Youth,* 415.

31. Ernest Hemingway, *For Whom the Bell Tolls* (New York, 1940), 160.

32. Hollingshead, *Elmtown's Youth,* 419.

33. Cantril, *Public Opinion* (note 9 above), 482.

34. Whyte, "A Slum Sex Code," 25–31; Hollingshead, *Elmtown's Youth,* 238–39.

35. Day, *Bloody Ground* (note 17 above), 31–32.

36. John W. Riley and Matilda W. Riley, "The Use of Various Methods of Contraception," *American Sociological Review,* December 1940, 894–95.

37. *Ibid.,* 890–903; see also "Birth Control in Massachusetts," *New Republic,* December 8, 1941, 759.

38. Whyte, "Slum Sex Code," 29.

39. Day, *Bloody Ground,* 31–32.

40. Hollingshead, *Elmtown's Youth,* 431–32.

41. Department of Health, Education, and Welfare (HEW), *Vital Statistics Rates in the United States 1940–1960* (Washington, D.C., 1968), 185; Bureau of the Census, *Vital Statistics of the United States, 1941, Part I* (Washington, D.C., 1944), 10–11.

42. West, *Plainville,* 196; see also Hollingshead, *Elmtown's Youth,* 116, 240.

43. Jane Ward, "What Everyone Should Know About Abortion," *American Mercury,* August 1941, 194–200.

44. Hollingshead, *Elmtown's Youth,* 429–30.

45. Wardell B. Pomeroy, *Dr. Kinsey and the Institute for Sex Research* (New York, 1972), 52–58.

46. *Ibid.,* 63–64.

47. Kinsey, *Human Male* (note 27 above), 144–47; Alfred C. Kinsey *et al., Sexual Behavior in the Human Female* (Philadelphia, 1953), 310.

48. This statistic might lead one to infer more promiscuous behavior than is warranted; it should not be taken to mean that half of unmarried women were sexually active at any time. Kinsey explained that many girls were active only with their fiancés, hence activity did not begin until a commitment to marriage had been made. On the other hand, 2,094 single girls in one sample had, by Kinsey's count, coitus some 460,000 times. See Kinsey, *Human Female,* 292, 327.

49. Kinsey, *Human Male,* 144–47, 339, 347, 587; Kinsey, *Human Female,* 142, 233, 282, 286, 416.

50. Hollingshead, *Elmtown's Youth,* 414.

51. *Time Capsule/1941* (New York, 1967), 160; Los Angeles *Times,* December 10, 1941.

52. The Council of State Governments, *The Book of the States,* 220–21; "Divorces While You Play," *Reader's Digest,* October 1941, 12–14.

53. Bureau of the Census, *Historical Statistics of the United States, Colonial Times to 1957* (Washington, D.C., 1960), 22, 30; *idem, Vital Statistics Rates,* 102.

54. Chicago *Tribune,* September 4, 1941.

55. Cantril, *Public Opinion* (note 9 above), 1044–45, 1052–53; Detroit *Free Press,* July 6, 1941.

56. Los Angeles *Times,* July 9, 1941.

57. *Ibid.,* July 3, 31, 1941; "Should Wives Work?" *Ladies' Home Journal,* January 1941, 4. See also Karen Anderson, *Wartime Woman: Her Roles, Family Relations, and the Status of Women During World War II* (Westport, Conn., 1981), 24.

58. William H. Chafe, *The American Woman: Her Changing Social, Economic and Political Role, 1920–1970* (New York, 1972), 136.

Eight. Another America

1. Population statistics appear in Bureau of the Census, *Historical Statistics of the United States, Colonial Times to 1957* (Washington, D.C., 1960), 11–12, 66.

2. Guy B. Johnson, in *Annals of the American Academy of Political and Social Science,* September 1941, cited in Jessie Parkhurst Guzman, ed., *Negro Yearbook: A Review of Events Affecting Negro Life 1941–1946* (Tuskegee, Ala., 1947), 316; see also Bureau of the Census, *Historical Statistics,* 23, 25, 218.

3. Richard Wright, *12 Million Black Voices: A Folk History of the Negro in the United States* (New York, 1941), 5.

4. Gunnar Myrdal, *An American Dilemma: The Negro Problem and Modern American Democracy,* 2 vols. (New York, *c.* 1944, Harper Torchbook ed., 1969), I: 358–59; Richard Sterner, *The Negro's Share: A Study of Income, Consumption, Housing and Public Assistance* (New York, 1943), 287–89; Richard Polenberg, *One Nation Divisible* (New York, 1980), 24.

5. Myrdal, *American Dilemma,* I: lxxi.

6. Bertram W. Doyle, *The Etiquette of Race Relations in the South* (Chicago, 1937), 143–46. See also Allison Davis, Burleigh B. Gardner, and Mary R. Gardner, *Deep South: A Social Anthropological Study of Caste and Class* (Chicago, 1941), 22–23; Charles S. Johnson, *Growing Up in the Black Belt* (Washington, D.C., 1941), 281.

7. Larry L. King, *Confessions of a White Racist* (New York, 1969), 55.

8. Myrdal, *American Dilemma,* I: 41, 108.

9. *Ibid.,* I: 57, 60, and II: 607.

10. Charles S. Johnson, *Patterns of Negro Segregation,* (New York, 1943), 219.

11. Leo C. Rosten, *Hollywood: The Movie Colony, The Movie Makers* (New York, 1941), 359.

12. Chicago *Defender,* May 31, 1941.

13. Cited in J. Fred MacDonald, *Don't Touch That Dial! Radio Programming in American Life, 1920–1960* (Chicago, 1979), 343. Although the show was broadcast in 1947, it projected attitudes that existed in 1941 and other years during the long course of the program.

14. Myrdal, *American Dilemma,* I: 75.

16. "I Got Plenty O' Nuthin'," lyrics by Ira Gershwin and Du Bose Heyward. © 1935 by Gershwin Publishing Co.; published in the United States by Gershwin Publishing Co. and Chappell & Company, Inc. Cited in Robert Kimball and Alfred Simon, *The Gershwins* (New York, 1973), 181.

16. Wright, *12 Million Black Voices* (note 3 above), 40.

17. Myrdal, *American Dilemma,* II: 928.

18. St. Clair Drake and Horace R. Cayton, *Black Metropolis: A Study of Negro Life in a Northern City,* 2 vols. (New York, *c.* 1945), II: 498; Johnson, *Growing Up in the Black Belt* (note 6 above), 270.

19. Chicago *Defender,* September 6, 1941.

20. Gerda Lerner, ed., *Black Women in White America: A Documentary History* (New York, 1972), 302.

21. James Baldwin, *Nobody Knows My Name,* (New York, 1961), 80.

22. Alex Haley and Malcolm X, *The Autobiography of Malcolm X* (New York, 1964; Ballantine edition, 1981), 52–54.

23. Cited in Myrdal, *American Dilemma,* II: 1431.

24. Haley and Malcolm X, *Autobiography of Malcolm X,* 49–51.

25. Wright, *12 Million Black Voices,* 128–29.

26. Myrdal, *American Dilemma,* II: 1431.

27. Haley and Malcolm X, *Autobiography of Malcolm X,* 50, 67.

28. *Ibid.,* 31, 45.

29. For examples, see Johnson, *Patterns of Segregation* (note 10 above), 44–45, 49–56, 66–67, 71–72.

30. Willie Morris, *North Toward Home* (Boston, 1967), 8–9.

31. Guzman, *Negro Yearbook, 1941–1945* (note 2 above), 58–59, 61, 70.

32. Myrdal, *American Dilemma,* II: 902–3.

33. Theodore Bilbo, "An African Home for our Negroes," *Living Age,* June 1940, 33. See also Virginius Dabney, *Below the Potomac: A Book About the New South* (New York, 1942), 209.

34. Guzman, *Negro Yearbook 1941–1946,* 265; Myrdal, *American Dilemma,* I: 479–85.

35. Davis, Gardner, and Gardner, *Deep South* (note 6 above), 16–17; Morris, *North Toward Home,* 78.

36. Johnson, *Growing Up in the Black Belt* (note 6 above), 17; Johnson, *Patterns of Segregation,* 138–39.

37. Johnson, *Growing Up in the Black Belt,* 319; Allison Davis and John Dollard, *Children of Bondage: The Personality Development of Negro Children in the Urban South* (Washington, 1940), 65–66.

38. Johnson, *Patterns of Segregation,* 267–69, 280–84.

39. Wright, *12 Million Black Voices* (note 3 above), 42.

40. Waller Wynne, *Culture of a Contemporary Rural Community: Harmony, Georgia* (Washington, D.C., 1943), 48.

41. J. C. Furnas, *How America Lives* (New York, 1941), 127–32.

42. Morris, *North Toward Home,* 80.

43. Johnson, *Growing Up in the Black Belt,* 299.

44. August Meier and Elliott Rudwick, *Black Detroit and the Rise of the U.A.W.* (New York, 1979), 5.

45. Claude Brown, *Manchild in the Promised Land* (New York, 1965), 7.

46. *Ibid.,* 7–8.

47. *Ibid.;* see also Sterner, *Negro's Share* (note 4 above), 42.

48. Haley and Malcolm X, *Autobiography of Malcolm X,* (note 22 above), 47–48.

49. Wright, *12 Million Black Voices,* 104; Haley and Malcolm X, *Autobiography of Malcom X,* 76.

50. Guzman, *Negro Yearbook, 1941–1946* (note 2 above), 312.

51. *Variety,* November 12 and December 10, 1941.

52. Haley and Malcolm X, *Autobiography of Malcolm X,* 88–90.

53. Drake and Cayton, *Black Metropolis* (note 18 above), II: 475–77.

54. *Variety,* October 8, 1941. For other activity in Bronzeville, see Drake and Cayton, *Black Metropolis,* II: 610, and virtually any edition of the Chicago *Defender.*

55. Haley and Malcolm X, *Autobiography of Malcolm X,* 40–43, 76–79.

56. Brown, *Manchild in the Promised Land* (note 45 above), 8.

57. Quoted in Herbert Garfinkel, *When Negroes March: The March on Washington Movement in the Organizational Politics for F.E.P.C.* (Glencoe, Ill., 1959), 17.

58. Johnson, *Patterns of Segregation* (note 10 above), 105–16; Neil A. Wynn, *The Afro-American and the Second World War* (New York, 1975), 41.

59. Director of Selective Service, *Selective Service in Peacetime: First Report of the Director of Selective Service, 1940–41* (Washington, D.C., 1942), 256–57.

60. Quoted in Johnson, *Patterns of Segregation,* 115–16; for statistics on recruitment of blacks see Director of Selective Service, *First Report,* 103, 254–57, 401–02.

61. Myrdal, *American Dilemma* (note 4 above); II: 419–21; Chicago *Tribune,* August 21, 1941; Chicago *Defender,* September 6, 1941.

62. Chicago *Defender,* February 1 and April 26, 1941.

63. *Ibid.,* February 16, 1941; Lerner, *Black Women in White America* (note 20 above), 300–303.

64. Chicago *Defender,* November 15, 1941; Wright, *12 Million Black Voices* (note 3 above), 143.

65. Langston Hughes, "What the Negro Wants," *Common Ground,* Autumn 1941, 52–54; Chicago *Defender,* January 25, 1941.

66. James M. Burns, *Roosevelt: The Soldier of Freedom* (New York, 1970), 123.

67. Garfinkel, *When Negroes March,* 39, 56–57.

68. Walter White, *A Man Called White* (New York, 1948), 169–70.

69. Joseph P. Lash, *Eleanor Roosevelt: A Friend's Memoir* (Garden City, N.Y., 1964), 217; White, *A Man Called White*, 189–90.

70. Cited in Wynn, *Afro-Americans* (note 58 above), 46.

71. Pittsburgh *Courier*, July 5, 1941.

72. Johnson, *Patterns of Segregation* (note 10 above), 111; Pittsburgh *Courier*, July 5 and September 6, 1941.

73. Wright, *12 Million Black Voices*, 146–47.

74. Chicago *Defender*, July 5, 1941.

Nine. Joe DiMaggio, Joe Louis, Joe Palooka . . .

1. For a survey of shows on Broadway see *Variety*, June 4, 1941; *Life*, February 7, 1941; and Abe Laufe, *Broadway's Greatest Hits* (New York, 1969), 38–40.

2. See, for example, "Goings on About Town," *New Yorker*, February 12, 1941, 2, 4, and *Variety*, October 15, 1941.

3. Jan Coss, "The 1,001 Night Clubs," *New York Times Magazine*, January 12, 1941, 12.

4. Sherwood Gates, "Radio in Relation to Recreation and Culture," *Annals of The American Academy of Political and Social Sciences*, January 1941, 9. For statistics, see Bureau of the Census, *Historical Statistics of the United States, Colonial Times to 1957* (Washington, D.C., 1960), 491, and J. Frederick Dewhurst & Associates, *America's Needs and Resources* (New York, 1947), 399.

5. See J. Fred MacDonald, *Don't Touch That Dial! Radio Programming in American Life, 1920–1960* (Chicago, 1979), 232, 275, and *Variety*, January 22, April 16, and October 22, 1941.

6. For a breakdown of program scheduling, see *Variety*, May 28, 1941.

7. *Ibid.*, October 15, 1941; *Time*, January 20, 1941, 58. See also John Dunning, *Tune in Yesterday: The Ultimate Encyclopedia of Old Time Radio 1925–1976* (Englewood Cliffs, N.J., 1976), 231–32, 419–20.

8. Jim Harmon, *The Great Radio Heroes* (Garden City, N.Y., 1967), 100.

9. *Variety*, May 28, 1941; *Time*, June 30, 1941.

10. *Time Capsule/1941*, 216. For other reviews, see *New Yorker*, July 5, 1941, 43; *Variety*, July 2, 1941; and Los Angeles *Times*, July 3, 1941.

11. Detroit *Free Press*, April 5, 1941.

12. For the Westerns' "Top Ten," see New York *Times*, December 28, 1941.

13. *Variety*, January 8, 1941.

14. *Life*, April 14, 1941, 32–33. See also Eric Barnouw, *A History of*

Broadcasting in the United States: 1933 to *1953, The Golden Web* (New York, 1968), 105–6.

15. *Variety,* April 30, 1941.

16. Mary Harden Looram, "The Movies Slide Down Toward the Condemned Class," *America: A Catholic Review of the Week,* October 18, 1941, 38–39.

17. *Ibid.*

18. *Variety,* October 22, 1941, 8.

19. *Ibid.,* December 3, 1941; see also *America,* December 13, 1941, and Los Angeles *Times,* December 7, 1941.

20. *Variety,* December 10, 1941. See also Otto Friedrich, *City of Nets: A Portrait of Hollywood in the 1940s* (New York, 1986), 125–36.

21. Chicago *Tribune,* August 2, 1941; *Variety,* August 6, 1941.

22. Chicago *Tribune,* September 10, 1941; *Variety,* September 10, 1941. See also Martin Quigley, Jr., and Richard Gertner, *Films in America 1929–1969* (New York, 1970), 111.

23. *Variety,* October 22, 1941.

24. Friedrich, *City of Nets,* 85.

25. *Variety,* April 16, 1941. For a more critical assessment see Edwin Schallert's review in Los Angeles *Times,* May 9, 1941.

26. Edwin Schallert in Los Angeles *Times,* July 8, 1941.

27. Detroit *Free Press,* January 27, 1941.

28. D. W. Brogan, *U.S.A.: An Outline of the Country, Its People and Institutions* (London, 1941), 108. For statistics on attendance, see Bureau of the Census, *Historical Statistics* (note 4 above), 224–25, and *Variety,* September 17, 1941, and January 7, 1942.

29. Brogan, *U.S.A.,* 107.

30. *Variety,* March 19, 1941; Leo C. Rosten, *Hollywood: The Movie Colony, The Movie Makers* (New York, 1941), 12.

31. *Life,* December 23, 1940, 64; Lana's story is told in Detroit *Free Press,* February 23, 1941.

32. Gerda Lerner, ed., *Black Women in White America: A Documentary History* (New York, 1972), 304–5.

33. August B. Hollingshead, *Elmstown's Youth* (New York, 1949), 380, 384–85; Rosten, *Hollywood,* 362; Detroit *Free Press,* March 24, 1941.

34. Rosten, *Hollywood,* 358–59.

35. *Ibid.,* 361.

36. Barry Ulanov, *A History of Jazz in America* (New York, 1972), 185,

196–98. See also Dave Dexter, Jr., *Jazz Cavalcade: The Inside Story of Jazz* (New York, 1946), 101–3.

37. George T. Simon, *The Big Bands* (New York, 1981), 24.

38. *Variety,* December 3 and 31, 1941.

39. *Ibid.,* October 1 and December 10, 1941.

40. "Juke-Box Clubhouse," *Parade Magazine,* in Nashville *Tennessean,* November 9, 1941, 11.

41. Simon, *Big Bands,* 13.

42. *Variety,* January 8 and March 26, 1941.

43. The remark about Dorsey appears in Herb Sanford, *Tommy and Jimmy: The Dorsey Years* (New Rochelle, N.Y., 1972), 58. Sinatra wrote the Foreword in Simon, *Big Bands,* xiii.

44. John Day, *Bloody Ground* (Garden City, N.Y., 1941), 239–41.

45. For a discussion of the development of country music, see Patrick Carr, *The Illustrated History of Country Music* (Garden City, N.Y., 1979), 49–80.

46. Hemingway to Maxwell Perkins, November 15, 1941, in Carlos Baker, ed., *Ernest Hemingway: Selected Letters, 1917–1961* (New York, 1981), 527–28.

47. Ernest Hemingway to Pauline Hemingway, July 19, 1941, in *ibid.,* 525.

48. Los Angeles *Times,* July 20, 1941. For reviews of bestsellers see New York *Times,* December 22, 1941; Encyclopaedia Britannica, *1942 Britannica Book of the Year* (Chicago, 1942), 551–52; and Alice P. Hackett, *70 Years of Best Sellers 1895–1965* (New York, 1967), 163.

49. Statistics appear in *1942 Britannica Book of the Year,* 482.

50. Walter Goldschmidt, *As You Sow* (New York, 1947), 120–21.

51. John Kobler, "Up, Up and Away," *Saturday Evening Post,* June 21, 1941, 14–15.

52. James Frank Vlamos, "The Sad Case of the Funnies," *American Mercury,* April 1941, 411–16; *Time,* February 24, 1941, 48.

53. Vlamos, "Sad Case of the Funnies," 416.

54. Joe Palooka appeared in many newspapers. This account is derived from Sunday editions of the Detroit *Free Press* in 1941. A brief discussion of Ham Fisher appears in Jerry Robinson, *The Comics: An Illustrated History of Comic Strip Art* (New York, 1974), 123–24.

55. *Variety,* February 19, March 5, and December 3, 1941; *Sporting News,* May 15, 1941. For polls on the popularity of baseball, see Hadley Cantril, *Public Opinion 1935–1946* (Princeton, N.J., 1951), 38.

56. Detroit *Free Press,* March 9, 1941.

57. Quoted in Richard C. Crepeau, *Baseball: America's Diamond Mind, 1919–1941* (Orlando, Fla., 1980), 168.

58. Los Angeles *Times,* June 3, 1941.

59. *Sporting News,* September 18 and December 4, 1941.

60. New York *Times,* December 21, 1941.

61. Joseph P. Lash, *Eleanor Roosevelt: A Friend's Memoir* (Garden City, N.Y., 1964), 259; Harry Truman to Bess Truman, September 18, 1941, in Robert H. Ferrell, ed., *Dear Bess: The Letters from Harry to Bess Truman 1910–1959* (New York, 1983), 464.

62. Anita Brenner, "Why Is a Dodger Fan?" *New York Times Magazine,* May 11, 1941, 10, 25.

63. Nashville *Tennessean,* September 30, 1941; *Time,* October 6, 1941, 53.

64. Nashville *Tennessean,* October 7, 1941.

65. Milton Bracker, "10,000,000 Fans Are Mad About It," *New York Times Magazine,* January 25, 1942, 12–13.

66. *Ibid.,* 12.

67. William F. Fox, Jr., "I'll Take Hoosier Hoopla," *Saturday Evening Post,* February 22, 1941, 16.

68. Hollingshead, *Elmtown's Youth,* (note 33 above), 193–94.

69. Brogan, *U.S.A.* (note 28 above), 114–15.

70. Chicago *Defender,* March 29, July 17, and October 4, 1941; see also William G. Nunn, "Joe Louis and His People," *Common Ground,* Autumn 1941, 63–64.

71. Joe Louis, with Edna Rust and Art Rust, Jr., *Joe Louis: My Life* (New York, 1978), 81–82.

72. Larry J. King, *Confessions of a White Racist* (New York, 1969), 7.

73. Russell Baker, *Growing Up* (New York, 1982), 204.

74. Detroit *Free Press,* March 24, 1941.

75. Nashville *Tennessean,* December 23, 1941; Detroit *Free Press,* July 5, 1941.

76. Detroit *Free Press,* June 19, 1941.

77. *Sporting News,* February 27, 1941.

Ten. "Hell, This Isn't a Pinochle Party We're Having—It's War!"

1. Philip Gibbs, *America Speaks* (Garden City, N.Y., 1942), 28–29.

2. Harold L. Ickes, *The Secret Diary of Harold L. Ickes,* vol. III: *The Lowering Clouds, 1939–1941* (New York, 1954), 524.

3. *Time Capsule/1941* (New York, 1967), 17.

4. *Catholic World,* August 1941, 1.

5. August 5, 1941, quoted in Rex Stout, ed., *The Illustrious Dunderheads* (New York, 1942), 56.

6. Los Angeles *Times,* July 13, 1941.

7. Nashville *Tennessean,* November 2 and 14, 1941.

8. Joseph E. Davies, *Mission to Moscow* (New York, c. 1941; Pocket Books edition, 1943), 450–51.

9. Diary entry, June 22, 1941, in David E. Lilienthal, *The Journal of David E. Lilienthal,* vol. I: *The TVA Years, 1939–1945* (New York, 1964), 343–44.

10. August 10, 1941, reprinted in Carl Sandburg, *Home Front Memo* (New York, 1942), 85.

11. Chicago *Tribune,* July 6 and August 9, 1941.

12. *Ibid.,* August 28, 1941.

13. *Ibid.,* quoted in Stout, *Illustrious Dunderheads,* 73.

14. Los Angeles *Times,* July 10, 1941.

15. Ickes, *Secret Diary* (note 2 above), 574; Los Angeles *Times,* June 29, 1941.

16. Eric Sevareid, *Not So Wild a Dream* (New York, 1946, 1976), 189.

17. Gibbs, *America Speaks* (note 1 above), 20, 31, 151.

18. Sevareid, *Not So Wild a Dream,* 194; Ickes, *Secret Diary,* 523.

19. Henry L. Stimson and McGeorge Bundy, *On Active Service: In Peace and War* (New York, 1947), 368–69.

20. James M. Burns, *Roosevelt: The Soldier of Freedom* (New York, 1970), 132.

21. New York *Times,* September 12, 1941; Chicago *Tribune,* September 13, 1941.

22. Burns, *Roosevelt,* 147–48.

23. Los Angeles *Times,* July 30, 1941.

24. Maurice Samuel, "Anti-Semitism Is a Christian Problem," *American Mercury,* July 1941, 63; Hadley Cantril, *Public Opinion 1935–1946* (Princeton, N.J., 1951), 1187.

25. Nashville *Tennessean,* November 17, 1941.

26. *Ibid.,* November 15, 1941; Cordell Hull, *The Memoirs of Cordell Hull,* 2 vols. (New York, 1948), II: 1062.

27. Dwight D. Eisenhower, *At Ease: Stories I Tell to Friends* (New York, 1967), 244–45.

28. Dean Acheson, *Present at the Creation: My Years in the State Department* (New York, 1969), 35.

29. *New Yorker,* December 13, 1941, 19.

30. As described in a letter to the editor from Private Jefferson G. Artz, *New Republic,* December 22, 1941, 863.

31. Lilienthal, *TVA Years* (note 9 above), 413.

32. *New Republic,* December 15, 1941, 815.

33. I. F. Stone, "War Comes to Washington," *Nation,* December 13, 1941, 603; Sevareid, *Not So Wild a Dream* (note 16 above), 205.

34. New York *Times,* December 8, 1941; Woody Guthrie, *Bound for Glory* (New York, *c.* 1943), 347, 349, 351.

35. Correspondents of *Time, Life,* and *Fortune, December 7: The First Thirty Hours* (New York, 1942), 6, 39, 41.

36. Russell Baker, *Growing Up* (New York, 1982), 207.

37. Jonathan Daniels, "A Native at Large," *Nation,* December 20, 1941, 643.

38. Correspondents of *Time,* etc., *December 7,* 195–99.

39. *Ibid.,* 201–2.

40. Meyer Berger, "War Comes to the Camps," *New York Times Magazine,* December 28, 1941, 4.

41. See remarks in New York *Times,* December 8, and *Nation,* December 20, 1941, 642.

42. See, for example, *Variety,* December 17, 19, and 24, 1941; Los Angeles *Times,* December 9 and 20, 1941.

43. Margaret Truman, *Harry S. Truman* (New York, 1973), 148.

44. *Sporting News,* December 18, 1941; see also Los Angeles *Times,* December 21, 1941.

45. New York *Times,* December 8, 1941.

46. New York *Times,* December 8, 1941.

47. George F. Kennan, *Memoirs 1925–1950* (Boston, 1967), 135.

48. New York *Times,* December 9, 1941.

49. Los Angeles *Times,* December 9 and 10, 1941; New York *Times,* December 10, 1941.

50. Los Angeles *Times,* December 10, 1941.

51. New York *Times,* December 10 and 11, 1941.

52. Richard E. Neuberger, "Reveille in the Northwest," *Nation,* December 20, 1941, 637.

53. Los Angeles *Times,* December 11, 1941.

54. *Ibid.,* December 10 and 15, 1941.

55. Jeanne Wakatsuki Houston and James D. Houston, *Farewell to Manzanar* (Boston, 1973), 5–8.

56. Guthrie, *Bound for Glory* (note 34 above), 349.

57. Joseph P. Lash, *Eleanor Roosevelt: A Friend's Memoir* (Garden City, N.Y., 1964), 262.

58. New York *Times,* December 25, 1941.

59. Letter to the editor of the Nashville *Tennessean,* December 29, 1941.

60. Los Angeles *Times,* December 28, 1941.

☆
Selected Bibliography
☆

While this study seeks to describe events of a single year, it is also a story of an era. For that reason I have allowed myself some latitudes in research. I did not hesitate to use material from a different year—a related period— if it helped explain conditions of 1941. For example, I occasionally used census reports of 1940, which were more complete than statistical studies of 1941, if there was good indication that the numbers had not changed much in a year. I used several firsthand contemporary accounts, such as *Bloody Ground,* that came partly from research conducted in the 1930s, because they described conditions that continued to exist in 1941. Other firsthand studies, such as *Elmtown's Youth, An American Dilemma,* and the volumes in the Kinsey Report, were in fact the result of research conducted in or about the year 1941, even though they carried a later publication date. The objective throughout has been to project conditions that existed in the last year before America's World War II, and I have used any material that might assist in that undertaking.

This book was written largely from statistical collections, memoirs, recollections, and articles and books contemporary to the period. Rather than list (or relist) all the pieces—143 articles and titles of 257 volumes—many of which appear in the notes, I have chosen only to list the newspapers, journals, and magazines from which the articles came and to mention but a small number of the books used, selected because they were the most helpful.

Not appearing in the documentation are interviews—discussions might be a better word—with dozens of individuals who remembered the period before World War II. Those people are not famous and were not involved in large decisions of government, and they will remain anonymous in this study, but they helped formulate my observations of America of 1941.

Newspapers

Chicago *Defender*

Chicago *Tribune*

Detroit *Free Press*

Evansville *Courier*

Kalamazoo *Gazette*

Los Angeles *Times*

Nashville *Tennessean*

New York *Times*

Pittsburgh *Courier*

Washington (Indiana) *Herald*

Washington (Indiana) *Democrat*

Periodicals

America: A Catholic Review of the Week

American City

American Journal of Sociology

American Mercury

American Sociological Review

Annals of the American Academy of Political and Social Science

Atlantic Monthly

Automotive Industries

Aviation

Catholic World

Christian Century

Coal Age

Common Ground

Country Life

Economic Geography

Fortune

Good Housekeeping

Graphic Survey

Harper's

Hygeia

Ladies' Home Journal

Life

Living Age

Michigan Alumnus Quarterly Review

Nation

New Republic

New Yorker

New York Times Magazine

Reader's Digest

Rural America

Rural Sociology

Saturday Evening Post

Sporting News

Time

Variety

Statistical Accounts

Most important, of course, are the various reports of the Bureau of the Census, especially the Census of 1940. A good single-volume compilation is *Historical Statistics of the United States: Colonial Times to 1957* (Washington, D.C., 1960). Many statistics appear also in Frederick J. Dewhurst & Associates, *America's Needs and Resources: A Twentieth Century Fund Survey* (New York, 1947). Useful for their contribution to special areas are Director of Selective Service, *Selective Service in Peacetime: First Report of the Director of Selective Service 1940–41* (Washington, D.C., 1942); Hadley Cantril, ed., *Public Opinion 1935–1946* (Princeton, N.J., 1951); and Joseph L. Reichler, ed., *The Baseball Encyclopedia: The Complete and Official Record of Major League Baseball* (New York, 1985).

Memoirs, Autobiography

For world affairs of the prewar period, see Harold Ickes, *The Secret Diary of Harold L. Ickes; Vol. III: The Lowering Clouds 1939–1941* (New York,

1954); Cordell Hull, *The Memoirs of Cordell Hull,* 2 vols. (New York, 1948); William L. Shirer, *Berlin Diary* (New York, 1941); and, for a feeling of the year especially, Eric Sevareid, *Not So Wild a Dream* (New York, 1976). Personal accounts by black people are Claude Brown, *Manchild in the Promised Land* (New York, 1965); Joe Louis, with Edna Rust and Art Rust, Jr., *Joe Louis: My Life* (New York, 1978); Alex Haley and Malcolm X, *The Autobiography of Malcolm X* (*c.* 1964, New York, 1973), the most helpful to this study; and Walter White, *A Man Called White* (New York, 1948). Excellent recollections of men growing up in the prewar period are Russell Baker, *Growing Up* (New York, 1982), in Baltimore; Willie Morris, *North Toward Home* (Boston, 1967), in a small town in Mississippi; and Curtis K. Stadtfeld, *From the Land and Back* (New York, 1972), on a farm in central Michigan.

Contemporary Descriptions

General accounts of conditions and attitudes in the United States are Denis W. Brogan, *U.S.A.: An Outline of the Country, Its People and Institutions* (London, 1941); Erskine Caldwell and Margaret Bourke-White, *Say, is this the U.S.A.* (New York, 1941); Philip Gibbs, *America Speaks* (Garden City, N.Y., 1942); and J. C. Furnas, *How America Lives* (New York, 1941), a collection of magazine pieces. Rex Stout's *The Illustrious Dunderheads* (New York, 1942) compiles remarks made by isolationists, and correspondents of *Time, Life,* and *Fortune* survey reaction to the attack at Pearl Harbor in *December 7: The First Thirty Hours* (New York, 1942).

The late 1930s and early 1940s was a time of extensive research into aspects of American society. Studies of localities are Walter Goldschmidt, *As You Sow* (New York, 1947), on Wasco, California; August Hollingshead, *Elmtown's Youth* (New York, 1949), on Morris, Illinois; James West (Carl Withers), *Plainville, U.S.A.* (New York, 1945), on a small town in Missouri; and two volumes in the Department of Agriculture series, *Culture of a Contemporary Rural Community: Irwin, Iowa* (Washington, 1942), by Edward O. Moe and Carl G. Taylor, and *Harmony, Georgia* (Washington, 1943), by Waller Wynne. See also W. Lloyd Warner and Paul S. Lunt, *The Social Life of a Modern Community* (New Haven, 1941); Arthur F. Raper and Ira De A. Reid, *Sharecroppers All* (Chapel Hill, N.C., 1941); and Otto Ernest Rayburn, *Ozark Country* (New York, 1941). Richest and most moving of all is John Day's account of life in Kentucky's hill country, *Bloody Ground* (Garden City, N.Y., 1941).

On social groups, see W. Lloyd Warner and Leo Srole, *The Social Systems of American Ethnic Groups* (New Haven, 1945), and William F. Whyte, *Street Corner Society* (Chicago, 1943), on Italians in the slums of Boston. Most extensively researched were black people in such volumes as Allison Davis *et al., Deep South: A Social Anthropological Study of Caste and Class* (Chicago, 1941); Allison Davis and John Dollard, *Children of*

Bondage: The Personality Development of Negro Youth in the Urban South (Washington, D.C., 1940); St. Clair Drake and Horace R. Cayton, *Black Metropolis: A Study of Negro Life in a Northern City,* 2 vols. (New York, 1945); Charles S. Johnson, *Growing Up in the Black Belt* (Washington, D.C., 1941), and *Patterns of Negro Segregation* (New York, 1943); and Richard Sterner, *The Negro's Share: A Study of Income, Consumption, Housing and Public Assistance* (New York, 1943). Finally there are Richard Wright's personalized account of the plight of his people, *12 Million Black Voices: A Folk History of the Negro in the United States* (New York, 1941), and the massive and incomparable work by Gunnar Myrdal, *An American Dilemma: The Negro Problem and Modern American Democracy,* 2 vols. (New York, *c.* 1944; Harper Torchbook ed., 1969).

Secondary Works

General accounts that touch upon politics and foreign policy include Geoffrey Perrett, *Days of Sadness, Years of Triumph: The American People 1939–1945* (New York, 1973); Charles C. Alexander, *Nationalism in American Thought 1930–1945* (Chicago, 1969); James M. Burns, *Roosevelt: The Soldier of Freedom* (New York, 1970); Mark Lincoln Chadwin, *The Warhawks: American Interventionists Before Pearl Harbor* (*c.* 1968; Norton ed., New York, 1970); Wayne S. Cole, *Charles A. Lindbergh and the Battle Against American Intervention in World War II* (New York, 1974); Robert Dalleck, *Franklin D. Roosevelt and American Foreign Policy, 1932–1945* (New York, 1979); and George O. Flynn, *Roosevelt and Romanism: Catholics and American Diplomacy, 1937–1945* (Westport, Conn., 1976).

For various social and economic problems, see Ronald H. Bayor, *Neighbors in Conflict: The Irish, Germans, Jews, and Italians of New York City, 1929–1941* (Baltimore, 1970); Russell A. Buchanan, *Black Americans in World War II* (Santa Barbara, Calif., 1977); Jessie Parkhurst Guzman, ed., *Negro Yearbook: A Review of Events Affecting Negro Life 1941–1946* (Tuskegee, Ala., 1947); Richard Polenberg, *One Nation Divisible: Class, Race and Ethnicity in the United States Since 1938* (New York, 1980); Carl C. Taylor *et al., Rural Life in the United States* (New York, 1949); and Walter W. Wilcox, *The Farmer in the Second World War* (New York, 1947).

On aspects of culture and entertainment, there are Erik Barnouw, *A History of Broadcasting in the United States,* vol. II, *The Golden Web, 1933 to 1953* (New York, 1968); John Dunning, *Tune in Yesterday: The Ultimate Encyclopedia of Old-Time Radio, 1925–1976* (Englewood Cliffs, N.J., 1976); Jim Harmon, *The Great Radio Heroes* (Garden City, N.Y., 1967); and J. Fred MacDonald, *Don't Touch That Dial! Radio Programming in American Life, 1920–1960* (Chicago, 1979). For films, see Otto Friedrich,

City of Nets: A Portrait of Hollywood in the 1940s (New York, 1986); Leo C. Rosten, *Hollywood: The Movie Colony, The Movie Makers* (New York, 1941); and Ken D. Jones and Arthur F. McClure, *Hollywood at War: The American Motion Picture and World War II* (New York, 1973). For other areas, helpful volumes include Patrick Carr, ed., *The Illustrated History of Country Music* (Garden City, N.Y., 1979); George T. Simon, *The Big Bands* (New York, 1967); Richard M. Crepeau, *Baseball: America's Diamond Mind, 1919–1941* (Orlando, Fla., 1980); and Alice P. Hackett, *70 Years of Best Sellers 1895–1965* (New York, 1967).

Important specialized studies are Irving Bernstein, *Turbulent Years: A History of the American Worker 1933–1941* (Boston, 1970); H. Wayne Morgan, *Drugs in America: A Social History, 1800–1980* (Syracuse, 1981); James T. Patterson, *America's Struggle Against Poverty 1900–1980* (Cambridge, 1981); Wardell Pomeroy, *Dr. Kinsey and the Institute for Sex Research* (New York, 1972); and Samuel A. Stouffer, *The American Soldier*, 2 vols. (Princeton, N.J., 1949).

Novels that project attitudes of the time are Ernest Hemingway, *For Whom the Bell Tolls* (New York, 1940); James Jones, *From Here to Eternity* (New York, 1951); Herman Wouk, *The Winds of War* (Boston, 1971); and Richard Wright, *Native Son* (New York, 1940).

Index